D1176085

TRANSLATION

Routledge Applied Linguistics is a series of comprehensive resource books, providing students and researchers with the support they need for advanced study in the core areas of English language and Applied Linguistics.

Each book in the series guides readers through three main sections, enabling them to explore and develop major themes within the discipline:

*   Section A, Introduction, establishes the key terms and concepts and extends readers' techniques of analysis through practical application.
*   Section B, Extension, brings together influential articles, sets them in context, and discusses their contribution to the field.
*   Section C, Exploration, builds on knowledge gained in the first two sections, setting thoughtful tasks around further illustrative material. This enables readers to engage more actively with the subject matter and encourages them to develop their own research responses.

Throughout the book, topics are revisited, extended, interwoven and deconstructed, with the reader's understanding strengthened by tasks and follow-up questions.

Translation:

*   examines the theory and practice of translation from a variety of linguistic and cultural angles, including semantics, equivalence, functional linguistics, corpus and cognitive linguistics, text and discourse analysis, gender studies and post-colonialism
*   draws on a wide range of languages, including French, Spanish, German, Russian and Arabic
*   explores material from a variety of sources, such as the Internet, advertisements, religious texts, literary and technical texts
*   gathers together influential readings from the key names in the discipline, including James S. Holmes, George Steiner, Jean-Paul Vinay and Jean Darbelnet, Eugene Nida, Werner Koller and Ernst-August Gutt.

Written by experienced teachers and researchers in the field, *Translation* is an essential resource for students and researchers of English language and Applied Linguistics as well as Translation Studies.

Basil Hatim is Professor of Translation and Linguistics at Heriot Watt University, UK and Professor of English and Translation at the American University of Sharjah, UAE. **Jeremy Munday** is Deputy Director of the Centre for Translation Studies, University of Surrey, UK.

ROUTLEDGE APPLIED LINGUISTICS

SERIES EDITORS

Christopher N. Candlin is Senior Research Professor in the Department of Linguistics at Macquarie University, Australia, and Professor of Applied Linguistics at the Open University, UK. At Macquarie, he has been Chair of the Department of Linguistics; he established and was Executive Director of the National Centre for English Language Teaching and Research (NCELTR); and was foundation Director of the Centre for Language in Social Life (CLSL). He has written or edited over 150 publications and from 2004 will co-edit the new *Journal of Applied Linguistics*. From 1996 to 2002 he was President of the International Association of Applied Linguistics (AILA). He has acted as a consultant in more than 35 countries and as external faculty assessor in 36 universities worldwide.

Ronald Carter is Professor of Modern English Language in the School of English Studies at the University of Nottingham. He has published extensively in applied linguistics, literary studies and language in education, and has written or edited over 40 books and 100 articles in these fields. He has given consultancies in the field of English language education, mainly in conjunction with the British Council, in over 30 countries worldwide, and is editor of the Routledge Interface series and advisory editor to the Routledge English Language Introductions series. He was recently elected a Fellow of the British Academy for Social Sciences and is currently UK Government Advisor for ESOL and Chair of the British Association for Applied Linguistics (BAAL).

FORTHCOMING TITLES IN THE SERIES

Intercultural Communication: An advanced resource book
Adrian Holliday, Martin Hyde and John Kullman, Canterbury Christ Church University College, UK

Translation: An advanced resource book
Basil Hatim, Heriot-Watt University, UK and the American University of Sharjah, UAE and Jeremy Munday, University of Surrey, Guildford, UK

Grammar and Context: An advanced resource book
Ann Hewings, Open University and Martin Hewings, University of Birmingham

Translation

An advanced resource book

Basil Hatim and Jeremy Munday

Routledge
Taylor & Francis Group

LONDON AND NEW YORK

First published 2004
by Routledge
2 Park Square, Milton Park, Abingdon, Oxon OX14 4RN

Simultaneously published in the USA and Canada
by Routledge
270 Madison Ave, New York, NY 10016

Routledge is an imprint of the Taylor & Francis Group

© 2004 Basil Hatim and Jeremy Munday

Typeset in Akzidenz, Minion and Novarese
by Keystroke, Jacaranda Lodge, Wolverhampton
Printed and bound in Great Britain
by TJ International Ltd, Padstow, Cornwall

British Library Cataloguing in Publication Data
A catalogue record for this book is available from the British Library

Library of Congress Cataloging in Publication Data
A catalog record for this book has been requested

ISBN 0-415-28305-1 (hbk)
ISBN 0-415-28306-x (pbk)

To Nuria,
who came into this world at the same time as this book

and to Sam and Lema,
we will make it up to you.

Contents

Contents

Contents cross-referenced

Series Editors' Preface

This series provides a comprehensive guide to a number of key areas in the field of applied linguistics. Applied linguistics is a rich, vibrant, diverse and essentially interdisciplinary field. It is now more important than ever that books in the field provide up-to-date maps of ever changing territory.

The books in this series are designed to give key insights into core areas. The design of the books ensures, through key readings, that the history and development of a subject is recognised while, through key questions and tasks, integrating understandings of the topics, concepts and practices that make up its essentially inter-disciplinary fabric. The pedagogic structure of each book ensures that readers are given opportunities to think, discuss, engage in tasks, draw on their own experience, reflect, research and to read and critically re-read key documents.

Each book has three main sections, each made up of approximately 10 units:

A: An **Introduction** section: in which the key terms and concepts are introduced, including introductory activities and reflective tasks, designed to establish key understandings, terminology, techniques of analysis and the skills appropriate to the theme and the discipline.

B: An **Extension** section: in which selected core readings are introduced (usually edited from the original) from existing books and articles, together with annotations and commentary, where appropriate. Each reading is introduced, annotated and commented on in the context of the whole book, and research/follow-up questions and tasks are added to enable fuller understanding of both theory and practice. In some cases, readings are short and synoptic and incorporated within a more general exposition.

C: An **Exploration** section: in which further samples and illustrative materials are provided with an emphasis, where appropriate, on more open-ended, student-centred activities and tasks, designed to support readers and users in undertaking their own locally relevant research projects. Tasks are designed for work in groups or for individuals working on their own.

This book also contains a glossary and a detailed, thematically organised A–Z guide to the main terms used in the book which lays the ground for further work in the discipline. There are also annotated guides to further reading and extensive bibliographies.

The target audience for the series is upper undergraduates and postgraduates on language, applied linguistics, translation and communication studies programmes as well as teachers and researchers in professional development and distance learning programmes. High-quality applied research resources are also much needed for teachers of EFL/ESL and foreign language students at higher education colleges and universities worldwide. The books in the Routledge Applied Linguistics series are aimed at the individual reader, the student in a group and at teachers building courses and seminar programmes.

We hope that the books in this series meet these needs and continue to provide support over many years.

THE EDITORS

Professor Christopher N. Candlin and Professor Ronald Carter are the series editors. Both have extensive experience of publishing titles in the fields relevant to this series. Between them they have written and edited over one hundred books and two hundred academic papers in the broad field of applied linguistics. Chris Candlin was president of AILA (International Association for Applied Linguistics) from 1997–2002 and Ron Carter is Chair of BAAL (British Association for Applied Linguistics) from 2003–6.

Professor Christopher N. Candlin,
Senior Research Professor
Department of Linguistics,
Division of Linguistics and Psychology
Macquarie University
Sydney NSW 2109
Australia

and

Professor of Applied Linguistics
Faculty of Education and Language Studies
The Open University
Walton Hall
Milton Keynes MK7 6AA
UK

Professor Ronald Carter
School of English Studies
University of Nottingham
Nottingham NG7 2RD
UK

Acknowledgements

Many people have helped us in the course of writing this book. Our thanks go to, amongst others, Dunstan Brown, Stephen Hutchings, Margaret Lang, Ana Cristina Llompart, Charles Mann, Michael O'Shea and Anat Vernitski. To series editors Chris Candlin and Ron Carter for their detailed comments on various stages. To Louisa Semlyen, Christy Kirkpatrick and Kate Parker at Routledge for their patience, support and hard work, and to copyeditor Kristina Wischenkämper for her keen attention to detail. To the Department of Linguistic, Cultural and Translation Studies, University of Surrey, for allowing one of the authors a period of teaching relief from January to June 2002.

We are grateful to the copyright holders of the following texts for permission to reproduce extracts in Section B:

R. Jakobson, 'On Linguistic Aspects of Translation', in R. A. Brower (ed.) *On Translation*, Harvard University Press. Reproduced by permission of The Roman Jakobson Trust u/w/o Krystyna Pomorska Jakobson.

J. S. Holmes, 'The Name and Nature of Translation Studies', in J. S. Holmes, *Translated! Papers on Literary Translation and Translation Studies*, Rodopi, 1988. Reproduced by permission of Rodopi BV.

G. Steiner, *After Babel: Aspects of Language and Translation*, 3rd edition, Oxford University Press, 1998. Reprinted by permission of Oxford University Press.

J.-P. Vinay and J. Darbelnet, *Comparative Stylistics of French and English*, pp 20–27, John Benjamins, 1995. Reproduced by permission of John Benjamins Publishing Company, Amsterdam/Philadelphia. www.benjamins.com.

J. C. Catford, *A Linguistic Theory of Translation*, Oxford University Press, 1965. Reprinted by permission of Oxford University Press.

M. L. Larson, *Meaning-Based Translation*, 2nd edition, University Press of America, 1998. Reproduced by permission of the University Press of America.

E. A. Nida, 'Science of Translation', in *Language* 45, 3, 1969. Reproduced by permission of the Linguistic Society of America.

E. A. Nida, *Toward a Science of Translating*, Brill Academic Publishers, 1964 (reprint 2003). Reproduced by permission of Brill Academic Publishers.

W. Koller, 'The Concept of Equivalence and the Object of Translation Studies, in *Target* 7:2, 1995. Reproduced by permission of John Benjamins Publishing Company, Amsterdam/Philadelphia. *www.benjamins.com*.

J. Levý, 'Translation as a Decision Process', in *To Honour Roman Jakobson II*, Mouton de Gruyter, 1967. Reproduced by permission of Mouton de Gruyter.

E.-A. Gutt, 'Pragmatic Aspects of Translation: Some Relevance-Theory Observations', in *The Pragmatics of Translation*, L. Hickey, Multilingual Matters, 1998. Reproduced by permission of Multilingual Matters Ltd.

K. Reiss, 'Text Types, Translation Types and Translation Assessment', in Andrew Chesterman (ed) *Reach ups in Translation Theory*, Suomalainen Kirjakauppa, 1989. Reproduced by permission of the publisher.

M. Gregory, 'Perspectives on Translation', in *META*, XXV.4, 1980. Reproduced by permission of Copibec.

C. James, 'Genre Analysis and the Translator', in *Target* 1:1, 1989. Reproduced by permission of John Benjamins Publishing Company, Amsterdam/Philadelphia. *www.benjamins.com*.

D. Bruce, 'Translating the Commune: Cultural Politics and the Historical Specificity of the Anarchist Text', in *Traduction, Terminologie, Redaction*, No. 1. Reproduced by permission of TTR, McGill University, Montreal, Canada.

P. Fawcett, 'Translation and Power Play', in *The Translator*, vol. 1, no. 2, 1995. Reproduced by permission of St Jerome Publishing.

T. Niranjana, *Siting Translation: History, Post-Structuralism and the Colonial Context*, University of California Press © 1991 The Regents of the University of California. Reproduced by permission of University of California Press.

D. J. Arnold, L. Balkan, S. Meijer, R. L. Humphreys and L. Sadler, *Machine Translation: An Introductory Guide*, Blackwells-NCC, 1994. Reproduced by permission of Douglas Arnold.

And to the following for permission to use examples and figures:

Georgetown University Press for Figure C5.1, a series of cup-like objects, from William Labov (1973) 'The Boundaries of Words and their Meanings';

Laboratoire RALI of the University of Montreal for the parallel concordance of the Canadian Hansard, produced with their TSrali system and used in Text A14.3;

Lou Bernard at the British National Corpus for Figures C5.2 and C5.3, sample concordances of *handsome* and *pretty*;

Milengo for Figure A14.1, The Localization Process;

TRADOS for Figure A14.2, the screenshot from the Translator's Workbench. Copyright © TRADOS Incorporated 2004. Used by Permission. All rights reserved.

Every effort has been made to trace the copyright holders but if any have been inadvertently overlooked the publishers will be happy to make the necessary arrangement at the first opportunity.

Jeremy Munday and Basil Hatim, February 2004

How to use this book

TRANSLATION

Translation, both commercial and literary, is an activity that is growing phe-nomenally in today's globalized world. The study of translation, an interdisciplinary field known as Translation Studies, has also developed enormously in the past twenty years. It interfaces with a wide range of other disciplines from linguistics and modern languages to Cultural Studies and **postcolonialism**. This book attempts to investigate both the practice and the theory of translation in an accessible and systematic way. It is designed specifically with the needs in mind of students of Masters degrees and final year undergraduates in translation or applied linguistics, research students beginning to investigate the field, and practising translators who wish to examine the theory behind the practice. It is hoped that it will also provide useful insights and examples for more experienced researchers.

The book is divided into three sections (A, B and C) and 14 units. Each unit is treated in each of the sections. **Section A** of each unit introduces the main concepts of each area of translation and presents reflective tasks to encourage the reader to think through the theory. Key concept boxes highlight and summarize the main points.

Section B, the extension stage, then presents one or two readings, which are extracts from key articles or books on the relevant subject. Each reading is accompanied by brief tasks: *Before you read* aids recall of the Section A concepts, *As you read* brings out the crucial elements of the reading and *After you read* recapitulates the main points and prepares for exploration.

Section C is the exploration section. It critiques and develops the previous sections with a series of tasks and projects that at first provide the reader with specific data to investigate and then encourage wider exploration and original research in the reader's own linguistic and cultural context.

A detailed glossary is supplied at the end covering central terms of Translation Studies, including some from Linguistics and Cultural Studies. These terms are **highlighted in bold** in the main text for ease of reference. Finally, a full bibliography brings together the theory references. A very focused Further reading list is given at the back of the book for each unit.

The many tasks and text examples are numbered to facilitate cross-reference. The following is illustrative of the format:

Example A2.6a ST French

Couvercle et cuves en polycarbonate. Matériau haute résistance utilisé pour les hublots d'avion.
[*Lid and bowls in polycarbonate. High resistance material used for aircraft windows.*]

A2.6b TT English

Workbowls and lid are made from polycarbonate, the same substance as the windows of Concorde.

 ### Task A2.4

➤ Look at the translation and reflect on the strategies employed by the translator to increase **comprehensibility**.

The text numbering refers to the section, unit and example. Thus, here the first text (A2.6a) is in Section A, Unit 2, and is example 6. The lower case **a** means the original text. This is followed by a close **back-translation**, bracketed and in italics. The actual translation is numbered A2.6b, the lower case **b** indicating that it is a version/translation of A2.6a. The accompanying tasks are ordered sequentially.

Of course, the study of translation inevitably presupposes knowledge of more than one language. However, the book has been designed for use by readers from any language background who have an advanced level of English, whether or not they are native speakers. In the translation examples, English is therefore always either the **source** (original) **language** or the **target language**. The other languages covered are varied, including the major European languages and Arabic. As in the illustrative example above, an italicized English **back-translation** of the source text is provided to facilitate analysis. A **back-translation** is a translation that is very close to the lexical and syntactic patterning of the **source text**. This enables the reader to compare the actual translation with the patterning of the original. For this reason, the original source texts have often been omitted, but for reference some of these are to be found on the book's website (see below).

The many different tasks that are part of the basic framework of the book are designed in such a way that they can be used either by readers working on their own, or in pairs or groups in a more formal teaching situation. Section A tasks are designed to encourage the reader to reflect on the validity and application of the theoretical concepts and to relate them to their own experience. In Section B, the

'After you read' tasks may lend themselves to an oral presentation by one member of a class, followed by discussion, or to a short essay-type response in the early stages of assessment. In Section C, the tasks are more extensive, especially the 'projects' which in some cases may develop into full-scale research projects and even doctoral theses! Although data are provided and a methodology suggested, the more complex projects will work best when the student actively researches new material and has the opportunity of interviewing or observing professional translators. Sometimes that professional may in fact be the teacher of a translation class.

The cross-referenced contents list describes each unit (1 to 14) and each section (A, B and C). This allows the book to be followed either 'vertically' or 'horizontally'. That is, it can be read *linearly* from beginning to end (all Section A units, then all Section B units, then all Section C units) or *thematically* through a unit (e.g. Unit 1 Section A, followed by Unit 1 Section B, Unit 1 Section C, and so on). Many readers or teachers may find the thematic order particularly useful, especially since Section C usually critiques the concepts presented in Section A and B of the same unit and which may then be further developed in Section A of the subsequent unit.

The book presents and explores many concepts, but these can only be properly extended by careful pursuit of the further reading and the research projects. The following reference books may prove to be of particular value in the initial stages of this research:

> Mona Baker (ed.) (1998) *The Routledge Encyclopedia of Translation Studies*, London and New York: Routledge.
> David Crystal (2003) *A Dictionary of Linguistics and Phonetics*, Oxford: Blackwell, 5th edn.
> Jeremy Munday (2001) *Introducing Translation Studies: Theories and applications*, London and New York: Routledge.
> Mark Shuttleworth and Moira Cowie (1997) *Dictionary of Translation Studies*, Manchester: St Jerome.
> Lawrence Venuti (ed.) (2000) *The Translation Studies Reader*, London and New York: Routledge.

We also recommend that the reader collect source material and text samples that may be valuable for the research projects. These could include one or more literary translations into the reader's first language (plus a copy of the foreign language **source text**), a translation of a classic work such as Shakespeare, **parallel texts** (either pairs of original texts with their translation or pairs of non-translated texts on the same subject in different languages) and other examples encountered of translation (good and bad).

A website for the book, and for the Routledge Applied Linguistics Series, can be found at <http://www.routledge.co.uk/rcenters/linguistics/series/ral/041528306X>. Further text examples, translations, illustrative material and updates on recent developments and events in Translation Studies will be posted there.

Finally, the following is a list of standard abbreviations that will be used throughout the book:

L1 the first (and normally native) language of the writer, reader, speaker, etc.

L2 the second language of the writer, reader, speaker. etc. (often their strongest foreign language)

SL source language (the language the text was originally written in)

ST source text (the original text)

TL target language (the language of the translation)

TT target text (the translated text)

SECTION A
Introduction

Unit A1
What is translation?

DEFINITIONS OF TRANSLATION

Translation is a phenomenon that has a huge effect on everyday life. This can range from the translation of a key international treaty to the following multilingual poster that welcomes customers to a small restaurant near to the home of one of the authors:

Example A1.1

Benvenuti!

Welcome!

Hi!

How can we then go about defining the phenomenon of 'translation' and what the study of it entails? If we look at a general dictionary, we find the following definition of the term *translation*:

Example A1.2

translation *n.* **1** the act or an instance of translating. **2** a written or spoken expression of the meaning of a word, speech, book, etc. in another language.

(*The Concise Oxford English Dictionary*)

The first of these two senses relates to translation as a **process**, the second to the **product**. This immediately means that the term *translation* encompasses very distinct perspectives. The first sense focuses on the role of the translator in taking the original or **source text** (ST) and turning it into a text in another language (the **target text**, TT). The second sense centres on the concrete translation **product** produced by the translator. This distinction is drawn out by the definition in the specialist *Dictionary of Translation Studies* (Shuttleworth and Cowie 1997: 181):

Example A1.3

Translation An incredibly broad notion which can be understood in many different ways. For example, one may talk of translation as a **process** or a **product**, and identify

3

such sub-types as literary translation, technical translation, **subtitling** and **machine translation**; moreover, while more typically it just refers to the transfer of written texts, the term sometimes also includes **interpreting**.

This definition introduces further variables, first the 'sub-types', which include not only typically written products such as literary and technical translations, but also translation forms that have been created in recent decades, such as **audiovisual translation**, a written **product** which is read in conjunction with an image on screen (cinema, television, DVD or computer game). Moreover, the reference to **machine translation** reveals that translation is now no longer the preserve of human translators but, in a professional context, increasingly a **process** and **product** that marries computing power and the computerized analysis of language to the human's ability to analyse sense and determine appropriate forms in the other language.

INTERLINGUAL, INTRALINGUAL AND INTERSEMIOTIC TRANSLATION

The final line of Shuttleworth and Cowie's definition also illustrates the potential confusion of translation with **interpreting**, which is strictly speaking 'oral translation of a spoken message or text' (1997: 83). Yet this confusion is seen repeatedly in everyday non-technical language use, as in the trial in the Netherlands of two Libyans accused of bombing an American Panam passenger jet over Lockerbie, Scotland, where defence lawyers protested at the poor 'translation' which, they said, was impeding the defendants' comprehension of the proceedings (reported in the *Guardian* 10 June 2000).

Even if **interpreting** is excluded, the potential field and issues covered by translation are vast and complex. *Benvenuti!* may be what many people expect as a translation of *Welcome!*, but how do we explain *Hi!*? Translation also exists between different varieties of the same language and into what might be considered less conventional languages, such as braille, sign language and morse code. What about the flag symbol being understood as a country, nationality or language – is that 'translation' too? Such visual phenomena are seen on a daily basis: no-smoking or exit signs in public places or icons and symbols on the computer screen, such as the hour-glass signifying 'task is under way, please wait' or, as it sometimes seems, 'be patient and don't touch another key!'

Example A1.4

J. K. Rowling's Harry Potter children's books have been translated into over 40 languages and have sold millions of copies worldwide. It is interesting that a separate edition is published in the USA with some alterations. The first book in the series, *Harry Potter and the Philosopher's Stone* (Bloomsbury 1997), appeared as *Harry Potter and the Sorcerer's Stone* in the USA (Scholastic 1998). As well as the title, there were other lexical changes: British *biscuits, football, Mummy, rounders* and the sweets *sherbet lemons* became American *cookies, soccer, Mommy, baseball* and *lemon drops*. The American edition makes a few alterations of grammar and **syntax**, such as replacing *got* by *gotten*, *dived* by *dove* and *at weekends* by *on weekends*, and occasionally simplifying the sentence structure.

Task A1.1

➤ Consider the changes listed above in Example A1.4 and how far you think these can be termed 'translation'.

In this particular case it is not translation between two languages, but between two versions or dialects of the same language. As we shall see below, this is termed '**intralingual translation**' in Roman Jakobson's **typology** and by other theorists may be known as a 'version'. Yet it does share some of the characteristics of translation between languages, notably the replacement of lexical items by other equivalent items that are considered more suited to the target **audience**.

Task A1.2

In the Hebrew translation of the same book, the translator chose to substitute the British with a traditional Jewish sweet, a kind of marshmallow.

➤ In what ways do you think this shows similar reasoning to that behind the American version?

In his seminal paper, 'On Linguistic Aspects of Translation' (Jakobson 1959/2000, see Section B, Text B1.1), the Russo–American linguist Roman Jakobson makes a very important distinction between three types of written translation:

1. **intralingual translation** – translation within the same language, which can involve rewording or paraphrase;
2. **interlingual translation** – translation from one language to another, and
3. **intersemiotic translation** – translation of the verbal **sign** by a non-verbal **sign**, for example music or image.

Only the second category, **interlingual translation**, is deemed 'translation proper' by Jakobson.

Task A1.3

➤ Look at the examples given in this section and think how they correspond to these three types of translation.

Translation between written languages remains today the core of translation research, but the focus has broadened far beyond the mere replacement of SL linguistic items with their TL **equivalents**. In the intervening years research has been undertaken into all types of linguistic, cultural and ideological phenomena around translation: in theatre translation (an example of translation that is written, but ultimately to be read aloud), for example, **adaptation**, of geographical or historical location and of dialect, is very common (see Upton ed. 2000). Where do we draw the line between 'translation' and '**adaptation**'? What about Olivier Todd's massive biography of the Algerian French writer Albert Camus (Todd 1996); the English edition omits fully one third of the French original. Yet **omission**, decided upon by the publisher, does not negate translation. And then there is the political context of translation and language, visible on a basic level whenever we see a bilingual sign in the street or whenever a linguistic group asserts its identity by graffiti-ing over the language of the political majority. More extremely, in recent years the differences within the Serbo–Croat language have been deliberately reinforced for political reasons to cause a separation of Croatian, and indeed Bosnian, from Serbian, meaning that translation now takes place between these three languages (Sucic 1996).

Developments have seen a certain blurring of research between the different types of translation too. Thus, research into **audiovisual translation** now encompasses **sign language**, **intralingual subtitles**, lip synchronization for **dubbing** as well as **interlingual subtitles**; the image–word relationship is crucial in both film and advertising, and there has been closer investigation of the links between translation, music and dance. In view of this complex situation and for reasons of space, in the present book we shall restrict ourselves mostly to forms of conventional written translation, including some **subtitling** and advertising, but excluding **interpreting**. We shall, however, examine a very wide range of types of written translation. These will include translation into the second language (see Campbell 1998), which does often take place in the context of both language learning and the translation profession, despite the general wisdom that the translator should always translate into his or her mother tongue or 'language of habitual use'.

Our threefold definition of the ambit of translation will thus be:

Concept box   The ambit of translation

1. The **process** of transferring a written text from SL to TL, conducted by a translator, or translators, in a specific socio-cultural **context**.
2. The written **product**, or TT, which results from that process and which functions in the socio-cultural **context** of the TL.
3. The **cognitive**, linguistic, visual, cultural and ideological phenomena which are an integral part of 1 and 2.

WHAT IS TRANSLATION STUDIES?

Jakobson's discussion on translation centres around certain key questions of linguistics, including **equivalence** between items in SL and TL and the notion of **translatability**. These are issues which became central to research in translation in the 1960s and 1970s. This burgeoning field received the name 'Translation Studies' thanks to the Netherlands-based scholar James S. Holmes in his paper 'The Name and Nature of Translation Studies', originally presented in 1972 but widely published only much later (Holmes 1988/2000, see Text B1.2 in Section B). Holmes mapped out the new field like a science, dividing it into 'pure' Translation Studies (encompassing **descriptive studies** of existing translations and general and partial translation theories) and 'applied' studies (covering translator training, **translator aids** and **translation criticism**, amongst others). More priority is afforded to the 'pure' side, the objectives of which Holmes considers to be twofold (1988: 71):

1. to describe the phenomena of translating and translation(s) as they manifest themselves in the world of our experience, and
2. to establish general principles by means of which these phenomena can be explained and predicted.

Here Holmes uses '*translating*' for the **process** and '*translation*' for the **product**. The descriptions and generalized principles envisaged were much reinforced by Gideon Toury in his *Descriptive Translation Studies and Beyond* (1995) where two tentative general '**laws**' of translation are proposed:

1. the **law** of growing **standardization** – TTs generally display less linguistic variation than STs, and
2. the **law** of **interference** – common ST lexical and **syntactic** patterns tend to be copied, creating unusual patterns in the TT.

In both instances, the contention is that translated language in general displays specific characteristics, known as **universals of translation**.

Concept box   Universals of translation

> Specific characteristics that, it is hypothesized, are typical of translated language as distinct from non-translated language. This would be the same whatever the language pair involved and might include greater **cohesion** and **explicitation** (with reduced ambiguity) and the fact that a TT is normally longer than a ST. See Blum-Kulka and Levenson (1983), Baker (1993) and Mauranen and Kujamäki (2004) for more on **universals**.

The strong form of this hypothesis is that these are elements that always occur in translation; the weaker form is that these are tendencies that often occur. Recent progress with **corpus-based** approaches have followed up suggestions by Baker (1993) to investigate **universals** using larger **corpora** (electronic databases of texts) in an attempt to avoid the anecdotal findings of small-scale studies. The TEC **corpus**, overseen by Mona Baker at the University of Manchester, UK, is one of these (<http://www.monabaker.com/tsresources/>).

DEVELOPMENTS IN TRANSLATION STUDIES

Although references are still to be found to the new or 'emerging' discipline (e.g. Riccardi 2002), since Holmes's paper, Translation Studies has evolved to such an extent that it is really a perfect interdiscipline, interfacing with a whole host of other fields. The aim may still be to describe translation phenomena, and in some cases to establish general principles, but the methods of analysis are more varied and the cultural and ideological features of translation have become as prominent as linguistics. Figure A1.1 illustrates the breadth of contacts:

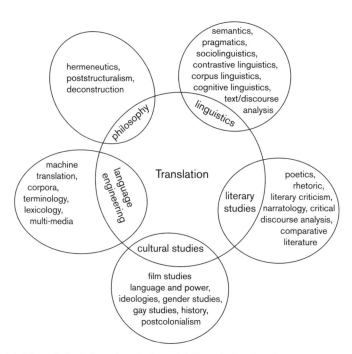

Figure A1.1 Map of disciplines interfacing with Translation Studies

The richness of the field is also illustrated by areas for research suggested by Williams and Chesterman (2002: 6–27), which include:

1. Text analysis and translation
2. Translation quality assessment
3. Translation of literary and other genres
4. Multi-media translation (audiovisual translation)
5. Translation and technology
6. Translation history
7. Translation ethics
8. Terminology and glossaries
9. The translation process
10. Translator training
11. The characteristics of the translation profession

Task A1.4

➤ In view of the diversity of contexts in which translation research is conducted, Figure A1.1 can never be fully comprehensive. Look at the different areas mentioned, look up definitions of any with which you are not familiar, and reflect on whether there are any areas which could be added.

Task A1.5

➤ Make a note of the terminology of translation used in this unit and keep the glossary updated as you cover more areas of Translation Studies. At various points throughout the book we will refer to this glossary.

This first unit has discussed what we mean by 'translation' and 'Translation Studies'. It has built on Jakobson's term 'interlingual translation' and Holmes's mapping of the field of Translation Studies. In truth we are talking of an interdiscipline, interfacing with a vast breadth of knowledge which means that research into translation is possible from many different angles, from scientific to literary, cultural and political. A threefold scope of translation has been presented, with a goal of describing the translation process and identifying trends, if not laws or universals, of translation.

Summary

Unit A2
Translation strategies

If we were to sample what people generally take 'translation' to be, the consensus would most probably be for a view of translating that describes the **process** in terms of such features as the literal rendering of meaning, adherence to **form**, and emphasis on general accuracy. These observations would certainly be true of what translators do most of the time and of the bulk of what gets translated. As we shall see as this book progresses, these statements require much refinement and betray a strongly **prescriptive** attitude to translation. But they are also the product of some of the central issues of translation theory all the way from Roman times to the mid-twentieth century.

FORM AND CONTENT

Roman Jakobson makes the crucial claim that 'all **cognitive** experience and its classification is conveyable in any existing language' (Jakobson 1959: 238, see Text B1.1). So, to give an example, while modern British English concepts such as the *National Health Service, public–private partnership* and *congestion charging*, or, in the USA, *Ivy League universities, Homeland Security* and *speed dating*, might not exist in a different culture, that should not stop them being expressed in some way in the target language (TL). Jakobson goes on to claim that only poetry 'by definition is untranslatable' since in verse the form of words contributes to the construction of the meaning of the text. Such statements express a classical dichotomy in translation between sense/**content** on the one hand and **form/style** on the other.

sense/ ◄───────────────────────────► form/

content   style

The sense may be translated, while the **form** often cannot. And the point where **form** begins to contribute to sense is where we approach un**translatability**. This clearly is most likely to be in poetry, song, advertising, punning and so on, where sound and rhyme and double meaning are unlikely to be recreated in the TL.

Task A2.1

➤ The spoken or written form of names in the Harry Potter books often contributes to their meaning. In *Harry Potter and the Chamber of Secrets*, one of
the evil characters goes by the name of Tom Marvolo Riddle, yet this name is
itself a riddle, since it is an anagram of 'I am Lord Voldemort' and reveals the
character's true identity. Think how you might deal with this **form–content**
problem in translation into another language.

In the published translations, many of the Harry Potter translators have resorted to
altering the original name in order to create the required pun: in French, the name
becomes 'Tom Elvis Jedusor' which gives 'Je suis Voldemort' as well as suggesting an
enigmatic fate with the use of the name Elvis and the play on words 'jeudusor' or
'jeu du sort', meaning 'game of fate'. In this way the French translator, Jean-François
Ménard, has preserved the **content** by altering the **form**.

LITERAL AND FREE

The split between **form** and **content** is linked in many ways to the major polar split
which has marked the history of western translation theory for two thousand years,
between two ways of translating: 'literal' and 'free'. The origin of this separation
is to be found in two of the most-quoted names in translation theory, the Roman
lawyer and writer Cicero and St Jerome, who translated the Greek Septuagint
gospels into Latin in the fourth century. In Classical times, it was normal for
translators working from Greek to provide a **literal, word-for-word** 'translation'
which would serve as an aid to the Latin reader who, it could be assumed, was
reasonably acquainted with the Greek source language. Cicero, describing his own
translation of Attic orators in 46 BCE, emphasized that he did not follow the **literal**
'word-for-word' approach but, as an orator, 'sought to preserve the general style and
force of the language' (Cicero 46 BC/1960: 364).

Four centuries later, St Jerome described his Bible translation strategy as 'I render
not **word-for-word** but sense for sense' (Jerome 395/1997: 25). This approach was
of particular importance for the translation of such sensitive texts as the Bible,
deemed by many to be the repository of truth and the word of God. A translator
who did not remain 'true' to the 'official' interpretation of that word often ran a
considerable risk. Sometimes, as in the case of the sixteenth-century English Bible
translator William Tyndale, it was the mere act of translation into the vernacular
that led to persecution and execution.

The **literal** and **free** translation strategies can still be seen in texts to the present day.
The shoe-cleaning machine example (Example C1.1) could be considered a **literal**
translation of the Spanish – so literal, it remains part Spanish! Example A2.1 below,
from a tourist brochure for a vintage train line in Mallorca, shows how a **literal**
translation may be the norm between two closely related languages, in this case ST

Catalan and TT Spanish. It is easy to see that the lexical and **syntactic** structures are almost identical:

Example A2.1

ST Des de 1912, el Ferrocarril de Sóller uneix les xiutats de Palma i Sóller
TT Desde 1912, el Ferrocarril de Sóller une las ciudades de Palma y Sóller
  [*Since 1912, the Railway of Soller joins the towns of Palma and Soller*
conservant encara el seu caràcter original.
conservando   su carácter original.
preserving still the its character original.]

Such a **literal** translation is not so common when the languages in question are more distant. Or, to put it another way, the term '**literal**' has tended to be used with a different focus, sometimes to denote a TT which is overly close or influenced by the ST or SL. The result is what is sometimes known as '**translationese**'.

Concept Box   Translationese

> A pejorative general term for the language of translation. It is often used to indicate a stilted form of the TL from calquing ST lexical or **syntactic** patterning (see Duff 1981). **Translationese** is related to translation **universals** (see Section A Unit 1) since the characteristics mentioned above may be due to common translation phenomena such as **interference, explicitation** and **domestication**. In Unit 13, we shall see how an alternative name, **translatese**, is employed by Spivak to refer to a lifeless form of the TL that homogenizes the different ST authors. Newmark (2003: 96) uses another term, 'translatorese', to mean the automatic choice of the most common 'dictionary' translation of a word where, in context, a less frequent alternative would be more appropriate.

To illustrate this, let us consider some typical examples of translated material (the English TTs of Arabic STs) which seem to defy comprehension. As you read through these TTs, try to identify features of the texts that strike you as odd, and reflect on whether problems of this kind are common in languages you are familiar with. For example, what are we to make of the request for donations in this welfare organization's publicity leaflet?

Example A2.2

Honorable Benefactor

After Greetings,
   [. . .] The organization hopefully appeals to you, whether nationals or expatriates in this generous country, to extend a helping hand. . . .
   We have the honour to offer you the chance to contribute to our programs and projects from your monies and alms so that God may bless you. [. . .]

In this example of what in English would be a fund-raising text, confusion sets in when 'making a donation' is seen as an honour bestowed both on the donor and on those making the appeal. There is a certain opaqueness and far too much power for a text of this kind to function properly in English.

In a way, this is not different from the advert for a French wine purchasing company which, instead of simply saying 'Now you too can take advantage of this wonderful opportunity' (Fawcett 1997: 62), actually had:

Example A2.3

Today, we offer you to share this position

In all these examples, the influence of poor **literal** translation is all too obvious. In this respect, perhaps no field has been more challenging to translators than advertising. Consider this advert promoting cash dispensing services:

Example A2.4

The Telebanking System

X Bank presents the banking services by phone. The Telebanking System welcomes you by the Islamic greeting 'assalamu 'alaykum', completes your inquiries/transactions within few seconds and sees you off saying 'fi aman allah'.

Not surprisingly, this publicity material was withdrawn since the advertising gimmick obviously did not work on a population consisting mostly of expatriates with little or no Arabic to appreciate the nuance. The advert has more recently re-appeared simply stating:

Example A2.5

X Islamic Bank, the first Islamic Bank in the world, is pleased to offer you a sophisticated service through Automated Teller Machine Cash Card.

The concept of literalness that emerges from these examples is one of exaggeratedly close adherence on the part of the translator to the lexical and **syntactic** properties of the ST. Yet, once again, the **literal–free** divide is not so much a pair of fixed opposites as a cline:

literal ⟵ free

Different parts of a text may be positioned at different points on the cline, while other variables, as we shall see in the coming units, are **text type, audience, purpose** as well as the general translation strategy of the translator.

 Task A2.2

➤ Reflect on examples of types of texts, **audience, purpose** or strategy that you have seen that have required a **literal** translation. For instance, it may be presumed that a legal text, such as a law, a treaty, or the International Declaration of Human Rights (see Example C13.3), might require a much closer, more **literal** translation than a piece of poetry.

 Task A2.3

The issues raised by almost all the above examples are certainly **semantic** and **syntactic** in origin. Upon closer scrutiny, however, they tend to reveal deeper conceptual problems closely bound up with such factors as competence in the foreign language and awareness of the target culture.

➤ Reflect on how some of the above **semantic** or **syntactic** problems take on socio-cultural values, and how you might go about the task of dealing with them in translation.

COMPREHENSIBILITY AND TRANSLATABILITY

Such **literal** translations often fail to take account of one simple fact of language and translation, namely that not all texts or text users are the same. Not all texts are as 'serious' as the Bible or the works of Dickens, nor are they all as 'pragmatic' as marriage certificates or instructions on a medicine bottle. Similarly, not all text receivers are as intellectually rigorous or culturally aware as those who read the Bible or Dickens, nor are they all as 'utilitarian' as those who simply use translation as a means of getting things done. Ignoring such factors as **text type, audience** or **purpose** of translation has invariably led to the rather pedantic form of **literalism**, turgid adherence to **form** and almost total obsession with accuracy often encountered in the translations we see or hear day in day out. We have all come across translations where the vocabulary of a given language may well be recognizable and the grammar intact, but the sense is quite lacking.

On the other hand, Example A2.6, from the packaging describing the components of a food processor, is an example of a much freer translation:

Example A2.6a ST French

Couvercle et cuves en polycarbonate. Matériau haute résistance utilisé pour les hublots d'avion. Résiste à de hautes températures et aux chocs.

Tableau de commandes simple et fonctionnel. 3 commandes suffisent à maîtriser Compact 3100.

[*Lid and bowls in polycarbonate. High resistance material used for aircraft windows. Resists high temperatures and shocks.*

Simple and functional control panel. 3 controls suffice to master Compact 3100.]

Example A2.6b TT English

Workbowls and lid are made from polycarbonate, the same substance as the windows of Concorde. It's shatterproof, and won't melt with boiling liquids or crack under pressure.

Technically advanced, simple to use : just on, off or pulse.

Task A2.4

➤ Look at the translation A2.6b and reflect on the strategies employed by the translator to increase **comprehensibility**.

The problem with many published TTs of the kind cited earlier is essentially one of impaired '**comprehensibility**', an issue closely related to '**translatability**'. **Translatability** is a relative notion and has to do with the extent to which, despite obvious differences in linguistic structure (grammar, vocabulary, etc.), meaning can still be adequately expressed across languages. But, for this to be possible, meaning has to be understood not only in terms of what the ST contains, but also and equally significantly, in terms of such factors as communicative purpose, target **audience** and **purpose** of translation. This must go hand in hand with the recognition that, while there will always be entire chunks of experience and some unique ST values that will simply defeat our best efforts to convey them across cultural and linguistic boundaries, translation is always possible and cultural gaps are in one way or another bridgeable. To achieve this, an important criterion to heed must be TT **comprehensibility**.

Is everything translatable? The answer, to paraphrase Jakobson (1959/2000, see Text B1.1), is 'yes, to a certain extent'. In the more idiomatic renderings provided above, the target reader may well have been deprived of quite a hefty chunk of ST meaning. But what choice does the translator have? Such insights as 'it is an honour both to appeal for and to give to charity, both to issue and to accept an invitation, both to offer and to accept a glass of wine, both to live and to die, etc.' are no doubt valuable. But what is the point in trying to preserve them in texts like fund-raising leaflets, adverts or political speeches if they are not going to be appreciated for what they are, i.e. if they do not prove to be equally significant to a target reader?

It is indeed a pity that the target reader of the modern Bible has to settle for 'to make somebody ashamed of his behaviour' when the Hebrew ST actually has 'to heap coal of fire on his head' (Nida and Taber 1969: 2), with the ultimate aim, we suggest, not so much of burning his head as blackening his face which in both Hebrew and Arab–Islamic cultures symbolizes unspeakable shame. But how obscure is one allowed to be in order to live up to the unrealistic ideal of full translatibility and how feasible is an approach such as Dryden's, who claimed to have endeavoured to make the ST author (Virgil in his case) 'speak such English as he would himself have spoken, if he had been born in England, and in this present age' (Dryden 1697/1992)?

Summary

Some of the main issues of translation are linked to the strategies of **literal** and **free** translation, **form** and **content**. This division, that has marked translation for centuries, can help identify the problems of certain overly **literal** translations that impair **comprehensibility**. However, the real underlying problems of such translations lead us into areas such as **text type** and **audience** that will become central from Unit 6 onwards.

Unit A3
The unit of translation

SYSTEMATIC APPROACHES TO THE TRANSLATION UNIT

Unit 2 focused on the age-old translation strategies 'literal' and 'free'. To a great extent, these strategies are linked to different **translation units**, 'literal' being very much centred on adherence to the individual word, while 'free' translation aims at capturing the sense of a longer stretch of language. In this unit we will begin to examine more systematic approaches to the **unit of translation**.

Concept box   The unit of translation

> This term refers to 'the linguistic level at which ST is recodified in TL' (Shuttleworth and Cowie 1997: 192). In other words, the element used by the translator when working on the ST. It may be the individual word, group, clause, sentence or even the whole text. In first discussing the word as a possible unit of translation, Vinay and Darbelnet (1958/1995) draw on Saussure's key concepts of the linguistic **sign**, defined by the **signifier** and **signified** (see the Concept box below).

Concept box   The linguistic sign

> The famous Swiss linguist Ferdinand de Saussure invented the linguistic term **sign** that unifies **signifier** (sound-image or word) and **signified** (concept). Importantly, Saussure emphasizes that the **sign** is by nature arbitrary and can only derive meaning from contrast with other signs in the same system (language). Thus, the **signifier** *tree* recalls the real-world **signified** plant with a trunk; it can be contrasted with **signifiers** such as *bush*, a different kind of plant. But the selection of *tree* for this designation is arbitrary and only occurs in the English-language system. In French, the **signifier** *arbre* is used for this plant (see Saussure 1916/1983: 65–70).

Vinay and Darbelnet reject the word as a **unit of translation** since translators focus on the **semantic field** rather than on the formal properties of the individual **signifier**. For them, the unit is 'the smallest segment of the utterance whose **signs** are linked in such a way that they should not be translated individually' (1958/1995: 21). This is what they call the lexicological unit and the unit of thought.

THE LEXICOLOGICAL UNIT

The lexicological units described by Vinay and Darbelnet contain 'lexical elements grouped together to form a single element of thought'. Illustrative examples they provide, to show the non-correspondence at word level between French and English, are: *simple soldat* = *private* (in the army) and *tout de suite* = *immediately*. Of course, the traditional structure of dictionaries, which divides a language into headwords, means that individual words do tend to be treated in isolation, being divided into different senses. Below is an adapted entry for the Spanish word *brote* in the Oxford Spanish bilingual dictionary (third edition, 2003):

Example A3.1

brote m
a (botanical) shoot; **echar brotes** to sprout, put out shoots
b (of rebellion, violence) outbreak
c (of an illness) outbreak

The bracketed descriptors, known as discriminators, summarize the main use, field or **collocation** for each translation **equivalent**. Thus, sense 'c' is the 'illness' sense, with the corresponding translation *outbreak*. On the other hand, sense 'a' is the botanical sense, with the translation *shoot*, of a plant. The example in sense 'a', *echar brotes*, is an example of a strong **collocation** in Spanish. This two-word unit may be translated in English by a single verb, *sprout*, or by a phrasal verb plus object, *put out shoots*, which demonstrates how the **translation unit** is not fixed to an individual word across languages. This is brought out even more strongly in the entry for *outbreak* on the English side of the dictionary:

Example A3.2

outbreak *n*
(of war) estallido *m*; (of hostilities) comienzo *m*; (of cholera, influenza) brote *m*; **at the outbreak of the strike** . . . al declararse *or* al estallar la huelga . . .; **there were outbreaks of violence/protest** hubo brotes de violencia/protesta

Task A3.1

➤ Reflect on what the **unit of translation** is in these translation **equivalents** and illustrative examples.

THE UNIT OF THOUGHT

Passengers flying from the United Kingdom to Madrid Barajas airport in March 2001 were presented with the following leaflet upon arrival:

Example A3.3a Spanish ST

Según OM nº 4295 de 2 de marzo de 2001

DEBIDO AL BROTE DE FIEBRE AFTOSA, ROGAMOS A LOS SEÑORES PASAJEROS DE LOS VUELOS CON ORIGEN EN EL *REINO UNIDO* O *FRANCIA*, DESINFECTEN SU CALZADO EN LAS ALFOMBRAS.

[*Due to the outbreak of foot-and-mouth disease, we ask ladies-and-gentlemen passengers of flights with origin in the United Kingdom or France, that they disinfect their footwear on the carpets.*]

Example A3.3b English TT

DUE TO THE OUTBREAK OF FOOT-AND-MOUTH DISEASE, ALL PASSENGERS ARRIVING FROM THE *UNITED KINGDOM* OR *FRANCE* ARE KINDLY REQUESTED TO DISINFECT THEIR FOOTWEAR ON THE SPECIAL CARPETS PROVIDED.

Example A3.3c French TT

À CAUSE DES PREMIERS SIGNES DE LA FIÈVRE APHTEUSE, NOUS PRIONS MESSIEURS LES PASSAGERS PROVENANT DU *ROYAUME UNI* OU DE *LA FRANCE* DE PASSER SUR LE TAPIS POUR DÉSINFECTER LEURS CHAUSSURES.

Task A3.2

➤ Look at the Spanish ST, using the back-translation as necessary. Think about what units of translation a translator might use when translating this.

If we focus on the first line of the ST, our particular interest is in the expressions *brote*, *fiebre aftosa* and *rogamos*. The first two have established **equivalents** in this scientific context, *outbreak* and *foot-and-mouth disease* respectively. Note that *fiebre aftosa* must be considered as a separate **translation unit**, a multi-word lexicological unit, and translated accordingly as *foot-and-mouth disease* and not *aphtose fever*, for example. The French has a multi-word unit that is similar in structure to the Spanish, *fièvre aphteuse*, and uses a two-word expression *premiers signes* ('first signs') to translate *brote*, a potential equivalent which is absent in most dictionaries. This shows that it is the specific context which determines the translation of a given unit.

When it comes to the word *rogamos* it can clearly be seen that it is impossible to translate the word individually. A translator needs to consider the whole structure *rogamos a los señores pasajeros . . . desinfecten su calzado* ('request-we ladies-and-gentlemen passengers . . . they disinfect their footwear . . .') and its politeness **function** in context before translating. It is in such instances that restructuring is most likely to occur. In this case, the English politeness formula prefers a passive (*are requested*) and the addition of the adverb *kindly* in order to reduce any abruptness that might be caused by a **literal** translation from the Spanish: *all passengers . . . are kindly requested to disinfect their footwear*. While a word such as *calzado* may be a **lexicological unit** which can be translated with its normal **equivalent** *footwear*, the phrase as a whole is a unit of thought and needs to be treated as such in the **process** of translation. Translation units, therefore, will vary according to the linguistic structure involved.

THE UNIT OF TRANSLATION AS A PRELUDE TO ANALYSIS

Division of ST and TT into the **units of translation** is of particular importance in Vinay and Darbelnet's work as a prelude to analysis of changes in translation, the **translation shifts** that will occupy us in Unit 4. As an illustration of how this division works, and how it might illuminate the **process** of translation, look at Example A3.4a, a poster located by the underground ticket office at Heathrow airport, London:

Example A3.4a

Travelling from Heathrow?
There are easy to follow instructions on the larger self-service touch screen ticket machines.

 Task A3.3

➤ Before reading further, imagine you have been asked to translate this poster into your first language (or main foreign language). Write down your translation and make a note of the translation units you use when dividing up the ST.

A translator approaching this short text will most probably break it down into the title (*Travelling from Heathrow?*) and the instructions in the second sentence. While that sentence will be taken as a whole, it might also in turn be sub-divided more or less as follows:

There are/
[easy to follow/instructions]/
[on the/larger/self-service/touch screen/ticket machines]

Here, the slashes (/) indicate small word groups with a distinct **semantic** meaning that might be considered separately, while the brackets ([. . .]) enclose larger units that a practised translator is likely to translate as a whole.

The actual French TT on the poster indicates how this operates in real life:

Example A3.4b

Vous partez de Heathrow?
Les distributeurs de billets à écran tactile vous fourniront des instructions claires et simples en français.

[You leave from Heathrow?
The distributors of tickets with screen touchable to-you provide-will some instructions clear and simple in French.]

The title is translated as a question, but with the grammatical subject filled out ('*You* leave from Heathrow?'). The second sentence has been restructured to produce an instruction that functions in French. The different ST–TT elements line up as follows, with Ø standing for an **omission** or 'zero translation':

There are	/ [easy to follow	/ instructions]	/ on / [the / larger /
[vous fourniront]	/ [claires et simples	/ des instructions]	/ Ø / [les / Ø /
self-service	/ touch screen	/ ticket machines	]
/ Ø	/ à écran tactile	/ distributeurs de billets]	/ en français

It is clear that the French has translated *the larger self-service ticket machines* as a single unit (*les distributeurs de billets*), with the solid-sounding *distributeurs* incorporating by implication not only the concept of *self-service* but also perhaps the comparator *larger* from the ST. Note also how the definite article *the* has necessarily been considered as part of the same translation unit as *ticket machines*, giving the plural form *les* in *les distributeurs de billets* in the French. *Easy to follow* has been rendered by two adjectives linked by an additive conjunction, *claires et simples* ('clear and simple'). There are two additions in the TT: *en français* ('in French'), to reassure the reader that the instructions will be easy to follow for them in their own language, and *vous fourniront* ('to you will provide'), which has taken over the function of the English existential verb form *there are*.

This simple text indicates how, in practice, the translation unit will typically tend to be not individual words but small chunks of language building up into the sentence, what the famous translation theorist Eugene Nida (1964: 268) calls 'meaningful mouthfuls of language'.

TRANSLATION AT DIFFERENT LEVELS

In his *Textbook of Translation* (1988), Peter Newmark discusses translation using in part a scale that has become well established in linguistics with the work of Michael Halliday (e.g. Halliday 1985/1994). It should be noted that Hallidayan linguistics also informs much of Mona Baker's influential *In Other Words* (1992), which, too, examines translation at different levels, although in Baker's case it is levels of **equivalence** (at the level of the **word**, **collocation** and idiom, grammar, **thematic** and **information structure**, **cohesion** and **pragmatics**).

Halliday's systemic analysis of English grammar is based on the following hierarchical **rank** scale, starting with the smallest unit (examples are ours and are drawn from Example A3.3b):

morpheme	– arriv-*ing*
word	– *arriving*
group	– *foot-and-mouth disease*
clause	– the whole of Example A3.3b
sentence	– the whole of Example A3.3b

Word and group are the **ranks** that we have discussed most so far in this unit. But Halliday's focus is on the clause as a representation of meaning in a communicative context and Newmark's is on the sentence as the 'natural' **unit of translation**. Newmark (1988: 165) states that **transpositions** and rearrangements may often occur, but that a sentence would not normally be divided unless there was good reason. He is careful to insist that any 'rearrangements' or 'recastings' must respect **Functional Sentence Perspective**.

Concept box   Functional Sentence Perspective (FSP)

A form of analysis of sentence and **information structure** created by the Prague School of Linguists (see Firbas 1992). **Syntactic structure**, known as linear modification, is an important structuring device. However, communication is driven forward primarily by 'communicative dynamism', that is, by elements that are context-independent and contribute most new information. These are most often, but not always, focused towards the end of a sentence. The part of the sentence containing the new information is known as the **rheme**, whereas '**old**' or '**given**' **information** is contained in the **theme**. It should be noted that this division of **theme** and **rheme** differs from a **Hallidayan** analysis, where **theme** is always realized in first position, in English grammar at least (Halliday 1985/1994: 38).

This can be illustrated by the following example in its different versions (the originals are dual, French and English, a not uncommon practice in large international organizations). The text is the Monaco statement on bioethics and the rights of the child, arising from the April 2000 symposium:

Example A3.5a Bioethics and the right of the child

The International Symposium on Bioethics and the Rights of the Child, jointly organized by the World Association of Children's Friends (AMADE) and UNESCO, was held in Monaco from 28 to 30 April 2000. It presents hereafter a number of considerations regarding the progress in biology and medicine with a view to reinforcing and implementing the protection of children's rights.

It acknowledged the issue of childhood, as a complex, evolving reality, which now merits specific consideration. Children are fragile beings. However, their autonomy should not be misconceived. [. . .]

(*Proceedings of the International Symposium AMADE – UNESCO on Bioethics and the Rights of the Child*, Monaco, 28–30 April 2000)

Task A3.4

➤ Study this example and consider how far the sentence would be the most appropriate unit of translation.

In a translation of Example A3.5a, rearrangements of elements would be possible in translation. Indeed, the Russian translation moved the details of the date and location of the meeting to first position but respected the link between the two sentences. Comparison of paragraph two in the French version and the English version shows that clause and sentence by no means necessarily correspond over languages, even if the development of the paragraph is maintained:

Example A3.5b Back-translation of French version of Bioethics text

It acknowledged that childhood is a complex, evolving reality and that it merits now a specific consideration. The child is a fragile being, but his autonomy should not therefore be disregarded. [. . .]

Task A3.5

➤ Compare Example A3.5b with A3.5a. Note the changes across clause and sentence boundaries and reflect on why these might have occurred and how the **information** structure has been preserved, or altered, in the process.

In the case of some texts, such as legal documents, or some authors, sentence length plays an important stylistic or **functional** role. Thus, Hemingway's preference for shorter sentences and avoidance of subordinate clauses, or Proust's tendency for long elaborate sentences, are fundamental not only to their style but also to the view of the world that is being depicted. A translator working with the sentence as the translation unit would therefore need to pay particular care to preserving the features of the STs.

Above the level of the sentence, Newmark considers paragraph and **text** (incorporating chapter and section) as higher units of translation. We shall discuss these in more detail in Units 9 to 11. At a **functional** level, as Reiss and Vermeer (1984) would argue, this means that the TT must perform the **purpose** associated with it: a translated piece of software must work perfectly on-screen and enable the user to perform the desired action; advertisements, most particularly, and poetry need to be translated at the level of the **text** (or even culture) and not the word if their message is to function in the target culture; and medicines and other foodstuffs must carry instructions and warning notices that satisfactorily alert the TT reader to possible dangers, such as the basic and simple one in Example A3.6:

Example A3.6   Warning notice on medicines

Keep out of reach of children

 Task A3.6

➤ Look at the corresponding warning notice printed on medicines and other products in your other language(s). Is the same wording always used whether or not the instructions are original SL or part of a translated text?

Of course, texts themselves are not isolated but function within their own socio-cultural and ideological environment. Equally importantly, at the **intertextual** level, texts are influenced reworkings of earlier texts. This concept of **intertextuality** will be discussed in far greater depth in Units 10 and 11, while the notion of culture as the **unit of translation**, argued by Snell-Hornby (1990), underpins Unit 13.

Summary

The **unit of translation** is normally the linguistic unit which the translator uses when translating. Translation theorists have proposed various units, from individual word and group to clause and sentence and even higher levels such as **text** and **intertextual** levels (e.g. Beaugrande 1978, see Unit 9). Importantly, Newmark (1988: 66–7) makes the crucial point that 'all lengths of language can, at different moments and also simultaneously, be used as units of translation in the course of the translation activity'. While it may be that the translator most often works at the sentence level, paying specific attention to problems raised by individual words or groups in that context, it is also important to take into account the **function** of the whole text and references to extratextual features. These are crucial areas that will be treated in more depth as this book develops. In the meantime, Unit 4 will go on to examine how the division of **translation units** can support an analysis of the changes or **shifts** that take place in the move from ST to TT.

Unit A4
Translation shifts

Unit 3 looked at the **unit of translation**, whether word, phrase or higher level. The present unit will now discuss models or taxonomies that have been proposed for examining the small changes or 'shifts' that occur between units in a ST–TT pair. A connecting theme of the examples is rail travel, perhaps a symbolic counterpoint to the best known **taxonomy** of **translation shifts**, devised by Vinay and Darbelnet and initially inspired by the study of bilingual road signs in Canada.

TRANSLATION SHIFTS

On some international trains in Europe, there is, or used to be, a multilingual warning notice displayed next to the windows:

Example A4.1

Ne pas se pencher au dehors

Nicht hinauslehnen

È pericoloso sporgersi

Do not lean out of the window

The warning is clear, even if the **form** is different in each language. The English, the only one to actually mention the window, is a negative imperative, while the French and German use a negative infinitive construction ('not to lean outside') and the Italian is a statement ('[it] is dangerous to lean out'). Of course, these kinds of differences are typical of translation in general. It is not at all the most common for the exact structure of the words to be repeated across languages and, even when the grammatical structure is the same (as in the French and German examples above), the number of word forms varies from six (*ne pas se pencher au dehors*) to two (*nicht hinauslehnen*).

The small linguistic changes that occur between ST and TT are known as **translation shifts**. John Catford was the first scholar to use the term in his *A Linguistic Theory of Translation* (1965, see Section B Text B4.1). His definition of **shifts** is 'departures from **formal correspondence** in the process of going from the SL to the TL' (Catford

1965: 73). The distinction drawn between **formal correspondence** and **textual equivalence** will be crucial and relates to Saussure's distinction between *langue* and *parole*:

Concept box *Langue, parole*

Language has two facets, one to do with the linguistic system (a fairly stable *langue*), the other with all that which a speaker might say or understand while using language (a variable *parole*). Noam Chomsky was probably right in categorically excluding activities such as translation from the purview of his own research into **syntactic** structures. And so-called 'linguistics-oriented' translation theory has not interacted well with translation practice simply because it has systematically sought neatness of categories at the expense of being true to what people say or do with language, which is what gets translated ultimately. In *parole*-oriented translation theory and practice, we are concerned not so much with the systemic similarities and differences between languages as with the communicative process in all its aspects, with conventions (both linguistic and rhetorical) and with translation as mediation between different languages and cultures.

Concept box Formal correspondence

A **formal correspondent** is defined by Catford as 'any TL category (unit, class, structure, element of structure, etc.) which can be said to occupy, as nearly as possible, the "same" place in the "economy" of the TL as the given SL category occupies in the SL' (Catford 1965: 27). In simplified terms, this means a TL piece of language which plays the same role in the TL system as an SL piece of language plays in the SL system. Thus, a noun such as *fenêtre* might be said generally to occupy a similar place in the French language system as the noun *window* does in English. **Formal correspondence** therefore involves a comparison and description of the language systems (Saussure's *langue*) but not a comparison of specific ST–TT pairs (**textual equivalence**).

Concept box Textual equivalence

A **textual equivalent** is defined as 'any TL text or portion of text which is observed [. . .] to be the equivalent of a given SL text or portion of text' (Catford 1965: 27). Whereas **formal correspondence** has to do with the

continued

general, non-specific, relationship between elements in two languages, **textual equivalence** focuses on the relations that exist between elements in a specific ST–TT pair (Saussure's *parole*). In Example A4.1, the English **textual equivalent** for *au dehors* is *out of the window*; the **formal correspondent** *outside* is not used. See Text B4.1 from Section B, which is taken from Catford's book.

Concept box   Translation shift

A **shift** is said to occur if, in a given TT, a translation **equivalent** other than the **formal correspondent** occurs for a specific SL element. This is what has occurred between the French and English texts in Example A4.1.

The following example, from a leaflet distributed on board Eurostar trains explaining the measures being taken to detect smoking, can illustrate these differences.

Example A4.2a   English

Please note that smoke detectors will be fitted on-board.

Example A4.2b   German

Beachten Sie bitte, daß die Züge mit Rauchdetektoren ausgestattet werden.

[*Note you please, that the trains with smokedetectors fitted will-be.*]

 ### Task A4.1

➤ Look at these two examples. How many departures from **formal correspondence** can you detect? How do you decide what a departure is?

Analysing these examples, it is clear that there are many formal correspondences at lexical and grammatical levels:

please	–	bitte
beachten	–	note
that	–	daß
smoke detectors	–	Rauchdetektoren
will be	–	werden

Systemic differences between the languages must be accepted. These include word-order changes and the construction of the German imperative with the addition of the pronoun *Sie* ['you']. However, there is a clear departure from **formal correspondence** in the translation of the ST *on-board* and the restructuring of the second clause. In this text, the only possible **textual equivalent** for *on-board* is *die Züge* ('the trains') which is added with a change of grammatical subject (ST *smoke detectors* to TT *die Züge*). The analyst then has to decide whether *ausgestattet* is a **formal correspondent** of *fitted*. A dictionary definition is not enough since some dictionaries may give *ausstatten* as a translation of *to equip* or *fit out* but not *fit*. However, the role occupied by *ausgestattet* and *fitted* in the two languages is very similar, so it is highly unlikely that we would class this as a **shift**.

Catford was the first to use the term **shift**, but the most comprehensive **taxonomy** of **translation shifts**, based on their 'translation **procedures**', was set out by the Canadians Jean-Paul Vinay and Jean Darbelnet in their *A Comparative Stylistics of French and English* (1958/1995). While it is true that they approach the subject from the point of view of comparative or contrastive **stylistics**, using parallel non-translated as well as translated texts, they describe a detailed and systematic model for the analysis and comparison of a ST–TT pair. The first step involves identification and numbering of the ST units and the **units of translation** (see Section A, Unit 3). This is followed by a matching of the two.

Task A4.2

➤ The Eurostar ST has been reproduced below together with the German translation. Look at the translation units that are matched up and, using the **back-translation** to help you, note any 'mismatches', denoting **shifts**.

Example A4.3a

Eurostar

Please note that smoke detectors will be fitted on-board. Any misconduct will result in necessary action being taken by rail staff and/or police.

Example A4.3b German

Beachten Sie bitte, daß die Züge mit Rauchdetektoren ausgestattet werden. Jeder Verstoß wird mit den erforderlichen Maßnahmen durch das Bahnpersonal und/oder die Polizei geahndet.

[*Note please that the trains with smokedetectors fitted will be. Each violation will-be with the necessary measures through the railstaff and/or the police punished.*]

ST	TT
1. please	bitte
2. note	beachten Sie
3. that	daß
	die Züge
4. smoke detectors	mit Rauchdetektoren
5. will be fitted	ausgestattet werden
6. on-board	
7. Any misconduct	Jeder Verstoß
8. will result in	wird . . . mit
9. necessary action	den erforderlichen Maßnahmen
10. being taken	geahndet
11. by rail staff	durch das Bahnpersonal
12. and/or	und/oder
13. police	die Polizei

Clear **shifts** in the second sentence can be seen in translation unit 7, where *any misconduct* becomes the more specific and stronger 'each violation' in the German, and in units 8 and 10, where *will result in . . . being taken* is altered to 'will . . . with . . . be punished'. Yet numerous issues arise when this type of analysis is undertaken, not least what the **translation unit** is. This is illustrated by the term *smoke detectors* in this and other versions (the leaflet also contained French and Flemish versions): the German and Flemish have a one word **equivalent** (*Rauchdetektoren* and *rook-detectoren* respectively) but the French needs the multi-word unit *détecteurs de fumée* ['detectors of smoke']. Few would argue that the translations are correct and close equivalents, but should the number of word forms used be taken into consideration when deciding if a **shift** has taken place? Similarly, has a **shift** occurred in the German because of the obligatory placing of the passive *werden* at the end of sentence 1? And how are we to decide if *Verstoß*, *infraction* (in the French) or *overtreding* (Flemish) involves a **shift** from ST *misconduct*?

Identifying that a **shift** has taken place leads to questions such as what kind of **shift**, what form of classification we can use and what the importance of the **shifts** is. As will begin to become clear in Section B Text B3.1, Vinay and Darbelnet's categorization of translation **procedures** is very detailed. They name two 'methods' covering seven **procedures**:

1. **direct translation**, which covers
    borrowing, calque and **literal** translation, and

2. **oblique translation**, which is **transposition, modulation, equivalence** and **adaptation**.

These **procedures** are applied on three levels of language:

i.   the **lexicon**

ii. the grammatical structures and

iii. the 'message', which is used to refer to the situational utterance and some of the higher text elements such as sentence and paragraphs.

At the level of message, Vinay and Darbelnet discuss such strategies as **compensation**, an important term in translation which is linked to the notion of **loss** and **gain**.

Concept box   Compensation, loss and gain

A translation technique used to **compensate** for translation **loss**. The translator offsets an inevitable **loss** at one point in the text by adding a suitable element at another point, achieving a compensatory translation **gain**. For example, an informal text in French using the second personal pronoun *tu* might be rendered in English by informal lexis or use of the first name or nickname. **Compensation** in an interpretive sense, restoring life to the TT, is the fourth 'movement' of Steiner's **hermeneutic** process (Steiner 1998: 39, see Part A, Unit 13).

These translation **procedures** have influenced later taxonomies by, amongst others, van Leuven-Zwart (1989, 1990), who attempts a very complex analysis of extracts from translations of Latin American fiction. However, despite a systematic means of analysis based on the **denotative** meaning of each word, the decision as to whether a **shift** has occurred is inevitably subjective since an evaluation of the **equivalence** of the ST and TT units is required. Some kind of evaluator, known in translation as a *tertium comparationis*, is necessary.

Concept box   *Tertium comparationis*

A non-linguistic, intermediate form of the meaning of a ST and TT. The idea is that an invariant meaning exists, independent of both texts, which can be used to gauge or assist **transfer** of meaning between ST and TT.

continued

This can be described graphically as follows:

This has long been a thorny issue in Translation Studies and no one measure has ever been accepted by all.

Task A4.3

➤ What means of comparison did you use when assessing **shifts** in Task A4.2 above? How objective do you feel this comparison was?

Attempts at objectifying the comparison have included van Leuven-Zwart's Architranseme concept where the dictionary meaning of the ST term was taken as a comparator and used independently to evaluate the closeness of the ST and TT term (van Leuven-Zwart 1989, 1990). However, the success of the Architranseme rests upon the absolute objective dependability of the decontextualized dictionary meaning and the analyst's ability to accurately and repeatedly decide whether a **shift** has occurred in the translation context. In view of the difficulty, not to say impossibility, of achieving this, many theorists have moved away from the *tertium comparationis* (see Snell-Hornby 1990). Gideon Toury is the Israeli scholar who has been the prime proponent of **Descriptive Translation Studies**, a branch of the discipline that sets out to describe translation by comparing and analysing ST–TT pairs. In his work, Toury initially used a supposed 'invariant' as a form of comparison (Toury 1980), but in his major work *Descriptive Translation Studies – and Beyond* (Toury 1995) he drops this in favour of a more flexible 'ad-hoc' approach to the selection of features, dependent on the characteristics of the specific texts under consideration. Importantly, he warns against 'the totally negative kind of reasoning required by the search for **shifts**' (Toury 1995: 84) in which error and failure and **loss** in translation are highlighted. Instead, for Toury **translation shift** analysis is most valuable as a form of 'discovery', 'a step towards the formulation of explanatory hypotheses' about the practice of translation (1995: 85). The relevance and applications of **translation shifts** are issues which we shall explore further in Sections B and C.

Summary

This unit describes a theoretical position that promotes the systematic analysis of the changes that take place in moving from ST to TT. A change, known technically as a 'shift', is generally any translation that moves away from **formal correspondence**. Analysis normally first requires identification of the **translation unit**. The best-known work in this area is by Catford, who first used the term **shift**, and by Vinay and Darbelnet, whose detailed **taxonomy** has influenced many theorists. But, as we shall see in Unit 11, shifts also occur on the higher levels of **text**, **genre** and **discourse**.

Unit A5
The analysis of meaning

The previous unit examined some of the problems in assessing **shifts** of meaning between a ST and its TT. One of the key problems for the analyst was in actually determining whether the ST meaning had been transferred into the TT. In the early 1960s, when a systematic, theory-based approach to many disciplines, including linguistics, was prominent, translation theory underwent a quantum leap with the work of the American Eugene Nida. Nida co-ordinated the translation of the Bible from English into a variety of African and South American indigenous languages, some of which had no written tradition. Many of those chosen to undertake the translation had little experience of the task and sometimes encountered difficulties with literary and metaphorical aspects of the English texts. Nida adopted some of the current theoretical ideas in linguistics (notably **Chomskyan linguistics**) and anthropology and incorporated them into his training of translators. These ideas form the basis of his *Towards a Science of Translating* (Nida 1964) and *The Theory and Practice of Translation* (Nida and Taber 1969). As the title of the first book suggests, this approach saw translation as a science that could be analysed systematically. Later work by Larson (1984/1998) has continued this tradition.

This unit will concentrate on such 'scientific' approaches to the analysis of linguistic meaning, specifically in relation to the analysis of individual words or phrases. This field, **semantics**, is 'the study of meaning' (Leech 1981: ix), its goal 'a systematic account of the nature of meaning' (1981: 4); by this, Leech initially avoids the circular conundrum of defining 'the meaning of meaning', a phrase that echoes the title of perhaps the best-known book on the subject, by Ogden and Richards (1923) who were the first of a series of famous proponents of the scientific study of meaning during the twentieth century. In the same vein, responding to the scientific mentality of other disciplines of the time, Nida (1964) and Nida and Taber (1969: 56) consider **semantics** to be the '*science* of meaning'. For Nida, analysis of meaning was a major practical problem because his inexperienced translators, some of them non-native speakers of English, were sometimes confused by the intricacies and ambiguities of the ST, especially multiple senses, figurative meanings and **near-synonyms**. Nida (1964) borrows Chomsky's **surface structure–deep structure** concepts in his **analysis–transfer–restructuring** model of translation that will be discussed in Unit 6. The **analysis** phase, which is of most interest in this chapter, involves examination of sentence structure and of two kinds of linguistic meaning: **referential** and **connotative**.

Concept box   Nida's two types of meaning

> **Referential meaning** (otherwise known as **denotation**), which deals with the words as signs or symbols, and
>
> **Connotative meaning** (**connotation**), the emotional reaction engendered in the reader by a word.

The key problem for the translator is the frequent lack of one-to-one matching across languages. Not only does the **signifier** change across languages but each language depicts reality differently (i.e. the **semantic field** occupied by individual **signs** often does not match, see the Concept box in Unit 3, p. 17). Some concepts are very language- or culture-specific; Jakobson (see Unit 1) may have claimed that any concept can be rendered in any language, but that still does not help the translator find an easily useable **equivalent** for *Halloween* in Mandarin Chinese nor an acceptable translation of *say* in the Chuj language of Guatemala (Larson 1984/1998: 117–8), where the truthfulness of the statement is crucial. Nida attempted to overcome this problem by adopting then current ideas from **semantics** for the **analysis** of meaning across languages.

REFERENTIAL MEANING

Various linguistic problems relating to **referential** meaning are described by Nida and Taber (1969: 58–9). For instance, the word *chair* is **polysemous** (has several meanings): as a noun, it can be an item of furniture, a university position as professor or the chairperson at a meeting, and, as a verb, can mean 'to preside over a meeting'. The word *spirit* also has a wide range of senses, including liquor, determination and ghost as well as the 'holy spirit' use more prevalent in the Bible. The correct sense for the translator is determined by the 'semotactic environment' or **co-text** (the other words around it). Some meanings are figurative and need to be distinguished from the literal meanings: *father* of a child, our *Father* in heaven, *Father* Murphy, *father* of an invention or a country, and so on, each perhaps requiring a different translation. Words such as *heart, blood* and *children* are frequently used figuratively in the scriptures: so, *children of wrath* does not mean 'angry children' but has a figurative sense of 'people who will experience God's wrath' (1969: 89). Problems posed by **near-synonyms** such as *grace, favour, kindness* and *mercy* are also discussed (p. 74). In all these cases, as a reader the translator first needs to **disambiguate** (differentiate between) the various possible senses of the ST term as a step towards identifying the appropriate TL **equivalent**. This is done by contrastive **semantic structure analysis**.

DISAMBIGUATION – SEMANTIC STRUCTURE ANALYSIS

Task A5.1

> An email in English from a Spanish-speaking country arrives in my inbox, tentatively inviting me to a conference. It begins:
>> 'We are writing to invite you to a conference. We expect you will attend.'

➤ **Reflect** on what the translation error is here, and what you think could be its cause.

The incorrect use of *expect* instead of the more normal *hope* (or *very much hope*) is caused because the SL term (in this case the Spanish verb *esperar*) covers a wider **semantic field** than the English. *Esperar* can correspond to *hope, want, expect* or even *look forward to*. In diagrammatic form this can be represented simply as:

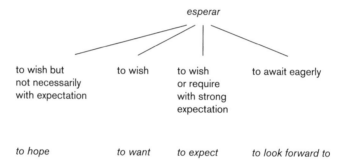

Figure A5.1 Semantic structure of *esperar*

The correct English translation will depend on the context and the force of the Spanish. In the example, *expect* is clearly far too emphatic for the intention of the message. Another, even clearer, example of non-correspondence of **semantic field** is given by Larson (1984/1998: 87): Russian has one word, *ruka*, for what in English is covered by the concepts of *arm* and *hand*, and also a single word, *noga*, for *leg* and *foot*. Translation from English to Russian requires **disambiguation** using **co-text** and **context** (the situation).

Incorrect selection of TL term, caused by non-native speaker confusion in the *esperar* example above, is also commonly seen where the translator has failed to **disambiguate** two terms in the SL that have the same **form** but different senses (i.e., are **homonyms**). One amazing example, with catastrophic consequences, concerned the destruction of the Monte Cassino monastery in Italy during the Second World War. The advancing Allies misinterpreted an intercepted German radio exchange that noted that 'Der Abt ist im Kloster'. The translator confused the word *Abt* (abbot) for an abbreviation of *Abteilung* (batallion) and rendered the sentence as 'The batallion is in the monastery', whereupon the Allies destroyed the building (Ezard 2000: 5).

This simple example can be expressed diagrammatically as:

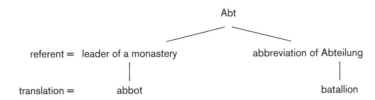

Figure A5.2 Semantic structure of *Abt*

These examples are relatively straightforward, but Nida and Larson use such visual representations of **semantic** structure to describe much more complex words such as *spirit* which we mentioned above.

HIERARCHICAL STRUCTURING AND COMPONENTIAL ANALYSIS

At other times the problem is more one of locating an **equivalent** on the same **level** in the TL. This occurs where one language has a wider range of specific terms for a given **semantic field** operating at various levels. Nida and Taber (1969: 68) give the example of a series of motion verbs under the generic verb *move*, which they ordered hierarchically:

Generic term	*move*
Lower level	*walk, run, skip, hop, crawl*
(more specific forms of *move*)	
Lower level	*march, stroll*
(more specific forms of *walk*)	

The generic term is known as the **superordinate** and the lower level terms as **hyponyms** – their more specific meaning is included within the meaning of the **superordinate**. Here analysis contrasts elements in the same **semantic** area, particularly on the same **semantic** level. *Walk* involves motion, on foot, moving legs alternately while always keeping at least one foot in contact with the ground; *run* involves motion on foot, moving legs in 1–2, 1–2 (left–right) fashion but not always keeping one foot on the ground, and so on. Both include the sense of motion, which can be described as a central or core component of meaning, and so can the use of the legs (or leg). But if we turn to the analysis of *crawl* we find that there is movement of legs and hands but not an upright posture, so this may cause us to modify what we consider to be central and what are supplementary features (Nida and Taber, 1969: 77). Distinguishing *run* from *skip* would conversely require the addition of more clearly differentiated supplementary components.

Task A5.2

➤ Reflect on what contrastive features are necessary to divide up the *move* list above (e.g. posture, movement of legs). Then consider other languages you know and how they differ in the division of the same **semantic field**. For example, do these languages have individual words for *hop* and *skip*? Do they commonly use other motion verbs?

Concept box   Componential analysis

> A technique of **semantic** analysis that examines the basic meaning components of a word and allows contrast with other terms in the same **semantic field**.

One of the prime elements of **componential analysis** is the notion of binary opposites: one sense of *bachelor* (a famous example in Katz and Fodor 1963) would be +human, +male, –married. This 'principle of contrast in identifying meaning' (Larson 1984/1998: 88) is crucial. It was initially used, and continues to have great currency, in anthropology for the mapping of **kinship terms** in different cultures. Examples can be seen in the reading from Larson in Text B 5.1.

CONNOTATIVE MEANING

The other area explored by Nida is **connotative meaning**, the emotional response evoked in the hearer. For instance, on various occasions in St John's gospel, the Greek word *gunai* is translated as *woman* in the old King James Version but as *mother* in the New English Bible. The justification for this change is the positive **connotation** of the Greek which, the translators felt, merited a similarly positive translation **equivalent** (1969: 95). This is a much more difficult area to investigate objectively. Nevertheless, Osgood, Suci and Tannenbaum (1957) did carry out an important study on what they term 'semantic space', asking respondents to assess words according to clines of evaluation (good to bad), potency (strong to weak) and activity (active to passive). This is taken up by Nida and Taber (1969: 94–6) who use the good–bad scale and add a scale of formality (Figure A5.3):

Figure A5.3 Scales of connotative meaning

Task A5.3

➤ Where on these scales would you place *woman* and *mother*, *girl* and *daughter*? Try doing the same with similar terms in other languages. Do their **connotations** correspond?

Nida and Taber discuss aspects other than single words or idioms that carry **connotative** associations, including pronunciation (some accents are more prestigious than others), **style** and subject matter when translated into a radically different cultural context. A striking example of the latter is the response from the Guaica people of Venezuela to Jesus's trial and death. For the Guaica, anyone in such a situation should have fought or tried to escape. They were thus unmoved by the story because they considered him to have exhibited extreme cowardice by not resisting arrest in the Garden of Gethsemane (Nida and Taber, 1969: 98).

The nature of meaning and how to analyse and evaluate it is crucial for a translator working on a text and for a theorist who is assessing the transference of meaning. This unit has examined forms of 'scientific' analysis adapted from English linguistics for the purposes of assessing translation. These include **disambiguation** of **referential meaning** through **semantic structure analysis** and **componential analysis**, and the gauging of **connotative meaning** using clines.

Summary

Unit A6
Dynamic equivalence and the receptor of the message

The previous unit focused on the 'scientific' analysis of linguistic meaning, particularly in relation to translation **equivalence** at the level of individual words and phrases. In this unit, we continue the discussion of **equivalence** but widen the focus on meaning and define it in terms of broader contextual categories such as **culture** and **audience** in both ST and TT. Specifically, we will deal with the **process of translation**, the problems of establishing **equivalent effect** in translation and how this factor, which draws heavily on **context**, affects meaning and determines the choice of translation method.

In Unit 2, we argued that to insist on full **translatability** across languages and cultures is to risk being incomprehensible (i.e. producing TTs that are confusing at best). Similarly, to insist on full **comprehensibility** in translation is to perpetuate the myth that there is no real difference between translation and other forms of communication. A more reasonable position to take is perhaps to see **translatability** and **comprehensibility** in relative terms. These two principles are not always in conflict, constantly pulling in opposite directions. In practice, an important assumption which translators entertain seems to be one epitomized by something Eugene Nida said many years ago, echoing Jakobson (1959/2000, see Section B, Text B1.1): 'Anything which can be said in one language can be said in another, unless the **form** is an essential element of the message (Nida and Taber1969: 4).'

The focus in this 'universalist' orientation to language use in translation is on the need to respond to the communicative requirements of the text receiver and, by implication, to the **purpose** of the translation, without necessarily losing sight of the communicative preferences of the original message producer or the **function** of the original text.

FORMAL EQUIVALENCE

This attitude to **translatability** and **comprehensibility** has given rise to **dynamic equivalence**, a translation method that may helpfully be seen in terms of its counterpart – **formal equivalence**. The latter (also referred to as 'structural correspondence'), is a relationship which involves the purely 'formal' replacement of one word or phrase in the SL by another in the TL. According to Nida, this is not the same as **literal** translation, and the two terms must therefore be kept distinct. For our purposes, one way of clarifying the distinction between 'formal' and 'literal' in this context is to suggest that:

> While **literal** translations tend to preserve formal features almost by default (i.e. with little or no regard for context, meaning or what is implied by a given utterance), a '**formal**' translation is almost always **contextually motivated**: formal features are preserved only if they carry contextual values that become part of overall text meaning (e.g. deliberate ambiguity in the ST).

Task A6.1

To illustrate this special use of **formal equivalence** defined here in terms of **contextual motivatedness**, consider the following example (Example A6.1), drawn from the *Newsweek* obituary of Sir Alec Guinness (the famous British actor who died on 5 August 2000). The text happens to be particularly opaque regarding one character trait of the great actor, Guinness's reticence, and whether it is to be regarded as 'condonable diffidence' or 'unforgivable arrogance'.

➤ Read through this excerpt and note features likely to be noteworthy regarding this issue. Reflect on how you would deal with this situation in translation.

Example A6.1

[. . .] a face so ordinary as to approach anonymity, a mastery of disguise so accomplished he could vanish without a trace inside a role and a wary intelligence that allowed him to *reveal the deepest secrets of his characters while slyly protecting his own.*
(*Newsweek* 21 August 2000 [italics added])

The general ambiguity, which is no doubt intended (i.e. it is **contextually motivated**) in a context such as that of an obituary, and which threads its way subtly throughout the text, must somehow be preserved in translation, and one way of doing this is perhaps through opting for **formal equivalence**. Any **explication** of *while slyly protecting his own*, for example, could seriously compromise intended meaning.

Preserving ST ambiguity is thus one legitimate use of **formal equivalence**. But there are other contexts. An extreme form of this kind of **equivalence** may be illustrated by St Jerome's oft-cited injunction in the context of Bible translation: 'even the order of the words is a mystery' (Jerome 395/1997: 25). More generally, however, Nida deals with such contexts in terms of focusing 'attention on the message itself, in both **form** and **content**' for whatever purpose (Nida 1964: 159). This is strictly the sense which Nida most probably intended for his **formal equivalence**.

Task A6.2

Many newspapers and magazines (e.g. *Readers' Digest, Newsweek*) publish so-called Quotable Quotes. These quotes are usually selected for their 'understatement', 'ironical twist', a 'look-who-is-talking' kind of sentiment, which makes the quote noteworthy.

➤ Focus on the significance of the element in bold in the following quote, and reflect on effective ways of dealing with it in translation.

Example A6.2

'If somebody messes with you, go to court. **That's the American way**.' *Bernard Adusei, who immigrated to the United States 21 years ago, criticizing a lawsuit in connection with a disputed lottery win.*

(*Newsweek* 21 May 2001 (bold in original))

DYNAMIC EQUIVALENCE

Given the sensitivity of **form** in the kind of message you have just considered in Example A6.2 above, **formal equivalence** must be our first port of call. To **explicate** *That's the American way* would be to give the game away and lose the sarcasm intended. Of course, a more **dynamic** approach may still have to be used, but only after we exhaust **formal** possibilities for conveying the intended effect.

Formal equivalence, then, is ideal for situations of this kind. It is a **contextually motivated** method of translation (i.e. a **procedure** purposefully selected in order to preserve a certain linguistic/rhetorical effect). We can sometimes preserve these effects in translation simply by doing nothing, which happens quite often when we do not need to interfere with the formal arrangement of words, structure, etc. But, even in such cases, the decision to opt for **formal equivalence** must always be a conscious decision (i.e. taken for a good reason and not gratuitously). The aim in this kind of adherence to **form** would be to bring the target reader nearer to the linguistic or cultural preferences of the ST.

Yet, for a wide variety of texts, and given a diverse range of readers and purposes of translation, there is often a need for some ST **explication** and **adjustment**. That is, if in the translator's judgement a form of words that is not sufficiently transparent in the TT is likely to pose a threat to **comprehensibility** and therefore result in unintended and unmotivated opaqueness, intervention on the part of the translator becomes inevitable. In such cases, the translator would need to resort to more 'dynamic' forms of **equivalence**.

Through **dynamic equivalence**, we can thus cater for a rich variety of contextual values and effects which utterances carry within texts and which a **literal** translation would simply compromise. These effects would not be so much **form**-bound, as **content**-bound. That is, we opt for varying degrees of **dynamic equivalence** when **form** is not significantly involved in conveying a particular meaning, and when a **formal** rendering is therefore unnecessary (e.g. in cases where there is no contextual justification for preserving ST opaqueness, ambiguity, etc.). Some of the defective translations examined in this book (e.g. Examples A2.2–A2.5, p. 13) illustrate how pointless this kind of unmotivated adherence to **form** can be.

Task A6.3

➤ Translate the Quote above (Example A6.2) and experiment with variant approaches to translating it. Reflect on whether there will be any differences of effect in terms of **formal** vs **dynamic**.

An important point to underline here is that opting for this or that form of **equivalence** is not an either/or choice. The distinction **dynamic** vs **formal equivalence** (or **dynamic** vs structural **correspondence**) is best seen in relative terms, as points on a cline. The two methods are not absolute techniques but rather general orientations. In fact, what experienced translators seem to do most of the time is to resort to a **literal** kind of **equivalence** initially, reconsider the decision in the light of a range of factors, and ultimately make a choice from **literal, formal** or **dynamic equivalence** in this order and as appropriate.

ADJUSTMENT

Adjustment or the gradual move away from **form**-by-**form** renderings and towards more **dynamic** kinds of **equivalence** is thus an important translation technique. In the search for **dynamic equivalence**, it is proposed by Nida (1964: 139) as an overall translation technique which may take several forms. In dealing with texts that are likely to produce a dense translation, for instance, we may opt for building in **redundancy, explicating** or even repeating information when appropriate. Alternatively, we may opt for **gisting**, a technique most useful in dealing with languages characterized by a noticeably high degree of repetition of meaning. Also as part of **adjustment**, we may at times have to re-order an entire sequence of sentences if the ST order of events, for example, does not match normal chronology, or proves too cumbersome to visualize.

Adjustment is also needed to cope with the wide range of **purposes** which translations might serve.

Task A6.4

➤ Look back at Example A2.2, a translation into English of a welfare organization's publicity leaflet originally addressed to Muslim donors.

➤ Reflect on the translation and 'adjust' it to serve the **purpose** of a translation addressed to potential *non-Muslim* donors.

There is thus a need for **adjustment** of various kinds (including a range of **compensation procedures**). These modification techniques will ensure that translation **equivalence** is upheld and access to the TT unimpeded. In this respect, it may be safe to assume that:

> The more **form**-bound a meaning is (e.g. a case of ambiguity through **word play**), the more **formal** the **equivalence** relation will have to be. Alternatively, the more context-bound a meaning is (e.g. an obscure reference to source culture), the more **dynamic** the **equivalence** will have to be.

This may be represented in diagram form as in Figure A6.1:

```
FE <<<<<<<<<<<<<       ADJUSTMENT        >>>>>>>>>>>> DE
FORM BOUND             MEANING            CONTEXT BOUND
```

Figure A6.1 Formal (FE) vs dynamic (DE) equivalence

 Task A6.5

➤ Consider the following flawed translation into English (Example A6.3a), so **literal** that it can easily be considered a **word-for-word back-translation**. This is followed by a more idiomatic translation (Example A6.3b).

➤ Reflect on the **adjustments** that have taken place in version B.

Example A6.3a

Preface

To strike a deal is not meant to be a 'strike'. Some people, in striking commercial deals, like to transform the whole process into dishonest transactions, claiming to be 'smart traders'. Their work is very far from that of smart people, because they transform right into wrong, finding in manoeuvring and deception an art that has to be mastered to win a deal, and feeling proud that they have 'stricken' their clients.

(Al-Jumriki, 1999)

Example A6.3b

Opinion

DEALERS AND DODGERS

We can strike a deal with someone, or we can deal them a blow. Yet there are those who enjoy deliberately confusing the two ideas. So where there should be honour and trust we find lies and deceit. It is these people who boast of being 'shrewd businessmen' and who seek to dress up the truth as falsehood – or rather, perhaps, the other way round. These artful dodgers of the business world see their underhand methods, and sometimes indeed their blatant lies, simply as a skill that they must hone and perfect.

THE TRANSLATION PROCESS: ANALYSIS, TRANSFER, RE-STRUCTURING

The **dynamically equivalent** version of the above editorial exhibits some of the following **adjustment** strategies:

■ Jettisoning less accessible ST items

  We can strike a deal with someone, or we can deal them a blow preserves the **word play** in the source.

■ Regulating **redundancy**

  There are those, however, who enjoy deliberately confusing the two ideas. So where there should be honour and trust we find lies and deceit establishes a contrast which enhances the relevance of the distinction introduced earlier.

These changes are introduced in the so-called '**restructuring**' stage, the last of three phases through which the **process** of translation is said to pass (Nida 1969: 484):

The translator . . .

(1) **Analyses** the SL message into its simplest and structurally clearest forms (or 'kernels')

(2) **Transfers** the message at this kernel level

(3) **Restructures** the message in the TL to the level which is most appropriate for the audience addressed

---

Figure A6.2 The Process of Translation (following Nida)

The 'analysis' phase begins with discovering the so-called 'kernels' (a term which Nida borrows from Chomsky's **transformational generative** grammar). Kernels are basic structural elements to which **syntactic**ally more elaborate **surface structures** of a language can be reduced. To return to an example examined in Unit 5, a phrase such as *children of wrath* yields 'God directs wrath at the transgressors' or 'the transgressors suffers God's wrath' as possible kernels representing the clearest understanding of ST meaning.

Kernel analysis is thus a crucial step in the process of moving from ST to TT. This is in keeping with the essentially universalist hypothesis to which Nida subscribes: languages 'agree far more on the level of the kernels than on the level of the more elaborate structures' (Nida and Taber 1969: 39).

Kernels consist of combinations of items from four basic **semantic** categories:

- object words (nouns referring to physical objects including human beings)
- event words (actions often represented by verbs)
- abstracts (qualities and quantities, including adjectives)
- relationals (including linking devices, gender markers)

Kernel sentences are derived from the actual source sentence by means of a variety of techniques including, most importantly, **back-transformation**. In **explicating** grammatical relationships, ST **surface structures** are 'paraphrased' into 'formulae' capturing the way in which elements from the various categories listed above are combined (Nida 1969: 485). Thus, the **surface structure** *will of God* may be back-transformed into a formula such as:

B (object, *God*) performs A (event, *wills*)

We move from ST to TT via a phase called **transfer**. This is the stage 'in which the analysed material is transferred in the mind of the translator from language A to language B' (Nida and Taber 1969: 33). What does this essentially 'mental' activity involve? It is important to remember that, during '**transfer**', kernels are not treated in isolation since they would already be marked temporally, spatially and logically. But they would still be raw material which the translator, in the light of his or her knowledge of TL structure, must now modify in preparation for **restructuring** (the stage of putting pen to paper, as it were). A SL word may have to be expanded into several TL words, or alternatively, a SL phrase re-moulded into a single TL word. Along similar lines, structural differences between SL and TL are reconciled at the sound, word, sentence or even **discourse** level. It is probably here that 'strategy' (or the translator's 'game plan') is worked out, and decisions regarding such matters as **register** and **genre** are initially taken. Thus, rather than a simple replacement exercise of actual SL elements with their most **literal** TL counterparts, 'transfer' is a dynamic process of 'reconfiguration' in the TL of sets of SL **semantic** and structural components.

The translator should now be ready for **restructuring** the transferred material, which hitherto has existed only in the form of **kernel** sentences. What is needed is a set of **procedures** by which the input accrued so far may be transformed into a 'stylistic form appropriate to the receptor language and to the intended receptors' (Nida and Taber 1969: 206). In particular, **restructuring** ensures that the impact which the translation is to have on its intended receptors is what the ST producer has intended (Nida 1969: 494–5): any message which does not communicate is simply useless. It is only when a translation produces in the **audience** a response which is essentially the same as that of the original **audience** that the translation can be said to be **dynamically equivalent** to its ST.

Summary

Within the linguistics paradigm, and with **equivalence** as the key concept in Translation Studies, Eugene Nida's work on the dynamic effect which translations produce on the reader has been extremely influential not only for Bible translation where Nida started, but also in dealing with a variety of text forms for a wide range of purposes. In this unit, we have examined **dynamic equivalence** and compared it with **formal equivalence** as two general orientations in the translation of texts. **Formal equivalence** is distinguished from 'literal' translation strictly in terms of '**contextual motivatedness**'. We have postulated this contextual criterion as a precondition for the success of **formal equivalence**. In the absence of the need for such forms of adherence to the ST, the translator either does nothing and ends up with a meaningless literalism, or actively seeks **equivalence** through **adjustment**. This subsumes a set of techniques for **restructuring** the ST message in the TL. In the translation **process** model outlined in this unit, the ST message is first broken down into its immediate constituents (or kernels), then mentally transferred, ultimately to undergo a process of **adjustment** that restores to the TT linguistic and stylistic appropriateness.

Unit A7
Textual pragmatics and equivalence

In Unit 6, we considered the process of **analysis** of the ST and the **restructuring** of the finished product to ensure linguistic **cohesion** and conceptual **coherence**. The process is dynamic and can respond to many different factors. The focus of the translation can be on ST **form**, **content** or on both, on the TT reader, the translator and his or her preferences, interests, **ideology**, or on the nature of the translation **brief** and the **purpose** of translation. It is this intrinsically variable nature of **equivalence** that will occupy us in this unit.

TRANSLATION PROPERLY DEFINED

While translation no doubt shares a number of significant features with a range of other text-processing activities that proceed from a source to a derived text (e.g. summarizing, explaining), mainstream translation theory suggests that fundamental differences exist between translation and these other activities. But the question that has not yet been answered satisfactorily is: what preconditions must be met for a text to be classified as translation proper? Koller proposes the following working definition of what he takes to be translation:

> Between the resultant text in L2 (the TL text) and the ST in L1 (the SL text) there exists a relationship which can be designated as a **translational**, or **equivalence**, relation.
>
> (1995: 196)

Note that '**translational**' (or 'translatory') can be glossed as 'strictly pertaining to translation' (as opposed to, say, original writing) and may thus be seen in terms of an **equivalence** relation that is different from the kind of relations obtaining under such conditions as 'deriving texts' in summaries or 'explaining' in a dictionary entry. We are still not told what '**equivalence**' is, but it is clear that translations are produced under conditions different from those obtaining in freer forms of writing. The translator confronts and resolves a number of problems not likely to feature in original writing, and vice versa. In translation, these limitations have a great deal to do with the need to reconcile differences in linguistic code, cultural values, the 'world' and how it is perceived, **style** and aesthetics, etc.

Task A7.1

➤ Select two comparable texts (perhaps covering the same topic), one freely composed in your own language, and the other translated into it. Informally analyse the differences. Consider features of so-called '**translationese**' (see Unit 2), the use of **calque**, etc., which are fairly common in translated texts.

LANGUE- ORIENTED VS *PAROLE*-ORIENTED EQUIVALENCE

In trying to work out a notion of **equivalence** that steers clear of either extreme – the narrowly quantitative approach vs the open-ended text-and-beyond view – Koller (1979) maintains a distinction between formal similarity at the level of virtual language systems (*langue*), and **equivalence** relations obtaining between texts in real time at the actual level of *parole*, a distinction we examined in relation to Catford in Unit 4.

Koller advocates that it is the latter, *parole*-oriented notion of **equivalence** (which the Germans call *Äquivalenz*) that constitutes the real object of enquiry in Translation Studies. **Textual equivalence** proper may thus be seen as obtaining not between the languages themselves at the level of the linguistic system but between real texts at the level of text in context (see again the discussion in Unit 4).

One way of reconciling the two extremes of *langue*- vs *parole*-oriented approaches to translation is to define **equivalence** in relative (not categorical) terms and in hierarchical (not static) terms. That is, **equivalence** is not an 'either/or' choice, nor is it an 'if X, then Y' formula. Translation approaches informed by **pragmatics** as the study of intended meaning are ideally suited for this **dynamic** view of **equivalence**, and the model of **equivalence** proposed by Koller is an excellent example of an approach that is variable and flexible in accounting for relationships between comparable elements in the SL and TL.

Task A7.2

➤ Look over the translation of a computer manual or a mobile phone user booklet translated into your own language.

➤ How useful is a quantitative, *langue*-oriented approach to **equivalence** in the translation of such texts?

➤ In this kind of text, is some knowledge of 'language as *parole*' necessary? Are there any cultural adjustments, an element of emotiveness, indeed a literary quality introduced to enhance the salesmanship tone of the ST or TT?

EQUIVALENCE: DOUBLE LINKAGE

Within the **equivalence** model to be outlined in this section, the scope of what constitutes an **equivalence** relation is limited in a number of important ways. Koller (1995) views **equivalence** as a process constrained on the one hand by the influence of a variety of potentially conflicting SL/TL *linguistic* textual and extra-textual factors and circumstances and on the other by the role of the *historical–cultural* conditions under which texts and their translations are produced and received.

Equivalence relations are differentiated in the light of this 'double-linkage', first to the ST and, second, to the communicative conditions on the receiver's side. A number of what Koller specifically calls 'frameworks of **equivalence**' (1989: 100–4) emerge. Linguistic-textual units are regarded as TL **equivalents** if they correspond to SL elements according to some or all of the following relational frameworks of **equivalence**. These 'frames of reference' are 'hierarchical' in that each type of **equivalence** (and the level of language at which translation **equivalence** is achieved) tends to subsume (i.e. retain and add to) features of the preceding level.

Let us work through these relations with the help of the following example. The text is one of the 'quotable quotes' with which we worked in Unit 6 (Example A6.2). This quote is by photographer Helmut Newton on his eye for the former British prime minister:

Example A7.1

'I had wanted for years to get Mrs Thatcher in front of my camera. **As she got more powerful she got sort of sexier.**'

(*Newsweek* 21 May 2001 [bold in original])

1. **Equivalence** is said to be fully achieved if SL and TL words happen to have similar orthographic or phonological features. This is the ultimate *formal equivalence*, where a SL form is strictly replaced by an identical TL form. Focusing on *sexier*, we need a language which deals with this item in the same way as many languages do with English words like *strategy, bureaucracy* (e.g. Arabic *stratiijiyya, biirokratiyya*). Obviously, this does not seem to be possible in the case of *sexy*, which means that we have to move up one level in the **equivalence** hierarchy.

2. When **formal equivalence** proves either unattainable or insufficient we tend to aim for the next level of *referential* or *denotative* equivalence. Here, a SL form is replaced by a TL form that basically refers to the same 'thing'. At face value, this is possible to achieve with the majority of words in any language. The *Newsweek* translator can conceivably opt for this level of **equivalence** in any language, with the relationship of 'sex–sexy' highlighted.

3. For a variety of linguistic, rhetorical and cultural reasons, the **referential** option may not do justice to sexy in the case of the Thatcher text. A denotative rendering may (as it certainly does in the case of Arabic) convey something like 'pornographic' if used on its own or trigger different associations in the minds of speakers of the two languages. In such cases, we should seek **equivalence** at the next higher level of 'similarity of association'. This is *connotative equivalence*, which in the case of sexy might yield a TT element which links *sexy*, say, with 'attractiveness'.

4. The **connotative** option goes some way towards a solution of the problem *sexy* in Arabic, but still falls short of an optimally satisfactory rendering. In this language, the **semantic** element 'attractiveness' can convey associations with the physical term 'gravity' that are too 'direct' and 'scientific' for this context. Here, we should seek **equivalence** at the higher level of textual context and aim for so-called *text-normative equivalence*. **Textual norms** are conventions which go beyond **connotations** and which enable us to work with the kind of language that is typical of a certain kind of text, a mood of writing, a certain attitude, etc. To account for this level of **equivalence** in the case of *sexy* or 'sexual attractiveness', for example, we need to bear in mind the communicative purpose of the ST and the use for which the TT is intended. This is the 'point' of the quote which, in this context, is perhaps to do with the incongruity emanating from the association of 'iron lady' with 'sexy'. To achieve this level of **equivalence** in the case of *sexy*, we might need to (a) jettison 'sexual' and modify 'sexual attractiveness' in favour of something like 'attractive femininity', and (b) **gloss** the translation with something like 'so to speak' which in a way also captures the ST *sort of* intended by the speaker as an apology for being too explicit with use of language, akin to saying 'for want of a better word'.

5. Contexts of use match in this case, and so does the effect on the TT reader which will here be sufficiently close to that experienced by the ST reader. To achieve similarity of effect and cater for reader expectations is to attain full *pragmatic* or *dynamic equivalence*.

Task A7.3

➤ As you read through the various frames of reference outlined above, apply the different procedures to your own language (or foreign language) situation and work out appropriate translation solutions.

Task A7.4

➤ Reflect on how far you need to go in terms of the **equivalence** hierarchy outlined above in the translation of: (1) the instructions on a medicine bottle, (2) a television commercial you have recently seen.

DECISION-MAKING

You will probably discover that in dealing with the medical instructions, levels 3, 4 and 5 would be taken care of by merely attending to levels 1 and 2. In the case of the commercial, however, levels 1, 2 and 3 are likely to be insufficient by themselves and, to do justice to the text, you would need to engage more closely with **equivalence** relations at levels 4 and 5.

Achieving **equivalence**, then, involves a complex decision-making process which the Leipzig-based translation theorist Jiři Levý (1967) defined in terms of moves as in a game of chess, and choices to make from several alternatives. In doing any kind of translation, there will always be a 'problem', and a number of possible 'solutions'. At every stage of the translation **process**, choices are made, and these obviously influence subsequent choices. At one level, this may be illustrated by Koller's **typology** of **equivalence** relations, with the translator opting for one kind of equivalence framework, then eliminating this option if it proves unworkable and trying out the next higher-level frame of reference.

Like all matters to do with text in context, however, translation decisions are rarely if ever so straightforward and 'sequential'. They tend to be highly complex and, as Koller intended his relational frameworks to be, 'hierarchical'. The hierarchy is in fact **iterative** in the sense that one progresses through the text, one can come back again and again to decisions already taken, reviewing and altering them. An important question now is: What motivates this kind of decision-making?

WHAT MOTIVATES TRANSLATOR DECISION-MAKING

Aesthetics

This hierarchical, **iterative** nature of decision-making (i.e. how decisions can be reviewed up and down the hierarchy, which decisions are overriding and which are minor, etc.) is often driven by a number of fairly subjective factors such as the translator's own 'aesthetic standards' (Levý 1967). In this UN text (Example A7.2a), for example, there is little justification to depart from a denotative kind of **equivalence**, except perhaps an idiosyncratic desire on the part of the translator to establish and maintain 'elegant' parallelism in the Arabic TT:

Example A7.2a

Preventing war

For the United Nations, there is no higher goal, no deeper commitment and no greater ambition than preventing armed conflict. The main short- and medium-term strategies for preventing non-violent conflicts from escalating into war, and preventing earlier wars from erupting again, are preventive diplomacy, preventive deployment and preventive disarmament.

(From a Report of the UN Secretary-General to the Foreign Affairs Committee of the Chinese People's Political Consultative Conference, in Beijing on 1 April 1998 (*United Nations Chronicle* 1998, vol. 1))

Example A7.2b (Back-translation from Arabic)

Preventing the eruption of wars

For the UN, preventing the eruption of armed conflicts represents a goal not possible to surpass by any other goal, a commitment not possible to sideline by any other commitment and an ambition not possible to overshadow by any other ambition. . . .

Task A7.5

➤ Read through the back-translation as though it were a ST that you are asked to translate into another language.

➤ What effect would the kind of language used have on you as a reader? What kind of text would you normally associate with this level of exhortation? Would you say that these added effects are justified and therefore worth preserving in translation? State your reasons.

Cognition and knowledge

A factor that is less subjective than aesthetics is the translator's own socio-**cognitive** system (the translator's culture and system of values, beliefs, etc.). This plays an important role in informing translation decisions and thus confirming the hierarchical-**iterative** and relative nature of **equivalence** relations.

In dealing with the following example, a group of translator trainees had serious difficulties appreciating what the concept of 'working for the government' could possibly mean in the context of the following argument:

Example A7.3a

Mismanaged Algeria

[. . .]
These strengths are being wasted. Some 180,000 well-schooled Algerians enter the job market every year. Yet a hobbled economy adds only 100,000 new jobs a year, **and some 45% of these involve working for the government**.

(*The Economist* 10 December 1988 [bold added])

Coming from an oil-rich Gulf state, the student translators could not **socio-cognitively** see how or why 'working for the government' should be abysmal, as intended by the ST. They therefore aimed for positive **connotation** which, to highlight, entailed **restructuring** the utterance to read as follows:

Example A7.3b

. . . and although 45% of those who do find jobs actually end up working for the government, this is still an abysmal record.

Yet it is clear that the concept of 'working for the government = abysmal' was crucial to the development of the argument and to the critical stance adopted by the editorial. The way the text was translated conveyed a totally different picture and certainly a much milder tone.

Task A7.6

➤ List some problems you have encountered in your language that are essentially cultural-conceptual (i.e. **socio-cognitive**).

➤ Reflect, for example, on the values assigned in English to such concepts as 'single-parent', 'farmer', 'bungalow', 'countryside', 'old and Victorian'?

➤ Identify the values assigned to the cultural concepts which you have listed above.

Commission

In addition to aesthetics, cognition and the criterion of knowledge base, the task specification agreed with clients could drastically influence decision-making. This raises issues of translation *skopos* or **purpose**, loyalty and conflict of interests, etc. We can now refer to this sense of **purpose** specifically as 'the **purpose** of *the* translation', and distinguish it from the **purpose** of *translation* (in the collective), which has to do with the skill involved in translating within a particular professional setting (e.g. **subtitling**).

The nature of the **commission** is a crucial factor in defining the **purpose** of the translation. For example, in translating a press release for the radical Palestinian group Hamas reporting one of their 'suicide' bombings and talking eulogistically about the carnage they caused, the translation **brief** had to be re-negotiated with Hamas who commissioned the translation. The translator suggested a more conciliatory tone, eradicating all references to bloody scenes for which credit was being claimed in the Arabic version. The suggestion was flatly refused by Hamas.

Task A7.7

➤ Do you think it is the translator's job to alert the client to problems of the kind outlined in the above vignette, or to negotiate a more favourable strategy for dealing with a situation that is likely to be controversial? Should the translator of the Hamas text have just gone ahead and translated what she was given? Or should the translator have simply doctored the document and deleted elements likely to cause offence?

TEXTUAL PRAGMATICS

By far the most concrete set of criteria for effective decision-making seems to be grounded in **text type**. Linguist and translation theorist Robert de Beaugrande sees **equivalence** relations in terms of the translation generally being 'a valid representative of the original in the communicative act in question' (1978: 88). The decision-making involved would thus be partly subject to system criteria such as grammar and diction, and partly to contextual factors surrounding the use of language in a given text (see *langue* vs *parole* on p. 49).

Task A7.8

➤ Show how the *parole*-dimension affects your reading and translation of this short text from an interview:

Example A7.4

NEWSWEEK: It is a bid [sic] odd, *isn't it*, that a journalist who was held captive by the Taliban would, several months later, be converting to Islam?

RIDLEY: I know, *you couldn't make it up*. It is strange.

(*Newsweek* 26 August 2002 [italics added])

In this example, there is a typo ('bid' for 'bit'), a minor performance error which can be rectified easily. But what about *isn't it?* Pragmatically, this feature suggests 'surely', another problem concept for many users of English as a foreign language. To render *isn't it?* into Arabic, for example, we need to **gloss** it by something like 'I am sure you will agree'. Similarly, we need to complement *you couldn't make it up* by something like 'even if you wanted to'. These pragmatic glosses are indispensable in any meaningful rendering of the above utterances, certainly into Arabic.

These considerations can only highlight the proposition, which we saw in Unit 3, that it is not the word which is the **unit of translation** but rather 'text in communication' (Beaugrande 1978: 91). This is a contentious issue, and one that has often been misunderstood. Fawcett sheds some useful light on the psychological reality of 'text' as a **unit of translation**:

> What professional and even novice translators actually do is relate the translation of the microlevel of words and phrases to higher textual levels of sentence and paragraph, and beyond that to such parameters as **register**, **genre**, **text** conventions, subject matter, and so on.
>
> (Fawcett 1997: 64)

Summary

Useful as the textual approach may generally be in clarifying the kinds of **resemblance** that are deemed appropriate, it is not yet clear what kind of constraints there are for determining what types of **resemblance** between original text and translation are most crucial, in what kinds of text, for what kind of reader and so on.

Formal **resemblance** (whether in Nida's 'contextually motivated' sense or in Koller's identical **form**-to-**form** relation) is a valid option; so is pragmatic **resemblance** (Nida's **dynamic equivalence** or Koller's higher levels of equivalence). But can there be any reliable means for ascertaining the precise **form–content** relationship in any coherent and useful way?

The question that is uppermost in the mind of the ST author or the translator must be: is it worth the target reader's effort to invest in the retrieval of something which would normally be opaque and therefore not straightforward to retrieve (a meaning, a nuance, an implication, a subtle hint, etc.)? This effort and reward is regulated by what Levý (1967) called the **Minimax** Principle: during the decision-making process, the translator opts for that solution which yields maximum effect for minimum effort. This principle has been recently resurrected by models of translation **relevance** to be dealt with in Unit 8.

Unit A8
Translation and relevance

FROM TEXT TO COGNITION

In the study of **equivalence**, what we have had to deal with so far is mostly texts or fragments of texts, and the notion of **equivalence** advocated (be this **dynamic**, **pragmatic** or textual) has been largely text-based. **Cognitive-linguistic** analysis of the translation **process** has shifted the focus from texts to **mental processes**. Translation is seen as a special instance of the wider concept of communication, and this, together with the decision-making process involved, is accounted for in terms of such **coherence** relationships as 'cause and effect'. These relations underpin the process of **inferencing**, a **cognitive** activity taken to be central to any act of communication and thus crucial in any act of reading or translation (Gutt 1991).

Example A8.1

Serge Cardin, a Canadian MP, had to apologize to the House for humming the theme song from 'The Godfather' while Public Works Minister Alfonso Gagliano, who is of Italian descent, addressed Parliament.

(*Newsweek*, Perspectives, 21 May 2001)

Task A8.1

➤ Consider the above example of intercultural communicative difficulties, and answer the following questions:

- ■ Why did the MP have to apologize? Is it for 'humming', which is a breach of parliamentary formality?
- ■ What is the **relevance** of the reference to *The Godfather*? Is it anything to do with the fact this film is a true classic?
- ■ Is 'descent' a relevant issue in this context? What is implied by this text?

The model of **relevance** to be introduced shortly would suggest that, in this context, to hum a tune from *The Godfather* is understood to imply a link between the allegedly corrupt practices of a government minister and those of the Italian Mafia.

Thus:

- the need to apologize is underpinned by another act of inference on the part of the reader: the ethnic slur causing hurt;
- the significance of humming a particular tune requires that the reader infer a particular kind of relationship between, say, *The Godfather* and a government minister;
- the minister happens to be of Italian descent.

To appreciate what is going on, then, hearers, readers or translators engage in some form of **inferencing**. This is put to the test when the episode is placed in the wider context of communication (e.g. will the analysis make sense in terms of such 'institutions' as racism and sexism?). Since a satisfactory translation must guide the target reader properly towards making appropriate inferences, this kind of inferential input is used as a basis for the decision-making involved regarding what to say and how to say it in the translation, as we shall see shortly.

 Task A8.2

➤ As a translator of Example A8.1, how would you deal with the subtle reference to racism? What kind of 'signals' would you use to enable the reader to engage in the appropriate **inferencing** without giving the game away?

INFERENCING AND RELEVANCE

Within **Relevance** Theory (Sperber and Wilson 1986), communication is usually sparked off by a 'stimulus', verbal or otherwise (e.g. humming of a theme song). These stimuli guide the hearer (or reader) through the maze of what one could infinitely mean. The ultimate aim is to enable the hearer to reach the speaker's 'informative' intention' (e.g. ethnic solidarity with/or condemnation of a government minister who is of Italian descent). This process is facilitated by the crucial ability of language users to convey and analyse inferences from the interaction of a range of stimuli (e.g. Minister of Public Works, *The Godfather*, corruption).

Inferencing necessarily involves context. But the kind of context recognized by **relevance** theory is not simply a catalogue of linguistic and situational features, including **socio-cultural norms** of appropriateness (polite, offensive, etc.). To the **relevance** theoretician, context involves those assumptions which language users mentally entertain vis-à-vis the world (e.g. the assumption that communication is 'intended' to perform certain acts, that these intentions and actions are properly signalled, and that, to process a given text act, certain assumptions are more accessible or plausible than others). The set of such assumptions surrounding utterances is referred to as the **cognitive environment** in which language and situation would certainly be important but only if they yielded the kind of explicit and implicit information which would significantly enhance interpretation without involving the **audience** in unnecessary effort.

Example A8.1 could potentially pose a problem of **relevance**. This would be compromised (gratuitously or meaningfully), if the interaction of stimulus (e.g. humming a particular tune), contextual assumptions (Godfather > Mafia > corrupt government minister > Italian descent, etc.) and interpretation (e.g. ethnic slur) were disturbed for any reason. This is precisely what often happens when we do not see the point or the joke or the irony.

The interaction of stimulus–assumptions–interpretation might also be disturbed if the **cognitive environment** of an utterance varied in the two languages. The Arabic translation of the *Newsweek* text above, for example, compromised **relevance** when it could not guide the target reader properly towards making the appropriate inferences. A 'literal' kind of rendering, without the proper 'signals', did indeed establish **relevance** but of the wrong kind. The translation managed only to elicit a response revolving around the commonsensical interpretation that the apology was for 'humming' being a breach of parliamentary convention. Here, despite **equivalence** of stimulus, we have two different **cognitive environments** yielding different contextual assumptions and consequently different interpretations.

Task A8.3

➤ Reflect on how the **cognitive environments** of a ST and a TT can be incompatible, and how **literal** translations can only compound the problem of incompatibility.

➤ Both **formal** and **dynamic equivalence** work in such situations. Attempt a translation of Example A8.1 aiming for different kinds of **equivalence**, and assess the differences in effect on the target reader.

But whether **intralingually** (within the same language) or **interlingually** (across languages), the interaction of stimulus, assumptions and interpretation would be drastically disturbed if the processing effort (which will be greater, the more implicit an assumption is) went unrewarded. That is, **relevance** would be compromised if the effort expended in retrieving a given assumption substantially exceeded the rewards obtainable (e.g. a silly joke, an over-the-top description).

Problems of this kind are captured by Jiři Levý's **Minimax** Principle. This is postulated as underpinning the complex decision-making process characteristic of translation.

Concept box   Minimax

This is a processing principle proposed by Levý (1967) as part of the decision-making process characteristic of any translation. According to **Minimax**, the translator in choosing between a number of solutions to a given problem ultimately settles for that solution which promises maximum effect for minimal effort. The kind of question the translator asks is: would preserving a certain feature of a ST (e.g. rhyme) be worth the target reader's effort? If rhyme turns out not to be essentially meaningful in the target context (i.e. not 'relevant'), the translation would have gratuitously upset the interaction of stimulus, contextual assumptions and interpretation.

 Task A8.4

➤ Illustrate **Minimax** from a domain such as translating humour by giving an example of a joke that is particularly difficult to tell in another language. Such a joke is likely to strain the effort–reward balance, since what we see as laughable can vary dramatically across languages.

Seen from the standpoint of text production and **reception**, then, **Minimax** suggests that writers tend to ensure, and readers expect, that any extra effort is justified and commensurately rewarded, and that such textual manifestations as opaque word order, repetition, the use of metaphorical language or any other form of implicitness are not gratuitously used.

Concept box   Functionality

To be meaningful, non-ordinariness of language use (i.e. textual **salience**) must always be communicatively motivated. Take a phenomenon such as repetition. This could occur in sloppy writing, could be an intention-less feature of languages with a great deal of 'residual orality' (Ong 1971), or could be there merely to uphold **cohesion** in the text. In such cases, repetition would not be significant, and the question of **contextual motivatedness** does not even arise. However, repetition can be **functional** if it is intended to serve particular **rhetorical purposes** within the text. In contexts of this kind, repetition becomes a marked feature of language use that must be accounted for (see **markedness** in Unit 9, pp. 69–70).

Task A8.5

➤ Reflect on this **functional**/ non-functional distinction in your own language and identify cases where **form** is not commensurate with **function** and vice versa. For example, a verb such as *declared* might be used when in fact merely *said* would do, or a verb like *announced* is used when no 'announcement' is forthcoming, or *noteworthy* is used for something that is not 'worth noting' at all.

➤ Examine news reports from the front page of your daily newspaper. Can you identify features that appear **marked** but are actually functionless?

To be communicated properly, **contextual motivatedness** (e.g. purposeful repetition) must first become part of the text-based information on which readers/ translators rely. This is important to the working of a principle such as **Minimax** and, by extension, to the assessment of '**relevance**'.

Task A8.6

➤ Reflect on such **form** vs **function** problems. Examine translated poetry, for example. How far and in what way is '**context**' invoked in dealing with what may appear to be a '**formal**' problem? Specifically, are there problems of effort and reward that can be explained adequately in terms of a complex network of contextual assumptions?

DESCRIPTIVE VS INTERPRETIVE

In dealing with these **form–content** problems, the **relevance** model of translation employs a range of **cognitive** tools, including inference and the ability to perceive and interact with textual **salience** functionally. An important distinction entertained by the text user relates to two ways of using language: '**descriptive**' and '**interpretive**'. These reflect the two ways our minds entertain thoughts. An utterance is said to be *descriptive* if it is intended to be true of a state of affairs in some possible world. On the other hand, an utterance is said to be *interpretive* if it is intended by the speaker not to represent his or her own thoughts but those of someone else.

To see the **descriptive** vs **interpretive** dichotomy in practical translation terms, let us consider two translation situations, one involving the production in English of a tourist brochure (with the instruction of producing a text that is ultra-functional in guiding tourists round a city), the other the production of an advert (with the instruction that the translation is for use by top planners of marketing strategy). Thus, while the resultant English tourist brochure could conceivably be composed without reference to the original, the translation of the advertisement would be crucially dependent on the ST.

The tourist brochure would be an instance of **descriptive** use in that the TT is intended to achieve **relevance** in its own right, whereas the advertisement translation could succeed only in virtue of its **resemblance** to some SL original. In practice, this points to a greater freedom enjoyed by the translator of the tourist brochure (hence the luxury of producing what is almost akin to an original text). The advertisement's translator, on the other hand, can work only **interpretively** (resigned to the limitations of a medium called translation).

 Task A8.7

➤ To what extent do you think 'interpretive' translation is tantamount to 'literal' translation, and 'descriptive' translation to 'free' translation?

➤ Find a tourist brochure and translate a portion into another language. Comment on whether your translation is **interpretive** or **descriptive**. Can you conceive of how the tourist brochure might sound, were you to adopt an alternative strategy?

Task A8.8

➤ What problems are likely to be encountered in translating a sacred text descriptively?

DIRECT VS INDIRECT TRANSLATION

The degree of latitude which translators enjoy may be seen in terms of another distinction which the **relevance** model of translation has had to adopt: **direct** and **indirect** translation. This dichotomy addresses the need 'to distinguish between translations where the translator is free to elaborate or summarize [i.e. indirectly] and those where he has to somehow stick to the explicit contents of the original' [directly] (Gutt 1991: 122). Obviously, this is not an either/or choice but rather the two ends of a continuum. **Indirect translations** are intended to survive on their own, and involve whatever changes the translator deems necessary to maximize relevance for a new **audience** (i.e. the predominantly 'descriptive' mode of the tourist brochure type of translation in the example discussed above). **Direct translations**, on the other hand, are more closely tied to the original, a case of what we have called 'interpretive' resemblance. Guided by a notion of **faithfulness**, the translator designs a **direct** translation in such a way that it resembles the original 'closely enough in relevant respects' (Sperber and Wilson 1986: 137).

Task A8.9

➤ Choose a translation of Shakespeare into a language you know well. Would you say that the translation is predominantly **direct** or **indirect**? If **indirect**, choose a passage and turn it into **direct**. If the translation is already **direct**, reflect on the situation and examine the notion of 'resembling the original closely enough in relevant respects'.

The **direct** vs **indirect** distinction is proposed in order to resolve the difficult choice between 'the need to give the receptor language **audience** access to the authentic meaning of the original, unaffected by the translator's own interpretation effort' (a case of **direct** translation), and 'the urge to communicate as clearly as possible' (Gutt 1991: 177).

Given the value placed on fluency throughout the history of translation practice, the decision in such cases has invariably been in favour of the latter, more communicative goal. The translation usually **explicates** information implicit in the ST, and explains any cultural material normally retrievable only by the SL **audience**. The context envisaged by the ST writer is made equally available to the TL **audience** as far as possible, hence the generous amount of additional explanatory information provided.

Task A8.10

➤ Examine the tourist brochure which you have most likely translated using the **indirect** strategy in Task A8.7 and reflect on the **procedures** you have employed.

While this form of **indirect** translation is still considered 'faithful' (Nida and Taber 1969), **relevance** theoreticians are adamant that, like the '**descriptive**' brand, this kind of translation is 'not translation at all' (Gutt 1991). But, should **indirect** translation be dismissed outright? Is it realistic to expect that a set of often alien assumptions intended by the communicator of the original text for his/her **audience** can always be communicated optimally to a different audience in a different language/culture?

To return to the question posed earlier: what if, in dealing, say, with sacred and sensitive texts, we are required to reproduce exactly not only what is said, but also how it is said (i.e. not only the **content** but also the **style** of what someone said or wrote in another language)? According to Gutt, this can be done with various degrees of approximation. With its commitment to total **interpretive resemblance**, **direct** translation ought to work well in this respect, and matters of **style** will feature prominently.

However, we must remember that the essential relationship between ST and TT will rest not in the formal features serving as stimuli or **communicative clues**, but in the resemblance of their intended interpretations. Stylistic features are extremely important, not so much in themselves as in the functions they serve while guiding the text receiver towards the intended interpretation.

A text may directly quote from another text, and this form of what we shall discuss in greater detail under **intertextuality** (Unit 11) can be stylistically problematic in translation. One source of difficulty is when the '**function**' of the stylistic feature is not heeded. An example of this is English translation Example A8.2.

Example A8.2

In comfort and in diversity, in suffering and in joy
(Cited in Dickins, Hervey and Higgins 2002: 142)

This conjures up the marriage service in the Book of Common Prayer (*for better for worse, for richer for poorer, in sickness and in health*). The ST, however, is the Muslim Brotherhood Oath of Allegiance!

 Task A8.11

➤ What should the translator do to avoid such unintended effects?

➤ Revise the above **literal** translation to avoid these particular unintended effects.

➤ Find similar problems of **intertextual** reference in languages other than English, and reflect on the translation problems involved.

COMMUNICATIVE CLUES

Direct translation has been likened to direct quotation, but with one important difference: while quotations preserve both **form** and meaning, enormous differences between languages, particularly at the formal level, make this untenable in the case of translation. In **relevance** theory, the notion of the **communicative clue** is proposed as a possible solution to the problem of inter-linguistic disparity (Gutt 1991: 127).

Relevance theory accords great importance to the stimuli which trigger communication and set **inferencing** in motion. One way of looking at a stimulus would thus be through the **cognitive** effects it yields (e.g. the implied meanings or the **implicatures** conveyed). But stimuli can also be seen in terms of their intrinsic linguistic properties or the perceptible phonic or graphic substance.

Task A8.12

How would you deal with a situation such as the following: the ST is a play partly written in colloquial Egyptian about an Egyptian housewife who has spent the last few years in Paris. She adopts a pseudo-French style of broken Arabic, on both the phonic and the grammatical levels.

The following example solves the problem by deliberately manipulating English spelling, pronunciation, etc.

➤ Are the stylistic values in this translation sufficiently transparent? Can you suggest other solutions to guide the reader to the intrinsic values of the linguistic properties?

Example A8.3

Full of extremely feelthy people zey eat zey sleep like zee peeg
(Cited in Dickins, Hervey and Higgins 2002: 46)

This is the domain of **direct** translation and an area of special interest in the translation of **style**. While it is certainly true, as Jakobson asserted (see Unit 1), that what can be said in one language can always be said in another, it is also true that this is often restricted to **semantic content**. In the area of stylistic properties, for example, linguistic features tend to be far from universal. To cope with this specificity, **relevance** theory has adopted the 'communicative clues' model. Stylistic properties are no longer seen in terms of their intrinsic value, but rather through the kind of *clues* they yield to guide the **audience** to the intended interpretation.

Task A8.13

Focal effects (emphasis, etc.) may be achieved by such formal means as stress in some languages, but not in others. Stress is a **communicative clue** which, if unavailable in the TL, may be replaced by other **syntactic** means that serve a similar **function** (e.g. **clefting** as in *it is his vision that was impaired*). In these TLs, **clefting** (like stress) would be a crucial **communicative clue**.

➤ Give examples of focal effects in texts in your own language. Will all **communicative clues** yielded be worth attending to? If not, what leads us to consider one **communicative clue** 'relevant' and others irrelevant?

Form vs **function** (or *how* something is said vs *what* is intended by it) has been a central theme in the discussion of translation strategy throughout the last fifty years or so of translation research and practice. The **relevance** model has presented itself as a **cognitive**-linguistic alternative to **formal** vs **dynamic equivalence** models which

Summary

had signalled a shift from the **form** of the message to the no less problematic idea of response. More significantly, **relevance** was seen as a corrective to theories which, out of **pragmatics**, had argued for the relative nature of **equivalence** (e.g. Koller) and, out of **text linguistics**, had postulated text as a **unit of translation** (e.g. Beaugrande). **Relevance** research has certainly shed light on a number of important issues including the role of such mechanisms as 'inference'. However, it is perhaps fair to say that **relevance** research has in turn raised more questions than it could answer. It has questioned the value of working with such concepts as 'intended readership' and 'equivalent effect', and has shown little concern with textual criteria such as **genre** membership. Yet, the **formal** vs **dynamic** distinction and the role of templates such as 'text type' in achieving **resemblance** have always featured as they are bound to do in accounts of the translation process informed by the **relevance** model itself. It is to some of these issues that we shall now turn our attention.

Unit A9
Text type in translation

As part of the 'form vs function' debate or whether we should be concerned with how something is said as opposed to what is intended by it, relevance research (e.g. Gutt 1991) took a 'cognitive' turn essentially to critique the 'textual' turn that was gaining momentum throughout the 1970s (e.g. Beaugrande 1978, Koller 1979). In the analysis of STs or the composition of TTs, the relevance model has drawn on mental resources such as 'inference' as a more viable alternative to taxonomic classifications such as text typologies. Yet, most theorizing by proponents of 'relevance' on translation strategy (descriptive vs interpretive, direct vs indirect), could not completely ignore macro-structures such as text type or genre. By the end of the 1990s, there was a clear admission that inference can only be enriched by awareness of the conventions governing the communicative event within which texts or genres occur (Gutt 1998). In Unit 7 of this book, we introduced the 'textual' dimension to the model of pragmatic equivalence and presented the main claims of the textual model. The present unit re-examines these claims and properly assesses the status of text type in the translation process.

STANDARDS OF TEXTUALITY

Translation theories informed by textual pragmatics (e.g. Thomas 1995) see 'equivalence' in relative and hierarchical terms (Koller 1995) and specifically view a 'translation' as a valid representative of ST communicative acts (Beaugrande 1978). Concepts such as 'valid representative' or 'communicative act', however, are problematical in that they can cover quite a range of translation phenomena, from producing a literal replica to a free paraphrase of sentences or entire texts.

From its very inception in the early 1970s, text linguistics has rejected the form–meaning split and the popular but counter-intuitive assumption that communicative contexts are simply too diffuse to yield meaningful generalizations regarding language use. From a textual perspective, context is seen as:

> A strategic configuration in which what things 'mean' coincides intention-ally and in systematic ways with what they are used for and with whatever else is going on in the situation.
>
> (Beaugrande 1991: 31)

This notion of context as **purpose** and **function** is underpinned by several **standards of textuality** which all well-formed texts (or their translations) must meet (Beaugrande 1980). **Cohesion** subsumes the diverse relations which transparently hold among the words, phrases and sentences of a text. Underlying these surface phenomena is **coherence** which taps a variety of conceptual resources, ensuring that meanings are related discernibly.

These aspects of **texture** link bottom-up with **situationality**, a cover term for the way utterances relate to situations. Situational appropriateness (together with efficiency and effectiveness provided by **cohesion** and **coherence**) is regulated by the principle of **informativity**, or the extent to which a text or parts of a text may be expected or unexpected, thus exhibiting varying degrees of **dynamism** (i.e. uncertainty or interestingness, see the '**markedness**' section on pp. 69–70). The entire communicative transaction is driven by the **intentionality** of a text producer, matched by **acceptability** on the part of a text receiver, which together ensure that the text is purposeful and that it functions in a particular way to serve the purposes for which it is intended. Finally, **intertextuality** ensures that texts or parts of texts link up in meaningful ways with other texts.

Example A9.1

She *woke* at midnight. She always *woke up* then without having to rely on an alarm clock. A wish that had taken root in her *awoke* her with great accuracy. For a few moments she was not sure she was *awake*. . . .

   Habit *woke* her at this hour. It was an old habit she had developed when young and it had stayed with her as she matured. She had learned it along with the other rules of married life. She *woke up* at midnight to await her husband's return from his evening's entertainment . . .

(N. Mahfouz (*Bayn al-Qasrayn*) *Palace Walk* (1962) [italics added])

 Task A9.1

➤ Consider Example A9.1 and answer the questions below. Pay particular attention to those elements in the text in italics.

- ■ What strikes you as interesting about the repetition of *woke, woke up*, etc.? (**Cohesion**)
- ■ How does this repetition help to sustain the narrative threading its way through the text? (**Coherence**)
- ■ What do you think is intended by the repetition? (**Intentionality**)
- ■ Can this function be appreciated for what it is by the average reader of the text? (**Acceptability**)
- ■ Is it normal and expected, or dynamic and unexpected? (**Informativity**)
- ■ What aspect of social life does the repetition underscore? (**Situationality**)

■ Does this kind of language, scene, etc., remind you of other texts? Does it sound like an argument, an explanation, a narrative, etc? (**Intertextuality**)

➤ In the light of this analysis, work out a strategy for translating the passage into a language of your choice.

As a general template for the study of **equivalence**, then, the textual-pragmatic scheme focuses our attention on the range of textual relations that can be established and must be accounted for in moving from a ST to a TT.

MARKEDNESS

One particular relationship worth noting in this respect is **markedness** or what we have so far referred to variously under such labels as textual **salience** and **dynamism**. The arrangement of words and sentences may take a 'preferred' or 'expected' form (i.e. unmarked), or a somewhat unfamiliar and unexpected form (i.e. **marked**, **salient**, **dynamic**).

Unmarked options confront us with no significant problems. But texts are rarely if ever so straightforward. There are situations in which language is deliberately used in a non-habitual, non-ordinary way, and it is this **dehabitualization** or non-ordinariness (i.e. **dynamism**) that usually proves particularly challenging in translation. The theoretical thinking on this issue in Translation Studies runs something like this: if **contextually motivated** (that is, if used ungratuitously), marked grammar and lexis must be accounted for in the processing of text and preserved in translation. Practice tells a different story.

Task A9.2

➤ Consider this specific example from an Arabic 'absurdist' drama (T. Al-Hakeem (1960) *al-Sultan al-Haa'ir, The Sultan's Dilemma*) which has seen two translations into English, one heavily **domesticated**, the other less so. Focus on the italicized elements in this respect, and reflect on the effect likely to be generated by the different renderings:

Example A9.2a (Version 1, italics added)

EXECUTIONER:	. . . Now that I have warned you of this condition, do you still want me to sing?
CONDEMNED MAN:	*Go ahead.*
E:	And you will admire and applaud me?
CM:	Yes.
E:	Is that a solemn promise?
CM:	*It is.*

Example A9.2b (Version 2, italics added)

EXECUTIONER:	. . . Now, having drawn your attention to the condition, shall I sing?
CONDEMNED MAN:	*Sing!*
E:	And will you admire me and show your appreciation?
CM:	Yes.
E:	You promise faithfully?
CM:	*Faithfully.*

Version 1 is from a translation which has opted for some form of **dynamic equivalence** (see Unit 6), drastically **gloss**ing the source utterance, while Version 2 is from a translation which predominantly uses **formal equivalence**, reproducing **form** for **form** and thus preserving such aspects of the text as the repetition considered here to be maximally motivated. Informed by **textual pragmatics**, we could say that the effect which the latter translation conveys is **defamiliarizing**: the translation seeks to preserve subtle aspects of ST meaning, such as the fact that the speaker in this text sounds 'ridiculous', 'absurd', etc.

But is preserving non-ordinariness in this way a valid solution all the time? Within the textual model, it is maintained that non-ordinariness should not be seen in static terms, with the non-ordinary forms of the original simply reconstructed or transferred more or less intact. Rather, a process is set in motion in which some form of negotiation takes place to establish what precisely is intended by the ST, and then to ascertain how the target reader may best be made aware of the intricacies involved. The communicative resources of the TL may have to be stretched, but this must always be interpretable. One way of enhancing this sense of interpretability is to exploit the target user's cultural experience and knowledge of his/her language. Text examples discussed in Unit 2 (e.g. Examples A2.2–2.5) show how interpretability can suffer irreparably sometimes.

TEXT-BASED INFORMATION

In dealing with issues such as **markedness** and **equivalence** from a **text-linguistic** point of view, a gradient may be proposed to capture how, specifically as a reader, the translator tends to move backwards and forwards between what may be called 'reader-supplied' information at one end, and information 'supplied by the text' at the other. Research into reading suggests that, as the reading process gets underway, there would ideally be *less* reliance on information supplied by the reader, and *more* on information which the text itself supplies. Indeed, according to Beaugrande (1978: 88), it is only when reading becomes almost entirely dependent on information dominated by the text that a 'truly objective translation' is possible, 'a translation which validly represents the perceptual potential of the original'.

What precisely is involved in 'text-based information'? This term is a misnomer, and the focus has been placed erroneously on '**form** or **content** *concretely present* in the text', which is not necessarily always the case. To appreciate this point, consider the following unidiomatic, published translation of an editorial:

Example A9.3a

EDITORIAL

A necessary move

Through Lebanese satellite's channels and newspapers we acknowledge and always emphasize the unity of the Lebanese and the Syrian tracks. [. . .]

We do not discuss the idea of the two tracks' coherence in spite of remarks about liberating South Lebanon. But we would like to point out that [. . .]

(Al-Watan 1999)

The translator is concerned with 'what the media are saying', etc., an area of **content** which, although physically present in the ST, is simply not relevant to what is intended. The reference to *satellite channels and newspapers*, for example, is a rhetorical way of talking which cannot be taken literally. The text producer is simply saying something like 'we have publicly acknowledged that . . .'. This is part of a concession which could be conveyed much more effectively by using an appropriate signal such as 'Certainly', 'Of course', followed by an adversative: 'However, this is not the issue'. If used, this format would naturally pave the way for a forthcoming contrast: 'The issue is . . .', ushering in the counter-claim.

Task A9.3

➤ With a clearer idea of what 'text-based information' means, edit and revise the published translation (Example A9.3a).

The **text-linguistic** view regarding what is said vs what is intended and how it is a combination of the two that can properly signal what text-based information is about, is stated clearly by Beaugrande (1978: 91): 'the word cannot be the **unit of translation**'. This claim is informed by a general stance which takes **text** to be the minimal unit of communication. In the above translations, a pragmatic reading of text-based information necessitates that we depart drastically from the surface manifestations of both **form** and **content** (i.e. from **surface structure** and **denotative** meaning).

This is consistent with the view that text-based information is yielded not by 'purely formal features, but rather as the result of an intense . . . evaluation of the communicative relevance of formal features' (Beaugrande 1978: 95). In the above example, the conditional structure or a word such as *discuss* is a striking example of how the **lexicogrammar** tends to communicate meanings that go beyond structural relationships and that must be placed within larger templates to be appreciated properly. This wider framework, we suggest, is provided by **text type**, a macro-structure which essentially encompasses the purposes for which utterances are used under what we will explain shortly as the **rhetorical purpose** of the text.

READER-SUPPLIED INFORMATION

Reader-supplied information is another potentially misleading term. It is best seen not as sole reliance on **form** or **content** but in terms of 'linguistic competence'. This competence in turn would not be in the mechanics of **syntactic** or **semantic** structures per se, but would relate to the individual's ability to operate within a set of constraints imposed by such macro-structures as **text type**. We are specifically concerned with real-life situations, and with the influence of variables such as socio-economic status, education and training, knowledge and beliefs. In dealing with the above text examples, for example, what the reader supplies would certainly relate to **content** and to knowledge of the grammar (say, of conditionals) and the **semantics** of words such as *satellite channels* and *newspapers*. But the focus would inevitably be much wider. It would cover how this content or **lexicogrammar** is deployed to serve higher-order value and belief systems to do with the **function** of text in context:

- serving social institutions and social processes (e.g. countering an adversary's claim subtly);
- maintaining relations of **power** and solidarity (e.g. issuing the counter-claim politely without alienating the adversary);
- making sense (conveying a semblance of a balance between claim and counter-claim cohesively and coherently).

Example A9.3a, for example, would now read something like:

Example A9.3b   (suggested amendment)

Certainly the Lebanese and Syrian tracks for peace with Israel run parallel and in perfect harmony. However, this is not the issue. The issue is [. . .]

Thus, it is the values yielded by these text-in-context relationships that collectively make up the 'perceptual potential' of the text which is the sole basis of '**textual equivalence**' (in Beaugrande's terms; compare with Catford's term in Unit 4). This is the outcome of an intricate interaction between **form** and **content** which we seek to preserve in translation. Let us examine what is involved in greater detail.

TEXT TYPOLOGY

The text-oriented models of the translation **process** that have emerged in recent years have all sought to avoid the pitfalls of categorizing **text** in accordance with situational criteria such as subject matter (e.g. legal or scientific texts). Instead, texts are now classified on the basis of a 'predominant contextual focus' (e.g. **expository**, **argumentative** or **instructional** texts). This has enabled theorist and practitioner alike to confront the difficult issue of **text hybridization**. That texts are essentially multi-functional is now seen as the norm rather than the exception.

Task A9.4

➤ What justifies the combination of reporting and commentary? Can you, for example, justify the use of a **cleft** structure (*it was . . . that*) and other emphatic devices in the following translation of an Arabic news report?

Example A9.4

It was the tension between the Blacks and Jewish communities in New York which ended in bloodshed in yesterday's clashes *that* glaringly exposed how precarious the relations are between the two groups. [. . .]

The tension *simply* began with a traffic incident when [. . .]

(*Al-Majalla* 1981 (italics added))

In this example, there is undoubtedly a certain amount of commentary. There are two points to make about this case of **hybridization**. First, the **evaluativeness** in this news report is justified in the light of a number of factors including, most importantly, the sensitivity of the issue reported. Second, despite the presence of evaluative material, we cannot fail to recognize the text for what it is: predominantly a news report. We are aware of this because we are familiar with what straight reporting (as opposed to commentary) looks or sounds like. But, perhaps more significantly, we are almost sure that reporting and commentary cannot be equally prominent. Since there is insufficient evaluation to turn the text into an editorial, the overall **purpose** of the text must be ultimately to report the news.

With the emphasis on contextual focus, the multi-functionality of all texts is thus no longer seen as a weakness of the **text type** model, nor indeed as a licence for an 'anything goes' attitude in the production or analysis of texts or translations. For example, it is recognized that, while a distinction may usefully be made between so-called **expressive** texts (of the creative, literary type) and **informative** texts (of the factual variety), texts are rarely if ever one or the other type. Yet it can safely be assumed that, unless there is a good reason to do otherwise, metaphors in predominantly **expressive** texts, for example, are best rendered metaphorically, while those in predominantly **informative** texts may if necessary be modified or altogether jettisoned (Reiss 1971: 62).

 Task A9.5

➤ Example A9.5 is an extract from the Charter of the Palestinian militant group Hamas. Given what charters should look or sound like, can you suggest some improvements on this translation, perhaps cutting down on the emotiveness that is allowed to feature too prominently. Would you, on the other hand, accept a reasonable measure of emotiveness in this particular context? Why?

Example A9.5

Article Nine

The state of truth has disappeared and was replaced by the state of evil. Nothing has remained in its right place, for when Islam is removed from the scene, everything changes. These are the motives.

As to the objectives: discarding the evil, crushing it and defeating it, so that truth may prevail and homelands revert to their owners [. . .]

(*The Hamas Charter* 1990 (trans Prof. R. Israeli))

Whether you have approved of or rejected the decision to preserve emotiveness in the Hamas text, your decision will have been informed by what the text is intended to do in a given context for a given text user. Central to **text typologies** of the kind advocated by context-sensitive theories of translation is the view that language use beyond the sentence may helpfully be seen in terms of **rhetorical purpose** (e.g. **exposition, argumentation, instruction**). This sense of **purpose** yields increasingly finer categories (e.g. report, counter-argument, regulation), and a variety of text forms identified on the basis of such factors as subject matter or level of formality (e.g. reporting, **argumentation** or **instruction** may be technical/non-technical, subjective/objective, spoken/written). But to reiterate, it is generally accepted that, in all cases, such a categorization is necessarily idealized and that, since all texts are in a sense hybrid, the predominance of a given **rhetorical purpose** in a given text is an important yardstick for assessing **text-type** 'identity'.

Models of translation informed by **text typology** have thus sought to encompass and account for the diversity of **rhetorical purposes** normally served in any act of communication. This entails that communicative values (related to such contextual factors as **situationality, intentionality, intertextuality**) are fully integrated into the way **text types** are used or produced. A set of constraints emerges, and **text types** are seen as 'guidelines' which text users instinctively refer to in adopting a given translation strategy with an eye on both sides of the translation divide – the ST and the TT.

Summary

In this unit, we have examined the minimal criteria which texts or their translations must meet to be effective, efficient and appropriate. But it may happen that the criteria are not followed either for no good reason (in which case we would be dealing with gratuitous 'violation') or with justification (**contextually motivated** 'flouting'). The **rhetorical purpose** of a text is thus an important yardstick by which to assess, first, whether the text is intended to **monitor** (view with detachment) or **manage** (evaluate) and, second, whether, within each of these broad categories, the text is intended to serve any of a number of sub-purposes such as counter- or through-**argumentation**, conceptual or narrative **exposition**. Finally, **rhetorical purpose** is important not only in defining **norms** but also in spotting deviations which (if **contextually motivated**) must be heeded and preserved in translation.

Unit A10
Text register in translation

In this and the next unit, we will examine the notion of **text type** from two distinct yet related angles. First, we will deal with **text type** in terms of how it accommodates the way language generally varies as situations vary (in the light of what has come to be known as **register**). The various patterns of **cohesion** which turn a sequence of disparate sentences into **coherent** texts, and dealing with these patterns in translation, are seen in relation to the immediate **context of situation**. Alongside this **register** dimension, **texts** (and their translations) may be seen from the vantage point of the wider **context of culture**. Here, factors such as the **communicative event** within which a **text** is embedded (**genre**) and the ideological statements which a **text** makes (**discourse**) become crucial parameters in the effective production and **reception** of texts and in the evaluation of translations.

USE AND USER OF LANGUAGE

In dealing with the **context of situation** from a translation perspective, we entertain the generally accepted socio-linguistic assumption that language use varies as its **context** varies, and that different language varieties emerge to cater for different contexts. The need to study this kind of variation was initially prompted by the idea that the concept of a 'whole' language was simply too diffuse to be operationally useful for many of our immediate purposes in such applied pursuits as language teaching (Halliday, Mcintosh and Strevens 1964). Translation Studies followed suit (Chau 1984) and began to recognize the need to appreciate, assess and, when appropriate, preserve, subtle text variation of the kind illustrated by these STs:

Example A10.1

THE FLOWER GIRL [subsiding into a brooding melancholy over her basket, and talking very low spiritedly to herself] I'm a good girl, *I am*.

[. . .]

THE FLOWER GIRL [still nursing her sense of injury] Aint no call to meddle with me, *he aint*.

(George Bernard Shaw (1916/2003) *Pygmalion*, Penguin Books, p. 35
[italics added])

Example A10.2

CHAIR: *Mr* Erlichman, *prior* to the *luncheon recess* you *stated* that . . .
From the Watergate transcripts, cited in Fairclough (1989) [italics added]

Task A10.1

➤ Consider the italicized features, the kind of variation involved, and the significance of such variation. Reflect also on ways of preserving the added values in translating these texts into another language.

Two dimensions may be recognized in the kind of variation shown by the above examples. The first has to do with who the speaker/writer is. Such user-related varieties are called 'dialects' (e.g. Example A10.1 above). The Flower Girl is a Cockney speaker (a geographical factor) who is also working class (a social factor) and a user of modern non-standard English (a temporal factor). These and similar contextual factors tend to find expression in the grammar and vocabulary of actual texts (see elements in italics).

The second dimension of variation relates not so much to the user as to the use of language. Essentially, use-related varieties (*registers*) have to do with such factors as the occupation of the speaker (e.g. lawyer, journalist) and whether the occasion of use is formal or informal. The speaker in Example A10.2 uses both legal-sounding language and formality. Language varieties distinguished on occupational grounds tend to attract labels such as 'legalese' or 'journalese', which reflect the status of these **registers** as 'languages' in their own right.

Task A10.2

➤ List a number of features we associate with legalese or journalese, and compare with an equivalent **register** (if such exists) in another language.

INSTITUTIONAL–COMMUNICATIVE CONTEXT

The use–user dimensions essentially indicate who is communicating with whom, what is being communicated, and how this is communicated, hence the institutional–communicative focus. Together with **intentionality** (covering such **pragmatic** factors as the force of an utterance, see Unit 7), and **intertextuality** (or how texts as '**signs**' conjure up images of other virtual or actual texts, see Unit 11), **register** mediates between language and situation (i.e. we use language **registers** to access situations). For example, the above texts serve institutional ends (the language of a working-class girl at a particular time and place, and that of the professional conduct of a tribunal). Simultaneously, these texts communicate certain values relevant to the situation to hand: the sense of identity (perhaps even the stigma and uncertainty attached to this kind of language use in the case of Example A10.1, and the sense of power and authority enjoyed by the Chair of a tribunal, in the case of Example A10.2).

The various strands of text in context may be represented diagrammatically as in Figure A10.1

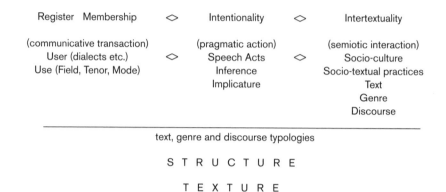

Figure A10.1   The three dimensions of context, adapted from Hatim and Mason (1990)

THE MYTH OF THE SINGLE REGISTER

The following text examples all relate to one particular situational setting – the Maastricht Treaty signed by the representatives of the twelve nations making up the European Community at the time. There was a stage in the development of **register** theory when the first three text examples would all have been glossed as 'legalese', leaving us with 'journalese' as the single **register** label of the last two. But, a closer look at these texts reveals that these texts differ from each other in a number of significant ways. What is involved may certainly cater for one subject matter, or one level of formality, but other systems of language variation are also clearly at work and must be heeded by the translator.

Example A10.3

Part Two

Citizenship of the Union

Article 8

Citizenship of the Union is hereby established. Every person holding the nationality of a Member State shall be a citizen of the Union. [. . .]

(From *The Treaty of Maastricht* (available online at http://europa.eu.int/abc/
obj/treaties/en/entr6c.htm))

Example A10.4

The treaty creates citizenship of the European Union. Everybody holding the nationality of a member state will be a citizen of the Union, with rights and duties conferred by the Treaty. (see note 10)

(Abridged by *The Independent* 11 October 1992)

Example A10.5

Note 10

This was designed to give the idea of the Union some meaning. But it has proved to be one of the most controversial elements in some countries, since it means that 'foreigners' get the vote.

(Annotation by *The Independent* 11 October 1992)

Example A10.6

European Community

Decommissioned

From our Brussels **Correspondent**

The mood inside the European Commission has not been so glum for almost a decade. Since 1985, when Jacques Delors became its president, the Commission has enjoyed seven years of growing power and influence. Its proposals, including those that created the single-market programme, made it the motor driving the European Community. But the recent wave of hostility to interference from 'Brussels' has badly dented the Commission's self-confidence. It is reluctant to make any proposal that could upset entrenched national interests, lest EC governments seek to trim its powers. The motor has all but stalled. [. . .]

(*The Economist* 10 October 1992)

Example A10.7

[. . .] Sir Leon Brittan and Martin Bengemann, whose responsibilities are respectively competition and the single market, argue that the Commission should risk courting unpopularity and push on with its legislative programmes. Other commissioners think that would be folly. Christine Scrivener, the taxation commissioner, has called for a legislative pause. Mr Delors, the President, now stresses the need for caution. [. . .]

(*The Economist* 10 October 1992)

Task A10.3

➤ Can you intuitively at this stage spell out the differences between the above examples? View these differences in terms of

- what is being communicated, by whom, to whom
- what is intended to be achieved, and
- what kind of 'other' texts you are reminded of while reading each of these texts.

You will have noted that Example A10.3 reflects the power and authority of the text producer to lay down the law and thus precisely define a future course of action. Example A10.4, on the other hand, displays the almost total absence of such power, since the text producer is merely 'summarizing', ideally with sole responsibility for the facts as he or she sees them.

Curiously enough, examples A10.5 (the annotated comment) and A10.6 (the concession-rebuttal) are not dissimilar to example A10.3 (the straightforward instruction). Each in its own way is aimed at the formation of future behaviour. There is one basic difference, however. Unlike A10.3, the text receiver of A10.5 or A10.6 is under no obligation to accept the views put forward. However, it has to be noted that, while the producer of Example A10.5 would not take exception to being ignored, as the argument is not really his but that of someone else (it is simply an annotation), the writer of Example A10.6 has put forward an argument that is exclusively her own and it is her credibility as an arguer that is at stake.

Nevertheless, as will become clear in the course of the following discussion, argument is not our Brussels correspondent's only card: she is able, for example, to assume a different role and achieve her overall persuasive objective through a different channel (e.g. in her capacity as a reporter in Example A10.3).

 Task A10.4

➤ Can it be said that even reporting can serve a persuasive appeal?

➤ Find two or three recent news reports and examine them carefully.

➤ Can you detect an element of persuasivess, emotiveness, etc., over and above the primary purpose of the news report which is to report the facts?

By themselves, then, user-related variables are not sufficient, hence the need for a different set of defining features which can capture the intricacies of use. Producers and receivers of texts operate within constraints imposed by the particular use to which they put their language. This aspect of variation caters for such variables as **field** (e.g. the legal domain of Example A10.3), **mode** of interaction (the example being written to be read reflectively), and **tenor** or level of formality (the example being formal, written in an almost 'frozen' style).

It is **tenor**, however, that is perhaps the crucial factor in regulating the complex interaction between addresser and addressee. In its simplest form, this is to do with the formal or informal stance which co-communicants adopt towards one another and which ranges from casual to deferential, from most intimate to most impersonal, and so on. Different terms have been used by different writers for this phenomenon: '**style**', 'status', 'attitude', 'relative social status', etc. However, the various terms all converge on the central point that, ultimately, **tenor** has to do with the level of formality of the relationship between the participants in the linguistic event.

FUNCTIONAL TENOR

The reason why **tenor** is a particularly privileged category in **register** analysis is to do with the overlap between formality and **field**, on the one hand, and between formality and **mode**, on the other. Diagrammatically, these interrelationships are represented in Figure A10.2:

TECHNICALITY/FORMALITY
FIELD
TENOR
MODE
FUNCTIONAL TENOR

Figure A10.2 Tenor vs. Field and Mode

It is important to note that the cross-fertilization taking place between **tenor** and **field** tends to give rise to technicality, an important aspect of variation: the more formal the occasion, the more technical the use of language. This is collectively viewed in terms of stabilized patterns of role relationships (e.g. student–teacher) which Halliday explains in the following terms:

> The language we use varies according to the level of formality, of technicality, and so on. What is the variable underlying this type of distinction? Essentially, it is the role relationships in the situation in question: who the participants in the communication group are, and in what relationship they stand to each other.
>
> (Halliday 1978: 222)

The overlap between **tenor** and **mode**, on the other hand, gives rise to what Gregory and Carroll (1978: 53) call '**functional tenor**': 'The category used to describe what language is being used for in the situation. Is the speaker trying to persuade? To exhort?'

Functional tenor (e.g. to persuade, to discipline, to inform) thus builds into the analysis a set of role relations different in both scope and nature from those identified under the level of formality/technicality. The participants (e.g. politician vs electorate, lawmaker vs public, reporter vs a particular readership) are now defined not only in terms of single-scale categories such as formal or technical, but also in terms of other aspects of interaction such as

- the informality of direct face-to-face encounters vs the formality of indirect writer-**audience** interaction;
- the semi-formality of the persuader vs the slightly more formal **tenor** of the informer (or the ultra-formality of the lawmaker).

 Task A10.5

➤ View Examples A10.3 to A10.7 above in terms of **functional tenor**: what kind of role relationships are involved in the production of each of these texts?

➤ Think about the implications these distinctions have for the translator. Focus on Examples A10.6 and A10.7.

Text producers enter into a diverse range of role relationships with their receivers, a factor which entails particular **shifts** in **functional tenor** (e.g. the reporter–arguer role-switching in Examples A10.6 and A10.7, obviously written by the same person and encountered in the same article). Institutional–communicative transactions thus acquire an interactive character which is the domain of the other level of **context**, of texts as **signs**, or **semiotics**.

SEMIOTIC INTERACTION: IDEATIONAL, INTERPERSONAL AND TEXTUAL METAFUNCTIONS

So far, our investigation of both **personal tenor** (e.g. casual, deferential) and **functional tenor** (detached reporting, involved persuasion), with technicality and role relationships (e.g. informer, arguer) forming the two basic aspects of **functional tenor**, has highlighted some basic differences in how language varies. This is an institutional issue and may thus be usefully viewed in terms of the use and user of language. However, for rhetorical goals such as persuading or informing to be properly pursued, and for role relationships to stabilize, language users must negotiate meanings in texts and thus deal with context more interactively. As Hatim and Mason point out from the perspective of **discourse** and the translator:

> Seeing the meaning of texts as something which is negotiated between producer and receiver and not as a static entity, independent of human processing activity once it has been encoded, is, we believe, the key to an understanding of translating, teaching translating and judging translations.
> (1990: 64–5)

This negotiation between speaker and hearer or writer and reader forms the basis of one fairly rudimentary level of **semiotic** interaction. Co-communicants do not merely exchange meanings which display a certain level of technicality, exhibit a certain degree of formality, or bear the features of a certain **mode** of interaction (spoken vs written). Rather, they perceive **field**, **tenor** and **mode** respectively in terms of:

- what is going on in and around the text (**ideational** resources);
- attitudes and assessment by speakers of what is happening around and through them (**interpersonal resources**);
- how **ideational** and **interpersonal** expression acquires **cohesion** and **coherence** in a given textual environment (**textual** resources).

Task A10.6

➤ Examine some of the above text examples from the specific perspective of how the text producers have

- **ideationally** represented what is going on around them (e.g. the use of active vs passive);
- **interpersonally** conveyed their attitudes (e.g. use of modals);
- **textually** ensured that the sequence of sentences hang together cohesively and coherently (e.g. the use of connectors).

➤ How would all this enhance the quality of your translation of these texts?

In general terms, then, **field** tends to focus on certain social processes and thus serves the interests of social institutions such as sexism and racism. **Tenor**, in turn, subsumes aspects of **power** and solidarity and thus caters for 'social distance'. Finally, **mode** concentrates on 'physical distance' between the interlocutors (e.g. the proximity of the footballer to the game when describing it on the pitch, as opposed to, say, a commentator on the game or indeed a journalist reporting the game the following day).

The **semiotic** domain of context, then, transforms institutional-communicative transactions into more meaningful interaction. The ways in which levels of basic communication (**field**, **mode** and **tenor**) acquire a **semiotic** specification may be represented diagrammatically as in Figure A10.3:

FIELD	IDEATIONAL RESOURCES	GENRE
MODE	TEXTUAL RESOURCES	TEXT
TENOR	INTERPERSONAL RESOURCES	DISCOURSE

Figure A10.3 The semiotics of field, mode and tenor

It is this complex web of relations that moves communication to a slightly higher level than that of speaker/hearer. Interaction now focuses on how the speaker interacts not only with the hearer, but also with the utterance produced. The hearer would similarly interact, not only with the speaker, but also with the utterance received. In this way, utterances become **signs** in the **semiotic** sense of 'meaning something to somebody in some respect or capacity', ultimately embodying the assumptions, presuppositions and conventions that reflect the way a given culture constructs and partitions reality.

The following text examples may make this point clearer.

Example A10.8

The University of X and Y University have a proven track record . . . which this collaborative venture *can only* enhance.

(Statement from Dean published in a university bulletin)

Example A10.9

The University of X and Y University have a proven track record . . . which this collaborative venture *is intended* to enhance.

(Report on the Dean's statement in a university bulletin)

Example A10.8 shows how the Dean complements the basic interaction between him and his **audience** (whom he probably took to be sceptical, eager, bored or whatever) by an attempt at raising the tempo of persuasiveness through an emphatic assertion. The reporter in Example A10.9, on the other hand, suppresses such a communicative desire, which is once again evidence of how interaction between him and his utterance underpins the customary interaction going on between him and his readers who are there to be informed and not entertained. This is all undertaken within a complex network of sociotextual practices which seem neatly to divide members of a given linguistic community into 'exhorters' and 'reporters'. It is as if by some divine linguistic convention that a notion of territoriality emerges to reflect this kind of division of labour. This territoriality is both well-charted and respected. Transgressions are immediately spotted and shunned as 'over the top' (a label which our reporter would have earned had he opted for *this venture can only enhance*) or as 'coy' (with which the Dean would have been described had he opted for the passive *this venture is intended to enhance*).

 Task A10.7

➤ Consider the translation or **interpreting** problems involved in dealing with such utterances.

> ➤ Does your own language signal the different thrust emerging from a text such as that of the Dean? Are there specific devices for conveying detachment?

Summary

Our concern with **text type** in Unit 9 led us to consider this unit of interaction from two distinct yet related perspectives. In the present unit, we covered the first of these perspectives: textual **registers**. This is seen in terms of linguistic variation giving rise to dialects as a reflection of the language user's geographical, historical and social provenance. What is perhaps more significant is that **register** variation can also be viewed from a language use vantage point. Here, we need to account for such aspects of the way language varies as **field** (involving both subject matter and social institutions served), **tenor**, catering for formality or informality and the way this gives rise to complex relationships of **power** and solidarity, and **mode**, covering the **cohesion** and **coherence** of texts. **Text types**, then, are recognized in terms of the **context of situation** and the **register** employed. In Unit 11 we turn to a different perspective and examine how **translation shifts** can occur in related areas of **text**, **genre** and **discourse**.

Unit A11
Text, genre and discourse shifts in translation

Alongside the focus on the **context of situation**, which we discussed in Unit 10, an important perspective from which texts may be viewed is the **context of culture**. Like other macro-structures such as **schemata** or **scripts**, texts are seen as vehicles for the expression of a range of socio-cultural meanings. These have to do with:

- ■ 'rhetorical purpose' in the case of what we can now technically call the unit **text**,
- ■ the conventional requirements of a set of '**communicative events**' or **genres**,
- ■ **ideology** (or other kinds of 'attitude') implied by adopting a particular **discourse**.

The focus in this unit will be on **translation shifts** (see Unit 4) within this **text–genre–discourse** framework.

Concept box   Intertextuality

> In its most basic form, communicative interaction involves the exchange of meanings as **signs** between speaker and hearer (or writer and reader). For an optimally effective expression of these meanings, however, text users tend to engage in higher-level interaction of utterances or texts with other utterances or texts. For example, the reference to Shakespeare's description of England as 'a precious stone set in the silver sea' as part of an argument on patriotism is not different from 'once upon a time, there was . . .' which conjures up images of fairy tales, or 'on your bike', a phrase that was made memorable in the 1980s by British politician Norman Tebbit and that still speaks volumes of Thatcherism. The principle which regulates this activity is **intertextuality**, a processing mechanism through which textual elements convey meaning by virtue of their dependence on other relevant texts (Bakhtin 1981; Beaugrande 1980).

With this notion of interaction of 'text with text' in mind, two basic types of **intertextual** reference may be distinguished (Fairclough 1989). First, **horizontal** intertextuality, involving concrete reference to, or straight quotation from, other texts (e.g. Shakespeare, Norman Tebbit).

Example A11.1a

'They had sworn to God previously that they would not turn their backs, and an oath to God must be answered for.'

(Al-Quran 33: 15)

The Guardian's translation rendered the verse as follows:

Example A11.1b

'They had made a covenant with God that they would not turn back in flight, and a covenant with God must be answered for.' [Koranic verse]

Task A11.1

In a broadcast letter to the Iraqi people in 2003, Saddam Hussein began with a Koranic verse. The translation of this essentially **horizontal intertextuality** by the Free Arab Voice rendered the verse as in Example A11.1a.

➤ If you were to choose between these two Koranic translations, which one would you choose for a translation of Saddam Hussein's speech? State the reasons why.

Second, effective **vertical intertextuality** is that which, in addition to quoting, contributes through the **intertextual** reference to:

- clarity of expression and accessibility of the intention (a **text** matter),
- the conventionality governing this mode of political speaking (**genre**),
- the sense of commitment to a cause conveyed (**discourse**).

These three factors move the reference along a continuum from mere 'quoting' to 'allusion'. Allusions (also called '**vertical intertextuality**') are more subtle than the essentially static quotative or '**horizontal**' form of **intertextuality**. They represent an 'echo' effect involving reference, not chapter and verse to the Bible or Shakespeare, for example, but to an entire 'mode of expression' (biblical style, Shakespearean tone). Consider the humorous online Example A11.2, a subtle example of **vertical intertextuality** echoing a **genre** with which most readers would probably be familiar.

Example A11.2

Position Title: Beverly's Lover

Position Available: Full Time; Part Time; Temporary; Seasonal;
Interns; and outpost: Positions around the Country.

Job Description: A General all round Companion, with duties
Including: hanging out; Listening to Beverly's Ranting and raving;

[. . .]

(http://www.snakegirl.net/personalADD.htm)

Task A11.2

➤ What makes this reference purely **vertical** rather than **horizontal inter-textuality**? What is the **intertextual** reference to? Reflect on the translation into your own language of this kind of **vertical intertextuality**. How would you deal with the mode of expression alluded to in the above example if no equivalent point of reference exists in the TL?

In the case of **vertical intertextuality**, conjuring up other texts 'virtually' in this way enables us to see a diverse range of linguistic/rhetorical devices (including emotive repetition and other forms of emphasis) as tokens of a type of textual occurrence. They are not necessarily concrete references to a text form we have actually encountered, but cues which conjure up images of other texts or **genres**. Our ability to recognize and catalogue such features of language use builds on a contextual awareness we possess as a basis of the way entire **socio-textual practices** evolve. These practices, which we will examine in terms of the triad **genre–text–discourse**, are crucial, particularly when they vary, sometimes drastically, from one language to another.

GENRE SHIFTS

As we have indicated on a number of occasions so far, 'genre' is a conventionalized form of speaking or writing which we associate with particular 'communicative events' (e.g. the academic abstract). Participants in these events tend to have set goals, with strict **norms** regulating what can or cannot be said within the confines of given **genre** settings. An effective orator opting aimlessly for coy impersonal constructions (such as the passive) or an over-the-top reporter waxing lyrical gratu-itously with emphatic constructions (such as repetition) would both be instances of mishandling **genre** in the context of an inauguration speech and a press release respectively. Similar transgressions may be noted when a letter of application begins with the words: 'Your Excellency, I am honoured and flattered to apply for a place on the MA programme at your esteemed University.' These can all be the result of poor translations or negative **interference** from the mother tongue.

Task A11.3

➤ A cursory glance at a sample of translated news reports into English would immediately reveal that the root cause of the bulk of errors is essentially flawed **genre** awareness rather than incompetence in grammar or lexis. Find your own examples by visiting a foreign news site which contains articles translated into English from your language or languages with which you are familiar. These are some examples of what you might find:

- ■ *It is worth mentioning* (when the news item in question is least noteworthy)
- ■ *On the other hand* (when no 'contrast' is stated or implied, and something like *meanwhile* should have been used)
- ■ *In parallel* (when 'also' is intended)
- ■ *The Minister assured, insisted, pointed out, that* (when 'said' would do)

TEXT SHIFTS

As a unit of communication and translation, **text** is a vehicle for the expression of conventionalized goals and functions. These are tied, not to **communicative events** as in **genre**, but rather to a set of specific rhetorical modes such as arguing and narrating. **Rhetorical purposes** of this kind impose their own constraints on how a sequence of sentences becomes a 'text', i.e. intended and accepted as a **coherent** and cohesive whole, and as such capable of realizing a set of mutually relevant communicative intentions appropriate to a given **rhetorical purpose**. Translators operate within these requirements which must be heeded. Look for example at the text discussed in Unit 11 (Example C9.3, p. 282) in which the translator failed to appreciate the function of the text-initial concessive *Certainly . . .*, and the adversative *But . . .*, compromising the informative text format and producing what read like an editorial.

These are some of the concessive and adversative signals that often go unheeded:

> Concessives: to be sure, of course, granted, naturally, no doubt, certainly
> Adversatives: still, but, however, nevertheless, yet

Such adversatives are perhaps fairly easy to identify. Problems arise when the adversative linkers are implicit (i.e. not stated but implied).

Task A11.4

To counter-argue is a **rhetorical purpose** which is realized in English through a Concessive – Adversative format (*Of course . . . However . . .*). This is a text structure which is particularly difficult for foreign users of English to appreciate.

➤ Examine the translations out of English, of editorials or feature articles, where counter-**argumentation** is commonly used.

➤ Compare STs and TTs and identify the kind of problems faced by translators in this respect.

DISCOURSE SHIFTS

Pursuing a given rhetorical goal in a text thus requires that the process be conducted within the confines of a particular **genre** structure. But to be a viable unit of communication, a text must also strike an ideological note of some kind. That is, in their attempt to pursue a given **rhetorical purpose**, within the dos and don'ts of a particular **genre**, producers and receivers of texts necessarily engage in the negotiation of attitudinal meanings and the espousal or rejection of a particular **ideology** (e.g. Euro-scepticism, Thatcherism, feminism). This attitudinal component which exhibits a range of **ideational**, **interpersonal** and **textual** values is what we shall now specifically call **discourse**. Cast your mind back to examples from *Mills & Boon* or similar kinds of popular fiction. Here, narration is certainly a dominant text mode, and the 'love story' is an important **genre** goal. More subtly, however, a particular kind of **discourse** emanates from the innocuous narration in what is essentially an entertaining **genre**. It is now established that *Mills & Boon* stories serve a sexist agenda. It is uncanny that the man's 'stomach always tightens' but the woman is always incapable of even doing the crying for herself, invariably having 'tears course down her cheeks'!

Apart from the heavy use of clichés in this particular **genre**, **inanimate** agents of the kind you have just seen in the above examples are systematically used to portray women as helpless, impulsive, etc. Here are further examples of ideologically motivated structures common in this kind of writing:

Example A11.3

A pain that could rend her in two . . . Her heart missed a beat . . . It took her breath away . . . Tears welled in her eyes . . . An answering pagan passion leapt to control her

Checking the Arabic translation of Example A11.3 for example, we found that **agency** was restored to the heroine and the **discourse** thrust compromised in 'she was possessed by a pagan passion'.

Task A11.5

➤ Take a *Mills & Boon* novel or any other work of popular fiction, and reflect on the use of '**inanimate agency**' (e.g. '*tears* coursed down her cheeks').

➤ Select a passage that illustrates the use of this particular device, and attempt a translation of your own.

➤ Comment on how you dealt with this translation issue.

Genres and **texts**, then, ultimately serve to 'enable' the expression of an attitude involved in a given **discourse**. Discoursal values relay **power** relations and help define **ideology**. This aspect of meaning is properly the domain of what Halliday (1978: 112) refers to as the 'participatory **function** of language, language as doing something'.

DISCOURSE SHIFTS: A CASE STUDY

Phenomena such as **text** and **genre shifts**, then, tend to implicate the third category in our **intertextual** triad – **discourse**. Kuhiwczak (1990) discusses a particularly interesting case of **manipulation** involving Czech writer Milan Kundera who is introduced by Bassnett and Lefevere in the following terms:

> Kundera writes novels in such a way that they may be too difficult for the average English-speaking reader to understand, and they must therefore be simplified, be made to read more like what the average reader (whoever s/he may be) is used to.
>
> (1990a: 6)

Focusing on Kundera's *The Joke*, Kuhiwczak points out that the English translation is both inadequate and distorted: 'an appropriation of the original, resulting from the translator's and publisher's untested assumptions about Eastern Europe, East European writing, and the ability of the western reader to decode complex cultural messages' (1990: 124).

Specifically, *The Joke*'s plot is not particularly complex; it reflects the writer's belief that novels should be about themes served by narratives which are 'polyphonic, full of seemingly insignificant digressions and carefully crafted repetitions' (1990: 125). The translator into English, however, saw in all of this a bewildering array of irrelevancies (i.e. an alien **poetics**) which must be tidied for the benefit of the prospective reader. Thus, for example, an important theme – the folk music cultural element – is jettisoned, sweeping away with it the very thing which Kundera intended by this particularly long digression: 'to illustrate the fragility of culture' (1990: 126).

Task A11.6

➤ Look at translations of *The Joke* into English and other languages you know, and examine the grounds on which Kundera crossed swords with his publishers and translators.

In similar vein, the Canadian translation theorist Donald Bruce examines the reasons for the state of critical neglect suffered by the nineteenth-century French writer Jules Vallès's trilogy *L'Enfant* (1879), *Le Bachelier* (1881) and *L'Insurgé* (1885). Bruce (1994: 48) shows that the reasons for the indifference are essentially discoursal, in the main due to 'attempts at ideological marginalization and delegitimization of these novels within the French educational apparatus itself'. An extract from Bruce's influential paper is to be found in Section B (Text B11.2), while **poetics** and '**manipulation**' will be central to the discussion in Unit 12.

Summary

In this unit, we have shown how texts tend to focus our attention on the **rhetorical purposes** pursued (to inform, to persuade). In the production (or **reception** and translation) of texts, the contextual focus may fluctuate between one end of a continuum emphasizing '**managing**' (a form of evaluation) to the other which caters for '**monitoring**' a given situation (or general detachment). But, at a slightly higher level of abstraction, texts may serve a different focus, this time on the dos and don'ts surrounding the way in which certain **communicative events** (e.g. the language of the cooking recipe, the academic abstract) may best be served. In these conventionally sanctioned text formats, the intention is certainly to serve a range of **rhetorical purposes** (to inform, etc.), a requirement that must be met for texts to function properly at all. The **rhetorical purposes** catered for, however, may not be ends in themselves, but a means to other communicative ends which transcend the specific purpose of the text. There is a **genre** structure to uphold. There is also an **ideology** to serve. The latter is the domain of **discourse** – the expression of attitude adopted towards areas of socio-cultural reality such as race, gender, entertainment.

Unit A12
Agents of power in translation

Consideration of the semiotic triad **text–genre–discourse** has led us to a discussion of **discourse shifts** in the previous unit. **Discourse** is seen as the expression of attitude towards areas of socio-cultural practice. Through our texts and **genres**, we adopt a 'stance', or a particular 'perspective' towards such issues as 'race' or 'gender'. The discoursal statements produced, say, on racism become a mouthpiece for entire social institutions and social processes. These institutions enjoy **power** and, through the process of exercising such **power**, **ideology** emerges and begins to play an important role in moulding a particular vision of reality. Language plays an important part in all of this, and it is to such textual practices that we will now turn.

THE POWER TO EXCLUDE

In the context of translating or assessing translations, one sense of **power** involves using language to 'include' or 'exclude' a particular kind of reader, a certain system of values, a set of beliefs or an entire culture. One cannot help but notice how, in some sense, the bulk of foreign literature translated into English and published in the west tends to sound the same, almost as though written by one writer and translated by one translator. This may indeed be explained in terms of translation 'universally' imposing its own constraints on the kind of language we use in translation (as opposed to original writing, for example). In **power** terms, however, this can also mean that somewhere, somehow, there is some exclusion of a reader (coerced to read in a particular way), an author (committed to oblivion) or a translator (doomed to be invisible). In the excerpts overleaf chosen at random from translated fiction, for instance, there is something too efficient, almost clinical, about the use of language which invites a particular kind of reading experience.

Task A12.1

As you read through these **back-translations** from Arabic (in italics) and the published translations, focus on the 'academic' veneer imposed on the TT. This manifests itself in such features of language use as:

- **cohesion** by lexical variation (as opposed to repetition, for example);
- over-simplicity of **syntax**;
- excessively explicit connectivity to signal text structure more transparently.

93

Supposedly, these devices are selected in the interest of 'readability' and to ensure that fluency is not impaired in any way.

➤ Do you think the 'readability' argument stands?

➤ How do you assess the readability of the **back-translations** provided?

Example A12.1a (Back-translation from Arabic)

What take root deep down are melancholy feelings which appear unobtrusive at first, only to become aggressive, with no hinges. At those moments of anger which recur so frequently, and which take innumerable forms . . .

(A. Munif *Endings* 1981)

Example A12.1b

Deep down, melancholy feelings take root. They may seem fairly unobtrusive at first. But people will often get angry. When this happens, these feelings burst out into the open, assertive and unruly. They can appear in a number of guises.

(A. Munif *Endings* (trans. Roger Allen), London: Quartet Books, 1998)

Example A12.2a (Back-translation from Arabic)

I was 24 years old and I was enamoured of gambling. The whole thing began in a very small way, like so many things in this world, such that you never dream that your whole life was going to change.

(A. Munif *Al-Ashjar* ('The Trees') London: Iraqi Cultural Centre 1973)

Example A12.2b

I was 24 years old and fond of gambling. Like so many things in this world, the whole thing started in a very small way. In such cases you never dream that your whole life is going to change as a result.

(A. Munif *The Trees*)

In reading through these translated texts, you may have noted a peculiar 'stability' of TT meanings which cannot possibly do justice to, or in any way accurately convey, the variety of **voices** and the multiplicity of tones characteristic of the STs in question.

This usurping of ST 'specificity' and 'uniqueness' may be explained in terms of a complex **power** structure at work in doing any translation. Particularly within prestigious translation traditions (e.g. the Anglo-American), translators are known to have been able to exercise absolute power to exclude a reader directly and consciously. This is achieved through selectively engaging in such innocent-sounding translation **procedures** as '**free**' translation, heavy **glossing**, **gisting**, or **compensation**. Similarly, real or imagined target **norms** can also turn translation into an ideological weapon for excluding an author, by resorting to such ostensibly harmless **procedures** as **omission** or **normalization**, often in the service of such seemingly noble goals as 'sustaining fluency', 'combating boredom'. Finally, translators themselves may fall victim to the exercise of power by ruthless editors or unthinking censors.

Concept box   Norms in translation

This term has had many uses in Translation Studies, but its most influential has been through the **descriptive translation** theorists, notably Gideon Toury, who view **norms** as translation behaviour typically obtaining under specific socio-cultural or textual situations (Toury 1995: 54–5). These TT-oriented **norms** encompass not only translation strategy but also how, if at all, a TT fits into the literary and social culture of the target system. Other **norms** are those proposed by Chesterman (1997), namely 'product and expectancy **norms**' (governed by the readers' expectations of what a translation should be) and 'professional **norms**' (governing the translator and the translation process).

Task 12.2

In reading through the above translated texts, did you in any way feel excluded? Similarly, did you feel that the authors themselves had been excluded? Finally, did you detect a uniformity of translation **style** across the various texts (almost as though the various translations had been produced by one and the same translator)?

➤ Re-read the excerpts and attempt to find linguistic evidence to support your views.

THE TRANSLATOR'S VOICE AS AN EXPRESSION OF POWER

Although there has been much debate about the status of the literary translator, and there seems to be general agreement that the translator should be more highly regarded, literary translators themselves have a varied view of their work. Gregory Rabassa, the renowned translator of Gabriel García Márquez's *One Hundred Years of Solitude* as well as many other classics of modern Spanish American fiction, considers that most translation solutions are 'instinctive' (Rabassa 1984: 23). Peter Bush, who has worked as an academic and as a literary translator, sees the translator's reading and writing as 'a complex mix of intuition and conscious choice involving thousands of decisions through which the translator is shaping and sustaining an interpretation' (Bush 1997: 15). Likewise, translators such as Margaret Sayers Peden (1987) and John Felstiner (1980), translator of the Chilean poet Pablo Neruda, concur in seeing the translator's role as uncovering the '**voice**' of the ST and reproducing this in translation.

Concept box   Voice

> Literary translators often talk about finding the '**voice**' of the author. This 'voice' is difficult to pin down, but normally refers to the narrative character and rhythm. In Sayers Peden's words (1987: 9), 'By "voice" I mean the way something is communicated: the way the tale is told; the way a poem is sung'. This **voice** guides all her decision-making, in the translation **process** which she herself describes metaphorically as the recreation of an ice cube that has melted and is reformed in translation.

But the translator also has a **voice**, or 'discursive presence' as it is called by Theo Hermans (1996: 27). Hermans approaches the problem from a narratological perspective and argues that the translator's **voice** is always present, even if it is sometimes obscured, and may manifest itself (1) because of temporal or geographical distance from the ST, (2) in 'self-referential' texts marked by wordplays, and (3) in cases of 'contextual overdetermination' where a complex chain of identification may lead to **omission** or explanation by footnote (1996: 40). For Hermans, 'it is only . . . the **ideology** of translation, the illusion of transparency and coincidence, the illusion of the one **voice**, that blinds us to the presence of [the translator's] **voice**' (1996: 27). Yet, when the translator feels he or she has more power, it is also true that the translating **voice** is much louder. This is the case with some authors who themselves are translators. One of the most striking examples is the Russian émigré author Vladimir Nabokov, whose translation into English of Pushkin's novel in verse *Onegin* very deliberately followed the ST structure closely and was full of academic footnotes:

> I want translations with copious footnotes, footnotes reaching up like skyscrapers to the top of this or that page so as to leave only the gleam of one textual line between commentary and eternity. I want such footnotes and the absolutely **literal** sense, with no emasculation and no padding.
>
> (Nabokov 1955/2000: 83)

Of course, Nabokov's translation approach is also ideologically informed, an expression of his favoured **poetics**, and is a demonstration of his power as an author-translator. Such translations are by their very nature élitist and deliberately marginalize readers who do not share Nabokov's view of language.

Task A12.3

➤ How aware are you of the '**voice**' or presence of the translator when reading translated works? For example, when reading a classic novel (Dostoyevsky, say) is there any way of determining how far the translator's linguistic choices (such as word order, repetitions, idioms, etc.) may have affected the **style**?

THE TRANSLATOR AND ETHICS

Perhaps as part of the power relations going on around the translator, organizations representing translators themselves have tried to assert their rights. Thus, the Translators Association in London proposes a model contract for literary translation based on recommendations to improve the status of translators passed by the general conference of UNESCO held in Nairobi in 1976. The translator undertakes to deliver a translation 'which shall be faithful to the [original] Work and rendered into good and accurate English', and guarantees s/he 'will not introduce into the translation any matter of an objectionable or libellous character which was not present in the Work'. At the same time, the translator's right to copyright over the translation is asserted as well as a moral right to be identified as the producer of the TT. This would guarantee a visibility and equality of the kind that, as Venuti (1995, 1998) has argued, has often been absent. The relevant clause in the contract is as follows:

Example A12.3

Translators Association Model contract

7. The Translator asserts his moral right to be identified as the Translator of the Work in relation to all such rights as are granted by the Translator to the Publishers under the terms and conditions of this Agreement. The Publishers undertake that the Translator's name shall appear on the title page and cover of their edition of the Translation and in all publicity material (catalogues, advertisements, etc.) concerning it, and shall use their best endeavours to ensure that this undertaking is adhered to also in other editions of the Translation and that the name of the Translator is mentioned in connection with all reviews and quotations of the Translation. The Publishers shall print the following copyright notice of the Translation: 'English language translation copyright © [Translator's name and date of publication].'

The Association also calls for a royalty of 2.5 per cent of the sale price to be paid to the translator in addition to a fee since the original author normally receives a lower royalty for translations.[1]

 Task A12.4

➤ How far would you agree with the Translators Association's proposals or do you feel that the translator's work cannot really be compared to that of the ST author?

➤ Are there other proposals you would want to add?

➤ In your country, are such proposals (or others) in effective use? What do they focus on?

Translators, editors, publishers and similar agents and victims of power form the basic elements of the analysis proposed by Peter Fawcett (1995, see Section B Text B12.1).

Another model of power analysis proposed by Susan Bassnett and Andre Lefevere (1990) approaches these relationships of power in socio-literary contexts, and sees translation as a form of **re-writing**, even **manipulation**, essentially driven by such all-pervasive power structures as **ideology** and **poetics**.

SYSTEMS WITHIN SYSTEMS

In any national language or literature, there has always been a dominant **poetics** (i.e. theories and practices which define literary creativity often in peculiarly elitist, exclusive ways) and a hierarchy of **canonized texts** (e.g. esteemed **discourses** and **genres**). This has invariably meant that qualities such as originality and aesthetic excellence are valued, often not on intrinsic merit but in accordance with certain preconceived and highly subjective criteria. These yardsticks see to it that at best only 'second-order' status is accorded to such 'less worthy' **genres** as children's literature, popular fiction and translation.

---

1 The fee is currently around £55–75 per thousand words in the United Kingdom, which is somewhat below the £70–100 fee typically charged for commercial translation. However, this does depend very much on the languages involved, the status of the translator (and the ST author) and on whether there is funding to pay for the translation. In many cases the reason a book is not translated is because a publisher is unable, or sometimes unwilling, to pay the translation costs of a text that may achieve only limited sales.

There is thus a constant struggle for domination aspired to by all systems, not only translation. But what is unique to translation is that the exercise of power tends to be easier to play out. Normally involved here are major and minor cultures, languages, and even varieties and **genres**, incessantly vying for recognition. A simple yet telling example might make this point clearer. For ideological reasons, Toury (1980) observes, Russian and German Jews preferred to read Russian and German texts in Hebrew translations, rather than in the originals which they were perfectly capable of reading. The observation can of course suggest that the phenomenon may simply point to national fervour: there is something 'symbolic' about these particular translations which meant something to those Jewish readers. More significantly, however, translations do enjoy a '**socio-semiotic**' of their own which does something to readers (e.g. translation as a **genre**, a linguistic issue discussed in Unit 11 and in Text B11.1). Whichever way the argument goes, one thing is certain: rightly or wrongly, translation is an effective means of self-assertion and a symbol of national identity. The Hebrew translations examined may have imparted to their readers that sense of belonging.

Task A12.5

➤ In your view, can translation be perceived as an ideological weapon?

➤ In the context of your own language and culture, what kind of status do translations enjoy?

REWRITING

One way of explaining the constant struggle for status referred to above is to see translation as a form of rewriting. Promoted by scholars such as Susan Bassnett and Andre Lefevere, this view has focused attention on a range of processes which translations must undergo and which, in one way or another, 'interpret' an original text. This analysis of what at times amounts to an act of **manipulation** purposefully designed to exclude certain readers, authors and ultimately translators, has thus shed a great deal of light on the range of socio-literary (ideological and poetic) constraints within which translation and indeed all forms of writing operate.

Task A12.6

➤ Recall the case of the French writer Vallès or the Czech writer Milan Kundera (Unit 11).

➤ Has any literary figure in your own language and culture met a similar fate?

➤ Do you share the view entertained by some cultural commentators that some **domestication** is a price worth paying for the universal recognition normally earned by what would otherwise be only a piece of minor indigenous literature?

Central to the 'translation as rewriting' thesis is the notion of **image**. This is understood as the desire to promote through translation a work, or an author (or, in the most general sense, an entire way of thinking or set of cultural values), in such a way that the translation can begin to exert a greater influence in the target culture than that which the original has had in its native culture. In fact, rewriting is taken in one definition to be 'anything that contributes to constructing the "image" of a writer and/or a work of literature' (Bassnett and Lefevere 1990: 10). This **image** construction, however, is never innocent. It is closely bound up with political and literary power structures operative in a given (usually target) language, culture and society.

In translation as rewriting (and the same no doubt applies to other forms of rewriting), two important constraints may be identified: **ideology** and **poetics** (Lefevere 1992). These manifest themselves in the way texts are consciously or unconsciously brought into line with dominant world views and/or dominant literary structures. Between them, political and literary pressures promote what the world or literature should be like.

PATRONAGE

Patronage is defined as 'the powers (persons, institutions) which help or hinder the writing, reading and rewriting of literature' (Lefevere 1992: 15). The powers involved in **patronage** can be individuals, a group, a social class, or a political or religious institution. The media have a role to play in all of this: the BBC, for example, is apparently the richest and largest patron in history. In each instance, the **patronage** will be called '**undifferentiated**' if the patron has control over **form** and subject matter, holds the purse strings and can legitimately grant or withhold status. This is a common occurrence when, genuinely or spuriously, the aim is to maintain the stability and moral fabric of society as a whole (e.g. English as a global language).

 Task A12.7

➤ Reflect on this sense of undifferentiated **patronage** and illustrate how this might function in texts produced by a state-run department of translation in a Ministry of Information.

On the other hand, **patronage** is '**differentiated**' when the economics of a project is divorced from any ideological considerations and when the agent is too concerned with commercial success to think of status. The notion of **differentiated patronage** is often invoked in making the point that, despite the 'conspiracy' theories which mythologize linguistic or cultural 'imperialism' (Venuti 1995), this kind of imperial-ism is mostly about money and more of a 'cock-up theory' than a conspiracy theory (Fawcett 1995).

Task A12.8

➤ Do you agree that the Anglo-American publishing industry is a good example of **differentiated patronage**? Or do you think that, as an institution, it is actually probably less **differentiated**, aspiring to higher ideals than economic success?

The separation between **poetics** and **ideology** is thus at best artificial. These con-ceptual systems are in constant interaction, with **patronage** serving as an area of interface between the poetic and the ideological. In the case of literature and literary translation, **patronage** is usually more concerned with **ideology** than with **poetics**. The latter usually matters less, put on hold as it were, with the patron 'delegating' authority to the interpreter. But the 'interpreter' would have been ideologically screened in the first place. That is, although **patronage** is essentially ideological, it ultimately acts as a constraint on what can or cannot be said and on how something is said (**form** and subject-matter). Finally, an element of status enters the **patronage** equation: granting and accepting **patronage** is a sure sign that someone has been admitted to an élitist circle with its own ethos and mores.

The power to exclude or include a reader, a writer or an entire **poetics** (a **genre**, a motif, etc.) is discussed in this unit from the perspective of both linguistics and cultural studies. To cast this in translation terms, we have viewed the various agents and power from the vantage point of **re-writing** (even **manipulation**) that goes on all the time and that has to be seen as an important factor in the way a powerful culture asserts itself in translation.

Summary

Unit A13
Ideology and translation

THE CULTURAL TURN IN TRANSLATION STUDIES

In the previous chapter we looked at power and commercial relations in and around literary translation, including work by the late André Lefevere. The volume *Translation, History and Culture* (1990), which Lefevere co-edited with Susan Bassnett, was a key text because it marked a specific move away from linguistic approaches to translation and, prompted by Snell-Hornby's 1990 article in the collection, coined the term '**cultural turn**' in Translation Studies.

Concept box   The cultural turn

> This is a metaphor that has been adopted by Cultural-Studies oriented translation theorists to refer to the analysis of translation in its cultural, political and ideological context.

In many ways, this 'turn' was presaged by the work on polysystems and translation **norms** by Even-Zohar and Toury (e.g. Even-Zohar 1978/2000; Toury 1980) and by the *Manipulation of Literature* volume edited by Theo Hermans (Hermans 1985). Since 1990, the turn has extended to incorporate a whole range of approaches from Cultural Studies and is a true indicator of the interdisciplinary nature of contemporary Translation Studies. These new studies go beyond a textual analysis of a ST–TT pair, although **ideology** can still be studied in that fashion as can be seen in the work of Hatim and Mason.

Concept box   Ideology

> For Hatim and Mason, **ideology** encompasses 'the tacit assumptions, beliefs and value systems which are shared collectively by social groups' (1997: 144). They make a distinction between 'the ideology of translating' and 'the translation of ideology'. Whereas the former refers to the basic orientation

chosen by the translator operating within a social and cultural context (the choice, for example, between Venuti's **domesticating** and **foreignizing** translation), in the translation of ideology they examine the extent of mediation supplied by a translator of sensitive texts. 'Mediation' is defined as 'the extent to which translators intervene in the **transfer** process, feeding their own knowledge and beliefs into processing the text' (Hatim and Mason 1997: 147). In many ways this is a parallel to the translator's discursive presence in literary texts discussed in Unit 12.

Task A13.1

Mediation concerns not only intervention by the translator in the **transfer** process but also by the ST writer in the drafting of the ST itself.

➤ Consider various forms of sensitive texts (for example, religious, political or legal documents, or indeed any document which seeks to persuade or convince).

➤ Reflect on how mediation might occur both in the ST and TT and how it could be researched.

Lexicogrammatical parameters of lexical choice, **cohesion** and **transitivity** (cf. Unit 10 on **register** analysis) are used by Hatim and Mason (1997: 15–22) to analyse a translation in the *UNESCO Courier* of a text about the proud history of the Mexican peoples. They show that the translator into English downplays the role of the indigenous peoples, making them seem less active and adopting a negative point of view: for example, *prolonged efforts* become *obstinate determination, indigenous man* becomes *pre-Columbian civilization* and details of the indigenous peoples' languages and cultures are omitted (1997: 153–9).

However, the move towards Cultural Studies has encompassed a much wider, interdisciplinary and problematizing field that includes Gender Studies, **post-structuralism**, **postmodernism** and **postcolonialism**. These are often interlinked, but we shall focus on gender and on **postcolonialism**, which are the most prominent.

GENDER AND TRANSLATION

Just as Venuti (1992, 1995) rails at the **invisibility** of translators in general, with their names often omitted from the title pages of their translations and with their work scarcely commented upon in reviews, so have feminist theorists and translators sought to make the female visible by examining the relationship between gender and translation. Chamberlain (1988/2000) applies feminist theories to traditional metaphors of translation, the ways in which authorship and originality are expressed in terms of the masculine and paternity, while translation, along with other artistic forms of expression such as the performing arts, is considered to be feminine and derivative. Typical of this is the metaphor of '*les belles infidèles*' that was first coined in the seventeenth century.

Concept box *Les belles infidèles* ('unfaithful beauties')

> This is a centuries-old metaphor which sees translations as being '*belles*' (beautiful) and '*infidèles*' (unfaithful). The word *traduction* is feminine in French, lending itself to be used in the metaphor which stressed the feminine and potentially untrustworthy nature of translation (the woman) compared to the masculine originality and trustworthiness of the source.

This metaphor harks back to the debate of that time about **free** (beautiful) or **literal** (**faithful**) translation. Chamberlain sees this as a 'sexualization of translation' (1988/2000: 315) and produces further examples to show how the feminine has been downgraded and degraded in writings on translation. She ends her paper with a list of ways in which feminists can challenge and subvert this dominant male **discourse**. One of the examples she gives is of Suzanne Jill Levine, the translator of a novel by the Cuban exile Cabrera Infante which is ideologically offensive to women. Chamberlain shows how, instead of rejecting the translation **commission**, Levine chooses instead 'to subvert the text, to play infidelity against infidelity, and to follow out the text's parodic logic' (1988/2000: 326). She does this first by choosing to translate the text and second by challenging the reader linguistically with new puns, forcing the reader to question the status of the original. As Levine herself describes it:

> Translation should be a critical act, however, creating doubt, posing questions to its reader, recontextualizing the **ideology** of the original text. Since a good translation, as with all rhetoric, aims to (re)produce an effect, to persuade a reader, it is, in the broadest terms, a political act.
>
> (Levine 1991: 3–4)

 Task A13.2

➤ Consider what kinds of texts might seem ideologically unsound to a translator (literary or non-literary).

➤ What are the choices facing a translator who is asked to translate such a text?

➤ Do you think it would be possible to translate such a text and still comply with the Code of Ethics presented in Unit 12, Section C, p. 305?

In the 1990s, a group of French Canadian feminist translators, including Barbara Godard, Suzanne de Lotbinière-Harwood and Luise von Flotow, undertook to challenge this dominant **discourse** with what they termed the '**translation project**'.

Concept box   The translation project

An approach to literary translation in which feminist translators openly advocate and implement strategies (linguistic and otherwise) to foreground the feminist in the translated text. See Simon (1996, Chapter 1) and van Flotow (1997).

The linguistic strategies they employed to make the female visible include the use of puns in a similarly creative way to Levine above. Barbara Godard's translations of the challenging fiction of the feminist Quebec writer Nicole Brossard use a variety of means to transfer the subversiveness of the original. These include mixing French and English and creating new puns that highlight the female. For example, the title *Amantes* (female, in this case lesbian, lover) is rendered as *LovHers*, and *L'Amer* as *These Our Mothers*. De Lotbinière-Harwood's translation of the French lesbian writer Michèle Causse regularly employs a bold font 'e' in the TT in an attempt to transfer the way Causse intentionally feminizes default-masculine words in French. So 'nulle ne l'ignore' ('no one (feminine) is unaware') becomes 'no one ignores . . .'. Elsewhere, *auteure* (female author) becomes *auther* (rather than 'author') and *amante* is translated as *shelove* (Simon 1996: 21), creatively highlighting the feminine gender in English translation.

It is important to note that the metaphor of the beautiful yet unfaithful woman/ translation is not the only one which has proved controversial in feminist circles. George Steiner, in *After Babel* (1975/1998), one of the first major works of modern translation theory, uses the following metaphors to describe the four-part **hermeneutic** (interpretative) process of translation:

1. initiative trust – the translator approaches the ST with trust that there is meaning there;
2. aggression (or penetration) – the translator takes over or 'captures' the foreign text;
3. incorporation (or embodiment) – the text becomes part of the translator's language; and
4. **compensation** (or restitution) – the translator restores something to the TT to **compensate** for what has been taken away.

(Steiner 1975/1998: 312–455)

Chamberlain (1998/2000: 320–1) is particularly critical of the male and sexual focus in Steiner's writing, notably the aggressive sexual imagery of male violence and penetration and the portrayal of translation as a special kind of communication in which 'eros and language mesh at every point' (Steiner 1975/1998: 39).

Clearly, the opposite of the **translation project** occurs when gender-marked works are translated in such a way that their distinctive characteristics are effaced. This is sometimes the case in the translation of 'camp' (gay) talk, as shown by Harvey (1998/2000). One of the examples given is from the French translation of Gore Vidal's *The City and the Pillar*. Gay lexis is translated inconsistently and in such a way as to reduce gay visibility or to add a pejorative tone. Thus, *pansies* (negative) and *queen* (more positive, though ironic) are both translated as *tante* (literally, 'aunt'); the gay-marked **collocation** *screaming pansies* becomes the mainstream **ces tantes si voyantes** [*these very glaring aunts*] and the gay word **butch** is rendered simply as the everyday *costaud* [*tough*] (Harvey 1998/2000: 458–9). Harvey suggests that the reason for these, and other, **shifts** in the text are ideologically based: 'I would like to suggest that the translator has (inevitably, one might say) produced a text that harmonizes with the prevailing view of human subjectivity that obtains in his – the target – culture' (1988/2000: 460).

 Task A13.3

➤ What other examples have you seen where the translator has toned down the ST subject in order to fit in with the TT culture?

➤ Can you think of examples where the opposite has occurred?

POSTCOLONIALISM AND TRANSLATION STUDIES

One of the most thriving points of contact between Cultural Studies and Translation Studies has been in the area of **postcolonialism**.

Concept box   Postcolonialism

> A broad cultural approach to the study of power relations between different groups, cultures or peoples, in which language, literature and translation may play a role.

Although the precise parameters of '**postcolonialism**', in some instances known as 'subaltern studies', are somewhat difficult to pin down and the term owes its origin to the studies of the former colonies of the European powers after independence, it is increasingly used in Translation Studies to refer to the study of power relations between different groups or cultures including a study of language, literature and translation. These often, but do not always, involve what are traditionally thought of as the former colonies.

While in the previous section we looked at the affirmation or erasure of gender identity, with **postcolonialism** it is national or ethnic identity which is at stake. Gender and postcolonial identity are not necessarily mutually exclusive as is shown in Gayatri Spivak's 'The Politics of Translation' (Spivak 1993/2000). She criticizes the lifeless '**translatese**' that comes from a translator of third-world feminist texts who is not fully at one with the 'rhetoricity' of the languages in question.

An alternative term for the stilted or standardizing **translationese** we discussed in Unit 2, **translatese** is viewed by Spivak as a 'a species of neo-colonialist construction of the non-western scene' since the dominant but characterless English that results (it is English that is the dominant TL) erases the speech patterns and differences of the huge range of 'third-world' feminist voices: 'In the act of wholesale translation into English there can be a betrayal of the democratic ideal into the law of the strongest' (1993/2000: 399–400). This has its echo in Venuti's criticism of Anglo-American publishing practices that favour **domesticating translation** (Venuti 1995).

Task A13.4

➤ Think of examples or scenarios you have encountered where translation into English has obscured the identity of a non-western culture. Do you feel it is possible to avoid this happening?

Written from the viewpoint of a translator (of Derrida) and a bilingual (Bengali and English), Spivak's essay is important in casting doubt on the value of translation between languages of different world status and on the comfortable assumptions underlying western feminism (or any other **ideology**) when it portrays the 'third world'. Her post-structuralist preference is for a **literal** translation with a strong understanding of the 'tough terrain' of the original and an awareness of the different cultural contexts: 'she [the translator] must be able to confront the idea that what seems resistant to the space of English may be reactionary in the space of the original language' (Spivak 1993/2000: 404).

Task A13.5

➤ What do you think Spivak means by the last quote above? What kind of ideological elements may be interpreted differently in two very different cultures?

The study of the power relations between different peoples is the central focus of **postcolonialism.** Edward Said's *Orientalism: Western conceptions of the Orient*

(1978/1995) is the most famous and pioneering example, describing the way the west's depiction of the east as 'irrational, depraved, childlike, different' (as opposed to Europe which is 'rational, virtuous, mature and normal' (p.40)) has pervaded western thinking since the 1800s and, driven by political forces, helped to create a mindset that was imperialist, racist and ethnocentric when dealing with other cultures (p. 204). Indeed, for Said as for other theorists, Orientalism is 'a kind of western projection onto and will to govern over the Orient' (p. 95). Orientalism, in the sense of a policy of teaching the subject peoples through their native language, and Anglicism (policies favouring education in English) are considered by Pennycook (1994: 74–80) to have gone hand-in-hand in colonial India, where only a minority were educated and were then expected to serve the colonizer. Translation, as described by Niranjana in her *Siting Translation* (1992), created and strengthened the image of the eastern Other by its distortions and in fact was a major tool of the colonial power. As part of her analysis, Niranjana borrows the term '**interpellation**' from the Marxist critic, Louis Althusser.

Concept box   Interpellation

> A term coined by Althusser to describe the way **ideology**, through institutions and laws, constructs and stereotypes people as suppressed social subjects. **Interpellation** now has a broader focus and is used to describe the reformulation of one perspective or **discourse** by another (cf. Fairclough 1992). In translation it refers to the subjection of a given people by the **discourse** of colonialism which constructs a stereotype of that people as inferior. Translation is a tool, sometimes *the* tool, in this process.

One example Niranjana gives is of Sir William Jones, a polyglot who combined a legal career (he was member of the Supreme Court in Calcutta from 1783 to his death in 1794) with translation of Arabic, Persian and Sanskrit literature and the ancient Sanskrit laws. The motive behind the work of Jones, and others, was that the British felt they needed to translate India's laws themselves and did not trust the interpretation given by locals. The colonizer-translator was thus the bearer of the 'true' meaning of the law, always operating from a position of assumed superiority.

Niranjana writes from a Marxist and post-structuralist perspective, that is, she seeks to undermine the liberal-humanist rhetoric of colonialism by questioning some of the basic unproblematic assumptions of earlier translation theory and practice such as the notion that the meaning of the original can be fixed and translated. Perhaps the most important move by Niranjana is to call for a strategy of resistance to the power of the colonizer's language. In the last chapter of her book (1992: 173–86), Niranjana discusses the English translations of a short extract from a *vacuna*, a twelfth-century spiritual poem from South India, written in Kannada. She criticizes earlier translators, including the famous translator-theorist A. K. Ramanujan, for their over dependence on western thought and their simplification of the text 'toward English and the Judeo-Christian tradition' and for re-creating the poem along the lines of the language of the Protestant *Pilgrim's Progress* (1992: 180). Ramanujan, for instance, is depicted as a post-Romanticist whose reading of a complex and 'unstable' poem revolves around a repeated light metaphor that suggests an illusion of transparency in the ST (1992: 184). Niranjana provides her own translation of the poem. From a **poststructuralist** point of view, and borrowing strongly from Walter Benjamin's (1923/1969) concept of **literal** translation allowing the original text to come through in the translation, Niranjana's prescription is to translate more literally and at times to **borrow** words into English. These include the philosophical term *linga* (italicized by Niranjana, translated as *light* by Ramanujan), which refers to the form of the normally formless god Śiva, and Guhēśvara, the name of the poet's god (given as *Lord of the Caves* by Ramanujan). This practice of translation, or **re-translation**, is described by Niranjana as 'speculative, provisional and interventionist' (p. 173).

Concept box   Resistance through re-translation

A (re-)translation practice of **postcolonialism** that aims to disrupt the comfortable orthodoxies and to subvert the myths and identities formed under colonialism by the **discourse** of westernized translation.

Task A13.6

Ramanujan (1989), in the description of his translation of a 2000-year-old Tamil poem, sees translation as an 'impossible task', yet it becomes possible because of universals of language, **intertextuality** and typicalities of poetry. His stated aim (pp. 60–1) is 'to translate linguistic relations not single words'.

➤ Given this approach to translation, how far do you consider Niranjana justified in criticizing Ramunajan's work?

The motive behind the **re-translation** strategy is to highlight the difference of cultures, to make the original visible using the colonizer's own language and to subvert the linguistic and political power structure. The most famous **postcolonial** theorist, Homi Bhabha, goes further and sees culture as untranslatable in the conventional sense. Rather than being an agglomeration of knowledge, culture is performed or *enunciated* and translation is a major creative aspect of this process. Bhabha's main interest is in **hybridity**, the 'Third Space' of never stable border cultures and always mobile migrants who exist 'in-between' languages and peoples and are always alien in some way, always Other. It is that 'in-between' space, in which translation operates, which 'carries the burden of meaning of culture' (Bhabha 1994: 38).

Concept box   'In-betweenness' (or hybridity, the Third Space)

> This describes the dynamic geographical, religious, ethnic, cultural and linguistic environment of migrant or border communities, where interaction and overlap highlight cultural difference and interrogate identity. This thereby subverts what may have been considered stable relations and meanings, including the conventional colonizer's traditional concept of (European) nationhood.

POSTCOLONIALISM REVIEWED

The **postcolonial** concepts reviewed here may have conveyed a view of translation as a damaging instrument of the colonizers who imposed their language and used translation to construct a distorted image of the suppressed people which served to reinforce the hierarchical structure of the colony. Critiquing **postcolonialist** translation theories, Robinson (1997: 105) makes the important point that the view of translation as purely a 'harmful and pernicious tool of empire' is inaccurate. For example, Vicente Rafael (1993), who writes about the mutual bafflement of the encounter between Spanish colonizer and Tagalog colonized in the Philippines, also describes the complex Tagalog participation in the process and their attempts to 'retranslate' themselves by placing a Tagalog veneer on Spanish Catholic terminology.

Many of the writers on **postcolonialism** mentioned in this unit have written from an Asian or, specifically, Indian perspective. Yet it is equally valid to treat the subject from a European point of view. Michael Cronin's *Translating Ireland* (1996), in which he describes the suppression of the Irish language by the English colonizers and its concomitant physical displacement of the rural Irish population, is one such example. Similar hierarchical issues arise with relation to the affirmation of identity through language in post-Franco Spain, where Basque, Catalan and Galician have official status along with the dominant variety, Castilian Spanish. A similar linguistic melting-pot exists in many of the countries of Eastern and Central Europe where Russian previously dominated over the subject peoples of the Soviet Union before the fall of the Berlin Wall.

Finally, and most prominently, the movement of large numbers of migrants from rural areas to the cities in developing countries, and from the poorer continents to Europe and the USA, has heightened that 'in-betweenness' described by Bhabha. Thanks to migration from the south, the number of Spanish speakers in the USA is currently estimated at up to 50 million, making them the largest minority group in the most powerful nation of the world that itself was formed by colonization and migration. In Europe, immigration is currently one of the most important political topics and is producing a more hybrid culture than ever before.

Summary

This unit has examined some of the major concepts introduced to translation from Cultural Studies. These challenge long-held stable orthodoxies of translation. In the case of those working from a Gender Studies angle, this involves challenging the subjection of the female or gay that occurs in translation metaphor and translation strategy where their identity-specific linguistic characteristics have been obscured. In the case of **postcolonialism**, this is achieved by unmasking the role of translation in subjecting the colonial people and by challenging this process using a strategy of **re-translation**, making the native visible, and by a celebration of hybrid cultures.

Unit A14
Translation in the information technology era

TRANSLATION, GLOBALIZATION AND LOCALIZATION

The volume of translation conducted worldwide has increased dramatically in the last fifty years. Even though English may have become a *lingua franca* of world trade, it is the increasing **globalization** and the advent of the internet that have meant that promotional literature, technical manuals, webpages and all ranges of other communication are being translated into other languages at a faster and faster pace.

Concept box   Globalization

> Globalization is a multi-level term that is used to refer to the global nature of the world economy with the all-pervasive spread of multinationals. In commercial translation it is often used in the sense of the creation of local versions of websites of internationally important companies or the translation of product and marketing material for the global market (see Esselink 2000: 4). Michael Cronin's *Translation and Globalization* (Cronin 2003) deals with some of the complex cultural, political and philosophical consequences of translation in the global age.

In addition, the growth of international organizations such as the United Nations and the European Union has made **interpreting** at meetings and translation of documentation a necessity. In the case of the European Union, the commitment to translate into all official languages of the Member States has seen the number of original pages of documentation translated by its Translation Centre in Luxembourg alone increase from 20,000 in 1995 to 280,000 in 2001 (European Communities Court of Auditors 2002). The turnover of the Translation Centre, employing 140 permanent staff and tendering out a portion of its work to commercial translation agencies, was almost 26 million euros in 2001 (European Court of Auditors 2002: 9). But this is just a small portion of the EU's translation and **interpreting** costs, estimated in 2001 at 2 billion euros per year (Austermühl 2001: 3).

Translation is thus big business. In fact, for many companies, translation has become part of what is known as the GILT business: Globalization, Internationalization, **Localization** and Translation. The acronym is sometimes reduced to GIL, since in many instances the translation part is subsumed under **localization**, defined as follows by the Localisation Standards Industry Association (LISA):

Concept box   Localization

> **Localization** involves taking a product and making it linguistically and culturally appropriate to the target locale (country/region and language) where it will be used and sold.
>   (Localisation Standards Industry Association 2003 (www.lisa.org))

LISA's website goes on to differentiate between **localization** and translation in its main field of computer software: it explains that, while **localization** involves translation of the linguistic **content**, it also involves adapting the size of screen dialogue boxes, colours and character sets (for languages such as Chinese, Korean and Japanese) to ensure correct display. Furthermore, visuals may need altering, with taxis, telephones, buses and so on needing to fit the local market. Dress codes of people featured will often be different in the target locale, while financial accounting packages may require tailoring to local conventions. Nevertheless, in business circles, the word *localize* may be taking the place of *translate*: a personal example of this is that one of the authors of this book was recently approached by a translation agency asking him to 'localize' two sixteenth-century Spanish poems into English.

Task A14.1

In **localization** process models, translation is just one element.

➤ Reflect on Figure A14.1, from milengo, a European and Asian **localization** alliance (http://www.milengo.com/), which shows the linguistic translation elements of a software **localization** project.

The website explains that there are four inputs to this process: (1) the new software to be translated; (2) the new documentation and Help files; (3) the translation of the previous software release; (4) the last documentation and Help files that were translated. The process is facilitated by the use of **Computer-Assisted Translation** (CAT); specifically, the previous software translation is incorporated into the **translation memory tool**. In the case of the reference manuals, the tool aligns the new and last version of the ST and TT and pinpoints which elements have changed. This process helps to assure consistency of terminology and means that the translators only need to translate the changed text. Finally, the text and dialogue boxes that are going to be visible to the user also need to be checked for functionality.

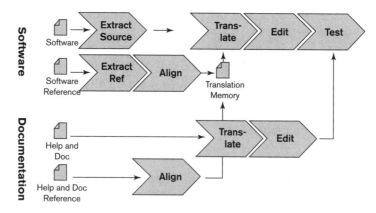

Figure A14.1 The Localization Process (Milengo 2003)

From this it is clear that the **translation memory tool** plays a key role in assisting the translator. This is typical of the translator's work nowadays. **Translation memory tools**, of which TRADOS's *Translator's Workbench* (www.trados.com) and ATRIL's *Déjà Vu* (www.atril.com) are the best known, compile a translation database as the translator is typing in the text. They then alert the translator to previously translated strings of text that are the same or very similar to a phrase or term currently being translated. At the same time they draw on the database of earlier translations to suggest possible translation **equivalents** which the translator can choose to accept or reject (see Figure A14.2).

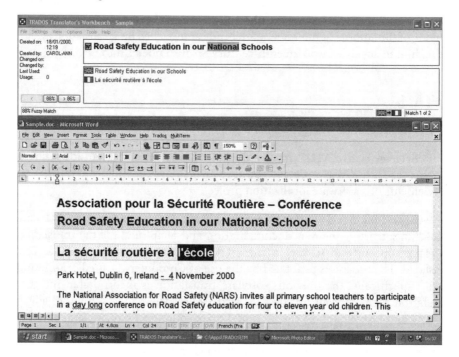

Figure A14.2 Screenshot from TRADOS's Translator's Workbench

In Figure A14.2, the Workbench has sought a translation for the phrase *Road safety education in our national schools*. In its memory of previous translations, it has found an imperfect or **fuzzy match** with *La sécurité routière a l'école*. The translator would almost certainly accept the proposed translation of the text up to the highlighted word *national*, the first non-exact match. At this point he or she would need to decide on a suitable translation for the new material. The downside to the assistance provided by the computer software is that translation commissions reduce the translation rate where documents contain exact and even **fuzzy matches**.

These tools are used in conjunction with **term banks** (for example, the EC's EURODICAUTOM or IATE database which we shall consider in Section C) and **glossaries** to allow an individual or group of translators to ensure consistency of terminology (i.e. that the same TL term is always used for the same SL term) and translate more quickly and efficiently.

THE MACHINE AND THE TRANSLATOR

Computer power is therefore being harnessed by the translation industry, but it still remains **Computer-Assisted Translation**. The goal of fully automatic or **Machine Translation** (MT) remains elusive although recent developments have been more promising. First a little history to put it into context:

Concept box   A brief history of early Machine Translation

The first real developments in **Machine Translation** (MT) took place after the Second World War, during which the first computers had been invented in the UK by Alan Turing's team as part of the now famous code-breaking operation at Bletchley Park (Hinsley and Stripp 1993). The beginning of the Cold War in the late 1940s prompted significant investment by the US government in automatic Russian–English translation systems for the military; France, Japan, the UK and the USSR had smaller programs. These first-generation systems were known as '**direct**' systems since they were basically word-based 'direct-replacement' systems; each ST word would be looked up and replaced by a corresponding TL term. As we have seen in Unit 2, **word-for-word** substitution is not a solid base for translation. Without significant progress, MT's reputation fell very low in the 1960s following damning criticism by Yehoshua Bar-Hillel in his *Report on the State of Machine Translation in the United States and Great Britain* (1959) and in the report published in 1966 by the Automatic Language Processing Advisory Committee (ALPAC). Instead the focus shifted to more basic questions of language processing, the field that became known as computational linguistics.

Bar-Hillel considered that real-world knowledge was necessary for translation and that this was impossible for a machine to replicate. He felt that the goal of a fully mechanized translation on a par with that produced by a professional translator was unrealistic. In his opinion, it would be more realistic to attempt to produce machines that worked in conjunction with humans.

In a brief overview of the history of the field, Martin Kay (1980/2003) discusses some of the obstacles to successful **Machine Translation** including 'words with multiple meanings, sentences with multiple grammatical structures, uncertainty about what a pronoun refers to, and other problems of grammar'. He uses a now well-known example (Example A14.1) to illustrate the problems:

Example A14.1

The police refused the students a permit because they feared violence.

 Task A14.2

➤ Translate this into your first language or first foreign language.

➤ Try translating it using an internet-based translation program.

➤ Reflect on what problems you think this sentence might pose to **Machine Translation** which is unable to infer textual relations from context.

Kay's analysis focuses on the pronoun *they*, which in Example A14.1 refers to the police and not the students. Translation into a gender-marked language such as French would require the feminine singular pronoun *elle*. However, if we change the verb that follows from *feared* to *advocated* we find that the pronoun *they* must refer to the students. The French translation would then be the masculine third person plural *ils* unless all the students were female in which case *elles* would be necessary. As Kay affirms, 'the knowledge required to reach these conclusions has nothing linguistic about it. It has to do with everyday facts about students, police, violence, and the kinds of relationships we have seen these things enter into' (Kay 1980/2003).

This is the kind of real-world knowledge referred to by Bar-Hillel in 1959. Despite this, from the late 1970s onwards, MT enjoyed more successful outcomes partly by focusing on very specific **genres** and situations. The most well-known of these success stories has been the Canadian METEO system which was developed at the University of Montreal; it translates automatically the weather bulletins for the Meteorological Service of Canada (www.msc-smc.ec.gc.ca/contents_e.html). A typical bulletin can be seen below, in this case for the locality of Yellowknife:

Example A14.2a   ST English

Yellowknife: *Issued 5: 00 AM MDT Friday 23 May 2003*
Today .. Sunny. Wind south 20 km/h. High 15. UV index 4 or moderate.
Tonight .. Increasing cloudiness. Wind southeast 20 km/h. Low 10.
Saturday .. Cloudy with 60 percent chance of showers. Wind south 30 km/h. High 19.
Sunday .. Sunny. Low 12. High 19.
Normals for the period .. Low 3. High 13.

Example 14.2b   TT French

Yellowknife: *Émises à 05h00 HAR le vendredi 23 mai 2003*
Aujourd´hui .. Ensoleillé. Vents du sud de 20 km/h. Maximum de 15. Indice uv de 4
ou modéré.
Ce soir et cette nuit .. Ennuagement. Vents du sud-est de 20 km/h. Minimum de 10.
Samedi .. Nuageux avec possibilité de 60 pour cent d´averses de pluie. Vents du sud
de 30 km/h. Maximum de 19.
Dimanche .. Ensoleillé. Minimum de 12. Maximum de 19.
Normales .. Minimum de 3. Maximum de 13.

Task A14.3

➤ Look at the ST–TT pair in Example A14.2 and identify some lexical and
conceptual features of the ST that you think have facilitated the production of
a functional TT.

This simple but effective system depends on careful pre-editing and the adoption
of very controlled lexis and **syntactic structures** (cf. Austermühl 2001: 163–4). The
system is also reversible, which means that automatic French>English translation
is possible with weather forecasts originating from Quebec.

MT developments over recent decades have focused on second-generation 'indirect'
systems, which add an intermediate phase between ST and TT. This is either an
interlingual approach, where the ST meaning is represented in an abstract form
before being reconstituted in the TT, or the rather more successful **transfer**
approach. The latter comprises three stages: (1) analysis and representation of ST
syntactic structure; (2) transfer into TL structure; (3) synthesis of output from that
structure (Somers 1998: 145).

The most widely used MT system, which is in many ways a mixture of first and
second generation systems, is SYSTRAN, which in fact uses a very large **lexicon** and
little **syntax**. SYSTRAN was originally developed privately in the USA and was trialled
at the European Commission in Luxembourg. It is now used extensively for 'instant'
translation of webpages. We shall examine SYSTRAN in more detail in Section C.

ELECTRONIC CORPORA AND TRANSLATION

From the 1990s onwards, a statistical approach to MT has become popular. This is based on the computer's analysis of statistical data from a large body of existing bilingual **parallel text** collections to determine the probability of matching given SL and TL expressions. The most statistically probable match is then chosen by the computer as the translation of the expression in a new document.

The best-known of these new systems is the Candide system developed at the IBM TJ Watson Research Center in the USA. The electronic documents, the '**corpus**', are the proceedings of the Canadian Parliament, known as the Canadian Hansard (for access, search at http://www.tsrali.com/index.cgi?UTLanguage=en). These are produced in English and French versions. Candide had at its disposal a **corpus** of 2,205,733 English– French sentence pairs from the Hansard. Sentence **alignment** and statistical analysis can lead to very useful conclusions, for instance that the most likely translation of 'le programme a été *mis en application*' is 'the program has been *implemented*', where the three-word unit *mis en application* (lit. *put into application*) has been translated by the single verb form *implemented*. Other computational uses of **parallel texts** are for the generation of natural language (e.g. Bateman, Matthiessen and Licheng 1999) and the automatic extraction of lexical **equivalences** (Boutsis, Pipiridis and Demiros 1999).

In fact, electronic **corpora**, which were originally formed to assist large-scale diction-ary projects first at COBUILD in Birmingham, UK, and then at other major publishers, are becoming increasingly used in research across the board in Translation Studies. There are now some very large reference **corpora** that are available online either free or by subscription. These include the bilingual French–English Canadian Hansard **corpus** (above), and large monolingual **corpora** such as the British National Corpus (http: //thetis.bl.uk/), the Bank of English (http: //titania.cobuild.collins.co.uk/), where the website also allows entry to a **corpus** of French and Spanish, and the Spanish Real Academia **corpus** (www.rae.es). One reason is simply that many more texts are produced electronically, so it is possible for researchers to access their own **corpora** of newspaper texts, bilingual versions of documents from international organizations and so on. Similarly, it is often possible for a researcher to put together a ST–TT such as a novel and its translation in electronic form (Kenny 2001).

The initial reason for using electronic **corpora** in dictionary compiling was that they provided up-to-date information on the current use of words and the patterns in which they occurred that was far superior to a lexicographer's intuition (Sinclair 1991: 4). Of course, this is still the case and **corpora** are a valuable aid to bilingual dictionary compilation as well, but there are additional advantages when using them for research into translation. Mona Baker's paper 'Corpora and Translation Studies' (Baker 1995) describes both the basic tools of the **corpus-based** approach and their potential uses in translation. The most important are:

1. The Key-Word-in-context or KWIC **concordance**, which allows the search word or term to be called up on screen and the patterns of its collocates to be viewed.

Task A14.4

➤ Look at the **concordance** of the words *handsome* and *pretty* that is given in Section C, Unit 5, p. 250.

➤ What kinds of grammatical and lexical patterns show up most clearly using a KWIC **concordance**?

➤ What kind of information may be absent from a **concordance**?

2. **Alignment** tools in some packages – e.g. Wordsmith (Scott 2003), ParaConc (Barlow forthcoming) and TSrali (see below) – allow the ST items and their corresponding TT **equivalents** to be viewed together. A further development is the construction of **parallel corpora**. Typically these comprise either a **corpus** of STs with the corresponding TTs, such as the Canadian Hansard, or a **corpus** of original texts of similar **genres** in two different languages (see Véronis 2000). Example A14.3 is an extract from the Canadian Hansard, produced using the TSrali alignment tool (search available at www.tsrali.com):

Example A14.3   (Example 3 is ST French. The others are ST English)

1. Human Resources **Development** and the Status of Persons with Disabilities
   Développement des ressources humaines et condition des personnes handicapées

2. The challenge was when it came to **development** assessment on a project . . .
   Le problème est le suivant: au moment d'évaluer les impacts d'un projet . . .

3. In order to promote responsible **development** activities, the assessment process must be uniform and predictable.
   Afin de favoriser des activités de développement responsables, l'homogénéité et la prévisibilité du processus d'évaluation sont essentielles.

4. They want to ensure that there is public input on the **development** of regulations and on the **development** of the Yukon environmental and socio-economic assessment board rules.
   Elles veulent s'assurer que la population participera à l'élaboration du Règlement et à la mise en place de l'Office d'évaluation environnementale et socioéconomique du Yukon.

5. It provides certainty to those doing the **development**.
   Cela donnera de l'assurance aux responsables.

6. The purpose of the act should ensure that **development** as a public good is considered during socio-economic assessment.
La mesure législative doit assurer que le développement s'effectue dans l'intérêt général et que cet aspect est pris en compte au moment de l'évaluation socio-économique.

(Reproduced with the kind permission of the RALI laboratory of the University of Montreal)

 Task A14.5

➤ What types of phenomena do you consider might be investigated using such software that allows ST and TT **equivalents** to be viewed simultaneously?

3. If whole ST–TT pairs are available in electronic form, the computer can easily calculate total word counts and provide access to data very quickly and accurately. This access can then lead to the testing of some long-held tenets of translation, such as 'TTs are always longer than STs' or '**cohesion** tends to be greater in TTs'.

Task A14.6

➤ Think how it would be possible to investigate the translation generalizations mentioned above using **corpus-based** tools.

Of course, the development of the internet, which in a way is a massive electronic **corpus** of texts of all manner of **genres**, means that a rough **corpus** is available to almost any translator or researcher with a computer. The search term needs simply to be entered within inverted commas into a search engine such as Google (www.google.com) that is configured to the language in question. The result is a list of sometimes thousands of current examples. However, at present there is a limited possibility of **concordancing** the search results or of configuring the search to select the specific **text types** or **genres** that are of interest. As we saw in Units 9 and 11, **text type** and **genre** are prime determiners of translation strategy; a general **corpus** will produce general results, so useful **equivalents** for specific contexts can only be unearthed by a trawl for the relevant **text type**.

Summary

This unit has briefly examined some of the most prominent uses of technology for translation and attempted to show that technology is now a commonplace in the translation workplace. These include **Machine Translation**, translation memory and terminology management tools and **corpus-linguistic** tools. Each has a different emphasis, designed to replace the translator, aid the translator or aid the translation theorist.

SECTION B
Extension

Unit B1
What is translation?

The two readings in this section consider the definition of translation and the study of the field. Both readings were crucial in determining the scope of research in the latter part of the twentieth century.

Text B1.1, by the famous Russian-American linguist Roman Jakobson, is from his paper 'On Linguistic Aspects of Translation', originally published in 1959. He considers three kinds of translation of the 'verbal **sign**': **intralingual** translation, **interlingual** translation and **intersemiotic** translation. Of these he classes **interlingual** translation as 'translation proper, [. . .] an interpretation of verbal **sign**s by means of some other language' (Jakobson 1959/2000: 114). As we saw in Section A, this is what is most commonly understood as written translation. However, Jakobson goes beyond the idea that translation involves the **word-for-word** replacement of linguistic items, insisting instead on substitution of 'entire messages in some other language'. This concept of **equivalence** between languages and its exact nature was to occupy translation theorists for several decades afterwards as we saw in Section A (Units 6 and 7).

Task B1.1.1

➤ Before you read Text B1.1, look back at Section A, Unit 1 and review the different definitions of translation.

➤ As you read, note examples of **intralingual** and **interlingual** translation given in the extract.

➤ What examples can you think of to illustrate **intersemiotic** translation?

➤ Make a note of the linguistic terminology used and add it to your **glossary**.

➤ Note the categorical statements made by Jakobson (e.g. '**equivalence** in difference is the cardinal problem of language'). Think of examples to support or challenge these statements.

Roman Jakobson (1959/2000) 'On Linguistic Aspects of Translation', in R. Brower (ed.) (1959) *On Translation*, **Cambridge MA: Harvard University Press, pp. 232-9, reprinted in L. Venuti (ed.) (2000), pp. 113-18.**

We distinguish three ways of interpreting a verbal sign: it may be translated into other signs of the same language, into another language, or into another, nonverbal system of symbols. These three kinds of translation are to be differently labeled:

1) Intralingual translation or *rewording* is an interpretation of verbal signs by means of other signs of the same language.
2) Interlingual translation or *translation proper* is an interpretation of verbal signs by means of some other language.
3) Intersemiotic translation or *transmutation* is an interpretation of verbal signs by means of signs of nonverbal sign systems.

The intralingual translation of a word uses either another, more or less synonymous, word or resorts to a circumlocution. Yet synonymy, as a rule, is not complete equivalence for example, 'every celibate is a bachelor, but not every bachelor is a celibate.' A word or an idiomatic phrase-word, briefly a code-unit of the highest level, may be fully interpreted only by means of an equivalent combination of code-units, i.e., a message referring to this code-unit: 'every bachelor is an unmarried man, and every unmarried man is a bachelor,' or 'every celibate is bound not to marry, and everyone who is bound not to marry is a celibate.'

Likewise, on the level of interlingual translation, there is ordinarily no full equivalence between code-units, while messages may serve as adequate interpretations of alien code-units or messages. The English word 'cheese' cannot be completely identified with its standard Russian heteronym 'сыр', because cottage cheese is a cheese but not a **сыр**. Russians say: **принеси сыру и творогу**, 'bring cheese and [sic] cottage cheese.' In standard Russian, the food made of pressed curds is called **сыр** only if ferment is used.

Most frequently, however, translation from one language into another substitutes messages in one language not for separate code-units but for entire messages in some other language. Such a translation is a reported speech; the translator recodes and transmits a message received from another source. Thus translation involves two equivalent messages in two different codes.

Equivalence in difference is the cardinal problem of language and the pivotal concern of linguistics. Like any receiver of verbal messages, the linguist acts as their interpreter. No linguistic specimen may be interpreted by the science of language without a translation of its signs into other signs of the same system or into signs of another system. Any comparison of two languages implies an examination of their mutual translatability; widespread practice of interlingual communication, particularly translating activities, must be kept under constant scrutiny by linguistic science. It is difficult to overestimate the urgent need for and the theoretical and practical significance of differential bilingual dictionaries with careful comparative definition of all the corresponding units in their intension and extension. Likewise differential bilingual grammars should define what unifies and what differentiates the two languages in their selection and delimitation of grammatical concepts.

Both the practice and the theory of translation abound with intricacies, and from time to time attempts are made to sever the Gordian knot by proclaiming the dogma of untranslatability. 'Mr. Everyman, the natural logician,' vividly imagined by B. L.

Whorf, is supposed to have arrived at the following bit of reasoning: 'Facts are unlike to speakers whose language background provides for unlike formulation of them.' In the first years of the Russian revolution there were fanatic visionaries who argued in Soviet periodicals for a radical revision of traditional language and particularly for the weeding out of such misleading expressions as 'sunrise' or 'sunset.' Yet we still use this Ptolemaic imagery without implying a rejection of Copernican doctrine, and we can easily transform our customary talk about the rising and setting sun into a picture of the earth's rotation simply because any sign is translatable into a sign in which it appears to us more fully developed and precise.

[. . .]

All cognitive experience and its classification is conveyable in any existing language. Whenever there is deficiency, terminology may be qualified and amplified by loanwords or loan-translations, neologisms or semantic shifts, and finally, by circumlocutions. Thus in the newborn literary language of the Northeast Siberian Chukchees, 'screw' is rendered as 'rotating nail,' 'steel' as 'hard iron,' 'tin' as 'thin iron,' 'chalk' as 'writing soap,' 'watch' as 'hammering heart.' Even seemingly contradictory circumlocutions, like 'electrical horsecar' (злектрйческая конка), the first Russian name of the horseless street car, or 'flying steamship' (*jena paragot*), the Koryak term for the airplane, simply designate the electrical analogue of the horse-car and the flying analogue of the steamer and do not impede communication, just as there is no semantic 'noise' and disturbance in the double oxymoron – 'cold beef-and-pork hot dog.'

No lack of grammatical device in the language translated into makes impossible a literal translation of the entire conceptual information contained in the original. [. . .] If some grammatical category is absent in a given language, its meaning may be translated into this language by lexical means. Dual forms like Old Russian брата are translated with the help of the numeral: 'two brothers.' It is more difficult to remain faithful to the original when we translate into a language provided with a certain grammatical category from a language devoid of such a category. When translating the English sentence 'She has brothers' into a language which discriminates dual and plural, we are compelled either to make our own choice between two statements 'She has two brothers' – 'She has more than two' or to leave the decision to the listener and say: 'She has either two or more than two brothers.' Again in translating from a language without grammatical number into English one is obliged to select one of the two possibilities – 'brother' or 'brothers' or to confront the receiver of this message with a two-choice situation; 'She has either one or more than one brother.'

As Boas neatly observed, the grammatical pattern of a language (as opposed to its lexical stock) determines those aspects of each experience that must be expressed in the given language: 'We have to choose between these aspects, and one or the other must be chosen.'[1] In order to translate accurately the English sentence 'I hired a worker,' a Russian needs supplementary information, whether this action was completed or not and whether the worker was a man or a woman, because he must make his choice between a verb of completive or noncompletive aspect – нанял or нанимал – and between a masculine and feminine noun – работника or работницу. If I ask the utterer of the English sentence whether the worker was male or female, my question may be judged irrelevant or indiscreet, whereas in the Russian version of this

---

1   [Jakobson's note] Franz Boas, 'Language', *General Anthropology* (Boston, 1938), pp. 132f.

sentence an answer to this question is obligatory. On the other hand, whatever the choice of Russian grammatical forms to translate the quoted English message, the translation will give no answer to the question of whether I 'hired' or 'have hired' the worker, or whether he/she was an indefinite or definite worker ('a' or 'the'). Because the information required by the English and Russian grammatical pattern is unlike, we face quite different sets of two-choice situations; therefore a chain of translations of one and the same isolated sentence from English into Russian and vice versa could entirely deprive such a message of its initial content. The Geneva linguist S. Karcevski used to compare such a gradual loss with a circular series of unfavorable currency transactions. But evidently the richer the context of a message, the smaller the loss of information.

Languages differ essentially in what they *must* convey and not in what they *may* convey. Each verb of a given language imperatively raises a set of specific yes-or-no questions, as for instance: is the narrated event conceived with or without reference to its completion? Is the narrated event presented as prior to the speech event or not? Naturally the attention of native speakers and listeners will be constantly focused on such items as are compulsory in their verbal code.

Task B1.1.2

'Languages differ essentially in what they *must* convey and not in what they *may* convey', says Jakobson.

➤ Now that you have read Text B1.1 look back at the examples given by Jakobson and think how they would work between English and a language other than Russian. Do your findings support Jakobson's claim?

➤ Jakobson sees a compelling need for 'differential' dictionaries and grammars to assist translation. What ideas do you have for how these could be constructed and how they would function? How far do current dictionaries fulfil this need?

Translation Studies initially struggled to be recognized as an academic discipline internationally. Indeed, it was in the translation section of the Third International Congress of *Applied Linguistics* that James S. Holmes, an Amsterdam-based lecturer and literary translator, presented his famous paper 'The Name and Nature of Translation Studies' in August 1972 (Holmes 1988/2000). The setting illustrated the fact that, at that time, outlets for researchers working on translation were to be found primarily in other, more established, disciplines. The paper was soon to be considered 'the founding statement of work in the field' (Gentzler 2001: 93). In it, Holmes ponders the impediments to the progress of the study of translation in the academic world which had long deemed translation to be a secondary or derivative activity. He suggests a name for this emerging discipline and maps out its possible 'scope and structure': 'theoretical' ('pure' and '**descriptive**') and 'applied'. In the extract below, Holmes classifies possible areas of research in 'pure' Translation Studies.

Task B1.2.1

➤ Before you read Text B1.2, review the terms 'theoretical', '**descriptive**' and 'applied' discussed in Section A, Unit 1, as they refer to Translation Studies. Look at the 'map' of the discipline, based on Holmes's paper, in Toury (1995: 10). This provides a useful overview and guide for this extract.

➤ As you read, list the different examples of research possibilities under the three headings (i) 'theoretical', (ii) '**descriptive**' and (iii) 'applied'.

James S. Holmes (1988/2000) 'The Name and Nature of Translation Studies', in *Translated! Papers on Literary Translation and Translation Studies* (2nd edition, 1988), pp. 67-80, reprinted in L. Venuti (ed.) (2000), pp. 172-85.

Text B1.2

J. S. Holmes

A greater impediment than the lack of a generally accepted name in the way of the development of Translation Studies is the lack of any general consensus as to the scope and structure of the discipline. What constitutes the field of Translation Studies? A few would say it coincides with comparative (or contrastive) terminological and lexicographical studies; several look upon it as practically identical with comparative or contrastive linguistics; many would consider it largely synonymous with translation theory. But surely it is different, if not always distinct, from the first two of these, and more than the third. As is usually to be found in the case of emerging disciplines, there has as yet been little meta-reflection on the nature of Translation Studies as such – at least that has made its way into print and to my attention. One of the few cases that I have found is that of Werner Koller, who has given the following delineation of the subject: 'Übersetzungswissenschaft ist zu verstehen als Zusammenfassung und Überbegriff für alle Forschungsbemühungen, die von den Phänomenen "Übersetzen" und "Übersetzung" ausgehen oder auf diese Phänomene zielen.' (Translation studies is to be understood as a collective and inclusive designation for all research activities taking the phenomena of translating and translation as their basis or focus).[1]

1.1

From this delineation it follows that Translation Studies is, as no one I suppose, would deny, an empirical discipline. Such disciplines, it has often been pointed out, have two major objectives, which Carl G. Hempel has phrased as 'to describe particular phenomena in the world of our experience and to establish general principles by means of which they can be explained and predicted'.[2] As a field of pure research – that is to say, research pursued for its own sake, quite apart from any direct practical

---

1 [Holmes's note] Werner Koller, 'Übersetzen, Übersetzung, und Übersetzer. Zu schwedischen Symposien über Probleme der Übersetzung', *Babel* 17 (1971): 3-11, quotation p. 4.

2 [Holmes's note] Carl G. Hempel, *Fundamentals of Concept Formation in Empirical Science* (Chicago: Chicago University Press, 1967; International Encyclopedia of Social Science, Foundation of the Unity of Sciences, II, Fasc. 7), p. 1.

Extension

application outside its own terrain – Translation Studies thus has two main objectives: (1) to describe the phenomena of translating and translation(s) as they manifest themselves in the world of our experience, and (2) to establish general principles by means of which these phenomena can be explained and predicted. The two branches of pure Translation Studies concerning themselves with these objectives can be designated *descriptive translation studies* (DTS) or *translation description* (TD) and *theoretical translation studies* (ThTS) or *translation theory* (TTh).

1.11

Of these two, it is perhaps appropriate to give first consideration to *descriptive translation studies*, as the branch of the discipline which constantly maintains the closest contact with the empirical phenomena under study. There would seem to be three major kinds of research in DTS, which may be distinguished by their focus as product-oriented, function-oriented, and process-oriented.

1.111

Product-oriented DTS, that area of research which describes existing translations, has traditionally been an important area of academic research in Translation Studies. The starting point for this type of study is the description of individual translations, or text-focused translation description. A second phase is that of comparative translation description, in which comparative analyses are made of various translations of the same text, either in a single language or in various languages. Such individual and comparative descriptions provide the materials for surveys of larger corpuses of translations, for instance those made within a specific period, language, and/or text or discourse type. In practice the corpus has usually been restricted in all three ways: seventeenth-century literary translations into French, or medieval English Bible translations. But such descriptive surveys can also be larger in scope, diachronic as well as (approximately) synchronic, and one of the eventual goals of product-oriented DTS might possibly be a general history of translations – however ambitious such a goal may sound at this time.

1.112

Function-oriented DTS is not interested in the description of translations in themselves, but in the description of their function in the recipient socio-cultural situation: it is a study of contexts rather than texts. Pursuing such questions as [to] which texts were (and, often as important, were not) translated at a certain time in a certain place, and what influences were exerted in consequence, this area of research is one that has attracted less concentrated attention than the area just mentioned, though it is often introduced as a kind of sub-theme or counter-theme in histories of translations and in literary histories. Greater emphasis on it could lead to the development of a field of translation sociology (or – less felicitous but more accurate, since it is a legitimate area of Translation Studies as well as of sociology – socio-translation studies).

1.113

Process-oriented DTS concerns itself with the process or act of translation itself. The problem of what exactly takes place in the 'little black box' of the translator's 'mind' as he creates a new, more or less matching text in another language has been the subject of much speculation on the part of translation's theorists, but there has been very little attempt at systematic investigation of this process under laboratory conditions. Admittedly, the process is an unusually complex one, one which, if I. A. Richards is correct, 'may very probably be the most complex type of event yet produced in the evolution of the cosmos'.[3] But psychologists have developed and are developing highly sophisticated methods for analysing and describing other complex mental processes, and it is to be hoped that in future this problem, too, will be given closer attention, leading to an area of study that might be called translation psychology or psycho-translation studies.

1.12

The other main branch of pure Translation Studies, *theoretical translation studies* or *translation theory*, as its name implies, is not interested in describing existing translations, observed translation functions, or experimentally determined translating processes, but in using the results of descriptive translation studies, in combination with the information available from related fields and disciplines, to evolve principles, theories, and models which will serve to explain and predict what translating and translations are and will be.

1.121

The ultimate goal of the translation theorist in the broad sense must undoubtedly be to develop a full, inclusive theory accommodating so many elements that it can serve to explain and predict all phenomena falling within the terrain of translating and translation, to the exclusion of all phenomena falling outside it. It hardly needs to be pointed out that a *general translation theory* in such a true sense of the term, if indeed it is achievable, will necessarily be highly formalized and, however the scholar may strive after economy, also highly complex.

Most of the theories that have been produced to date are in reality little more than prolegomena to such a general translation theory. A good share of them, in fact, are not actually theories at all, in any scholarly sense of the term, but an array of, axioms, postulates, and hypotheses that are so formulated as to be both too inclusive (covering also non-translatory acts and non-translations) and too exclusive (shutting out some translatory acts and some works generally recognized as translations).

1.122

Others, though they too may bear the designation of 'general' translation theories (frequently preceded by the scholar's protectively cautious 'towards') are in fact not general theories, but partial or specific in their scope, dealing with only one or a few of the various aspects of translation theory as a whole. It is in this area of partial theories that the most significant advances have been made in recent years, and in fact it will probably be necessary for a great deal of further research to be conducted in them before we can even begin to think about arriving at a true general theory in the sense I have just outlined. *Partial translation theories* are specified in a number of ways. I would suggest, though, that they can be grouped together into six main kinds.

---

3   [Holmes's note] I. A. Richards 'Toward a Theory of Translating', in Arthur F. Wright (ed.), *Studies in Chinese Thought* (Chicago: University of Chicago Press, 1953), pp. 247-62.

1.1221

First of all, there are translation theories that I have called, with a somewhat unortho-dox extension of the term, *medium-restricted translation theories*, according to the medium that is used. Medium-restricted theories can be further subdivided into theories of translation as performed by humans (human translation), as performed by computers (machine translation), and as performed by the two in conjunction (mixed or machine-aided translation). Human translation breaks down into (and restricted theories or 'theories' have been developed for) oral translation or interpreting (with the further distinction between consecutive and simultaneous) and written transla-tion. Numerous examples of valuable research into machine and machine-aided translation are no doubt familiar to us all, and perhaps also several into oral human translation. That examples of medium-restricted theories of written translation do not come to mind so easily is largely owing to the fact that their authors have the tendency to present them in the guise of unmarked or general theories.

1.1222

Second, there are theories that are area-restricted. *Area-restricted theories* can be of two closely related kinds; restricted as to the languages involved or, which is usually not quite the same, and occasionally hardly at all, as to the cultures involved. In both cases, language restriction and culture restriction, the degree of actual limitation can vary. Theories are feasible for translation between, say, French and German (language-pair restricted theories) as opposed to translation within Slavic languages (language-group restricted theories) or from Romance languages to Germanic lan-guages (language-group pair restricted theories). Similarly, theories might at least hypothetically be developed for translation within Swiss culture (one-culture restricted), or for translation between Swiss and Belgian cultures (cultural-pair restricted), as opposed to translation within western Europe (cultural-group restricted) or between languages reflecting a pre-technological culture and the languages of contemporary western culture (cultural-group pair restricted). Language-restricted theories have close affinities with the work being done in comparative linguistics and stylistics (though it must always be remembered that a language-pair translation grammar must be a different thing from a contrastive grammar developed for the purpose of language acquisition). In the field of culture-restricted theories there has been little detailed research, though culture restrictions, by being confused with language restrictions, sometimes get introduced into language-restricted theories, where they are out of place in all but those rare cases where culture and language boundaries coincide in both the source and target situations. It is moreover no doubt true that some aspects of theories that are presented as general in reality pertain only to the western cultural area.

1.1223

Third, there are *rank-restricted theories*, that is to say, theories that deal with discourses or texts as wholes, but concern themselves with lower linguistic ranks or levels. Traditionally, a great deal of writing on translation was concerned almost entirely with the rank of the word, and the word and the word group are still the ranks at which much terminologically oriented thinking about scientific and technological translation takes place. Most linguistically oriented research, on the other hand, has until very recently taken the sentence as its upper rank limit, largely ignoring the macro-structural aspects of entire texts as translation problems. The clearly discernible trend away from sentential linguistics in the direction of textual linguistics will, it is to be hoped, encourage linguistically oriented theorists to move beyond sentence-restricted translation theories to the more complex task of developing text-rank (or 'rank-free') theories.

1.1224

Fourth, there are *text-type* (or discourse-type) *restricted theories*, dealing with the problem of translating specific types or genres of lingual messages. Authors and literary scholars have long concerned themselves with the problems intrinsic to translating literary texts or specific genres of literary texts; theologians, similarly, have devoted much attention to questions of how to translate the Bible and other sacred works. In recent years some effort has been made to develop a specific theory for the translation of scientific texts. All these studies break down, however, because we still lack anything like a formal theory of message, text, or discourse types. Both Bühler's theory of types of communication, as further developed by the Prague structuralists, and the definitions of language varieties arrived at by linguists particularly of the British school provide material for criteria in defining text types that would lend themselves to operationalization more aptly than the inconsistent and mutually contradictory definitions or traditional genre theories. On the other hand, the traditional theories cannot be ignored, for they continue to play a large part in creating the expectation criteria of translation readers. Also requiring study is the important question of text-type skewing or shifting in translation.

1.1225

Fifth, there are *time-restricted theories*, which fall into two types: theories regarding the translation of contemporary texts, and theories having to do with the translation of texts from an older period. Again there would seem to be a tendency to present one of the theories, that having to do with contemporary texts, in the guise of a general theory; the other, the theory of what can perhaps best be called cross-temporal translation, is a matter that has led to much disagreement, particularly among literarily oriented theorists, but to few generally valid conclusions.

1.1226

Finally, there are *problem-restricted theories*, theories which confine themselves to one or more specific problems within the entire area of general translation theory, problems that can range from such broad and basic questions as the limits of variance and invariance in translation or the nature of translation equivalence (or, as I should prefer to call it, translation matching) to such more specific matters as the translation of metaphors or of proper names.

Task B1.2.2

➤ Holmes describes what he terms the 'ultimate goal' of a 'full, inclusive theory of translation'. Having read Text B1.2, what kinds of phenomena and predictions do you think that such a theory, if possible, might consist of?

➤ Holmes provides many examples of different categories of research. Give further examples of possible similar research projects involving your languages which would illustrate each category.

SECTION
B

Unit B2
Translation strategies

As we saw in Section A of this unit, the debate on whether translation should be **literal** or **free** continued to dominate (some would say 'plague') translation theory until well into the twentieth century. Nevertheless, writings on translation began to become more systematic and George Steiner's *After Babel* is one of the classics of modern translation theory, written at a time before Translation Studies became firmly established (the first edition appeared in 1975). Steiner was working from a general humanistic and philosophical perspective, bringing together key issues of literary translation. In this extract, Steiner discusses the arguments for and against **translatability**. His own firm view is that, except perhaps for poetry, translation is always possible (after all, it does occur in daily practice). Later in the book, he goes further, railing against the sterility of the **literal** vs **free** debate, and proposes his own model of the **hermeneutic movement**, that is, the act of interpretation and transfer of meaning that is involved in translation.

Task B2.1.1

➤ Before you read Text B2.1, review the section on **translatability** from Section A of this unit.

➤ As you read, list the arguments for and against **translatability** discussed by Steiner.

➤ Make a list of the metaphors and other images used by Steiner to discuss translation.

Text B2.1
G. Steiner

George Steiner, (1998, 3rd edition) *After Babel*, Oxford: OUP, pp. 251-64 (abridged).

The perennial question whether translation is, in fact, possible is rooted in ancient religious and psychological doubts on whether there ought to be any passage from one tongue to another. So far as speech is divine and numinous, so far as it encloses revelation, active transmission either into the vulgate or across the barrier of languages is dubious or frankly evil. Inhibitions about decipherment, about the devaluation which must occur in all interpretative transcription – substantively each and every act of translation leads 'downward', to one further remove from the immediate moment of the *logos* – can be felt in Saint Paul. I Corinthians 14, that remarkable excursus on *pneuma* and the multiplicity of tongues, is ambivalent. If there is no interpreter present, let the alien speaker be silent. But not because he has nothing to say. His discourse is with himself and with God: 'sibi autem loquatur et Deo'. Moreover, where such speech is authentic, there must be no translation. He who has been in Christ and has heard unspeakable words – 'arcana verba' – shall not utter them in a mortal idiom. Translation would be blasphemy (II Corinthians 12: 4). An even more definite taboo can be found in Judaism. The M*egillath Ta'anith* (*Roll of Fasting*), which is assigned to the first century AD, records the belief that three days of utter darkness fell on the world when the Law was translated into Greek. In most cases, and certainly after the end of the fifteenth century, the postulate of untranslatability has a purely secular basis. It is founded on the conviction, formal and pragmatic, that there can be no true symmetry, no adequate mirroring, between two different semantic systems. But this view shares with the religious, mystical tradition a sense of wastage. The vital energies, the luminosity and pressure of the original text have not only been diminished by translation; they have been made tawdry. Somehow, the process of entropy is one of active corruption. Traduced into French, said Heine, his German poems were 'moonlight stuffed with straw'. Or as Nabokov puts it in his poem 'On Translating "Eugene Onegin"':

What is translation? On a platter
A poet's pale and glaring head,
A parrot's screech, a monkey's chatter,
And profanation of the dead.

Because all human speech consists of arbitrarily selected but intensely conventionalized signals, meaning can never be wholly separated from expressive form. Even the most purely ostensive, apparently neutral terms are embedded in linguistic particularity, in an intricate mould of cultural-historical habit. There are no surfaces of absolute transparency. *Soixante-dix* is not arrived at semantically by the same road as *seventy*; English can reproduce the Hungarian discrimination between the elder and the younger brother, *bátya* and *öcs*, but it cannot find an equivalent for the reflexes of associative logic and for the ingrained valuations which have generated and been reinforced by the two Hungarian words. 'Thus not even "basic notions", central points in a human sphere of experience, stand outside the area of arbitrary segmentation and arrangement and subsequent conventionalization; and the extent to which semantic boundaries as determined by linguistic form and linguistic usage coincide with absolute boundaries in the world around us is negligible.'[1]

[. . .]

[. . .]

The case *for* translation has its religious, mystical antecedents as well as that against. Even if the exact motivations of the disaster at Babel remain obscure, it would be sacrilege to give to this act of God an irreparable finality, to mistake the deep pulse of ebb and flow which marks the relations of God to men even in, perhaps most

---

1 [Steiner's note] Werner Winter, 'Impossibilities of Translation', in William Arrowsmith and Roger Shattuck (eds), *The Craft and Context of Translation* (Anchor Books, New York, 1964), p. 97.

especially in, the moment of punishment. As the Fall may be understood to contain the coming of the Redeemer, so the scattering of tongues at Babel has in it, in a condition of urgent moral and practical potentiality, the return to linguistic unity, the movement towards and beyond Pentecost. Seen thus, translation is a teleological imperative, a stubborn searching out of all the apertures, translucencies, sluice-gates through which the divided streams of human speech pursue their destined return to a single sea. We have seen the strength, the theoretic and practical consequences of this approach in the long tradition of linguistic Kabbalism and illumination. It underlies the subtle exaltation in Walter Benjamin's view of the translator as one who elicits, who conjures up by virtue of unplanned echo a language nearer to the primal unity of speech than is either the original text or the tongue into which he is translating.

[. . .]

We *do* speak of the world and to one another. We *do* translate intra- and inter-lingually and have done so since the beginning of human history. The defence of translation has the immense advantage of abundant, vulgar fact. How could we be about our business if the thing was not inherently feasible, ask Saint Jerome and Luther with the impatience of craftsmen irritated by the buzz of theory. Translation is 'impossible' concedes Ortega y Gasset in his *Miseria y esplendor de la traducción*. But so is all absolute concordance between thought and speech. Somehow the 'impossible' is overcome at every moment in human affairs. Its logic subsists, in its own rigorous limbo, but it has no empirical consequences: 'no es una objeción contra el posible esplendor de la faena traductora.'[2] Deny translation, says Gentile in his polemic against Croce, and you must be consistent and deny all speech. Translation is, and always will be, the mode of thought and understanding: 'Giacchè tradurre, in verità, è la condizione d'ogni pensare e d'ogni apprendere.'[3] Those who negate translation are themselves interpreters.

The argument from perfection which, essentially, is that of Du Bellay, Dr. Johnson, Nabokov, and so many others, is facile. No human product can be perfect. No duplication, even of materials which are conventionally labelled as identical, will turn out a total facsimile. Minute differences and asymmetries persist. To dismiss the validity of translation because it is not always possible and never perfect is absurd. What does need clarification, say the translators, is the *degree* of fidelity to be pursued in each case, the tolerance allowed as between different jobs of work.

[. . .]

Task B2.1.2

> Steiner points to the obvious fact that translated texts do exist and thereby prove the feasibility of translation. However, he goes on to stress that 'what does need clarification, say the translators, is the *degree* of **fidelity** to be pursued in each case, the tolerance allowed as between different jobs of work'. Look back at the

2   [Steiner's note] J. Ortega y Gasset (1937) Obras Completas I, Madrid: Revista de occidente, pp. 427–55.
3   [Steiner's note] G. Gentile, 'Il diritto e il torto delle traduzioni' (*Rivista di Cultura*, I, 1920), p. 10.

text examples from Section A and consider how this degree of **fidelity** might be defined.

➤ Summarize the points specifically related to religious texts. Try and find other examples of the translation of sacred or otherwise sensitive texts and see how they fit with what Steiner says.

➤ The metaphors Steiner uses for the translation process are discussed further in Section A, Unit 13 on **ideology** and translation. Read over that discussion and keep an ongoing log of metaphors you come across in your reading on translation theory.

Unit B3
The unit of translation

Because of the difficulty of analysing the translation process, there is no full agreement as to what the **unit of translation** is. As is clear in Section A (Unit 11), some theorists stress that the major unit must be the text itself, that it is impossible to translate well unless the significance of the whole text has been established. Yet practising translators are often required to undertake a translation without having had the time (or, in some instances, the opportunity) to read or access the whole of a lengthy text.

Vinay and Darbelnet's *Comparative Stylistics of French and English* first appeared in 1958. Though a study in contrastive analysis of the two languages, its subtitle, *A Method in Translation*, indicates its desired influence in the field of translation. In this extract, the authors define their **unit of translation** as 'the smallest segment of the utterance whose signs are linked in such a way that they should not be translated individually'. They attempt to move beyond the word (although 'this concept cannot be abandoned altogether') and consider **unit of translation** to be equivalent to 'unit of thought' and 'lexicological unit'.

 Task B3.1.1

> Vinay and Darbelnet begin by discussing the value of the word as a **translation unit**. They draw on Saussure's concept of the **linguistic sign** (see Section A of this unit).

> ➤ Before reading Text B3.1, look up Saussure's own description (Saussure 1916/1983: 66), or find a summary of it in a reference book on linguistics. Look up also the definition of 'word' in different dictionaries. Does it vary across the languages you know?

> ➤ Vinay and Darbelnet equate '**unit of translation**' with 'unit of thought' and 'lexicological unit', each approaching the issue from a different point of view. As you read, make a note of the characteristics of the different units discussed by the authors.

Text B3.1
J.-P. Vinay and
J. Darbelnet

Jean-Paul Vinay and Jean Darbelnet (1958/95) *Comparative Stylistics of French and English*, **trans. J. Sager and M-J. Hamel, Amsterdam and Philadelphia: John Benjamins, pp. 20-7 (abridged).**

Translation units

For any science, one of the essential and often the most controversial preliminary step is defining the units with which to operate. This is equally true of translation, where until recently attention was concentrated on words, as if these segments of the utterance were so obvious that they did not require definition. But we only have to glance through the pages of the main linguistic journals over the last twenty years to see that nothing is less clearly defined than the concept 'word'; some linguists, notably Delacroix, have gone so far as describing the word as a *'nébuleuse intellectuelle'*, or even refused to consider it as having any concrete existence at all.

It is obvious that, despite its apparent convenience, the word on its own is unsuitable for consideration as the basis for a unit of translation. It is unlikely, however, that this concept can be abandoned altogether: after all, in written language utterances are divided into words by blank spaces and dictionaries are compiled on the principle of such units as words. But even in written language, the limits of a word are not always very clear. There is first of all the capricious use of the hyphen: the French write *'face à face'*, but *'vis-à-vis'*, *'bon sens'*, but *'non-sens'* and *'contresens'*, *'portefeuille'*, but *'porte-monnaie'*, *'tout à fait'*, but *'sur-le-champ'*. These irregularities are just as common in English, with the added complication that there is variance in the use of the hyphen between British English and American English, which uses hyphens more sparingly. The following sentence would seem ludicrous to a British reader without a hyphen, yet its absence is perfectly normal to an American.

His face turned an ugly   Son visage prit une vilaine

brick(-)red   couleur rouge brique.

Observing spoken language utterances, we note that, at least in French, the beginnings and endings of words merge into one another. The units we distinguish aurally are not words but syllables and phonetic groups which may be longer or shorter than words and whose boundaries do not always coincide with the boundaries of words. French in particular has very few phonological features which allow a clear distinction of one word from another. We are therefore faced with the problem of defining units, something de Saussure spent a lot of time researching:

Units – Planes

Language then has the strange, striking characteristic of not having entities that are perceptible at the outset and yet of not permitting us to doubt that they exist and that their functioning constitutes it. (Saussure (trans. Wade Burkin) 1960: 149)

What makes us hesitate about adopting the word as a unit is that the double structure of the sign then no longer seems clear to us, and the signifier takes on a more important role than the signified. Translators, let us remind ourselves, start from the meaning and carry out all translation procedures within the semantic field. They therefore need a unit which is not exclusively defined by formal criteria, since their work involves form only at the beginning and the end of their task. In this light, the

Text B3.1
J.-P. Vinay and
J. Darbelnet

unit that has to be identified is a unit of thought, taking into account that translators do not translate words, but ideas and feelings.

For the purpose of this book we shall consider the following terms to be equivalent: **unit of thought**, **lexicological unit**, and **unit of translation**. For us, these terms convey the same concept, but with emphasis on different points of view. The units of translation we postulate here are lexicological units within which lexical elements are grouped together to form a single element of thought. It would be more correct to say: the unit of translation is the predominant element of thought within such a segment of the utterance. There may be superposition of ideas within the same unit. For example, 'to loom' conveys both the idea of a ghost hanging in mid-air and, at the same time, that of imminence or threat, but, whether seen as a single lexical item in a dictionary or from the point of view of the morpho-syntactic structure in which the word might occur, the two ideas cannot be separated. They are superimposed. It is what Bally refers to as an accumulation of meanings. In such cases the translation may be able to retain only one signified, preferably that which in the context has priority. This is the reason why it is almost impossible to fully translate poetry.

We could define the unit of translation as the smallest segment of the utterance whose signs are linked in such a way that they should not be translated individually. With such a definition we clearly touch upon what separates the stylistic analysis proposed in the following chapters from structural analysis. Given that translators have to be concerned more with semantics than structure, it is obviously preferable to have a unit whose definition originates in a distinction of meaning rather than in syntactic functions.

According to the particular role they play in the message, several types of units of translation can be recognised:

a. **Functional units**, i.e. units whose elements have the same syntactic function, e.g.:

Il habite	He lives
Saint-Sauveur,	at Saint-Sauveur,
à deux pas,	a short distance away
en meublé,	in furnished rooms
chez ses parents.	with his parents

b. **Semantic units**, i.e. units of meaning, e.g.:

le grand film	the main feature
prendre place	to sit (or: to stand)

c. **Dialectic units**, i.e. expressing a reasoning, e.g.:

en effet	really
puisque, aussi, bien	since, however, also, well

d. **Prosodic units**, i.e. units whose elements have the same intonation:

You don't say!	Ça alors!
You're telling me!	Vous ne m'apprenez rien!

The last three categories constitute units of translation. Unless they are very short, functional units may contain more than a single unit of thought.

If we now look at the relationship between units of translation and words within a text, three different cases can arise:

Text B3.1
J.-P. Vinay and
J. Darbelnet

a. Simple units

These units correspond to a single word. It is obviously the simplest case and listed here in first place because it is widely used and also because it enables us to give a better definition of the remaining two. In the following sentences there are as many units as there are words and each word can be replaced individually without changing the sentence structure.

Il gagne cinq mille dollars.	He earns five thousand dollars.
Elle reçoit trois cents francs.	She receives three hundred francs.

b. Diluted units

These units extend over several words which together form a lexicological unit, because the whole group of words expresses a single idea. We take our examples from both languages:

simple soldat	private
tout de suite	immediately

c. Fractional units

These units consist of only a fraction of a word, which means that the speaker is therefore still aware of the constituent elements of the word, e.g.:

Two units	*One unit*
relever quelqu'un qui est tombé	relever une erreur [spot, point out]
re-cover [recouvrir]	recover [recouvrer]

In English, wordstress can reveal the difference between single and multiple units, e.g. 'black 'bird vs 'black-bird.

The identification of units of translation also depends upon another classification in which the degree of cohesion between the elements is taken into account. Unfortunately, this involves a variable criterion and the categories we shall try to establish are, above all, fixed points between which we may expect to find intermediary cases which are more difficult to classify.

a. **Unified groups**, in contrast to one-word units, refer to highly coherent units of two or more words such as idioms. The unity of meaning is very clear and is often marked by a syntactic characteristic such as the omission of an article before a noun. In general, even the least experienced translators can detect this kind of unit without any difficulty.

à bout portant	point-blank

b. **Affinity groups** are units whose elements are more difficult to detect and in which the cohesion between the words is less evident. We identify five separate types:

   i. Phrases of Intensity

   focused around a noun:

une pluie diluvienne	a downpour

Text B3.1
J.-P. Vinay and
J. Darbelnet

focused around an adjective, a past participle, or a verb:

grièvement blessé	seriously injured
réfléchir mûrement	to give careful consideration

Such groupings exist in both languages, but they can only rarely be translated literally. For example, English has its own special tendency to reinforce an adjective, e.g.:

Drink your coffee while it is nice and hot.	Buvez votre café bien chaud.
He was good and mad.	Il était furieux.

The reinforcement of 'big' by 'great' is reminiscent of children's language. Certain English adjectives are intensified by another adjective, e.g.:

stone deaf	sourd comme un pot

ii. Verbal phrases

In these cases a verb followed by a noun (e.g. *faire une promenade*) corresponds, in principle, to a simple verb (e.g. *se promener*) of the same family as the noun:

faire une promenade	to take a walk
pousser un soupir	to heave a sigh

The simple verb without its associated complement may be quite rare, e.g. the case of 'heave', or not occur at all. Groups formed by a noun and verb with a single meaning within the sentence should also be considered as units of thought. The verb does not necessarily have a literal correspondent.

passer un examen	to take an exam

Many simple English verbs correspond to French verbal phrases, e.g.:

mettre en danger	to endanger
fermer à clef	to lock

iii. Many French adjectival and adverbial phrases form units in the same way as their English counterparts do in the form of single words, e.g.:

sans condition	unconditionally

iv. Many units consist of a noun and an adjective, but without the intensification noted above. The adjective is often an everyday word which acquires a more technical meaning, e.g.:

les grands magasins	department stores
un haut fourneau	a blast furnace

v. Beyond these easily defined units, translators are faced with a maze of phrases in which they have to try and identify the lexicological units. Dictionaries give numerous examples of these, but there are no complete lists, and all for good reason. The following examples have been selected at random to illustrate the variety of these units.

le régime des pluies	the rainfall
mettre au point	to overhaul, perfect, clarify

Text B3.1
J.-P. Vinay and
J. Darbelnet

The translation of a word usually depends upon its context. A unit of translation provides a limited context; it forms a syntactic unit where one element determines the translation of the other. For example, in '*régime des pluies*', '*régime*' corresponds to 'fall'. On the other hand, the context is created by the usage, and it is unlikely that these words should recur in the same order with a different meaning association. At the same time, the unit of translation is anchored in the system of the language, for it is also a memory association.

Task B3.1.2

➤ The examples in the many categories of unit and sub-unit of translation are drawn exclusively from English and French. Find examples of these units in your own languages. How far do your findings suggest that the **unit of translation** may vary depending on language?

In Vinay and Darbelnet's opinion, 'Given that translators have to be concerned more with **semantics** than **structure**, it is obviously preferable to have a unit whose definition originates in a distinction of meaning rather than in **syntactic functions**.'

➤ What does this indicate about the authors' views of translation? How does this compare to the theorists such as Jakobson and Steiner, whom we discussed in previous units? How does it fit with your own experience of translation?

Unlike Vinay and Darbelnet, Newmark (1988: 66) introduces the concept of text authority, considering that 'the more authoritative the text, the smaller the **unit of translation**'.

➤ Look for texts which seem to support or challenge this argument. How far is it possible to link text authority (or even **text type**) and the **unit of translation**?

SECTION
B

Unit B4
Translation shifts

In Section A of this unit, we looked at the concept of **translation shift** and at some of the **taxonomies** that have been proposed for describing the changes that occur in a specific ST–TT pair. The readings in this section are from perhaps the most noted theorists in this area: John Catford, who was the first to use the term 'translation shift' in his *A Linguistic Theory of Translation*, published in 1965; and Jean Vinay and Jean-Paul Darbelnet, whose *A Comparative Stylistics of French and English* (1958/1995) still remains the most comprehensive categorization of differences between a pair of languages. The extract from Catford (Text B4.1), describes the two kinds of **translation shifts** in his model: **level shifts** (between the **levels** of grammar and **lexis**) and **category shifts** (**unbounded** and **rank-bounded**).

 Task B4.1.1

➤ Before you read Text B4.1, look back at Section A, Unit 4 and make sure you are familiar with the term **translation shift**.

➤ What would you say would be the aim of **translation shift** analysis?

➤ What were some of the problems with **shift** analysis discussed at the end of Section A of this unit? Do you agree that these really are problems?

➤ As you read the text below, make a list of examples of the different kinds of **shifts** described by Catford. Note the difference between **level shifts** and **category shifts**.

Text B4.1
J. C. Catford

J. C. Catford (1965) *A Linguistic Theory of Translation*, Oxford: OUP, Chapter 12, pp. 73-82.

1.1   *Level shifts*. By a shift of level we mean that a SL item at one linguistic level has a TL translation equivalent at a different level.

We have already pointed out that translation between the levels of phonology and graphology – or between either of these levels and the levels of grammar and lexis – is impossible. Translation between these levels is absolutely ruled out by our theory, which posits 'relationship to the same substance' as the necessary condition of translation equivalence. We are left, then, with shifts from *grammar* to *lexis* and vice-versa as the only possible level shifts in translation; and such shifts are, of course, quite common.

1.11 Examples of level shifts are sometimes encountered in the translation of the verbal aspects of Russian and English. Both these language have an aspectual opposition – of very roughly the same type – seen most clearly in the 'past' or *preterite* tense: the opposition between Russian *imperfective* and *perfective* (e.g. *pisal* and *napisal*), and between English *simple* and *continuous* (*wrote* and *was writing*).

There is, however, an important difference between the two aspect systems, namely that the *polarity of marking* is not the same. In Russian, the (contextually) marked term in the system is the *perfective*; this explicitly refers to the *uniqueness* or *completion* of the event. The *imperfective* is unmarked – in other words it is relatively neutral in these respects (the event may or may not actually be unique or completed, etc., but at any rate the imperfective is indifferent to these features – does not explicitly refer to this 'perfectiveness').[1]

In English, the (contextually and morphologically) marked term is the *continuous*; this explicitly refers to the development, the *progress*, of the event. The 'simple' form is neutral in this respect (the event may or may not actually be in progress, but the simple form does not explicitly refer to this aspect of the event).

We indicate these differences in the following diagram, in which the marked terms in the Russian and English aspect systems are enclosed in rectangles:

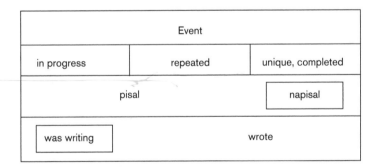

1.12 One result of this difference between Russian and English is that Russian *imperfective* (e.g. *pisal*) is translatable with almost equal frequency by English *simple* (*wrote*) or *continuous* (*was writing*). But the *marked* terms (*napisal* – *was writing*) are mutually untranslatable.

A Russian writer can create a certain contrastive effect by using an imperfective and then, so to speak, 'capping' this by using the (marked) perfective. In such a case, the same effect of explicit, contrastive, reference to *completion* may have to be translated into English by a change of lexical item. The following example[2] shows this:

---

1   [Catford's note] My attention was first drawn to this difference between English and Russian by Roman Jakobson in a lecture which he gave in London in 1950.
2   [Catford's note] From *Herzen*, cited by *Unbegaun* in Grammaire Russe, p. 217.

'Čto že *delal* Bel'tov v prodolženie etix des'ati let? Vse ili počti vse. Čto on *sdelal*? Ničego ili počti ničego.'

Here the imperfective, *delal*, is 'capped' by the perfective *sdelal*. *Delal* can be translated by either *did* or *was doing* – but, since there is no contextual reason to make explicit reference to the progress of the event, the former is the better translation. We can thus say 'What *did* Beltov do . . .?' The Russian perfective, with its marked insistence on *completion* can cap this effectively: 'What did he *do and complete*?' But the English marked term insists on the *progress* of the event, so cannot be used here. ('What *was* he *doing*' is obviously inappropriate.) In English, in this case, we must use a different lexical verb: a lexical item which includes reference to completion in its contextual meaning, e.g. *achieve*.[3] The whole passage can thus be translated:

What did Beltov do during these ten years? Everything, or almost everything. What did he achieve? Nothing, or almost nothing?

1.13 Cases of more or less incomplete shift from grammar to lexis are quite frequent in translation between other languages. For example, the English: *This text is intended for* . . . may have as its French TL equivalent: *Le présent manuel s'adresse à* . . . Here the SL modifier, *This* – a term in a *grammatical* system of deictics – has as its TL equivalent the modifier *Le présent*, an article + a lexical adjective. Such cases are not rare in French, cf. also *This may reach you before I arrive* = Fr. *Il se peut que ce mot vous parvienne avant mon arrivée*. Once again the grammatical item *this* has a partially lexical translation equivalent *ce mot*.[4]

1.2 *Category shifts*. In 2.4 we referred to *unbounded* and *rank-bound* translation: the first being approximately 'normal' or 'free' translation in which SL–TL equivalences are set up at whatever rank is appropriate. Usually, but not always, there is sentence–sentence equivalence,[5] but in the course of a text, equivalences may shift up and down the rank-scale, often being established at ranks lower than the sentence. We use the term 'rank-bound' translation only to refer to those special cases where equivalence is *deliberately limited* to ranks below the sentence, thus leading to 'bad translation' = i.e. translation in which the TL text is either not a normal TL form at all, or is not relatable to the same situational substance as the SL text.

In normal, unbounded, translation, then, translation equivalences may occur between sentences, clauses, groups, words and (though rarely) morphemes. The following is an example where equivalence can be established to some extent right down to morpheme rank:

Fr. SL text   J'ai laissé mes lunettes sur la table
Eng. TL text   I've left my glasses on the table

---

3 [Catford's note] Another possibility would be '*What did he get done?*', but this would be stylistically less satisfactory.
4 [Catford's note] Examples from Vinay et Darbelnet, *Stylistique Comparée du français et de l'anglais*, p. 99.
5 [Catford's note] W. Freeman Twaddell has drawn my attention to the fact that in German-English translation, equivalence may be rather frequently established between the German *sentence* and an English unit greater than the sentence, e.g. *paragraph*.

Text B4.1
J. C. Catford

Not infrequently, however, one cannot set up simple equal-rank equivalence between SL and TL texts. An SL *group* may have a TL *clause* as its translation equivalent, and so on.

Changes of rank (unit-shifts) are by no means the only changes of this type which occur in translation; there are also changes of *structure*, changes of *class*, changes of *term* in systems, etc. Some of these – particularly *structure-changes* – are even more frequent than rank-changes.

It is changes of these types which we refer to as *category-shifts*. The concept of 'category-shift' is necessary in the discussion of translation; but it is clearly meaningless to talk about category-shift unless we assume some degree of formal correspondence between SL and TL; indeed this is the main justification for the recognition of formal correspondence in our theory. Category-shifts are *departures from formal correspondence* in translation.

We give here a brief discussion and illustration of category-shift, in the order *structure-shifts*, *class-shifts*, *unit-shifts* (rank-changes), *intra-system-shifts*.

1.21 *Structure-shifts*. These are amongst the most frequent category shifts at all ranks in translation; they occur in *phonological* and *graphological* translation as well as in *total translation*.

1.211 In *grammar*, structure-shifts can occur at all ranks. The following English–Gaelic instance is an example of *clause-structure shift*.

SL text   *John loves Mary*   = SPC [Subject, Predicate, Complement]
TL text   *Tha gradh aig Iain air Mairi* = PSCA [A = Adjunct]

(A rank-bound word-word back-translation of the Gaelic TL text gives us: *Is love at John on Mary*.)

We can regard this as a structure-shift only on the assumption that there is formal correspondence between English and Gaelic. We must posit that the English elements of clause-structure S, P, C, A have formal correspondents S, P, C, A in Gaelic; this assumption appears reasonable, and so entitles us to say that a Gaelic PSCA structure as translation equivalent of English SPC represents a *structure-shift* insofar as it contains different elements.

But the Gaelic clause not only contains different elements – it also places two of these (S and P) in a different sequence. Now, if the sequence S$\overrightarrow{P}$ were the only possible sequence in English (as P$\overrightarrow{S}$ is in Gaelic) we could ignore the *sequence* and, looking only [at] the particular elements, S and P, say that the English and Gaelic structures were the same as far as *occurrence* in them of S and P was concerned. But sequence *is* relevant in English and therefore [we] count it as a feature of the structure, and say that, in this respect, too, structure-shift occurs in the translation.

[1.212 . . .]

1.213 Structure-shifts can be found at other ranks, for example at group rank. In translation between English and French, for instance, there is often a shift from MH (modifier + head) to (M)HQ ((modifier +) head + qualifier), e.g. A *white house* (MH) = *Une maison blanche* (MHQ).

1.22 *Class-shifts*. Following Halliday, we define a *class* as 'that grouping of members of a given unit which is defined by operation in the structure of the unit next above'.

Text B4.1
J. C. Catford

Class-shift, then, occurs when the translation equivalent of an SL item is a member of a different class from the original item. Because of the logical dependence of class on structure (of the unit at the rank above) it is clear that structure-shifts usually entail class-shifts, though this may be demonstrable only at a secondary degree of delicacy.

For example, in the example given in 1.213 above (*a white house* = *une maison blanche*), the translation equivalent of the English *adjective* 'white' is the French adjective 'blanche'. Insofar as both 'white' and 'blanche' are exponents of the formally corresponding class *adjective* there is apparently no class-shift. However, at a further degree of delicacy we may recognize two sub-classes of adjectives; those operating at M and those operating at Q in Noungroup structure. (Q-adjectives are numerous in French, very rare in English.) Since English 'white' is an M-adjective and French 'blanche' is a Q-adjective it is clear that the shift from M to Q entails a class-shift.

In other cases, also exemplified in the translation of Ngps from English to French and vice-versa, class-shifts are more obvious: e.g. Eng. *a medical student* = Fr. *un étudiant en médecine*. Here the translation equivalent of the adjective *medical*, operating at M, is the adverbial phrase *en médecine*, operating at Q; and the lexical equivalent of the adjective *medical* is the noun *médecine*.

1.23 *Unit-shift*. By unit-shift we mean changes of rank – that is, departures from formal correspondence in which the translation equivalent of a unit at one rank in the SL is a unit at a different rank in the TL.

[. . .]

We use the term *intra-system shift* for those cases where the shift occurs *internally*, within a system; that is, for those cases where SL and TL possess systems which approximately correspond formally as to their constitution, but when translation involves selection of a non-corresponding term in the TL system.

It may, for example, be said that English and French possess formally corresponding systems of *number*. In each language, the system operates in *nominal groups*, and is characterized by concord between the exponents of S and P in clauses and so on. Moreover, in each language, the system is one of two terms – *singular* and *plural* – and these terms may also be regarded as formally corresponding. The exponents of the terms are differently distributed in the two languages – e.g. Eng. *the case/the cases* = Fr. *le cas/les cas* – but as terms in a number system *singular* and *plural* correspond formally at least to the extent that in both languages it is the term *plural* which is generally regarded as morphologically marked.

In translation, however, it quite frequently happens that this formal correspondence is departed from, i.e. where the translation equivalent of English *singular* is French *plural* and vice-versa.

e.g. advice   = des conseils
     news   = des nouvelles
     lightning   = des éclairs
     applause   = des applaudissements
     trousers   = le pantalon
     the dishes = la vaisselle
     the contents = le contenu etc.[6]

---

6 [Catford's note] cf. Vinay et Darbelnet, pp. 119–23.

Text B4.1
J. C. Catford

Again, we might regard English and French as having formally corresponding systems of deictic, particularly *articles*; each may be said to have four articles, *zero*, *definite*, *indefinite* and *partitive*. It is tempting, then, to set up a formal correspondence between the terms of the systems as in this table:

	French	English
Zero	–	–
Definite	le, la, l', les	the
Indefinite	un, une	a, an
Partitive	du, de la, de l', des	some, any

In translation, however, it sometimes happens that the equivalent of an article is not the formally corresponding term in the system:

e.g.

Il est – professeur.	He is *a* teacher.
Il a *la* jambe cassée.	He has *a* broken leg.
L'amour	Love
Du vin	Wine

In the following table we give the translation-equivalents of French articles found in French texts with English translations. The number of cases in which a French article has an English equivalent at word-rank is 6958, and the figures given here are percentages; the figure 64.6 against *le* for instance, means that the French definite article (le, la, l', les) has the English definite article as its translation equivalent in 64.6% of its occurrences.[7] By dividing each percentage by 100 we have equivalence probabilities – thus we may say that, within the limitations stated above, French *le*, etc., will have Eng. *the* as its translation equivalent with probability .65.

French		English			
	zero	the	some	a	(other)
zero	**67.7**	6.1	0.3	11.2	4.6
le	14.2	**64.6**	–	2.4	18.9
du	**51.3**	9.5	11.0	5.9	22.4
un	6.7	5.8	2.2	**70.2**	15.1

It is clear from this table that translation equivalence does not entirely match formal correspondence. The most striking divergence is in the case of the French partitive article, *du*, the most frequent equivalent of which is *zero* and not *some*. This casts doubt on the advisability of setting up *any* formal correspondence between the particular terms of the English and French article-systems.

---

7   [Catford's note] I am indebted to Dr. R. Huddleston for this information.

Task B4.1.2

Catford claims that 'cases of more or less incomplete shift from grammar to lexis are quite frequent in translation between other languages' and gives the example of the English deictic *this* being translated by the French lexical adjective *présent*.

➤ Can you think of other examples of this happening in ST–TT pairs in languages you know and in translations you have seen?

➤ From your own observations of translation, find examples from languages you know of the 'group-to-clause equal-**rank equivalence**' of which Catford speaks.

Vinay and Darbelnet's detailed list of 'translation **procedures**' is the **taxonomy** that has been most frequently employed by those investigating **translation shifts**. The following extract presents a summary of their seven **procedures**, divided into two methods: (1) **direct** or **literal** translation and (2) **oblique** translation.

Task B4.2.1

➤ Before you read Text B4.2, look back at Section A and Section B of Unit 3 (on the **unit of translation**) which discuss Vinay and Darbelnet's analysis of the **translation unit** as a preparation for **translation shift** analysis. What were the different translation segments proposed? Which seemed most logical to you?

➤ Look back at Section A, Unit 2 and make sure you are familiar with the discussion on **literal** and **free** translation. You will note that Vinay and Darbelnet's use of the term below is somewhat different.

➤ As you read the following text, give examples of each of the seven **procedures** set out in the extract and summarize the reasons the authors advance for using each.

➤ Make a note of the translation and linguistic terminology used by the authors and add this to your terminological glossary with a short definition you find useful.

Text B4.2
J.-P. Vinay and
J. Darbelnet

Jean-Paul Vinay and Jean Darbelnet (1958/1995) *Comparative Stylistics of French and English*, **trans. J. Sager and M-J. Hamel, Amsterdam and Philadelphia: John Benjamins, pp. 30-41 (abridged).**

Generally speaking, translators can choose from two methods of translating, namely direct, or literal, translation and oblique translation. In some translation tasks it may

Text B4.2
J.-P. Vinay and
J. Darbelnet

be possible to transpose the source language message element by element into the target language, because it is based on either (i) parallel categories, in which case we can speak of structural parallelism, or (ii) on parallel concepts, which are the result of metalinguistic parallelisms. But translators may also notice gaps, or 'lacunae', in the TL which must be filled by corresponding elements, so that the overall impression is the same for the two messages.

It may, however, also happen that, because of structural or metalinguistic differences, certain stylistic effects cannot be transposed into the TL without upsetting the syntactic order, or even the lexis. In this case it is understood that more complex methods have to be used which at first may look unusual but which nevertheless can permit translators a strict control over the reliability of their work: these procedures are called oblique translation methods. In the listing which follows, the first three procedures are direct and the others are oblique.

Procedure 1: Borrowing

To overcome a lacuna, usually a metalinguistic one (e.g. a new technical process, an unknown concept), borrowing is the simplest of all translation methods. It would not even merit discussion in this context if translators did not occasionally need to use it in order to create a stylistic effect. For instance, in order to introduce the flavour of the SL culture into a translation, foreign terms may be used, e.g. such Russian words as 'roubles', 'datchas' and 'apparatchik', 'dollars' and 'party' from American English, Mexican Spanish food names 'tequila' and 'tortillas', and so on. [. . .]

Procedure 2: Calque

A calque is a special kind of borrowing whereby a language borrows an expression form of another, but then translates literally each of its elements. The result is either:

i.   a lexical calque, as in the first example below, i.e. a calque which respects the syntactic structure of the TL, whilst introducing a new mode of expression; or
ii. a structural calque, as in the second example, below, which introduces a new construction into the language, e.g.:

English-French calque
Compliments of the Season   : Compliments de la saison!
Science-fiction   : Science-fiction

Procedure 3: Literal translation

Literal, or word for word, translation is the direct transfer of a SL text into a grammatically and idiomatically appropriate TL text in which the translators' task is limited to observing the adherence to the linguistic servitudes of the TL.

I left my spectacles on   : J'ai laissé mes lunettes sur la
the table downstairs   table en bas.

If, after trying the first three procedures, translators regard a literal translation [as] unacceptable, they must turn to the methods of oblique translation. By unacceptable we mean that the message, when translated literally:

i. gives another meaning
ii. has no meaning, or
iii. is structurally impossible, or
iv. does not have a corresponding expression within the metalinguistic experience of the TL, or
v. has a corresponding expression, but not within the same register.

Procedure 4: Transposition

The method called Transposition involves replacing one word class with another without changing the meaning of the message. Beside being a special translation procedure, transposition can also be applied within a language. For example: 'Il a annoncé qu'il reviendrait' [He announced he would return], can be re-expressed by transposing a subordinate verb with a noun, thus: 'Il a annoncé son retour' [He announced his return]. In contrast to the first expression, which we call the base expression, we refer to the second one as the transposed expression. From a stylistic point of view, the base and the transposed expression do not necessarily have the same value. Translators must, therefore, choose to carry out a transposition if the translation thus obtained fits better the utterance or allows a particular nuance of style to be retained. Indeed, the transposed form is generally more literary in character.

Procedure 5: Modulation

Modulation is a variation of the form of the message, obtained by a change in the point of view. This change can be justified when, although a literal, or even transposed, translation results in a grammatically correct utterance, it is considered unsuitable, unidiomatic or awkward in the TL.

As with transposition, we distinguish between free or optional modulation and those which are fixed or obligatory. A classical example of an obligatory modulation is the phrase, 'The time when . . .', which must be translated as 'le moment où . . .' [the moment where . . .]. The type of modulation which turns a negative SL expression into a positive TL expression is more often than not optional, even though this is closely linked with the structure of each language, e.g.:

It is not difficult to show . . .   : Il est facile de démontrer . . .
                                       [lit. It is easy to show . . .]

Procedure 6: Equivalence

We have repeatedly stressed that one and the same situation can be rendered by two texts using completely different stylistic and structural methods. In such cases we are dealing with the method which produces equivalent texts. The classical example of equivalence is given by the reaction of an amateur who accidentally hits his finger with a hammer: if he were French his cry of pain would be transcribed as 'Aïe!', but if he were English this would be interpreted as 'Ouch!'.

Most equivalences are fixed and belong to a phraseological repertoire of idioms, clichés, proverbs, nominal or adjectival phrases, etc. In general, proverbs are perfect examples of equivalences, e.g.:

Like a bull in a china shop   : Comme un chien dans un jeu de quilles.
                                  [lit. Like a dog in a game of skittles]

Too many cooks spoil the broth	: Deux patrons font chavirer la barque.
	[lit. *Two skippers make the boat capsize*]

Text B4.2
J.-P. Vinay and
J. Darbelnet

The method of creating equivalences is also frequently applied to idioms. For example, 'To talk through one's hat' and 'as like as two peas' cannot be translated by means of a calque.

Procedure 7: Adaptation

With this seventh method we reach the extreme limit of translation: it is used in those cases where the type of situation being referred to by the SL message is unknown in the TL culture. In such cases translators have to create a new situation that can be considered as being equivalent. Adaptation can, therefore, be described as a special kind of equivalence, a situational equivalence. [They] are particularly frequent in the translation of book and film titles, e.g.:

Trois hommes et un couffin	: Three Men and a Baby
[*Three men and a Moses basket*]	
Le grand Meaulne	: The Wanderer
[The *Big Meaulne* – a character's name]	

Task B4.2.2

➤ How does Vinay and Darbelnet's definition of literal translation fit with the definition given in Section A, Unit 2?

➤ Translate the examples in this extract into other languages you know. Do the same **shifts** occur in those languages or are there important differences? What might this suggest about the language-sensitivity of **shifts**?

➤ If possible, locate the fuller description of translation **procedures** in Vinay and Darbelnet (1958/1995) or the chapter in Venuti (2000). Note the most important additional subdivisions of **procedures** and add these to your translation **glossary** with a short definition you find useful.

Unit B5
The analysis of meaning

Section A of Unit 5 dealt with some of the ways in which a more systematic measurement of meaning was introduced into Translation Studies by Eugene Nida in the 1960s. He adapted for the analysis of translation some of the techniques in use at the time in linguistics. These included **disambiguation** using **semantic structure** analysis and **componential analysis**.

Although Nida's 'scientific' approach to translation has been heavily criticized by some translation scholars (for example, Gentzler 2001) for failing to account for the cultural implications of translation, it continues to exert influence notably for the many practical translation examples that it provides. The extract in this section is from Mildred Larson's *Meaning-Based Translation*, first published in 1984 with a revised second edition in 1998. Larson follows Nida's description of translation as 'a process which begins with the ST, analyses this text into **semantic structure**, and then restructures this **semantic structure** into appropriate receptor language forms in order to create an equivalent receptor language text' (Larson 1984/1998: 519). Text B5.1 below looks at some of the ways of analysing the **semantic structure** of the ST, and of comparing the range of SL terms with corresponding TL terms, in preparation for the **restructuring** phase. The whole three-fold process is examined in more detail in Section A, Unit 6.

 Task B5.1.1

➤ Before you read Text B5.1, look back at Section A, Unit 5 and consider the different **semantic** problems described and the techniques discussed for coping with them. Make sure you are clear on the difference between **referential** and **connotative** meaning.

➤ Whilst reading Text B5.1, list the different ways described by Larson for 'discovering' meaning.

➤ Make a note of limitations or **prescriptive** statements made by the author for this type of analysis. What factors does the author state are necessary when using these techniques?

Mildred L. Larson (1984/1998) *Meaning-Based Translation*, **2nd edition Lanham, New York and Oxford: University Press of America, pp. 87-95.**

Text B5.1
M. L. Larson

Discovering meaning by grouping and contrast

The meaning of a lexical item can only be discovered by studying that particular item in contrast to others which are closely related. There is no meaning apart from significant differences or contrasts. By grouping together words which are related to one another and then systematically looking at the contrast between these words, one is able to determine the meaning. The shared meaning components and the contrastive meaning components can thus be described more precisely. Lexical items are related in various ways and occur in various kinds of semantic sets.

Part–whole relations

One way in which languages group words is by the relationship known as part-whole. For example, in English *chin, cheek, forehead, nose,* and *ear* are all parts of the *head. Head, hand, neck, trunk, arms, legs,* and *feet* are part of the *body.* There are many sets made up of words in a part-whole relationship in any language. There will be sets of words describing parts of a house, parts of a machine, parts of a village, the structural organization of a country, political organizations, and many others. When a translator is studying the part-whole groupings of two languages, it will often become clear that there is no exact equivalent for some of the words. Some will be missing in one language or another. The reason for this is that languages classify and subdivide broad areas of knowledge in different ways. Slavic languages, for example, do not have separate words for *arm* and *hand.* The Russian word *ruka* includes both the *arm* and the *hand.* In the same way, the word *noga* includes both *leg* and *foot.* One word in Russian covers the part of the body which in English is represented by two lexical items.

Contrastive pairs

Contrastive pairs may be very helpful in determining the meaning of particular words. For example, a person who is translating Russian terminology will need to discover the difference between a *party congress* and a *party conference,* a *worker* and an *employee,* a *technical school* and a *trade school,* and a *territory* and a *national area.* When the source language has closely related pairs like these, it will be very important for the translator to find the components of meaning which distinguish the one from the other if he is to translate accurately.

In English, the words *meat* and *flesh* represent distinctions which are not shared by many languages of the world where only one word is used to cover both areas of meaning. The word *meat* has an added component of meaning, i.e., *food.* The Aguaruna word *neje* must be used to translate both *flesh* and *meat.* The context will make it clear if food is meant.

The principle of contrast in identifying meaning is very important. However, before any two lexical items are to be compared, they must belong to a system of some kind. There would be no advantage to comparing the word *leg* with the word *house.* They do not make a pair for comparison. On the other hand, a great deal can be learned about the meaning of words by comparing *leg* with other body parts and comparing *house* with other kinds of buildings. Therefore, in order to study meaning, it is necessary to have words in sets which share some features of meaning and have some contrastive features as well.

SECTION B

Extension

Text B5.1
M. L. Larson

There are pairs of words in all languages which differ from one another only by a single component of meaning. For example, *show* and *see* contrast only in that *show* has the additional meaning of *cause to*. That is, *show* means *to cause to see*. Other words with this same relationship would be *drop* and *fall* and *make* and *be*. To *drop* is *to cause to fall*, and *to make* is *to cause to be*. There is a common component of meaning, *causative*, in *show*, *drop*, and *make*. It is not uncommon that a language will have no exact equivalent, no word, for *show*, *drop*, and *make*. Rather, there will be some form which will indicate *causative* which will be used with *see*, *fall*, and *be*.

Componential analysis

The meaning components of words may also be more easily isolated by looking at lexical matrices. The pronominal systems of the source and receptor languages should be compared to see where there are differences between the two systems which might cause problems in translation. Once the systems are understood, there is the additional need to study the function of pronominal forms in the discourse of the language. When displaying a lexical set in a chart, the words go into the boxes, and the columns are labeled by the meaning components which are the basis of contrast between the words. Notice, for example, Displays 5.1, 5.2, 5.3, and 5.4 of the subject pronoun systems of a number of languages (Strange and Deibler 1974: 18-19):

English

	singular			plural
1st person	*I*			*we*
2nd person	*you*			
3rd person	masculine	feminine	neuter	
	he	*she*	*it*	*they*

Display 5.1

Greek

	singular			plural		
1st person	εγώ			ἡμεῖς		
2nd person	σύ			ὑμεῖς		
3rd person	masculine	feminine	neuter	masculine	feminine	neuter
	αὐτός	αὐτή	αὐτό	αὐτοί	αὐταί	αὐτά

Display 5.2

Pidgin

	singular	dual	plural	
			inclusive	exclusive
1st person	*mi*	*mitupela*	*yumi*	*mipela*
2nd person	*yu*	*yutupela*	*yupela*	
3rd person	*em*	*tupela*	*ol*	

Display 5.3

Text B5.1
M. L. Larson

Upper Asaro	singular	plural
1st person	naza	laza
2nd person	gaza	lingine
3rd person	aza	ingine

Display 5.4

Note that English and Greek distinguish gender. Pidgin of Papua New Guinea does not indicate gender but does have an additional member contrast, dual, and also differentiates *inclusive* and *exclusive* in *first person*. In Upper Asaro (Papua New Guinea), free pronouns distinguish neither *gender, dual member,* nor *inclusive* and *exclusive.*

It may be helpful to the translator to make displays which show the contrastive features of meaning for certain areas of vocabulary. Such mapping is arrived at by **componential analysis**. (For a more complete discussion, see Nida 1975.) **Componential analysis** has often been used to analyse kinship systems (see Lounsbury 1956).

Certain areas of a language lend themselves to **componential analysis** better than other areas. It can be very helpful for those areas where it does apply. It is essential that the words have a relationship one to another which is based on shared and contrasting features. In order to do **componential analysis** of this kind, there needs to be some non-linguistic behavior that shows the contrast between the symbols. For example, the contrast between generation in kinship can be observed, like the contrast between older and younger, and male and female.

Displays 5.5 and 5.6 show the mapping of English kinship terms and Aguaruna kinship terms. The lexical items are in the boxes of the chart and the labels show the contrast in meaning of these lexical items. Because we can correlate each lexical item with people in the non-linguistic world and what they call one another or how they refer to one another, it is possible to analyse these terms.

English	lineal		colineal		ablineal
	masculine	feminine	masculine	feminine	
second generation previous	grandfather	grandmother	uncle	aunt	cousin
previous generation	father	mother			
same generation	ego		brother	sister	
next generation	son	daughter	nephew	niece	
second generation following	grandson	granddaughter			

Display 5.5

Notice that English has two words, *brother* and *sister*, which in Aguaruna [see following page] are three words – *yatsug, ubag,* and *kaig.* Which of the three words is used depends on who is talking. A male calls his sister *ubag* and his brother *yatsug;* whereas, a female calls her sister *kaig* and her brother *ubag.* There are languages in which one cannot simply say *brother* because there may be two or more words to choose from.

Javanese divides this same area of meaning into three terms, but with different components. The forms are *mas* for 'older brother,' *emhag* for 'older sister,' and *adig* for

Aguaruna

	Own lineage		Other lineage	
	masculine	feminine	feminine	masculine
second generation previous	apach	dukuch		diich
previous generation	apag	dukug		
same generation — ego — male	yatsug	ubag	antsug	saig
same generation — ego — female	ubag	kaig	yuag	antsug
next generation	uchi	nawantu	nuwasa	ajika
second generation following	tijagki			

Display 5.6

'younger sibling.' A translator must carefully study and compare the kinship terminology of the source language and the receptor language. Each time a kinship term
needs to be translated, the translator should consider carefully the referent in the
nonlinguistic world, and how that person would be referred to, rather than simply
translating literally the word that looks like the closest equivalent.

The kind of analysis we have been talking about points to the fact that each word
is a bundle of meaning components, and that we can discover these by contrasting
one word with another when these words are part of a system; that is, when they are
related in some way. There would be no point in comparing words if there were not
some shared components. In order to form a set, all of the words must contain a
generic component in common. For example, all of the above have the shared
component of KINSHIP.

Kinds of meaning components

We can make a display for the English words *man*, *woman*, *boy*, and *girl*, because they
are all human beings. They have a generic component which they share as the central
component, HUMAN BEING (see Display 5.7).

	MALE	FEMALE
ADULT	man	woman
YOUNG	boy	girl

Display 5.7

In addition to the central component, each word will have contrastive components
which distinguish it from all other words of the set. *Man* has the contrastive
components ADULT and MALE, *woman* has the contrastive components ADULT and
FEMALE, *boy* has the contrastive components YOUNG and MALE, and *girl* has the
contrastive components YOUNG and FEMALE. Each word contrasts with every other
word by at least one contrastive component.

The meaning component which unites any semantic set of this kind is called the generic component or the central component. The meaning components which distinguish them one from the other, and have been used as labels for the displays, are contrastive components. These are the components which help in distinguishing one word from another in the set.

Very often two languages will have the same set as far as the generic component is concerned, but the contrastive components will be different. There may be more lexical items or less lexical items in the set, and the contrastive components may not match. For example, the set for HUMAN in English is given in Display 5.7 and the set for Aguaruna is given in Display 5.8.

		MALE	FEMALE
ADULT	married	*aishmang*	*nuwa*
	unmarried	*datsa*	
YOUNG		*uchi*	*nuwauch* (female-little)

Display 5.8

Notice that there is an added contrast in Aguaruna for ADULT MALE in that there are two words, one having the added contrastive component of MARRIED and the other of UNMARRIED. Also notice that the contrast between ADULT FEMALE and YOUNG FEMALE can only be indicated by adding a suffix *-uch* to the word for ADULT FEMALE. This suffix means *little* so that the word for FEMALE CHILD is *little woman*. (However, the suffix is clearly related in form to the word for YOUNG MALE.)

In the previous chapter, we discussed hierarchical relationships between words; that is, taxonomies. Here, also, the taxonomy is based on the shared generic components and contrastive components which distinguish one lexical item from another. For example, notice Display 5.9 (Beekman and Callow 1974: 70).

Display 5.9

Notice that all of the words in this set belong to the generic class of *furniture*. The contrastive components which separate *table, chair, wardrobe, cabinet*, and *cupboard* will have to do with the shape and the use of these particular pieces of furniture. *Chair* is then the generic component for *armchair, rocking chair, deck chair*, and *baby chair*. The meaning of these phrases again depends upon contrastive components which have to do with shape and use. If a translator is working on a text which includes terminology relating to the generic class of *furniture* he will need to think very carefully through the contrastive components in the source language vocabulary and in the receptor language vocabulary in order to choose the best equivalent. If there is no exact equivalent, he may need to include the right components by restating, as indicated previously, when the contrast is focal to the meaning of the sentence or paragraph. If not, he will simply choose the nearest equivalent without further detail.

In looking at the meaning of the lexical items which belong to the same semantic set, one needs to first identify the class to which it belongs (the generic term). Then the individual lexical items belonging to that class can be studied in contrast, the one with the other. For example, *command, promise, rebuke, ask, reply,* and *announce* are ways of speaking; that is, they all belong to the generic class termed *speak*. Because they belong to a common set, the meaning of each can be identified by contrast. Another language may also have a set of lexical items which are part of the semantic domain *speak*, but they may be very different from this set in English. For example, the Waiwai language of Guyana (data from Hawkins 1962) does not have verbs meaning *promise, praise,* and *deny*. The meaning is simply included in the content of the quotation which goes with the verb *say*.

The generic, or central, meaning component can be said to be more prominent than the other components. Within the word *boy*, the meaning component HUMAN BEING is more prominent than MALE or YOUNG which simply delimits HUMAN. In the sentence 'The boy is here,' the component of HUMAN is used with natural prominence. However, in certain contexts, one of the contrastive components may come into focus and, therefore, carry marked prominence. For example, in the sentence 'The boy, not the girl, lost the race,' marked prominence is on MALE which is a noncentral component; that is, it is a contrastive component. In the sentences 'A boy cannot accomplish this task. It will take a man to do it,' marked prominence is on YOUNG (immaturity), the other noncentral component.

The components of meaning found in the word boy can be diagrammed as shown in Display 5.10:

Display 5.10

The relationship between the two contrastive components and the central component, HUMAN, is one of delimitation, that is, HUMAN is delimited to refer only to a HUMAN that is YOUNG and MALE. The relationship between the central component and the contrastive components is always one of delimitation; the contrastive components delimit (narrow down the meaning of) the central component.

In addition to the central component and the contrastive components, there are often incidental (or supplementary) components. Their presence or absence is incidental for the contrast needed to differentiate a certain set of terms. At another level of study (more specific), these same components may be contrastive components. What is generic, contrastive, or incidental depends on the level of focus of the analysis. It depends on the level of the taxonomic hierarchy at which one is looking.

For example, in contrasting *kinds of furniture*, it is not relevant if the object has *arms* or not. *Chair* is *something to sit on* in contrast to *table, bed*, etc. However, if one is describing the semantic set *kinds of chairs*, then having *arms* is no longer incidental but is contrastive. Also, in moving up from *kinds of furniture* to a more generic class of *human artifacts*, the component *to sit on* which was contrastive for *furniture* is no longer contrastive but only incidental. Since the translator is concerned with the meaning of words, he will often need to investigate minute differences between words in a semantic set. It is the contrastive components that he will want to focus on.

Task B5.1.2

➤ Look at the examples given by Larson to illustrate the discovery techniques. Select some of the examples and consider how these would be translated into languages that you know. Are there languages for which the discovery techniques do not work?

Text B5.1 extract begins with the words 'The meaning of a lexical item can only be discovered by studying that particular item in contrast to others which are closely related. There is no meaning apart from significant differences or contrasts.'

➤ Consider Section A of this unit as well. Make a list of the forms of contrast that have been used. What meaning concepts in this unit do not lend themselves to analysis by contrast?

The techniques described by Larson generally presuppose a rather static form of meaning or of the relation between a given term and the real world.

➤ Think how these techniques might be expanded to encompass the shades of meaning acquired by language in its socio-cultural context.

Unit B6
Dynamic equivalence and the receptor of the message

In Section A, Unit 6, we presented **dynamic equivalence**, compared it with **formal equivalence** and discussed the search for the appropriate kind of equivalence in terms of a three-stage model of the translation process: **analysis, transfer** and **re-structuring**. The approach, developed by American Bible translator and linguist Eugene Nida, is broadly informed by psycho- and socio-linguistics. On the psycho-linguistic front, the model seems to have followed the then fashionable **trans-formational generative** linguistics, and, as with other 'applications' of linguistics, this was perhaps to the detriment eventually of the richness of the application. However, as a model which for the first time explicitly captures the process of translation, Nida's approach has beyond any doubt been extremely influential to the present day. It has inspired research in this area of Translation Studies and has specifically guided the study of Bible translation contexts around the globe (see reports published regularly by the United Bible Societies, for example, http://www.ubs-translations.org/).

It is in fact within the ambit of this approach that Nida's central thesis concerning **equivalence** and text receiver response may best be understood. Raising these issues from an essentially socio-linguistic perspective has helped significantly in widening the focus on the analysis of 'meaning' to take into account a variety of textual, contextual and cultural factors seen in relation to the translation process. While still working within dynamic equivalence as a general framework, translators and translation analysts have explored a number of new avenues in an attempt to achieve **dynamic equivalence** and attain the promised 'fluency' without necessarily sacrificing authenticity (e.g. Hu 1994).

The texts below are drawn from Nida's own work and deal with two subjects: (1) the process model of translation, and (2) the notion of dynamic equivalence.

 Task B6.1.1

➤ Before you read Text B6.1, refer back to Sections A and B, Unit 5 ('The analysis of meaning') for a description of basic concepts such as **denotation** (**referential meaning**) vs **connotation** (**emotive meaning**). Using good dictionaries of linguistics and translation (see Introduction), look up these concepts and also prepare brief statements on **syntactic** vs **semotactic** structures.

➤ Using basic reference works in Translation Studies (see Introduction), read up on the important three-way distinction: **literal/formal/dynamic equivalence**. Revise the distinctions between **literal** and **free translation** presented in Section A, Unit 2.

➤ Reflect on how **formal equivalence** should not be equated exclusively with **denotational meaning**, and list the differences. Features of **style** and **genre**, for example, are at some level 'formal' and can indeed be accommodated within **formal equivalence**. Similarly, '**dynamic**' continues to cater for formal aspects of ST meaning, alongside **connotational meaning** and **audience** response.

➤ Whilst reading the following text, make a list of features of what the author takes to be formal and functional aspects of **connotation, denotation, style, genre**, etc.

➤ Identify activities associated with the various processing stages. For example, **analysis** involves assessing ST **style** or **genre**.

➤ Focus on procedures normally resorted to in the stage of '**restructuring**' the target message. Create a list of these. If you can, check them with a fellow student.

Eugene A. Nida (1969) 'Science of Translation', *Language* 45.3, pp. 483-98.

Text B6.1
E. A. Nida

A careful analysis of exactly what goes on in the process of translating, especially in the case of source and receptor languages having quite different grammatical and semantic structures, has shown that, instead of going directly from one set of surface structures to another, the competent translator actually goes through a seemingly roundabout process of analysis, transfer, and restructuring. That is to say, the translator first analyses the message of the SOURCE language into its simplest and structurally clearest forms, transfers it at this level, and then restructures it to the level in the RECEPTOR language, which is most appropriate for the audience which he intends to reach. Such a set of related procedures may be represented diagrammatically as in *Figure* 6.1.

Figure 6.1

[. . .]

Connotative meaning of syntactic and semotactic structures

The analysis of a text in the source language must not be limited to a study of the syntactic relationships between linguistic units or to the denotative (or referential) meanings of these same units. Analysis must also treat the emotive (or connotative) values of the formal structure of the communication. At this point, however, we specifically exclude the emotive response to the thematic content of the communication. This is something outside the realm of linguistics though quite naturally one's enthusiasm for or dissatisfaction with the theme of a communication tends to color the emotive reactions to the syntactic and semantic structures of the message.

The connotative evaluation of the formal structures of the message is essentially an analysis of the style of the communication. But to accomplish this, one must obviously not be restricted to the sentence as the upper level of linguistic relevance. Stylistic factors affect the total form of any message, from the level of sound symbolism to the limits of the discourse. However, the principal area of stylistic concern is the discourse, not primarily the pleasing sound patterns or the juxtaposition of semotactically felicitous phrases. The analysis and evaluation of the stylistic features of a message involve a number of highly complex techniques, which cannot be treated within the scope of this paper. What is, however, perhaps even more important is a delineation of the essential elements involved in such an analysis. This will help materially in pointing out the essential parallelism between the two sets of formal features: the syntactic and the semotactic.

[. . .]

Restructuring

Describing the process of analysis and transfer is much easier than dealing with the processes of restructuring, for the latter depends so much upon the structures of each individual receptor language. Moreover, there are two principal dimensions of such restructuring (formal and functional) which must be fully considered if one is to understand something of the implications of this essential procedure.

The first formal dimension requires one to determine the stylistic level at which one should aim in the process of restructuring. In general there are three principal alternatives: technical, formal, and informal (for some literary genres, there are also casual and intimate levels of language). Perhaps the greatest mistake is to reproduce formal or informal levels in the source language by something which is technical in the receptor language. This is what has happened consistently in the translation of Paul's letters to the early churches. Rather than sounding like pastoral letters, they have turned out to be highly technical treatises. Such a shifting of levels is an almost inevitable consequence of not having thoroughly understood the original intent of a message, for when there is any appreciable doubt as to the meaning of any message, we almost instinctively react by raising its literary language level.

The second formal dimension involves the literary genre, e.g. epic poetry, proverbs, parables, historical narrative, personal letters, and ritual hymns. Though languages with long literary traditions have much more highly standardized literary genres, even some of the seemingly most primitive peoples have quite elaborate forms of oral literature, involving a number of distinct types; hence there is much more likelihood of formal correspondence than most people imagine. However, the real problems are not in the existence of the corresponding literary genres, but in the manner in which such diverse forms are regarded by the people in question. For example, epic and didactic poetry are very little used in the western world, but in many parts of Asia they are very popular and have much of the same value that they possessed in biblical times. But for most [people] in the western world, presenting the prophetic utterances of the Old Testament in poetic form, as the closest formal equivalence, often results in serious lack of appreciation [of] the urgency of the prophet's message, which was put into poetic form in order to enhance its impact and to make the form more readily remembered. Such poetic forms are often interpreted by [people] in the western world as implying a lack of urgency, because poetic forms have become associated with communications which are over-aestheticized and hence not relevant to the practical events of men's daily lives.

In addition to two formal dimensions in restructuring, one must also reckon with a functional, or dynamic, dimension, related in many respects to impact. At this point especially, the role of the receptor is crucial, for a translation can be judged as adequate only if the response of the intended receptor is satisfactory.

By focusing proper attention upon the role of the receptors of any translation, one is inevitably led to a somewhat different definition of translation than has been customarily employed. This means that one may now define translating as 'reproducing in the receptor language the closest natural equivalent of the message of the source language, first in terms of meaning and second in terms of style'.

Task B6.1.2

Having read Text B6.1, consider this important claim by Nida:

We specifically exclude the emotive response to the thematic content of the communication. This is something outside the realm of linguistics though quite naturally one's enthusiasm for or dissatisfaction with the theme of a communication tends to color the emotive reactions to the syntactic and semantic structures of the message.

➤ Do you agree with Nida that this kind of emotive response to thematic content should be excluded from the purview of what we translate? What about a writer's (or a translator's) own **ideology**? Is this an aspect of writing/translating that can be ignored? Justify your response.

Consider Nida's statement: 'Stylistic factors affect the total form of any message, from the level of sound symbolism to the limits of the discourse.'

➤ What are the two principal dimensions of **restructuring** (formal and functional) which must be considered?

➤ Assuming corresponding literary **genre**s exist in the SL and TL, identify any other factors that determine the success of reproducing the ST **genre** in the TL.

Task B6.2.1

As we saw in the discussion in Section A, Unit 2, in analysing a text to be translated, **form** vs **content** is an important distinction. Before you read Text B6.2 note the important claim that 'in the same way as there is no form-less content, there is no content-less form'.

➤ Can you find support for this from your own experience as a translator?

➤ Is it helpful to work with the idea that, in a given context, although **form** and **content** are inextricably linked, the two aspects are not necessarily always equally prominent? Adhering to one or the other, that is, **form** or **content**, can therefore be an important choice to make. Give examples to support your answer.

➤ From your own experience as a student of translation or as a translator, propose examples where an author's **purpose** and a translator's **purpose** are similar or at least compatible, and where the two may diverge.

➤ In the absence of a clear specification of a target readership, what kind of virtual audience would you as a translator normally envisage?

➤ As you read Text B6.2, update your **glossary** with the different types of translation referred to in this reading. Note for example the many more grades of translating than these **literal–free** extremes imply.

➤ Make notes on how different types of translation may be distinguished in terms of (a) the nature of the message, (b) the **purpose** of the author and (c) the type of **audience**. Demonstrate whether such factors cannot be equally prominent in any act of translating, using examples from translations with which you are familiar.

Text B6.2
E. A. Nida

Eugene A. Nida (1964) *Toward a Science of Translating*, **Leiden, Netherlands: E.J. Brill, pp. 156-71.**

Different types of translations

No statement of the principles of correspondence in translating can be complete without recognizing the many different types of translations (Herbert P. Phillips 1959). Traditionally, we have tended to think in terms of free or paraphrastic translations as contrasted with close or literal ones. Actually, there are many more grades of translating than these extremes imply. There are, for example, such unilateral translations as interlinears while others involve highly concordant relationships, e.g. the same source-language word is always translated by one – and only one – receptor-language word. Still others may be quite devoid of artificial restrictions in form, but nevertheless may be over-traditional and even archaizing.

Some translations aim at very close formal and semantic correspondence, but are generously supplied with notes and commentary. Many are not so much concerned with giving information as with creating in the reader something of the same mood as was conveyed by the original.

Differences in translations can generally be accounted for by three basic factors in translating (1) the nature of the message, (2) the purpose or purposes of the author and, by proxy, of the translator, and (3) the type of audience.

Messages differ primarily in the degree to which content or form is the dominant consideration. Of course, the content of a message can never be completely abstracted from the form, and form is nothing apart from content; but in some messages the content is of primary consideration, and in others the form must be given a higher priority. For example, in the Sermon on the Mount, despite certain important stylistic qualities, the importance of the message far exceeds considerations of form. On the other hand, some of the acrostic poems of the Old Testament are obviously designed to fit a very strict formal 'straitjacket.' But even the contents of a message may differ widely in applicability to the receptor-language audience. For example, the folk tale of the Bauré Indians of Bolivia, about a giant who led the animals in a symbolic dance, is interesting to an English-speaking audience, but to them it has not the same relevance as the Sermon on the Mount. And even the Bauré Indians themselves recognize the Sermon on the Mount as [being] more significant than their favourite 'how-it-happened' story. At the same time, of course, the Sermon on the Mount has greater relevance to these Indians than have some passages in Leviticus.

In poetry there is obviously a greater focus of attention upon formal elements than one normally finds in prose. Not that content is necessarily sacrificed in the translation of a poem, but the content is necessarily constricted into certain formal moulds. Only rarely can one reproduce both content and form in a translation, and hence in general the form is usually sacrificed for the sake of the content. On the other hand, a lyric poem translated as prose is not an adequate equivalent of the original. Though it may reproduce the conceptual content, it falls far short of reproducing the emotional intensity and flavour. However, the translating of some types of poetry by prose may be dictated by important cultural considerations. For example, Homer's epic poetry reproduced in English poetic form usually seems to us antique and [odd] – with nothing of the liveliness and spontaneity characteristic of Homer's style. One reason is that we are not accustomed to having stories told to us in poetic form. In our western European tradition such epics are related in prose. For this reason, E.V. Rieu chose prose rather than poetry as the more appropriate medium by which to render *The Iliad* and *The Odyssey*.

The particular purposes of the translator are also important factors in dictating the type of translation. Of course, it is assumed that the translator has purposes generally similar to, or at least compatible with, those of the original author, but this is not necessarily so. For example, a San Blas story-teller is interested only in amusing his audience, but an ethnographer who sets about translating such stories may be much more concerned [to give] his audience an insight into San Blas' personality structure. Since, however, the purposes of the translator are the primary ones to be considered in studying the types of translation which result, the principal purposes that underlie the choice of one or another way to render a particular message are important.

The primary purpose of the translator may be information as to both content and form. One intended type of response to such an informative type of translation is largely cognitive, e.g. an ethnographer's translation of texts from informants, or a philosopher's translation of Heidegger. A largely informative translation may, on the other hand, be designed to elicit an emotional response of pleasure from the reader or listener.

A translator's purposes may involve much more than information. He may, for example, want to suggest a particular type of behaviour by means of a translation. Under such circumstances he is likely to aim at full intelligibility, and to make certain minor adjustments in detail so that the reader may understand the full implications of the message for his own circumstances. In such a situation a translator is not content to have receptors say, 'This is intelligible to us.' Rather, he is looking for some such response as, 'This is meaningful for us.' In terms of Bible translating, the people might understand a phrase such as 'to change one's mind about sin' as meaning 'repentance.' But if the indigenous way of talking about repentance is 'spit on the ground in front of,' as in Shilluk[1] spoken in the Sudan, the translator will obviously aim at the more meaningful idiom. On a similar basis, 'white as snow' may be rendered as 'white as egret feathers,' if the people of the receptor language are not acquainted with snow but speak of anything very white by this phrase.

A still greater degree of adaptation is likely to occur in a translation which has an imperative purpose. Here the translator feels constrained not merely to suggest a possible line of behaviour, but to make such an action explicit and compelling. He is not content to translate in such a way that the people are likely to understand; rather, he insists that the translation must be so clear that no one can possibly mis-understand.

In addition to the different types of messages and the diverse purposes of translators, one must also consider the extent to which prospective audiences differ both in decoding ability and in potential interest.

Decoding ability in any language involves at least four principal levels: (1) the capacity of children, whose vocabulary and cultural experience are limited; (2) the double-standard capacity of new literates, who can decode oral messages with facility but whose ability to decode written messages is limited; (3) the capacity of the average literate adult, who can handle both oral and written messages with relative ease; and (4) the unusually high capacity of specialists (doctors, theologians, philosophers, scientists, etc.), when they are decoding messages within their own area of specialization. Obviously a translation designed for children cannot be the same as one prepared for specialists, nor can a translation for children be the same as one for a newly literate adult.

Prospective audiences differ not only in decoding ability, but perhaps even more in their interests. For example, a translation designed to stimulate reading for pleasure will be quite different from one intended for a person anxious to learn how to assemble a complicated machine. Moreover, a translator of African myths for [people] who simply want to satisfy their curiosity about strange peoples and places will produce a different piece of work from one who renders these same myths in a form acceptable to linguists, who are more interested in the linguistic structure underlying the translation than in cultural novelty.

---

1 [Nida's note] This idiom is based upon the requirement that plaintiffs and defendants spit on the ground in front of each other when a case has been finally tried and punishment meted out. The spitting indicates that all is forgiven and that the accusations can never be brought into court again.

Two basic orientations in translating

Since 'there are, properly speaking, no such things as identical equivalents' (Belloc 1931 and 1931a: 37), one must in translating seek to find the closest possible equivalent. However, there are fundamentally two different types of equivalence: one, which may be called formal, and another, which is primarily dynamic.

Formal equivalence focuses all attention on the message itself, in both form and content. In such a translation one is concerned with such correspondences as poetry to poetry, sentence to sentence, and concept to concept. Viewed from this formal orientation one is concerned that the message in the receptor language should match as closely as possible the different elements in the source language. This means, for example, that the message in the receptor culture is constantly compared with the message in the source culture to determine standards of accuracy and correctness.

The type of translation which most completely typifies this structural equivalence might be called a 'gloss translation,' in which the translator attempts to reproduce as literally and meaningfully as possible the form and content of the original. Such a translation might be a rendering of some Medieval French text into English, intended for students of certain aspects of early French literature not requiring a knowledge of the original language of the text. Their needs call for a relatively close approximation to the structure of the early French text, both as to form (e g. syntax and idioms) and content (e.g. themes and concepts). Such a translation would require numerous footnotes in order to make the text fully comprehensible.

A gloss translation of this type is designed to permit the reader to identify himself as fully as possible with a person in the source-language context, and to understand as much as he can of the customs, manner of thought, and means of expression. For example, a phrase such as 'holy kiss' (Romans 16: 16) in a gloss translation would be rendered literally, and would probably be supplemented with a footnote explaining that this was a customary method of greeting in New Testament times.

In contrast, a translation which attempts to produce a dynamic rather than a formal equivalence is based upon 'the principle of equivalent effect' (Rieu and Phillips 1954). In such a translation one is not so concerned with matching the receptor-language message with the source-language message, but with the dynamic relationship, that the relationship between receptor and message should be substantially the same as that which existed between the original receptors and the message.

A translation of dynamic equivalence aims at complete naturalness of expression, and tries to relate the receptor to modes of behaviour relevant within the context of his own culture; it does not insist that he understand the cultural patterns of the source-language context in order to comprehend the message. Of course, there are varying degrees of such dynamic-equivalence translations. One of the modern English translations which, perhaps more than any other, seeks for equivalent effects is J. B. Phillips' rendering of the New Testament. In Romans 16: 16 he quite naturally translates 'greet one another with a holy kiss' as 'give one another a hearty handshake all around.'

Between the two poles of translating (i.e. between strict formal equivalence and complete dynamic equivalence) there are a number of intervening grades, representing various acceptable standards of literal translating. During the past fifty years, however, there has been a marked shift of emphasis from the formal to the dynamic dimension. A recent summary of opinion on translating by literary artists, publishers, educators, and professional translators indicates clearly that the present direction is toward increasing emphasis on dynamic equivalences (Cary 1959).

Task B6.2.2

➤ In formal translations, what methods may be used to enhance accessibility?

Of course, the **content** of a message can never be completely abstracted from the **form**, and **form** is nothing apart from **content**; but in some messages the content is of primary consideration, and in others the **form** must be given a higher priority.

➤ Can you think of some examples from your own experience (as a translator or translation analyst) where **form** has had to take priority over **content**? Is this the case only with a particular class of texts, or is it a valid assumption across the board?

Of course, it is assumed that the translator has purposes generally similar to, or at least compatible with, those of the original author, but this is not necessarily so.

➤ Can you think of some examples from your own experience in which the translator has had to depart from the author's intended **purpose**? If justified, what is the justification?

Unit B7
Textual pragmatics and equivalence

The 1970s saw the continued dominance of the linguistics paradigm, and the central issue in Translation Studies continued to be **equivalence**. There was a slight shift of focus, however, and models of translation began to show the influence not only of psycho- and socio-linguistics, but also and much more prominently of **pragmatics** – the study of the purposes for which utterances and texts are used. Encouraged by the so-called 'contextual turn' in linguistics, translation theorists like Werner Koller and Robert de Beaugrande argued vigorously for the new focus on textual **pragmatics** in translation.

In this body of theory and practice, we note in particular how formal uniformity is no longer so much emphasized: **form** is no longer so highly rated over **meaning**, nor the language system over **communicative context**. As we saw in Section A, Unit 7, the relevant issue for Koller was: what is translation and how does it essentially differ from other activities of re-working texts (e.g. intercultural **gloss**es, summaries, commentaries)? **Equivalence** has therefore had to be seen in relative terms, and translation decisions as hierarchical and **iterative**. The issue of decision-making is crucial in any discussion of **equivalence** and the translation **process**. This had already occupied another translation theorist – Jiří Levý, whose **Minimax** model is presented in the second extract of this unit (Text B7.2).

Task B7.1.1

Before you read Text B7.1, think about the historical and cultural conditions under which texts are produced and translated in totalitarian regimes. Provide a written response to the following questions:

➤ How similar or different are such practices to those common in the west? In your own linguistic and cultural situation, what kind of texts are normally produced and translated? What different kinds of pressure would translators come under?

➤ It is fairly easy to pinpoint and explain linguistic (e.g. **syntactic**, **semantic**) differences between, say, English and other languages with which you are familiar. It is not so easy to identify and analyse differences of a more textual or **rhetorical** nature. Reflect on the kind of linguistic-textual areas of contrast likely to be encountered in translating a sample text from such widely used sources as *The Economist, Newsweek*. Write brief notes on the following issues: structural properties; the 'world'; **norms**, **stylistic** and aesthetic properties.

➤ Review your notes on **formal equivalence** as defined by Nida and as presented in this book, specifically in Section A, Unit 6. Write down the differences between the two approaches: the **formal** and the **dynamic**.

➤ Read relevant articles in encyclopaedias or dictionaries of linguistics and translation on such areas of linguistic/translation enquiry as **pragmatics**, **norms**, **form** and meaning, and provide in note form definitions of the areas – in no more than ten lines.

 Task B7.1.2

➤ As you read through the list of the SL/TL linguistic-textual and **extra-linguistic** factors and conditions that need to be reconciled in the following passage, pause at each item and think of a plausible example to illustrate the phenomenon in question. For example:

Factor: SL/TL structural properties, possibilities and constraints
Example: English **cataphora** and how, unless rhetorically motivated to convey suspense, for example, the use of this device is discouraged in many languages

➤ Label the kind of **equivalence** relation likely to be involved in each of the equivalence frameworks listed by Koller below, and illustrate. For example:

Framework: the **extra-linguistic** circumstances conveyed by the text
Equivalence relation: **formal equivalence**

➤ With Nida's definition of types of **equivalence** in mind, make careful notes on what Koller specifically means by 'formal'. Identify the similarities or differences.

Text B7.1
W. Koller

Werner Koller (1995) 'The Concept of Equivalence and the Object of Translation Studies', *Target* **7:2: 191-222.**

Translation from a linguistic and textual perspective: The conditioning factors, double linkage, and the equivalence frameworks of translation

[. . .]

Equivalence is a relative concept in several respects: it is determined on the one hand by the historical-cultural conditions under which texts (original as much as secondary ones) are produced and received in the target culture, and on the other by a range of sometimes contradictory and scarcely reconcilable linguistic-textual and extra-linguistic factors and conditions:

■ The source and the target languages with their structural properties, possibilities and constraints
■ The 'world', as it is variously classified in the individual languages
■ Different realities as these are represented in ways peculiar to their respective languages
■ The source text with its linguistic, stylistic and aesthetic properties in the context of the linguistic, stylistic and aesthetic norms of the source language
■ Linguistic, stylistic and aesthetic norms of the target language and of the translator
■ Structural features and qualities of a text
■ Preconditions for comprehension on the part of the target-language reader
■ The translator's creative inclinations and understanding of the work
■ The translator's explicit and/or implicit theory of translation
■ Translation tradition
■ Translation principles and the interpretation of the original text by its own author
■ The client's guidelines and the declared purpose of the translation
■ The practical conditions under which the translator chooses or is obliged to work

Fundamental to any linguistic-textual approach in descriptive translation studies is the assumption that translations are characterised by a *double linkage*: first by their link to the *source text* and second by the link to the *communicative conditions* on the *receiver's* side. This double linkage is central in defining (and this means in particular: in differentiating) the equivalence relation. The process of differentiating this double linkage, and of thereby rendering it operational, is achieved by distinguishing between various *frameworks of equivalence*; at this stage, (translational) equivalence merely means that a special relationship – which can be designated as the translation relationship – is apparent between two texts, a source (primary) one and a resultant one.

The specification of the equivalence relation follows from the definition of *relational frameworks*; its application presupposes that the relational frameworks be specified. Linguistic/textual units which differ in nature and range are regarded as *target-language equivalents* if they correspond to source-language elements according to the equivalence relations specified in a set of relational frameworks. Target-language equivalents answer to *translational units* in the source text; both the similarities and the differences between the units of the source-language and their target-language equivalents result from the degree to which the values assigned to the relational frameworks are preserved.

From a linguistic-textual standpoint, the following equivalence frameworks are of particular significance:

1. The *extra-linguistic circumstances* conveyed by the text
2. The *connotations* (with a multiplicity of connotative values) conveyed by the text via the *mode of verbalization*
3. The *text and language norms* (usage norms) which apply to parallel texts in the target language
4. The way the *receiver* is taken into account
5. *Aesthetic* properties of the source-language text

These equivalence frameworks, which I shall not on this occasion elucidate further, are based on theoretical and empirical studies concerned with the heterogeneity of individual languages in their textual manifestation (more precisely: individual European languages and most notably German). With regard to the theoretical and descriptive objectives of certain inquiries within the field of Translation Studies (including translation criticism) these equivalence frameworks both can and must be expanded upon, differentiated, refined and modified, and, in particular, examined against concrete translational phenomena. The necessity of such an examination – and of the subsequent theoretical work – is revealed by the fact that a number of meaning components can be accommodated in this model of equivalence frameworks only with difficulty, or not at all. I have in mind here particularly the inter-linguistic, intra-textual and socio-cultural meanings, which can become such a headache for the translator of literary texts, since the use of commentary is for the most part inappropriate (see Koller 1992: 267ff., 287ff.).

According to the approach discussed here, it is the source-language text, in terms of its linguistic-stylistic structure and its meaning potential, which is regarded as the fundamental factor in translation and hence in Translation Studies. Due to the link that exists between the translation and the conditions on the receiver's side, however, a linguistic and text-theoretical approach, when describing and analysing translation samples, will also have to consider the other factors that contribute to the production and reception of a translation.

In contrast to the (relatively) broad linguistic approach, as represented by the author of this article, we find a number of (relatively) narrow approaches, among them computer linguistics, as understood in the context of machine translation research. It can, incidentally, be seen as an oddity of the translation debate that I myself have occasionally been counted among this 'hard linguistic core', against which a stand is taken in, for example, the volume edited by Mary Snell-Hornby in 1986. This so-called 'new orientation in Translation Studies' pretends to be an answer 'to the present disenchantment with purely linguistic-oriented Translation Studies' (jacket text) [Trans. P.C.]. The following description of translation is cited there as 'Koller's definition of translation':

> *Linguistically* translation can be described as a *recoding* or substitution: elements $a_1, a_2, a_3 \ldots$ from the inventory of linguistic symbols L_1 are replaced by elements $b_1, b_2, b_3 \ldots$ from the inventory of linguistic symbols L_2.
> (Snell-Hornby 1986: 13) [Trans. P.C.]

It must be stressed, however, that, within the framework of the respective linguistic approach, this definition of translation is utterly legitimate and fruitful, as shown by the results of research on machine translation, which are of importance not only for descriptive linguistics but also for linguistic theory. Nonetheless, I am given far too much credit for this definition: it appears in the context of a chapter (in Koller 1972), which presents diverse approaches to translation (of research as it stood at the end of the 60s!).

An approach which I understand to be narrowly linguistic is that of Wolfgang Klein (1991), which concentrates on the semantic aspect and for which the process of translation entails 'nothing which need take us beyond the study of language and of the use of language' (1991: 105); in Klein's opinion Translation Studies as an independent discipline could possibly be justified on organizational grounds but not on the basis of content. The ability to translate is part of human linguistic competence,

Text B7.1
W. Koller

and once the scope of linguistics has been broadened so far as to include a compre-hensive account of human linguistic competence, it should also be in a position to describe the ability to translate:

> The problems of Translation Studies, insofar as these are of a systematic nature and thereby amenable to systematic scientific analysis, are the problems of linguistics itself, and once the latter have been solved, then so have the former.
> (Klein 1991: 122)

According to Klein, the 'specific problems of translation' are of a genuine linguistic nature and have to do with 'the systematic relationship between two texts which, in one respect, are the same (they express the same thing) in another respect not (namely in terms of the means by which they express that which remains the same)' (1991: 107) In other words, the problems of translation are open to description and explanation in a framework of theories of meaning and contrastive linguistics. Klein's conclusion, however, is somewhat sobering: since linguistics is still a long way from solving its own problems, it cannot contribute much to Translation Studies.

My reason for regarding this approach as being 'narrowly' linguistic is that, by confining itself to semantics, it acknowledges only one – albeit central – aspect of a linguistic-textual nature, one which is a consequence of the link between the trans-lation and the source text and of the linguistic-stylistic and textual properties of the target language. What remains largely ignored, however, is the link that exists between the translation and the conditions of communication in the target language – a link which has immediate consequences of a linguistic-textual nature and which must therefore be taken into account by any (broader) linguistic approach. This in turn does not mean that the semantic approach is not of vital significance for translation theory: if linguistics succeeds in answering the questions which Klein asks about translation, then it will indeed have solved a range of translation theory's most fundamental problems.

Task B7.1.3

> Statements such as the following have been the root cause of much mis-understanding of the **equivalence** paradigm in general, and Koller's approach in particular:

> According to the approach discussed here, it is the source-language text, in terms of its linguistic-stylistic structure and its meaning potential, which is regarded as the fundamental factor in translation and hence in Translation Studies.

➤ In the context of Text B7.1, can this claim by Koller be taken to mean exclusive concern with the ST? Or do you think that Koller is equally cognisant of the TT? Justify your answer.

> The following description of translation is often cited as 'Koller's definition of translation':

Linguistically a translation can be described as a *recoding* or substitution: elements a_1, a_2, a_3 ... from the inventory of linguistic symbols L_1 are replaced by elements b_1, b_2, b_3 ... from the inventory of linguistic symbols L_2.

(Snell-Hornby 1986: 13)

➤ Is this a fair representation of Koller's views on what translation is? Justify your response in the light of the above reading.

If in doubt regarding where Koller stands on these issues, re-read the above text with these issues in mind.

Before you read the following passage (B7.2), note the non-technical use of the term 'pragmatic' in Levý's text (denoting 'practical'), and compare this with its use in the text from Koller, where '**pragmatic**' is used technically as 'relating to the study of the purposes for which utterances are used'.

 Task B7.2.1

➤ As you read Text B7.2, take detailed notes on **Minimax**, the cornerstone of Levý's model. What **procedures** and what strategies does this principle involve? How helpful do you believe them to be? Justify your answer. Define and describe **Minimax** as an overall translation **procedure** and **strategy**.

Text B7.2
J. Levý

Jiři Levý (1967/2000) 'Translation as a Decision Process', in: *To Honour Roman Jakobson II*, pp. 1171-82, reprinted in L. Venuti (ed.) (2000), pp. 148-59.

From the teleological point of view, translation is a PROCESS OF COMMUNICATION: the objective of translating is to impart the knowledge of the original to the foreign reader. From the point of view of the working situation of the translator at any moment of his [or her] work (that is, from the pragmatic point of view), translating is a DECISION PROCESS: a series of a certain number of consecutive situations – moves, as in a game – imposing on the translator the necessity of choosing among a certain (and very often exactly definable) number of alternatives.

[. . .]

Translation theory tends to be normative, to instruct translators on the OPTIMAL solution; actual translation work, however, is pragmatic; the translator [resorts to] that one of the possible solutions which promises a maximum of effect with a minimum of effort. That is to say, he intuitively [invokes] the so-called MINIMAX STRATEGY.

For example, there can hardly be any doubt that a verse translation which would preserve in rhymes the vowels of the original would be preferable, since the expressive values of vowels may play a minor part in the whole emotional pattern of the poem.

Text B7.2
J. Levý

The price a translator would pay for complicating his task in this way would, however, be so great that modern translators prefer to renounce it. In a less conspicuous way, the same policy is pursued by translators of prose: they are content to find for their sentence a form which expresses more or less all the necessary meanings and stylistic values, though it is probable that, after hours of experimenting and rewriting, a better solution might be found.

[. . .]

An investigation into the following problems, for example, would benefit from the application of minimax procedures (especially if pursued in a more rigorous way than could be done here):

1 What degree of utility is ascribed to various stylistic devices and to their preservation in different types of literature (e.g. prose, poetry, drama, folklore, juvenile literature, etc.)?

2 What is the relative importance of linguistic standards and of style in different types of literature?

3 What must have been the assumed quantitative composition of the audiences to whom translators of different times and of different types of texts addressed their translations? With contemporary translators, the assumptions manifested in their texts could be confronted with results of an empirical analysis of the actual predilections of the audience.

Task B7.2.2

One stylistic feature of popular fiction such as Mills & Boon is the use of **inanimates** in subject position when a proposition relates to activity by women. Thus, Mills & Boon's women do not 'cry'; rather, 'tears course down their cheeks' (see Section A, Unit 11 pp. 90–1).

➤ With this particular feature in mind, re-examine and illustrate the problem situations identified by Levý as areas where **Minimax** procedure might be usefully applied. One problem situation revolves round the question Levý asks: 'Are given ST stylistic devices recognized as equally utilizable in the TL, i.e. worth the effort expended in trying to preserve it?'

Unit B8
Translation and relevance

Up to the late 1980s, what we had to work with in the analysis of translation **equivalence** (be this **dynamic**, **pragmatic** or **textual**) were texts or fragments of texts. **Text typologies** and **equivalence** classifications had been the order of the day. Then, the focus shifted in a number of directions. The **pragmatics** of 'relevance' was one perspective from which to research the **cognitive** aspect of what happens in translation and what it is that regulates the elusive notion of **equivalence**. Gutt (1991: 20) describes the new focus in the following terms: 'Relevance theory . . . tries to give an explicit account of how the information-processing faculties of our mind enable us to communicate with one another. Its domain is therefore mental faculties rather than texts or processes of text production.'

Research into **relevance** in translation is informed by a model of **relevance** originally proposed by Sperber and Wilson in their 1986 book *Relevance: Communication and Cognition*. In addition, work in this area of Translation Studies owes a great deal to pioneering work on **relevance** by the American language philosopher and pragmatician Paul Grice who, in a number of ground-breaking papers (e.g. 'Logic and Conversation', 1975), outlined what has since become an indispensable framework for both research and practice in the **pragmatics** of 'language as action'.

It might be helpful to recall at this point that **relevance** is one of the 'maxims' which Paul Grice lists under what he calls the 'co-operative principle' in communication. This principle revolves around four basic maxims:

a. Quantity: Make your contribution as informative as is required;
b. Quality: Do not say that for which you lack adequate evidence;
c. Relevance: Be relevant;
d. Manner: Be communicatively orderly.

According to Grice, disturbance of co-operativeness can be a case of lack of knowledge ('breaking' a maxim), failure on the part of a speaker to secure a hearer's uptake or **acceptability** ('violating' a maxim) or, perhaps more significantly, disobeying a maxim in a deliberate, **contextually motivated** manner ('flouting' a maxim). This 'flouting' of the co-operative principle gives rise to so-called 'implicatures', the implied meaning that is tacit yet discernible when any of the maxims is not totally adhered to.

Task B8.1.1

➤ There are several excellent introductions to **pragmatics**, including those of Yule (1996) and Thomas (1995). Read relevant material on the co-operative principle, and suggest possible applications to translation.

It might also be helpful to document the position on the role of **text typologies** which Gutt adopted in the earlier phases of developing his **relevance** theory of translation. This is one of the earliest statements:

> [I]f it turns out that each individual phenomenon – which here is not only each text, but potentially each instance of translating it for a particular audience – may require its own theory of equivalence, then this means that these phenomena cannot be accounted for in terms of generalizations at all, and that they actually fall outside the scope of theory. Thus recognition of the potential need for single-text based 'theories' of translation equivalence entails a possible *reductio ad absurdum* of the notion of 'theory' itself.
>
> (Gutt 1991: 12)

Task B8.1.2

➤ As you read Text B8.1, make a list of features characterizing **interpretive** use of language, and **interpretive** translation. Pay particular attention to the reasoning behind the ruling out of **descriptive** use as an adequate representation of the translation **process**. Note carefully what is meant by **text type**, what examples are given, and whether the forms cited might be better referred to under different labels.

Ernst-August Gutt (1998) 'Pragmatic Aspects of Translation: Some Relevance-Theory Observations', in Leo Hickey, *The Pragmatics of Translation*, Clevedon: Multilingual Matters, pp. 41-53.

Text B8.1
E.-A. Gutt

Interpretive and descriptive use of language

One of the important claims of relevance theory is that there are two psychologically distinct modes of using language: the descriptive use and the interpretive use. Since these two terms are not necessarily self-explanatory they are now briefly introduced.

A language utterance is said to be *used descriptively* when it is intended to be taken as true of a state of affairs in some possible world.

An utterance is said to be *used interpretively* when it is intended to represent what someone said or thought.[1]

---

1 [Gutt's note] For a more detailed and technical introduction to these notions, see Sperber and Wilson (1986: 224ff).

Example 1

(a) Melody: 'Fred and Judy have got a divorce.'
(b) Melody: 'Harry said, "Fred and Judy have got a divorce."'

Both examples contain the utterance 'Fred and Judy have got a divorce'. In the first example Melody uses that utterance to claim that the state of affairs it describes is true. In other words, she maintains that it is true that Fred and Judy have got a divorce. She is using that utterance descriptively. She would be wrong if Fred and Judy were not divorced.

In example (1b) however, Melody does not (necessarily) claim that Fred and Judy have got a divorce; all she does is report what someone else said. Therefore, here the utterance is used *interpretively*. Melody's utterance in (1b) would not be wrong if Fred and Judy had not got a divorce, but it would be wrong if Harry had not, in fact, made that statement.

Interpretive resemblance and faithfulness

The crucial factor in interpretive use is that there [should] be a relationship of *interpretive resemblance* between the original utterance and that used to represent it. Such interpretive resemblance between utterances consists in the sharing of explicatures and implicatures. This implies that resemblance is a matter of degree.

Thus, two utterances interpretively resemble each other more closely, the more explicatures or implicatures they share.[2] A direct quotation, as in example (1b), shows the highest degree of resemblance to the original: it shares all explicatures and implicatures of the original, though only under one important condition, to which we shall return below: that is, that the direct quotation is interpreted in the same context as the original.

By contrast, excerpts, paraphrases, summaries etc. can vary a great deal as to the degree and kind of resemblance they show. Thus, if asked about the content of a particular lecture, the respondent or reporter would have a range of options open for his or her reply:

Example 2

(a) She could give a report with much detail of the lecture, which would show a high degree of interpretive resemblance.
(b) She could give a detailed report of one part of the lecture, summarizing the rest.
(c) She could give a brief summary of the main points.

These raise the important question of what will determine which kind of report the speaker will give? Being engaged in interpretive use, the speaker will aim at interpretive resemblance to the original; being constrained by the principle of relevance, she will aim at resemblance in those aspects which she believes will satisfy the expectation of optimal relevance.[3] Thus, in interpretive use, the utterance of the speaker comes with a claim to *faithfulness*:

---

2   [Gutt's note] See Sperber and Wilson (1986: 228f) and Gutt (1991: 44).
3   [Gutt's note] This claim is understood to hold within the limits of her own 'abilities and preferences' (Sperber and Wilson 1995: 270).

The speaker guarantees that her utterance is a faithful enough representation of the original: that is, resembles it closely enough in relevant respects.

(Wilson and Sperber, 1988: 137)

So if the reporter knows that the recipient is quite interested in the lecture as a whole, she will use option (2a), giving much detail. If she is aware that there is only one part which the recipient would find relevant, she is likely to choose option (2b), concentrating on that part of the lecture. Hence we find that relevance theory comes with a ready-made, context-sensitive concept of faithfulness, applying to the interpretive use of language in general.

THE PRAGMATIC ROLE OF THE NOTION OF 'TRANSLATION'

Translation as an interpretive use of language

From the relevance-theory point of view, translation falls naturally under the interpretive use of language: the translation is intended to restate in one language what someone else said or wrote in another language. In principle it is, therefore, comparable to quoting or speech reporting in intra-linguistic use. One of its primary distinctions setting it off from intra-lingual quoting or reporting is that original text and translation belong to different languages.

It follows that, as an instance of interpretive use, translation will also be constrained by the notion of faithfulness introduced above. In other words, the translator will design her translation in such a way that it 'resembles [the original] closely enough in relevant respects' (Wilson and Sperber, 1988: 137).

Up to here things might have seemed straightforward enough were it not for the term and concept called 'translation'. In order to understand the rather ambivalent function of this term, let us consider the role of labels for types of texts or acts of communication in general.

Text typologies as guides to relevance

As for many other phenomena in our world, so also for communication, people have coined particular terms to distinguish between particular kinds of texts or utterances. For example, we talk about eulogies and summaries, novels and comic strips, commentaries and abstracts, text books and hymn books and so on.

From a general communication point of view, such terms can serve a significant purpose: they can help to coordinate the intentions of the communicator with the expectations of the audience. For example, when the communicator presents her utterance as a 'report', this will trigger different expectations in the audience than if she called it a 'satire' or a 'curriculum vitae'. In this way labels referring to different kinds of communication can fulfil an important pragmatic function in coordinating the activities of communicator and audience.

From the relevance-theory point of view, by the appropriate use of such labels the communicator can guide the audience in their search for optimal relevance; for example, when given something called 'a novel' to read, one would be looking for the plot, for the way in which characters are portrayed, for values, attitudes and so on. One would not necessarily seek the intended relevance of such a book to lie in historical accuracy, objectivity of presentation, quality and quantity of source materials used

Text B8.1
E.-A. Gutt

and the like, all of which would be of high relevance for a historical reference work, for example.

So, by labelling her work a 'novel' rather than a 'historical reference work', the author guides the potential audience to the ways in which she intends her work to achieve relevance. Hence, such typological labels can be helpful in guiding the audience towards the intended interpretation, thus reducing the processing cost for the audience. In this sense, text-typological labels can serve to increase the relevance of a text or utterance, hence performing a pragmatic function.

Naturally, this relevance-increasing effect of text-type labels crucially depends on how well the types used by communicator and audience respectively agree with each other. The less they agree the less helpful they will be in the communication process. For example, if your publisher's idea of an abstract significantly differs from your own, then the chances are that the abstract you have written of a paper of yours will not be satisfactory to him and vice versa.

 Task B8.1.3

True translations seek to guarantee that a TT utterance is a sufficiently **faithful** representation of the original, i.e. that it resembles it closely enough in relevant respects. This is precisely what Gutt takes translation to be.

➤ With the help of an example, discuss what is meant by this notion of '**resemblance**'. How prominently does '**faithfulness**' feature, and what constrains it? Think about the issues involved and illustrate from a ST that it would be possible to translate in at least two different ways.

To assist with this task, consider the following: the amount of detail with which you provide the addressee depends on the degree of interest shown; so, if you know that the recipient is quite interested in what you have to say, you will give much more detail; if you become aware that there is only one part which the recipient would find relevant in what you have to say, you are more likely to concentrate on that part.

➤ What will happen if you exceeded (or fell short of) the amount of detail required? How does this relate to Grice's co-operative scheme outlined above?

➤ Reflect on the issue of **text typology** and on how this has been viewed by research into relevance and translation. The following quote may be useful:

As for many other phenomena in our world, so also for communication people have coined particular terms to distinguish between particular kinds of texts or utterances. For example, we talk about eulogies and summaries, novels and comic strips, commentaries and abstracts, text books and hymn books and so forth.

(Gutt 1998: 46)

Unit B9
Text type in translation

In the mid-1980s, Edinburgh-based translation theorists Basil Hatim and Ian Mason (separately and together) proposed a comprehensive model of translation grounded in the notion of **text type** (Werlich 1976; Beaugrande and Dressler 1981) and **critical discourse analysis** (Fowler 1986; Fairclough 1989). The basic concepts underpinning these developments are presented in Section A, Unit 9.

The text used in the present extension section comes out of an earlier and indeed particularly noteworthy attempt to classify texts and their translations. The text is drawn from the work of German linguist and translation theorist Katharina Reiss. In the text classification proposed, the overriding criterion relates not so much to *text* **purpose** (Hatim and Mason's **rhetorical purpose**) as to the crucial aspect of *translation* **purpose**.

Initially, Reiss sought to establish a correlation between **text type** and translation method, arguing for the need to preserve the predominant function of the text in translation. Thus, what the translator must do in the case of **informative** texts is to focus on **semantic** relationships within the text and only secondarily on **connotative meanings** and aesthetic values. In the case of **expressive** texts, the main concern of the translator should be to try and preserve aesthetic effect alongside relevant aspects of the **semantic content**. Finally, **operative** texts require the translator to heed the **extra-linguistic** effect which the text is intended to achieve even if this has to be undertaken at the expense of both **form** and **content**.

Task B9.1.1

➤ To familiarize yourself with the notion of **text typology**, read the relevant chapters in Crystal and Davy's valuable book on **stylistics** (1969) and in Beaugrande and Dressler's introduction to **text linguistics** (1981).

➤ Familiarize yourself with the various types of **intertextuality** (see also Section A, Unit 11). Focus on two main kinds:

   ■ one essentially involving quotation (called **horizontal intertextuality** by some scholars);

■ the other more akin to allusion or a subtle echo – **vertical intertextuality**. Here, the reference could be to an entire mode of writing or genre, for example. This is the basis on which **text type**s evolve.

➤ Review an old textbook on practical translation or a translator's guide or manual in use in your country. Examine the kinds of passages selected for translation practice. What method of classification is used: 'subject matter' (e.g. education, the environment), 'province' (legal, scientific), 'mode of expression' ('functional language' as in a technical manual), 'literary language' etc.? Do you find such classifications useful or is the difference between, say, a text on education and a scientific text mainly to do with 'terminology'?

➤ Think about the role which metaphors or other forms of 'embellishment' could possibly play in a text that is factual and intended to inform.

 Task B9.1.2

➤ As you read Text B9.1, fill in the empty slots in the following grid with labels of three **text type**s of **functions** recognized by the various scholars whose work is cited in the text. As you go through the various classifications, note Reiss's focus on 'dominance' in the sense that the various categories are not mutually exclusive (i.e. they overlap).

BÜHLER	1	2	3
STIEHLER	1	2	3
COSERIU	1	2	3

➤ Make an 'identity card' for each of the **text type**s discussed. The grid for each type will have the categories listed below on the left. The example is for Reiss's **'informative' text type**:

CONTEXT	Plain communication of facts
LINGUISTIC LEVEL	Semantic-syntactic
ASPECT OF MESSAGE	Topic
TEXT TYPE	Informative
TRANSLATION STRATEGY	Transmit the original information in full

Katharina Reiss (1977/1989) 'Text-types, Translation Types and Translation Assessment', trans. by Andrew Chesterman (ed. 1989), pp. 105-15, original German (1977) 'Texttypen, Übersetzungstypen und die Beurteilung von Übersetzungen', *Lebende Sprachen* 22.3: 97-100.

Text B9.1
K. Reiss

Language has long been classified intuitively, according to the predominant mode of expression, as functional language, literary language, etc. In the 1930s the psychologist Karl Bühler (1934/1965) distinguished three functions of a linguistic sign: informative (*Darstellung*), expressive (*Ausdruck*) and vocative (*Appell*). The semanticist Ulrich Stiehler (1970: 32) associated these three language functions with the realization of three types of human cognition: thinking (or perceiving), feeling and willing. The Tübingen linguist Eugenio Coseriu (1970: 27) sees the three functions in terms of their relative dominance in linguistic utterances, and thus distinguishes three language forms: 'a descriptive, declarative or informative language form, the main object of which is providing information about a given topic; an expressive or affective or emotive form, mainly expressing the speaker's state of mind or feeling; and a vocative or imperative form which primarily seeks to bring out certain behaviour in the hearer.' This classification thus basically relates the main objective of a language form to one of the three main elements in the communicative process: sender (= speaker, writer); receiver (= hearer, reader); and topic (= information).

This tripartite aspect of language itself suggests a similar tripartite division of basic verbal communicative situations; moreover, the many verbal constituents of the secondary system of language (i.e. its written form) can also be seen in terms of three broad types.

According to their communicative intention, verbal texts thus display three possible communicative functions, correlating with the dominance of one of the three elements of a communicative act as mentioned above. In this way we can distinguish the following three basic types of communicative situation.

(a) Plain communication of facts (news, knowledge, information, arguments, opinions, feelings, judgements, intentions, etc.); this is also taken to include purely phatic communication, which thus does not constitute a separate type: the actual information value is zero, and the message is the communication process itself (see Vermeer 1976). Here the *topic* itself is in the foreground of the communicative intention and determines the choice of verbalization. In the interest of merely transmitting information, the dominant form of language here is functional language. The text is structured primarily on the semantic-syntactic level (cf. Lotmann 1972). If an author of such a text borrows aspects of a literary style, this 'expressive' feature is nevertheless only a secondary one – as, for example, in book and concert reviews, football reports and the like. The text type corresponding to this basic communicative situation is the 'informative' type.

(b) Creative composition, an artistic shaping of the content. Here the *sender* is in the foreground. The author of the text writes his topics himself; he alone, following only his own creative will, decides on the means of verbalization. He consciously exploits the expressive and associative possibilities of the language in order to communicate his thoughts in an artistic, creative way. The text is doubly structured: first on the syntactic-semantic level, and second on the level of artistic organization (Lotmann 1972). The text type corresponding to this communicative situation can be referred to as 'expressive'.

Text B9.1
K. Reiss

(c) The inducing of behavioural responses. Texts can be conceived as stimuli to action or reaction on the part of the reader. Here the form of verbalization is mainly determined by the (addressed) receiver of the text by virtue of his being addressable, open to verbal influence on his behaviour. The text is doubly, or even triply structured: on the syntactic-semantic level, (in some circumstances, but not necessarily, on the level of artistic organization) and on the level of persuasion. The corresponding text type may be called the 'operative' one.

(One consequence of this threefold division is of course that in addition to these linguistic functions, an expressive text must also fulfil an artistic function in translation, and an operative text a psychological one.)

2. We now have three basic types which are relevant to translation. If we now apply this classification to the *assessment* of translations, we can state that a translation is successful if it:

■   guarantees direct and full access to the conceptual content of the SL text in an informative text;
■   transmits a direct impression of the artistic form of the conceptual content in an expressive text;
■   produces a text form which will directly elicit the desired response in an operative text.

In other words:

(a) If a text was written in the original SL communicative situation in order to transmit news, facts, knowledge, etc. (in brief: information in the everyday sense, including the 'empty' information of phatic communion), then the translation should transmit the original information in full, but also without unnecessary redundancy (i.e. aim *in the first place* at invariance of content). (This relates to the controversy about target text additions or omissions vis-à-vis the source text – see, for example, Savory 1957: 49.)

An example, from Ortega y Gasset (1937/1965: 18-19): – *'es usted una especie de último abencerraje, último superviviente de una fauna desaparecida.'* – 'you are a kind of last "Abencerraje", a last survivor of an extinct fauna.' This translation is inadequate, because the English reader lacks the Spanish reader's understanding of what the name *Abencerraje* signifies (a famous Moorish family in Granada).

(b) If the SL text was written because the author wished to transmit an artistically shaped creative content, then the translation should transmit this content artistically shaped in a similar way in the TL (i.e. aim *in the first place* at an analogy of the artistic form).

An example: two translations of a line from Rilke's first *Duineser Elegie*: *'Ein jeder Engel ist schrecklich'*.

(i)   'Round every angel is terror' (trans. by Wydenbruck)
(ii)   'Each single angel is terrible' (trans. by Leishman and Spender).

This second version mirrors the form of the original. (Cf. Reiss 1975: 57f.)

(c) If the SL text was written in order to bring about a certain behaviour in the reader, then the translation should have this same effect on the behaviour of the TL reader (i.e. aim in the first place at the production of identical behavioural reactions).

Text B9.1
K. Reiss

An example: an advertisement '*Füchse fahren Firestone-Phoenix*'. If this slogan is translated only 'informatively', as 'Foxes drive (use) Firestone', the psychologically persuasive ('operative') alliterative element is lost and false associations are evoked: metaphorically, *Fuchs* is not equivalent to 'fox'. Suggested version, preserving alliteration: 'Profs prefer Firestone-Phoenix'. If a given translation fulfils these postulates which derive from the communicative function of a text, then the translator has succeeded in his overall communicative task.

Of course, the full achievement of this goal entails not only a consideration of the text type in question – this only indicates the general translation method – but also the specific conventions of a given text variety (*Textsorte*). Text varieties have been defined by Christa Gniffke-Hubrig (1972) as 'fixed forms of public and private communication', which develop historically in language communities in response to frequently recurring constellations of linguistic performance (e.g. letter, recipe, sonnet, fairy-tale, etc.). Text varieties can also realize different text types; e.g. letter: private letter about a personal matter – informative type; epistolary novel – expressive type; begging-letter – operative type. Limitations of space prohibit a further discussion of this in the present context, but see Reiss (1974) on the problem of text classification from an applied linguistic viewpoint.

The three text types mentioned cover in principle all forms of written texts. However, one must not overlook the fact that there are also compound types, where the three communicative functions (transmission of information, of creatively shaped content, and of impulses to action) are all present, either in alternate stages or simultaneously. Examples might be a didactic poem (information transmitted via an artistic form), or a satirical novel (behavioural responses aroused via an artistic form).

[. . .]

Task B9.1.3

Having read Text B9.1, consider the following questions:

➤ Coseriu's work cited is of interest: what is the major claim made?

➤ How do the various **typologies** relate to the 'communicative process'?

➤ Once we go beyond the imparting of information, we get into multi-levels in the structure of the message. Explain and illustrate.

➤ How does Reiss's **typology** fit within the scheme of **intertextuality**?

➤ **Hybridization** or the fact that texts are essentially multifunctional has been the Achilles' heel of those **text typologies** which seek 'rigour' at the expense of genuinely reflecting how texts are actually produced and received. How does a model such as Reiss's fare in this regard?

➤ In current theorizing on translation, there is disenchantment with earlier text typologies. They were envisaged either within classification schemes such as

Unit B10
Text register in translation

Register theory has been one of the more significant contributions to our under-standing of the interaction between translation and linguistics. The remarkable influence which **register analysis** has had on language and Translation Studies is in part due to the numerous revisions which the notion of **register** has undergone over the years, incorporating new and valuable insights into the major thesis that people speak in many registers. This comprehensive view of language variation which has emerged counters the prevalent myth of 'one situation = one language'.

Cast in more practical terms, these issues have given rise to a number of relevant questions: What are the criteria for judging one kind of language (or one trans-lation) as appropriate or inappropriate for a particular situation or context? In what way does our reaction to appropriateness form part of our textual competence as language users or translators? Are these critical skills teachable or learnable? How can awareness of these communicative variables help translators and interpreters deal more efficiently with the rich variety of texts they encounter in professional life?

Task B10.1.1

The language of weather bulletins is a good example of a restricted register.

➤ Before reading Text B10.1, conduct a simple **register analysis** of language in this or a similarly restricted domain: list commonly used vocabulary items and find examples of the casual, almost chatty tone characteristic of the delivery of this kind of text (see also the discussion of the restricted vocabulary of Example A14.2, a written bulletin produced by **Machine Translation**).

➤ Reflect on the many kinds of English there can be in terms of geography, history, social class, etc., and provide examples.

➤ Look up the term 'idiolect' in a good dictionary of linguistics or **stylistics** terms. Do you think it is normally necessary to translate this fairly marginal type of variation which invariably consists of individual mannerisms? What criteria might be invoked to ascertain the significance of idiolectal variation? Would idiolect acquire more significance in the more creative kinds of writing? Is 'creativity' restricted to the literary domain? Justify your response.

➤ As you read Text B10.1, note features and types of language variation identified according to the language user.

➤ Note features and types of language variation identified according to language use. Organize your notes under such headings as **field**, **tenor** and **mode**.

➤ Underline problem situations encountered in literary translation regarding idiolect and dialect.

Text B10.1
M. Gregory

Michael Gregory (1980) 'Perspectives on translation from the Firthian tradition', *Meta* 25.4: 455-66.

There has also, during the last fifteen years, been considerable work done on the concept of, and description of, varieties within a language. This was inspired by Firth's frequent remarks about restricted languages and is keenly relevant to questions of translation. Catford himself pointed out that 'The concept of a "whole language"' is so vast and heterogeneous that it is not operationally useful for many linguistic purposes, descriptive, comparative and pedagogical. It is therefore desirable to have a framework of categories for the classification of sub-languages or *varieties* within a total language.'[1] In several publications,[2] colleagues and I have attempted to explicate and develop such a framework, and our terminology and schemata have been widely accepted. Some of the categories which we use are of long standing in philological study: these are those which are related to constant features of *users* in language situations. *Temporal, geographical* and *social dialects* are sets of linguistic habits corresponding to the temporal, geographical and social provenances of speakers and writers. *Idiolect* is the individual dialect: the variety related to the personal identity of the user. It is not always necessary to translate idiolects: the personal identity of the user may not be relevant situationally: it usually is not, for example, in scientific or 'official' texts: however, this is not always the case, particularly in plays and novels. Many of Shakespeare's greatest characters are strongly marked linguistically as individuals: Richard III, Falstaff, Hamlet, Iago, Juliet's Nurse, Beatrice, Cleopatra, to mention but a few: and the work of Dickens is full of linguistic curiosities. In such instances I suggest that in the search for 'equivalence' the translator has a responsibility to try to distinguish them linguistically as being individual in the Target Language: of course, the markers of individuality will not be 'the same' or probably even parallel in the two languages.

1. [Gregory's note] J. C. Catford, *A Linguistic Theory of Translation*, London, Oxford University Press, 1965, p.88.
2. [Gregory's note] John Spencer and Michael Gregory, 'An Approach to the Study of Style,' in N. Enkvist, J. Spencer and M. Gregory, *Linguistics and Style*, London, Oxford University Press, 1964: M. Gregory 'Aspects of varieties differentiation', *Journal of Linguistics* 3: 177–98, 1967: J. Benson and W. Greaves, *The Language People Really Use*, Agincourt, Ontario, Book Society of Canada, 1973: M. Gregory and S. Carroll, *Language and Situation*: Language varieties in their social context, London: Routledge and Kegan Paul, 1978.

Text B10.1
M. Gregory

Dialects themselves also present translation problems. Many languages, as Catford points out,[3] have a 'standard' or literary dialect which shows only slight variation (in its written form at least) from one locality to another and over long stretches of time. For translation purposes it may be regarded as unmarked, and unmarked text in the unmarked dialect of the Source Language can usually be translated into an equivalent unmarked Target Language dialect. If there is no such dialect the translator may have the exciting task of helping to create a literary dialect for the Target Language.

When a text has passages in a dialect other than the unmarked dialect, and this is not uncommon in literary works, particularly in the dialogue of novels and plays, the translator may have to select an equivalent Target Language dialect. Care and good sense are necessary. In relation to the dialects of the British Isles, Cockney is a southeastern geographical dialect. However, in translating Cockney dialogue into French, most translators would quite rightly select Parigot, which is a northerly dialect of French. Catford has pointed out that 'the criterion here is the "human" or "social" geographical one of "dialect of the metropolis" rather than a purely locational criterion'.[4] Interesting here too is that Cockney is marked chiefly by phonological features presented in conventionalized graphological forms, while Parigot is marked chiefly at the lexical level in the use of argot items. In Catford's terms the translation equivalence is set up in this instance between varieties of language, not between phonological and lexical features as such.

[. . .]

Newer categories than dialect relate to constant features of speakers' and writers' use of language in situations: these are the *diatypic varieties: field, mode,* and *personal* and *functional tenors of discourse* and the more abstract and powerful concept of *register*. In *Language and Situation*, Suzanne Carroll and I described *field of discourse* as the linguistic 'consequence of the user's purposive role' in the language event, 'what his language is about, what experience he is verbalizing'.[5] This means, among other things, that languages such as English and French which reflect highly developed scientific and technical cultures and a *world* experience, have a wide variety of strongly marked fields of discourse, particularly as regards their lexis. Even such an ancient language as Hindi faces the problem of creating equivalent scientific and technical fields of discourse, as also does Hausa as it emerges more and more as a national language in Nigeria: on the other hand, English has problems coping with 'the myriad praise names of the Yoruba *Oba*' and the complex generic–semantic structure of surrounding *isu*, Yoruba for yam.[6] Firth's proposed situation-inclusive translation may be the only answer in such cases.

Modes of discourse are the linguistic consequences of users' relationships to language's two mediums, speech and writing. The relationship can initially be seen as the simple one of which is being used, but as soon as we consider relationships such as those

---

3. [Gregory's note] J. C. Catford, *A Linguistic Theory of Translation*, London, Oxford University Press, 1965, p 38.
4. [Gregory's note] *Ibid.*, p. 87–118.
5. [Gregory's note] M. Gregory and S. Carroll, *Language and Situation: Language Varieties in their Social Contexts*, London, Routledge and Kegan Paul, 1978, p.7.
6. [Gregory's note] O. Osundare, *Bilingual and Bicultural Aspects of Nigerian Prose Fiction*, Ph.D. York University, Toronto, 1979, pp. 123, 127.

between lectures and articles, between conversations in real life and dialogue in novels, and especially plays, distinctions amongst modes of discourse, if they are to be useful and revealing, have to be more delicate than the simple spoken–written dichotomy. Within speaking I have distinguished between *speaking spontaneously* or *non-spontaneously*.[7] Spontaneous speech may be *conversing*, that is when there is the expectation of verbal exchange, or *monologuing* (where there is no such expectation). Non-spontaneous speech is more complex. It may be *reciting*, a technical term for the performance of what belongs to an oral tradition, or it may be *the speaking of what is written*. What has been written may itself have been *written to be spoken as if not written*, as are the scripts of plays and films, much radio and television, or just *written to be spoken* with no such pretence, as are most lectures and some sermons. In the English texts my colleagues and I have examined there are significant lexical and grammatical as well as phonological markers of these sub-modes of speech: it is, however, unfortunate how many poor translations of the classics of European theatre there are in English, translations which have, as Firth might have said, no implication of *utterance* in English, although they might pass as *written* texts.

Tenors of discourse result from the mutual relations between the relationship the user has with his audience, and the language used. When the relationship is looked at as a personal one, variations in English and other languages can be seen to range from extreme degrees of formality to similar degrees of informality by way of virtually unmarked norms. These are what are known as *personal tenors of discourse*. When the relationship is viewed functionally, concerned with what the user is trying to do with language to his audience, whether he is teaching, persuading, amusing, controlling and so on, we can discern *functional tenors of discourse*. Tenor of discourse is certainly an area in which the translator has to keep his head. A North American young man may easily talk to his father in an informal personal tenor: indeed his father might suggest he was being 'taken for a ride' if he did otherwise: but an Oriental young man may have to use honorific forms in such a situation. Certainly filial respect and affection are likely to be both present in both situations but respect is usually not *linguistically* relevant for the North American in this situation; it is for most Orientals. The translator has to decide what sort of equivalence he wants here. If when translating into English he uses a formal English tenor, he would probably do well to use it consistently so the reader begins to appreciate that in the particular culture the book is about, this formality of language is the norm in that situation.

In some cases a change of personal tenor involves a corresponding change of dialect or even language: classical Arabic is not really compatible with an informal tenor: and some of the most proficient Nigerian users of English have problems with the more informal tenors – indeed when they do use them they often sound curiously old-fashioned as though they have stepped out of a novel about the Bright Young Things of the 'twenties' or ' thirties', by P.G. Wodehouse or Evelyn Waugh. That may be where they have picked up their informal repertoire rather than in day-to-day interchange. Several Nigerian colleagues and students of mine have told me that most English-speaking Nigerians switch to their indigenous language when speaking informally at home and with friends: and my own observation in Nigeria bears this out. This of course means that they are not as experienced in informal tenors as they

---

7. [Gregory's note] M. Gregory and S. Carroll, *Language and Situation: Language Varieties in their Social Contexts*, London, Routledge and Kegan Paul, 1978, pp. 39–45.

are in other varieties of the language and this influences their creative writing and their creative translations.

There remains one other important category concerned with language varieties, that of *register*. Many texts can be located similarly as regards field, modes and tenors: lectures on geography, sermons, cooking recipe books, legal depositions, sports reports – such recurring configurations of field, mode, personal and functional tenor constitute registers, the varieties according to use of which a given text is an instance. M.A.K. Halliday has aptly pointed out that 'There's not a great deal one can predict about the language that will be used if one knows only the field of discourse or only the mode or the tenor. But if we know all three then we can predict quite a lot.'[8] Register is, therefore, an important sociolinguistic and semantic concept with pertinent relevance to translation. Consistency of register together with what has been referred to as internal cohesion is what makes a text hang together, function as a unit in its environment. Halliday has abstractly described register as 'the configuration of semantic resources that the member of a culture typically associates with a situation type. It is the meaning potential that is [linguistically] accessible in a given social context'.[9]

The establishment of register equivalence can be seen then as the major factor in the process of translation: the problems of establishing such equivalence is a crucial test of the limits of translatability.

Task B10.1.2

➤ Summarize Gregory's view on the indispensability of **register** awareness in such domains as the use of idiolect and dialect in literary translation.

➤ How does Gregory deal with translation from or into languages which have a 'standard' or literary dialect that shows only slight variation (in its written form at least) from one locality to another and over long stretches of time?

➤ What is Gregory's recommendation regarding situations where there is no equivalent dialect, say, to literary Arabic (a dialect which does not vary much in that language)?

➤ What does Gregory suggest for dealing with the translation of geographical or social dialects such as working-class Cockney?

➤ Discuss the following statement from Halliday (1978: 223): 'There's not a great deal one can predict about the language that will be used if one knows only the field of discourse or only the mode or the tenor. But if we know all three then we can predict quite a lot.'

---

8. [Gregory's note] M. A. K. Halliday, *Language as a Social Semiotic: the social interpretation of language and meaning*, London, Edward Arnold, 1978, p. 223.
9. [Gregory's note] *Ibid.*, p. 111.

Unit B11
Text, genre and discourse shifts in translation

As we have explained in Unit 11, Section A, recent developments in relevance research have signalled a shift back to **text typologies**. These are now seen as important templates for the alignment of communicator intentions with **audience** expectations, thus guiding the text receiver in the search for optimal **relevance**. For example, one would not seek intended **relevance** in a novel's historical accuracy of detail the way one would in an historical reference book.

A glance at the list of the various **text typologies** rehabilitated by the **relevance** model, however, reveals that the term 'textual' is used in a fairly generic sense, covering quite an assortment of textual products: eulogies, summaries, novels, comic strips, commentaries, abstracts, text books, hymn books, historical reference books, etc. Strictly speaking, these are not all **text types**. While some of these forms are **texts** proper (e.g. summaries, commentaries), others belong to what we have called **genres** (e.g. eulogies, novels, comic strips), and still others form part of **discourse** (e.g. textbooks, historical reference books).

Genre occupies Carl James in his study of **translation shifts** (James 1989, see Text B11.1). James's study may be credited with being the first to recognize, from an essentially applied-linguistic perspective, the distinction between two levels of abstraction in approaching the notion of **genre** in translation. Translation itself may be seen as a **genre** *in the abstract*. This is a function of the total effect of choices made and felt to be intrinsic to any act of translation (i.e. the *translational* sense of **genre**, as in 'all translation intrinsically seems foreign or contrived'). There is, on the other hand, the detailed *more concrete* sense of **genre**. This subsumes all kinds of purposeful activities with which translation, like any other form of text production, deals and which revolve around conventionalized communicative events (i.e. the *linguistic* sense of **genre**, as in the cooking recipe, the academic abstract).

The second extract in this unit (Text B11.2) shifts the focus from **genre** to **discourse**, and from Applied Linguistics to Cultural Studies, the discipline which examines the cultural ramifications of issues such as conventions and attitudes. In this field of inquiry, two basic research trends may be identified: one simply unsympathetic to linguistics or even to discourse analysis, the other cognisant of the contribution of discourse studies to the study of culture and translation. The latter approach may be illustrated by the work of the Canadian cultural commentator and translation theorist Donald Bruce which, while firmly grounded in Cultural Studies, has nevertheless branched out in a number of interesting ways to include discursive models and socio-political theory. Specifically, it is the focus on **discourse** alongside other types of **sign** (**genre**, **text**, etc.) which has primarily motivated our choice of this reading at this point in our discussion.

But, whatever the brand, Cultural Studies is credited with raising an important question in the study of translation. This relates to which texts to translate and which to ignore. This sensitive decision is closely bound up with the translation strategy favoured by a given translation tradition. For example, within the Anglo-American translation tradition, careful selection has ensured that only those texts which lend themselves to a **domesticating** strategy are included, while other texts which resist such a strategy are all but totally excluded. The question of what determines whether a text will be translated and published or not is thus at the heart of cultural politics, a topic that Donald Bruce addresses in his study of discourse shifts.

Task B11.1.1

➤ James (and linguists such as Tannen) relates **coherence** to **intertextuality**. Before you read Text B11.1, recall the seven standards of textuality (Section A, Unit 9) and reflect on how these cross-fertilize meaningfully (e.g. **coherence** is underpinned by **intertextuality** and realized by **cohesion**).

➤ Review your notes on the two types of **intertextuality** – the **horizontal** and the **vertical** (Section A, Unit 1) and provide further examples to illustrate each.

➤ Reflect on the following distinction:

■ What goes on '*in* translation', i.e. in STs and TTs as '**texts**'

as opposed to

■ What is essentially '*of* translation', i.e. entailed in translating as an activity that exists in and by itself and that stands in contrast with such activities as original writing.

➤ As you read Text B11.1, note the various definitions of **genre** and the examples used to illustrate them.

➤ Focus on how the seven **standards of textuality** are met in Koller's definition of the technical text cited in this extract.

➤ Under two separate headings, note details of '*translation as a genre*' and details of '*genre in translation*'.

➤ Note details of parody as evidence for the existence of translation as a genre.

Text B11.1
C. James

Carl James (1989) 'Genre Analysis and the Translator', *Target* 1.1: 21-41.

Intertextuality, constituting a claim that one text relates to another text or one text-part relates to another part, has much in common with the notion of *coherence* which is an 'underlying organizing structure making the words and sentences into a unified discourse that has cultural significance for those who create or comprehend it' (Tannen 1984: xiv). Now, the most coherent texts are those that are perceived as instances of genres, so much so that genre-compliance on the part of a speaker or writer (or translator) is marked by an ability to maintain coherence. The most coherent genres will thus fall into the two classes of technical text or everyday prosaic text (OBITUARY, NEWSCAST, etc.), while the least coherent are literary texts, which derive their interest from innovative violation of the expectations held by readers: then we have 'poetic license' of course.

One writer (Koller 1981: 277) invokes similar arguments to these when he defines a technical text as one about which the reader entertains six expectations, that it will: (i) carry the expected information or have 'topic-relevance'; (ii) be in a conventional format; (iii) have logical sentence connectivity; (iv) have the expected 'impact'; (v) be appropriate in style; and (vi) be intelligible to him as reader. Exactly the same applies, of course, to technical translations. It is to translation and its relationships with genre analysis that we now turn.

Genre study in translator training

In this section I want to consider some of the possible 'applications' of genre analysis in translator training, as well as their relevance to translation theory in general. We start with the latter, and pose the first question: is a translation to be regarded as a genre in the same sense as a RECIPE, TESTIMONIAL, or READER'S LETTER to a newspaper? I suggest there is a genre TRANSLATION, but that it has a special status. The existence of what Toury (1982a: 69) calls 'ideological translation' is one relevant fact: Toury describes Russian and German Jews who preferred 'for ideological reasons' to read Hebrew translations of German and Russian texts rather than the originals which they could just as easily have read. Analogously, there are people in Wales today who prefer to read European classics in Welsh rather than in English – so in their case it is not so much a matter of turning their backs on the originals as insisting that what is lost in translation is no greater when the target language text is Welsh than if it were English.

Further support for the claim that there is a genre TRANSLATION also comes (indirectly) from Toury's work, and involves his idea of pseudo-translations, these being defined as 'target-language texts which are presented as translations although no corresponding source texts in another language, hence no factual translational relationships, exist' (Toury 1982b: 67). The point is that it is only when humans recognize the existence of an entity and become aware of its characteristics that they can begin to imitate it. A particular kind of imitation is of course the PARODY, which we have already identified as a genre. But its existence is of dual significance: PARODY not only exists as a genre *per se* but its very existence depends on the assumed existence and the real knowledge of other genres which get parodied: examples would be Peter Sellers' parodies of the SERMON and the POLITICAL SPEECH genres. We must draw the same conclusions about TRANSLATION: it too has dual significance. The two strands of evidence for the generic status of TRANSLATION secondarily imply that translators are aware of the existence of other genres to be translated, just as Peter

Sellers' cultivation of PARODY relied heavily on himself and his audience having shared beliefs about the existence and the critical features of those other genres that he so grotesquely contorted.

The first point – that TRANSLATION is at least potentially a genre – is reminiscent of Savory's (1957: 50) famous paradox:

> A translation should read like an original work,

> and

> A translation should read like a translation.

Both of these propositions are true, and the implication for the student of translation is that he must be thoroughly familiarized with both original works and translations: only in this way will he be able to refine his sensitivity to and the appropriateness of his response to TRANSLATION. The second point – that translations are translations of other genres – means that the student must receive genre-based experience. The translation of an individual text must start with the identification of its genre type. To refer back to what we said earlier, translators neglect the TOP-DOWN direction of the information processing at their peril. It is not enough for the translator to take care of the words and phrases in a BOTTOM-UP manner, hoping that the larger discourse units, and ultimately the genre-fidelity will thereby automatically take care of themselves: this will not happen, and the result will be genre-infelicities which read like weak parodies. We already have sufficient compelling evidence from the fast-developing field of Contrastive Rhetoric (e.g. Connor and Kaplan, 1987) to know that such optimism is ill-founded.

The suggestion that all texts belong to their generic class and genre has implications for syllabus design in translator training, and the case for a text-typological approach to syllabus design for translator training was well stated by Hatim (1984). First, we might recognize the tripartite division: literary, technical and everyday class of genre, and organize the year's work around this scheme. Students would thus receive systematic exposure to the three categories of genre. Then the central genres of each class could be studied (in SL and in TL texts) and their salient formal features learnt. The next step would be to learn to recognize and translate the hybrid genres such as REVIEW-ARTICLE or DISCUSSION-DOCUMENT: in this way the student of translation would have more than merely his intuitions to rely upon for his recognition of the genre-type of any text he is called upon to translate. He would be given opportunities to discover these distinctive features for himself and to make conscious note of them 'for future reference'. Such a programme would go some way toward the learning targets set by Wilss: 'The ability by the student cognitively to describe, explain and evaluate SLT micro- and macrostructure under syntactic, semantic and pragmatic aspects' (Wilss 1982: 183).

Task B11.1.2

➤ With what kind of **intertextuality** is James mostly concerned? Is it of the **vertical** or the **horizontal** type? State exactly how, and illustrate.

➤ Having now read Text B11.1, do you accept as valid the notion of 'translation as a **genre**'? How does the concept of **intertextuality** support this view? What evidence can one derive from **pseudo-translations** and ideological translation (Toury)?

 Task B11.2.1

Do **style** characteristics such as 'journalistic' or 'referential' diminish the quality of a literary work? In this regard, it may be useful to read or re-read some of George Orwell's writings (e.g. the short story 'The Elephant') which have come under attack for their use of journalistic devices, for example.

In **discourse** terms and from the vantage point of creative writing, to 'problematize' is the opposite of 'to generate escapism' (morbid vs entertaining and cheerful).

➤ Reflect on this distinction in relation to realistic vs popular fiction. How does popular fiction such as Mills & Boon convey escapism? How do Dickens's realistic writings 'problematize'?

➤ As you read Text B11.2, note details of interdiscursive phenomena.

➤ List all guidelines given to translators.

Text B11.2
D. Bruce

Donald Bruce (1994) 'Translating the Commune: Cultural Politics and the Historical Specificity of the Anarchist Text', *Traduction, Terminologie, Rédaction* **1: 47-76.**

Why then is there nothing or at least so little of Vallès's work in English? The first and foremost reason is ideological: as outlined above, Vallès's anarchist links to the Commune, his biting analysis of the role of educational institutions in maintaining the *status quo*, as well as his insightful critique of the oppressive social function of humanistic culture have made his writings that of a 'persona non grata' in the French educational system. In turn, the traditional dependence of foreign educators on anthologies, *manuels*, literary histories, etc. produced in France has as a result effectively banished Vallès's writings from non-French consciousness by inadvertently reproducing the cultural politics of *l'hexagone*: at least in native French-speaking areas popular editions are available to fill in the gap created by institutional exclusion. Beyond that there are other possible reasons which may have contributed to the ghettoization of Vallès's writings. Amongst these one might consider the following:

■ Stylistically, the texts incorporate many *journalistic* devices, Vallès himself having been a well-known journalist of his day (editor of *Le Cri du peuple*). This has made them seem 'inferior' in the eyes of those who have a 'belletristic', highly evaluative vision of literature. Of course, in the past the same criticism has been leveled at Dickens, Balzac and other writers associated with serialized publication.

- The texts are strongly *referential* and become increasingly so as one reads through towards L'*Insurgé* which portrays the explosion of the Commune. Yet they are no more referential than Flaubert's L'*Éducation sentimentale* or Hugo's *Quatre-vingt-treize*, both of which are virtually indecipherable for the foreign reader without socio-historical contextualization.
- These are also very political novels which, instead of providing escape, bring us back to the realities of social conflict and oppression as seen through the eyes of a nineteenth-century anarcho-socialist. Again, the belletristic approach has tended to avoid overtly political literary texts which indeed problematize the political, ideological and institutional functions of literature.
- Finally, I would also suggest that there have simply not been enough informed readers of Vallès due to his exclusion from the canon. In this sense the de-legitimization process has worked very well, for his writing has remained largely unknown not only among anglophone students of French literature but also among their professors: the only Vallès text ever mentioned at all as a candidate for the undergraduate curriculum is *l'Enfant*, and that is because it appears to be a relatively innocuous story about an unhappy childhood (in the style of *Poil de carotte* and *Petite chose*). In my own university department, few of my colleagues have ever read or taught the novels and many would not have any idea as to how to situate Vallès's work in the XIXth century context. The anthologies which colleagues use in undergraduate classes (e.g. Lagarde et Michard) do not include Vallès and many colleagues would argue that exclusion must necessarily indicate inferior literary value. In this manner the cycle of exclusion engendered by cultural politics is both consciously and unconsciously perpetuated.

For all of these reasons, most of which are fundamentally ideological in nature, there exists today no complete translation of *Jacques Vingtras* in English and little knowledge about Vallès's writing amongst anglophone French literature specialists.

[. . .]

Elements relating discourse theory to translation

The studies undertaken in the analysis of the discourse of the Commune are based upon theoretical work done in discourse theory. These studies constitute a specific application of its principles.[1] This activity has been undertaken within the framework of an *interdiscursive* model, one which seeks to map the exchanges, transformations, and subversions which take place when discursive material passes from one discursive formation to another. This is of particular importance for translation since these transfers are historically specific: if their 'sense' is to be communicated to a contemporary reader the translator must clearly be the first to understand it in the source text and reproduce it in the target text.

In order to clarify the theoretical framework of this model I will briefly present a few operative definitions before discussing the historically specific elements found in the discourse of the Commune:[2]

---

1 [Bruce's note] In particular, Richard Terdiman and Kristin Ross have done much to elaborate discourse theory in relation to XIXth century literature, as have Marc Angenot, Régine Robin, Ross Chambers and Dominique Maingueneau.

2 [Bruce's note] My point of departure for these definitions is the very insightful work done by Marc Angenot on both theoretical and practical aspects of discourse analysis.

i. *Discourse*: 1) a dispersion of texts whose historical mode of inscription allows us to describe them as a space of enunciative regularities; 2) a set of anonymous, historically situated rules (e.g. generic systems, repertoires of topoï, actantial schemes, principles of narrative syntax which determine the way *énoncés* are linked) which are determined by a given epoch, and which in turn determine the conditions of enunciation for a given social or linguistic field. These are the largely implicit principles which determine what is *sayable* within a specific discourse. It is also essential to recognize that discourse is *embodied* in texts and that texts make up discourse: 'the relation between discourse and text is one of *emergence*; discourse emerges in and through texts' (Kress, 1985, p. 29; my emphasis). Discourse, then, goes beyond the aggregate of texts: it is, to a large extent, the abstract structure as related to the material conditions which are at the basis of the articulation of meaning. A translator must be aware of the characteristics which define the discourse in which a text is located if any sense of historical or semantic identity is to be maintained.

ii. *Text*: is a specific articulation of discourse, a semiotic space within which discourse emerges. Thus text and discourse are not synonymous, yet they are inextricably interconnected and interdependent. Individual texts concretize discursive characteristics in multiple ways.

iii. *Interdiscursivity*: since any given text contains a mix of discourses, this is where the notion of interdiscursivity becomes crucial to the translator. It can be defined as 'the reciprocal interaction and influence of contiguous and homologous discourses' (Angenot, 1983, p. 107), i.e. the interaction of the fundamental regulative principles of specific discourses. No discourse type is 'pure'; all contain elements which find their origins in other discourses: the recognition of this is essential in the translator's attempt to define ambiguous meanings.

iv. *Intertextuality*: this is a more punctual phenomenon, and can be defined as 'the circulation and transformation of ideologems' (Angenot, 1983, p. 106). These are one-to-one relationships of varying kinds. This is the more readily explicable referential network within which the text is located, the sense of which the translator can most immediately transmit to the culturally, temporally or spatially distanced reader (by means of notes, paraphrases, etc.).

v. *Ideologem*: can be defined as a small signifying unit possessing the attribute of acceptability within a given doxa (Angenot, 1983, p. 107). It contains within itself both the logical basis for its probability and the implicit argumentative structure which realizes it. What is particularly significant about an ideol is its ability to migrate from one discourse to another and to undergo successive re-semanticizations which result in its variability (Angenot, 1989, pp. 902–903). The translator must come to recognize those ideologems which are typical of a particular discourse and period in order to use them in reconstructing the semantic relations in the target text.

Task 11.2.2

➤ Recall the distinction established by Bruce between **text** and **discourse** and compare this view with those held by **text linguist**s such as Beaugrande and applied to translation by theorists such as Hatim and Mason (Units 9 and 10). Comment on the views by relating to your own experiences in translation.

➤ Does the idea of 'socio-textual practices' outlined in Unit 11 (Sections A and C) shed any useful light on Bruce's use of interdiscursivity vs **intertextuality**? Justify your answer by relating the distinction to translation.

Unit B12
Agents of power in translation

The marginal status of translators and translations is to a great extent precipitated by such factors as the adherence to outmoded notions of **equivalence** and the insistence on the supremacy of the original. Challenging this status quo, groups of mostly literary scholars have declared an interest in the **norms** and constraints which govern the production and **reception** of translations and which can explain acts of **re-writing**, even deviation and **manipulation**, that have become part and parcel of translating texts and translating cultures. Susan Bassnett and André Lefevere (1990), for example, assert that all translation involves some form of manipulation of the ST. This can be purposeful, and is often the work of a translator prompted by a variety of motives, including a legitimate response to the pressures of different linguistic, literary and cultural codes impacting on one another.

Power play is an important theme for these cultural commentators and translation scholars. In both the theory and practice of translation, **power** resides in the deployment of language as an ideological weapon for 'excluding' or 'including' a reader, a value system, a set of beliefs, or even an entire culture. As the following extract by British linguist and translation theorist Peter Fawcett shows, translators working within certain translation traditions can and often do exercise absolute power directly and consciously to exclude a reader or an author through selectively engaging in such innocent-sounding translation **procedure**s as **free translation** or **compensation**. This reader exclusion is often underpinned by real or imagined target **norms** invoked in the name of **relevance** for a target reader, language or culture. The exercise of **power** in this way is carried out by translators, but these practitioners themselves are not immune to power being directed against them. Armies of editors and censors often unthinkingly modify and even jettison those parts of the translator's work that do not fit in within schemes promoted by given target languages or translation traditions.

 Task 12.1.1

➤ Before you read Text B12.1, consider how target **norms** and conventions may militate against an author or an entire source culture (e.g. literary translations produced within the so-called Anglo-American translation tradition).

> The translator's own work is usually submitted to copy editors and translation revisers who normally exercise considerable influence in shaping the final **product**. Reflect on how this may not always be a bad thing (e.g. translations into English produced in non-English-speaking parts of the world, and published without proper editing).

> As you read, look up the definition of '**paratext**' in a linguistics reference book. Note two reasons given in the extract for why we should strive to provide paratextual information in translations, particularly in dealing with academic-oriented texts.

> Note a real translation example of a reader 'excluded'.

> Note the case of Milan Kundera as an example of author excluded.

> Note an example of harm done and another of good done by editors 'interfering' with submitted translations.

Peter Fawcett (1995) 'Translation and Power Play', *The Translator* **1.2: 177-92.**

Text B12.1
P. Fawcett

The main actors and victims of power play: reader, author, translator

The use of language to exclude some and include others is not new in translation, of course. One of the arch proponents of such power play was the 15th century translator Niclas von Wyle, who tells us that in some of his translations he has not attempted to be comprehensible to the common man, writing instead for the high-born, for whom his translations are 'uf das genewest dem latin nach gesetz' (set as close as possible to the Latin; von Keller 1861: 8-9). It is in fact in this domain, namely the use of language (not necessarily foreign) angled towards certain kinds of reader and away from others, that translators themselves are sometimes directly and consciously responsible for exercising absolute power to exclude the reader, especially when they are academically inclined. If a translator has understood and savoured the appearance in the original text of a resounding phrase such as *catastrophisme eschatologique* (taken from a sociological discussion of French leftists), the temptation is great to demonstrate one's conceptual sophistication by producing a literal translation, in this case scarcely more than a transcription, assuming without further reflection that readers will just have to work it out for themselves. This is a fairly widespread attitude among translators, students as well as professionals. In discussing with trainee translators the options involved in translating two allusions, one being *l'aventure du radeau de la Méduse* (the incident of the Medusa raft) from a philosophical discussion of cannibalism, and the other *Il meurt 'sans jeter un cri' comme le loup d'Alfred de Vigny* (he [the villain presented as heroic] dies without uttering a cry, like Alfred de Vigny's wolf) from a text on violence in films, there will always in my experience be a fair number who will insist on a literal translation, with no paratext of any kind, saying that the reader who does not understand should go and look it up. This attitude fails to take account of two things: firstly, the vast majority of English readers do not understand these allusions, as my own experience in teaching generations of English students suggests; and second, it is not at all obvious where such readers should go for an explanation and how much effort they have to expend in the process. An English reader who encounters *the Medusa raft* in a translation and goes to the encyclopedia for enlightenment will find no illumination of the darkness whatsoever under the entry *raft* and will probably fare no better with *Medusa*. Again s/he will have been excluded in the name of some ideology of textual purity, or perhaps intellectual arrogance.

This question of translating to exclude or include readership has always been a driving force in translation, and it is this power struggle which lies at the heart of the literal vs free debate. It was the big stick with which translators would cudgel one another in the old days. Rener (1989: 28-9) gives an account of one such hostile exchange between Jerome and Rufinus, where claims were made to the Authority of Antiquity; Kelly (1979: 100), referring to the same exchange, rightly points out that the appeal to authority betrays some dishonesty, and that both translators were unable, for some reason, to admit that their translations were probably dictated more by the constraints of the restricted or extended code of the intended readership. It is even possible, as Copeland does, to relate this dispute to 'a much larger issue, the conflict over disciplinary hegemony waged between grammar and rhetoric' (1991: 2). And it is almost in these latter terms (*ut interpres, ut orator*: like an interpreter or like an orator) that the polemic is resurfacing in France as a battle between *sourciers* or SL-oriented translators and *ciblistes* or TL-oriented translators (Ladmiral 1979). This time, the dispute is between the literary and the linguistic hegemonists, or between the mystics and the craftsfolk as some would have it.

1. *Exercising power against the author*

Power in translation is not always exercised against the reader, of course; it can also be directed against the original text or author, and sometimes in the most mundane of ways, as in the unthinking use of target language norms or in-house conventions. The translator of Henriette Walter's *Les Français dans tous les sens* (Walter 1988) dealt with the bibliographical references by adopting the in-house publishing convention of citing the authors by surname and initials only, a strategy which caused the author considerable distress, since for her it was a matter of courtesy to provide the first name in full.

The same book offers another example where the absence of translation served as a kind of power play against the author of the original. Ms Walter felt that the many examples cited to illustrate the French language should have been translated for the English audience, whereas the publisher decided that they should not, partly in consideration of the intended reader, who would be presumed to have or be able to acquire painlessly the required knowledge, and partly, no doubt, with an eye to the economics. The book would have almost doubled in length.

In some ways comparable, because it concerned both norms and economies, was the case of the French author of a book on Third World economics who made frequent use of the word *maldéveloppement*. The translator applied the English frequency norm of using the negating prefix *mis-* rather than *mal-*, since the dictionary clearly indicates that *mal-* is quite rare in this function. By the time the author saw what had happened and demanded a change to *mal-* (presumably because it was *his* concept), it was, economically speaking, too late: the book had already reached proof stage and it would have been far too expensive to make the change.

Text B12.1
P. Fawcett

The application of real or imagined target norms and conventions in translation can result in a much more devastating form of power play. Kuhiwczak (1990) provides an account of the way in which the chronological order of events and chapters in Milan Kundera's novel *The Joke* was rearranged by its first translators. This is yet another move which can also take place intralingually. When the film *Once Upon a Time in America* was originally released in the States, its chronology was felt to be too difficult for an American audience and a new version was prepared in which all analepsis and prolepsis were removed.

Accounts of this type may well provoke feelings of outrage in many readers but the kind of power moves they demonstrate are among the oldest in the history of translation. Aelfric tells us: 'You must know that we have abbreviated the more prolix martyrdoms, for the refined and delicate reader would be overcome with boredom if there were as much prolixity in our own language as in Latin' (original in Amos 1920/1973: 5: my translation). As Rener (1989: 233) explains, 'The prevention of boredom becomes thus an important issue not only in rhetoric but also in translation' and frequently the 'remedy is omission', although the examples I have cited so far show that other 'remedies' can also be called upon. This is the mirror image of the strategies we have seen employed in the treatment of 'delicate' or taboo matter: whereas there the intention or the effect was to produce an excluded reader, here the aim is to include the reader, albeit yet again to the detriment of the original text. This, of course, was the motive behind the *belles infidèles* of the kind quoted by von Stackelberg (1971: 588), where the French reader is spared the combined tedium and indecorum of making sense of a local accent or direct speech as they appear in the mouth of a lower class character in an 18th century novel: the translator, the eighteenth-century French novelist Prévost, simply hands the whole lot over to the reported speech – in polished French – of the upper class narrator.

2. *Exercising power against the translator*

Translators themselves are no more immune from power displays than are the reader and the original text and author. The appearance of the words *Translated by* on the title page deceives both reader and critic, since most readers (although critics ought to know better) do not realize that the text of a translation in the case of published books in particular is rarely all the translator's own work; it is usually submitted to a copy editor or other translation reviser, who normally exercises considerable influence in shaping the final product. The influence of these editors on translation has prompted a fierce diatribe from Pergnier (1990: 219), who objects to the fact that translators are increasingly losing control of their translations, especially when they are handed over to the publishers. He accuses copy editors in particular of trying to 'faire joli' (prettify) and 'donner du piquant' (spice up) translated texts (ibid). Again, this is a matter on which the evidence is hard to come by and it would be helpful if more translators were more forthcoming with information. I can personally report from my own experience that I was on one occasion cheerfully informed by a copy editor that she had felt quite free to rewrite my 'stodgy bits'. 'My way of working on this book', she wrote, 'was to think back to my student days, studying linguistics textbooks and thinking: I'm sure this does not need to sound this complicated or stodgy'. It felt like an unkind cut at the time, but in hindsight I could scarcely complain: in the lengthy process of revision, I had set up a three-way fax conversation between translator, editor and author which occasionally seemed to have the unintended side-effect of marginalizing the author

Text B12.1
P. Fawcett

from her own work. The results of power play in translation can frequently be hilarious – but not for everyone.

It must, in any case, be pointed out that onslaughts such as Pergnier's are rather one-sided, since we have to admit that many published translations would be worse than they are if they had not been looked at by another pair of eyes. It is, after all, possible in translation to become the victim of a double bind: one's own sense of mission, which can become arrogance, as the torch-bearer of the foreign tongue, and the force of inertia emitted by one's own words once they are written on the page. If the copy editor of the French translation of Barry Hines' novel *Kes* had done a better job (or been able, perhaps, to read English), s/he might have avoided the embarrassment of the book beginning with a mistranslation in the very first sentence, a mistranslation that quite considerably undermines what that sentence is intended to achieve: 'There were no curtains up' (Hines 1969: 7) is intended from the outset to symbolize a lifestyle which is in many ways impoverished, whereas the French translation, 'Les rideaux étaient fermés' (the curtains were drawn; Hines, trans. 1982: 9) suggests the opposite. Similarly, better copy editing of the English translation of Sartre's L'*Etre et le néant* and the French translation of *The Secret Diaries of Adrian Mole* might mean that academics could not use the first as a source of translation mistakes for teaching purposes (as I myself do) and the second as a source of similar data for learned papers.

 Task B12.1.2

More academically oriented translations tend to be 'exclusive' of the reader (and even the author).

➤ After you read Text B12.1, examine a sample of such translations (e.g. the UNESCO *Courier*) and identify the translation strategies used (**free**, **literal**, etc.).

However, not all academically oriented translations are inevitably exclusive of the reader. Consider the following extract, taken from a medical novella by Oliver Sacks, known for a style of writing intended to be part of 'the conversation of mankind', communicating specialized knowledge to the widest possible kind of readerships.

. . . The notion of there being 'something the matter' did not emerge until some three years later, when diabetes developed. Well aware that diabetes could affect his eyes, Dr P. consulted an ophthalmologist, who took a careful history, and examined his eyes closely. 'There is nothing the matter with your eyes', the doctor concluded. 'But there is trouble with the visual parts of your brain. You don't need my help, you must see a neurologist.' And so, as a result of this referral, Dr P. came to me.

From Oliver Sacks (1985) *The Man who Mistook His Wife for a Hat*

➤ Translate the extract into your own language, aiming for a use of language that is more 'inclusive of the reader'.

Unit B13
Ideology and translation

Section A of Unit 13 examined some of the interdisciplinary links between translation and Cultural Studies, including Gender Studies and **postcolonialism**. The reading in this section narrows the focus to **postcolonialism** and is taken from Tejaswini Niranjana's influential book *Siting Translation* (1992) which considers translation to have played a key role under British colonial rule in 'interpellating' India (fixing the image of India as inferior, thus contributing to its subjection). The extract is from the beginning of the book and is typical of the style of an approach that is avowedly **poststructuralist**. The complex linguistic structures, terminology and concepts are designed to call into question the comfortable and apolitical assumptions of earlier debate on translation that was merely concerned with the degree of linguistic equivalence of two static texts. The extract begins with a quote from Charles Trevelyan as an example of the colonialist **discourse** which Niranjana is attacking before it moves on to discuss the relation between translation and colonialism.

 Task B13.1.1

➤ Before you read Text B13.1, look again at the main concepts discussed in Section A of Unit 13. In particular, focus on the description of **postcolonialism** and the concepts of **interpellation** and **poststructuralism**.
Following Derrida and de Man, Niranjana writes from a **poststructuralist** perspective which aims to subvert the 'reasonable' neocolonialist construction of India (and the non-western world as a whole). Look at encyclopaedias or other sources (e.g. Belsey 2002) to familiarize yourself with the main ideas of **poststructuralism** and of these authors before reading Niranjana.

The reading is broken up at key points with 'reflection' boxes linked to specific translation concepts. The two 'as you read' tasks below relate to the whole of the text.

➤ List the general ways in which Niranjana considers that the west fixes the colonial subject as inferior.

➤ Note the specific assertions with regard to translation. Summarize them in your own words.

Text B13.1
T. Niranjana

Tejaswini Niranjana (1992) *Siting Translation: History, post-structuralism and the colonial context,* **Los Angeles and Oxford: University of California Press, pp. 1-3 and 8-11 (abridged).**

Introduction: History in translation

> The passion for English knowledge has penetrated the most obscure, and extended to the most remote parts of India. The steam boats, passing up and down the Ganges, are boarded by native boys, begging, not for money, but for books. [. . .] Some gentlemen coming to Calcutta were astonished at the eagerness with which they were pressed for books by a troop of boys, who boarded the steamer from an obscure place, called Comercolly. A Plato was lying on the table, and one of the party asked a boy whether that would serve his purpose. 'Oh yes,' he exclaimed, 'give me any book; all I want is a book.' The gentleman at last hit upon the expedient of cutting up an old *Quarterly Review,* and distributing the articles among them.
>
> (Charles Trevelyan, *On the Education of the People of India*)

SITUATING TRANSLATION

In a postcolonial context the problematic of *translation* becomes a significant site for raising questions of representation, power, and historicity. The context is one of contesting and contested stories attempting to account for, to recount, the asymmetry and inequality of relations between peoples, races, languages. Since the practices of subjection/subjectification implicit in the colonial enterprise operate not merely through the coercive machinery of the imperial state but also through the discourses of philosophy, history, anthropology, philology, linguistics, and literary interpretation, the colonial 'subject' – constructed through technologies or practices of power/knowledge – is brought into being within multiple discourses and on multiple sites. One such site is translation. Translation as a practice shapes, and takes shape within, the asymmetrical relations of power that operate under colonialism. What is at stake here is the representation of the colonized, who need to be produced in such a manner as to justify colonial domination, and to beg for the English book by themselves. In the colonial context, a certain conceptual economy is created by the set of related questions that is the problematic of translation. Conventionally, translation depends on the western philosophical notions of reality, representation, and knowledge. Reality is seen as something unproblematic, 'out there'; knowledge involves a representation of this reality; and representation provides direct, un-mediated access to a transparent reality.

Reflection   Box 1

> Niranjana sees translation as part of the 'colonial enterprise' of subjection of the native peoples. Note the link between the power relations she describes and our discussion of the agents of power in Section B, Unit 12.

continued

> The western concepts of reality and representation can be traced back to classical Greek and Roman writings (see Kelly 1979 and Robinson 1997). The fallacy of unmediated and transparent translation has already been discussed in Section A of this unit.

Classical philosophical discourse, however, does not simply engender a practice of translation that is then employed for the purposes of colonial domination; I contend that, simultaneously, translation in the colonial context produces and supports a conceptual economy that works into the discourse of western philosophy to function as a philosopheme (a basic unit of philosophical conceptuality). As Jacques Derrida suggests, the concepts of metaphysics are not bound by or produced solely within the 'field' of philosophy. Rather, they come out of and circulate through various discourses in several registers, providing a 'conceptual network in which philosophy *itself* has been constituted.'[1] In forming a certain kind of subject, in presenting particular versions of the colonized, translation brings into being overarching concepts of reality and representation. These concepts, and what they allow us to assume, completely occlude the violence that accompanies the construction of the colonial subject.

Translation thus produces strategies of containment. By employing certain modes of representing the other – which it thereby also brings into being – translation reinforces hegemonic versions of the colonized, helping them acquire the status of what Edward Said calls representations, or objects without history.[2] These become *facts* exerting a force on events in the colony: witness Thomas Babington Macaulay's 1835 dismissal of indigenous Indian learning as outdated and irrelevant, which prepared the way for the introduction of English education.

In creating coherent and transparent texts and subjects, translation participates – across a range of discourses – in the *fixing* of colonized cultures, making them seem static and unchanging rather than historically constructed. Translation functions as a transparent presentation of something that already exists, although the 'original' is actually brought into being through translation. Paradoxically, translation also provides a place in 'history' for the colonized. The Hegelian conception of history that translation helps bring into being endorses a teleological, hierarchical model of civilizations based on the 'coming to consciousness' of 'Spirit,' an event for which the non-western cultures are unsuited or unprepared. Translation is thus deployed in different kinds of discourses – philosophy, historiography, education, missionary writings, travel-writing – to renew and perpetuate colonial domination.

NOTES abridged version of those used in Niranjana's original text.

1. Derrida, 'White Mythology: Metaphor in the Text of Philosophy,' in *Margins of Philosophy*, trans. Alan Bass (Chicago: University of Chicago Press, 1987), p. 230.
2. Said, discussion with Eugenio Donato and others ('An Exchange on Deconstruction and History,' *Boundary* 28, no. 1 [Fall 1979]: 65–74).

Reflection Box 2

Jacques Derrida's work is central to translation theorists working from a post-structuralist angle. He has applied his concept of **deconstruction** (the interrogation and subversion of established ideas of language and representation) to translation in several articles, for example 'Des Tours de Babel' (1985).

For further discussion on British policies towards language in colonial India, and Malaysia, see Pennycook (1994, Chapter 3).

Niranjana mentions several different types of writing associated with translation. An interesting study of the image of the colonized through travel-writing (not all of which is translated) is to be found in Pratt (1992).

[. . .]

The postcolonial (subject, nation, context) is therefore still scored through by an absentee colonialism. In economic and political terms, the former colony continues to be dependent on the ex-rulers or the 'west.' In the cultural sphere (using *cultural* to encompass not only art and literature but other practices of subjectification as well), in spite of widely employed nationalist rhetoric, decolonization is slowest in making an impact. The persistent force of colonial discourse is one we may understand better, and thereby learn to subvert, I argue, by considering translation.

By now it should be apparent that I use the word *translation* not just to indicate an interlingual process but to name an entire problematic. It is a set of questions, perhaps a 'field,' charged with the force of all the terms used, even by the traditional discourse on translation, to name the problem, to translate translation. *Translatio* (Latin) and *metapherein* (Greek) at once suggest movement, disruption, displacement. So does *Übersetzung* (German). The French *traducteur* exists between *interprète* and *truchement*, an indication that we might fashion a translative practice *between* interpretation and reading, carrying a disruptive force much greater than the other two. The thrust of displacement is seen also in other Latin terms such as *transponere*, *transferre*, *reddere*, *vertere*. In my writing, *translation* refers to (a) the problematic of translation that authorizes and is authorized by certain classical notions of representation and reality; and (b) the problematic opened up by the poststructuralist critique of the earlier one, and that makes translation always the 'more,' or the *supplement*, in Derrida's sense.[3] The double meaning of *supplement* – as providing both what is missing as well as

---

3. In *Positions* (trans. Alan Bass [Chicago: University of Chicago Press, 1981]), Derrida defines *supplement* as an 'undecidable,' something that cannot any longer 'be included within philosophical (binary) opposition,' but that resists and disorganizes philosophical binaries '*without ever* constituting a third term . . .; the *supplement* is neither a plus nor a minus, neither an outside nor the complement of an inside, neither an accident nor essence' (p. 43).

Extension

something 'extra' – is glossed by Derrida thus: 'The *overabundance* of the signifier, its *supplementary* character, is the result of a finitude, that is to say, the result of a lack which must be *supplemented*.'[4] Where necessary, however, I shall specify narrower uses of *translation*.

Reflection Box 3

> The disruption and displacement involved in translation is crucial for Niranjana's argument. Note how this relates to the '**in-betweenness**' of border cultures discussed by theorists such as Bhabha (Section A, Unit 13). Translation is an inherent element of geographical, cultural and virtual border cultures.
>
> The ideas underpinning the *supplement* are linked and draw on Walter Benjamin's famous essay 'The Task of the Translator' (Benjamin 1923/1969), where translation is claimed to possess the power to revitalize. In Benjamin's view, this can be accomplished best by an **interlinear translation**, half way between ST and TT, allowing the language of the original to 'shine through' rather than erasing traces of the SL and bringing its culture into the TL. As becomes clear in the next section of the reading, Niranjana's focus is exactly on this gap between the two cultures. At the end of her book she goes on to propose a form of translation that resembles Benjamin's, **calquing** the **lexis** of the ST and enabling the source culture elements to enter the TL. This is what we might now call **foreignization** (Venuti 1995, 1998).

My study of translation does not make any claim to solve the dilemmas of translators. It does not propose yet another way of theorizing translation to enable a more foolproof 'method' of 'narrowing the gap' between cultures; it seeks rather to think through this gap, this difference, to explore the positioning of the obsessions and desires of translation, and thus to describe the economics within which the sign of translation circulates. My concern is to probe the absence, lack, or repression of an awareness of asymmetry and historicity in several kinds of writing on translation.

[. . .]

The postcolonial distrust of the liberal-humanist rhetoric of progress and of universalizing master narratives has obvious affinities with poststructuralism.[5] Derrida's critique of representation, for example, allows us to question the notion of re-presentation and therefore the very notion of an origin or an original that needs to be re-presented. Derrida would argue that the 'origin' is itself dispersed, its 'identity'

4. Derrida, 'Structure, Sign, and Play in the Discourse of the Human Sciences,' in *Writing and Difference*, trans. Alan Bass (Chicago: University of Chicago Press, 1978), p. 290.
5. In fact, I use even the terms *postcolonial* and *Third World* with some hesitation, since they too can be made to serve a totalizing narrative that disregards heterogeneity.

Text B13.1
T. Niranjana

undecidable. A representation thus does not re-present an 'original'; rather, it re-presents that which is always already represented. The notion can be employed to undo hegemonic 'representations' of 'the Hindus,' like, for example, those put forward by C. W. F. Hegel and James Mill.

[. . .]

My concern here is not, of course, with the alleged misrepresentation of the 'Hindus.' Rather, I am trying to question the withholding of reciprocity and the essen-tializing of 'difference' (what Johannes Fabian calls a denial of coevalness) that permits a stereotypical construction of the other. As Homi Bhabha puts it: 'The stereo-type is not a simplification because it is a false representation of a given reality. It is a simplification because it is an arrested, fixated form of representation that, in denying the play of difference (that the negation through the Other permits), constitutes a problem for the *representation* of the subject in significations of psychic and social relations.'[6]

The 'native boys' about whom Charles Trevelyan, an ardent supporter of English education for Indians, wrote in 1838, are 'interpellated' or constituted as subjects by the discourses of colonialism, Trevelyan shows, with some pride, how young Indians, without any external compulsion, beg for 'English.'[7]

'Free acceptance' of subjection is ensured, in part, by the production of hegemonic texts about the civilization of the colonized by philosophers like Hegel, historians like Mill, Orientalists like Sir William Jones.[8] The 'scholarly' discourses, of which literary translation is conceptually emblematic, help maintain the dominance of the colonial rule that endorses them through the interpellation of its 'subjects.' The colonial subject is constituted through a process of 'othering' that involves a teleological notion of history, which views the knowledge and ways of life in the colony as distorted or immature versions of what can be found in 'normal' or western society. Hence the knowledge of the western orientalist appropriates 'the power to represent the Oriental, to translate and explain his (and her) thoughts and acts not only to Europeans and Americans but also to the Orientals themselves.'[9]

6. Bhabha, 'The Other Question,' *Screen* 24, no. 6 (November–December 1983): 27.
7. Under colonial rule, 'the individual is interpellated as a (free) subject in order that he shall submit freely to the commandments of the Subject, i.e. in order that he shall (freely) accept his subjection, i.e. in order that he shall make the gestures and actions of his subjection "all by himself"' (Louis Althusser, 'Ideology and Ideological State Apparatuses,' in *Lenin and Philosophy, and Other Essays*, trans. Ben Brewster [New York: Monthly Review Press, 1971], p. 182; emphasis in original). Interpellation is a term used by Althusser to describe the 'constitution' of subjects in language by ideology.
8. I do not mean to lump together Hegel's idealism, Mills utilitarianism, and Jones's humanism-romanticism. Their texts are, however, based on remarkably similar premises about India and the Hindus. For a discussion of how these premises led eventually to the introduction of English education in India, see my 'Translation, Colonialism and the Rise of English,' *Economic and Political Weekly* 25, no. 15 (1990): 773-79. I am grateful to Rajeswari Sunder Rajan for her perceptive criticism of my attempt to relate translation to the beginnings of 'English' in India.
9. Ronald Inden, 'Orientalist Constructions of India,' *Modern Asian Studies* 20, no. 3 (1986): 401-46.

Task 13.1.2

The last section of Text B13.1 deals with the danger of stereotypical representation of the subject peoples who are re-invented in translation by the colonizers in such a way that their otherness is concealed. This fits with the focus of Niranjana's argument which is 'to probe the absence, lack, or repression of an awareness of asymmetry and historicity in several kinds of writing on translation'.

➤ Look at other examples (whether or not in translation) where a colonizer portrays the colonized (e.g. Joseph Conrad's novels or accounts by the Spanish conquistadors such as Cortés or Bernal Díaz of their conquest of the Aztec empires).

➤ How far is the otherness of the subject peoples portrayed or destroyed by their re-presentation?

Unit B14
Translation in the information technology era

The extract in this section discusses why **Machine Translation** (MT) is important and sets out to counter some of the myths surrounding it. Although published in 1994, it provides general background to MT which is still valid today.

Task B14.1.1

Look back at Section A of this unit and familiarize yourself with the definitions of globalization, **localization**, MT and **parallel texts**.

➤ Revise the different types of **MT** systems and what their strengths and weaknesses are.

➤ What are you own opinions about the feasibility of **MT**?

➤ As you read Text B14.1, list the key criticisms of **MT** and the way that these are countered. How do these criticisms differ from those mentioned in Section A?

➤ List the advantages of **MT** according to the authors.

D. J. Arnold, Lorna Balkan, Siety Meijer, R. Lee Humphreys and Louisa Sadler (1994) *Machine Translation: an Introductory Guide*, **Blackwells-NCC, London, pp. 4-12.**

Available online at <http://www.essex.ac.uk/linguistics/clmt/MTbook/ PostScript/>

Text B14.1
D. J. Arnold,
L. Balkan,
S. Meijer,
R. L. Humphreys
and L. Sadler

Why MT Matters

The topic of MT is one that we have found sufficiently interesting to spend most of our professional lives investigating, and we hope the reader will come to share, or at least understand, this interest. But whatever one may think about its intrinsic interest, it is undoubtedly an important topic – socially, politically, commercially, scientifically, and intellectually or philosophically – and one whose importance is likely to increase as the 20th century ends, and the 21st begins.

Text B14.1
D. J. Arnold,
L. Balkan,
S. Meijer,
R. L. Humphreys
and L. Sadler

The *social* or *political* importance of MT arises from the socio-political importance of translation in communities where more than one language is generally spoken. Here the only viable alternative to rather widespread use of translation is the adoption of a single common 'lingua franca', which (despite what one might first think) is not a particularly attractive alternative, because it involves the dominance of the chosen language, to the disadvantage of speakers of the other languages, and raises the prospect of the other languages becoming second class, and ultimately disappearing. Since the loss of a language often involves the disappearance of a distinctive culture, and a way of thinking, this is a loss that should matter to everyone. So translation is necessary for communication – for ordinary human interaction, and for gathering the information one needs to play a full part in society. Being allowed to express yourself in your own language, and to receive information that directly affects you in the same medium, seems to be an important, if often violated, right. And it is one that depends on the availability of translation. The problem is that the demand for translation in the modern world far outstrips any possible supply. Part of the problem is that there are too few human translators, and that there is a limit on how far their productivity can be increased without automation. In short, it seems as though automation of translation is a social and political necessity for modern societies which do not wish to impose a common language on their members.

This is a point that is often missed by people who live in communities where one language is dominant, and who speak the dominant language. Speakers of English in places like Britain, and the Northern USA are examples. However, even they rapidly come to appreciate it when they visit an area where English is not dominant (for example, Welsh-speaking areas of Britain, parts of the USA where the majority language is Spanish, not to mention most other countries in the world). For countries like Canada and Switzerland, and organizations like the European Community and the UN, for whom multilingualism is both a basic principle and a fact of every day life, the point is obvious.

The *commercial* importance of MT is a result of related factors. First, translation itself is commercially important: faced with a choice between a product with an instruction manual in English, and one whose manual is written in Japanese, most English speakers will buy the former – and in the case of a repair manual for a piece of manufacturing machinery or the manual for a safety critical system, this is not just a matter of taste. Secondly, translation is expensive. Translation is a highly skilled job, requiring much more than mere knowledge of a number of languages, and in some countries at least, translators' salaries are comparable to other highly trained professionals. Moreover, delays in translation are costly. Estimates vary, but producing high quality translations of difficult material, a professional translator may average no more than about 4-6 pages of translation (perhaps 2000 words) per day, and it is quite easy for delays in translating product documentation to erode the market lead time of a new product. It has been estimated that some 40-45% of the running costs of European Community institutions are 'language costs', of which translation and interpreting are the main element. This would give a cost of something like £300 million per annum. This figure relates to translations actually done, and is a tiny fraction of the cost that would be involved in doing all the translations that could, or should be done.[1]

---

1 [Arnold *et al.*'s note] These estimates of CEC translation costs are from Patterson (1982).

Text B14.1
D. J. Arnold,
L. Balkan,
S. Meijer,
R. L. Humphreys
and L. Sadler

Scientifically, MT is interesting, because it is an obvious application and testing ground for many ideas in Computer Science, Artificial Intelligence, and Linguistics, and some of the most important developments in these fields have begun in MT. To illustrate this: the origins of Prolog, the first widely available logic programming language, which formed a key part of the Japanese 'Fifth Generation' programme of research in the late 1980s, can be found in the 'Q-Systems' language, originally developed for MT.

Philosophically, MT is interesting, because it represents an attempt to automate an activity that can require the full range of human knowledge – that is, for any piece of human knowledge, it is possible to think of a context where the knowledge is required. For example, getting the correct translation of *negatively charged electrons and protons* into French depends on knowing that protons are positively charged, so the interpretation cannot be something like 'negatively charged electrons and negatively charged protons'. In this sense, the extent to which one can automate translation is an indication of the extent to which one can automate 'thinking'.

Despite this, very few people, even those who are involved in producing or commissioning translations, have much idea of what is involved in MT today, either at the practical level of what it means to have and use an MT system, or at the level of what is technically feasible, and what is science fiction. In the whole of the UK there are perhaps five companies who use MT for making commercial translations on a day-to-day basis. In continental Europe, where the need for commercial translation is for historical reasons greater, the number is larger, but it still represents an extremely small proportion of the overall translation effort that is actually undertaken. In Japan, where there is an enormous need for translation of Japanese into English, MT is just beginning to become established on a commercial scale, and some familiarity with MT is becoming a standard part of the training of a professional translator.

[. . .]

1.3 *Popular conceptions and misconceptions*

[. . .]

■ 'MT is a waste of time because you will never make a machine that can translate Shakespeare'.

The criticism that MT systems cannot, and will never, produce translations of great literature of any great merit is probably correct, but quite beside the point. It certainly does not show that MT is impossible. First, translating literature requires special literary skill – it is not the kind of thing that the average professional translator normally attempts. So accepting the criticism does not show that automatic translation of non-literary texts is impossible. Second, literary translation is a small proportion of the translation that has to be done, so accepting the criticism does not mean that MT is useless. Finally, one may wonder who would ever *want* to translate Shakespeare by machine – it is a job that human translators find challenging and rewarding, and it is not a job that MT systems have been designed for. The criticism that MT systems cannot translate Shakespeare is a bit like criticism of industrial robots for not being able to dance Swan Lake.

■ 'There was/is an MT system which translated *The spirit is willing, but the flesh is weak* into the Russian equivalent of *The vodka is good, but the steak is lousy*, and *hydraulic ram* into the French equivalent of *water goat*. MT is useless.'

Text B14.1
D. J. Arnold,
L. Balkan,
S. Meijer,
R. L. Humphreys
and L. Sadler

The 'spirit is willing' story is amusing, and it really is a pity that it is not true. However, like most MT 'howlers' it is a fabrication. In fact, for the most part, they were in circulation long before any MT system could have produced them (variants of the 'spirit is willing' example can be found in the American press as early as 1956, but sadly, there does not seem to have been an MT system in America which could translate from English into Russian until much more recently – for sound strategic reasons, work in the USA had concentrated on the translation of Russian into English, not the other way round). Of course, there are real MT howlers. Two of the nicest are the translation of French *avocat* ('advocate', 'lawyer' or 'barrister') as *avocado*, and the translation of *Les soldats sont dans le café* as *The soldiers are in the coffee*. However, they are not as easy to find as the reader might think, and they certainly do not show that MT is useless.

■ 'Generally, the quality of translation you can get from an MT system is very low. This makes them useless in practice.'

Far from being useless, there are several MT systems in day-to-day use around the world. Examples include METEO (in daily use since 1977 at the Canadian Meteorological Center in Dorval, Montreal), SYSTRAN (in use at the CEC, and elsewhere), LOGOS, ALPS, ENGSPAN (and SPANAM), METAL, GLOBALINK. It is true that the number of organizations that use MT on a daily basis is relatively small, but those that do use it benefit considerably. For example, as of 1990, METEO was regularly translating around 45 000 words of weather bulletins every day, from English into French for transmission to press, radio, and television. In the 1980s, the diesel engine manufacturers Perkins Engines was saving around £ 4 000 on each diesel engine manual translated (using a PC version of WEIDNER system). Moreover, overall translation time per manual was more than halved from around 26 weeks to 9-12 weeks – this time saving can be very significant commercially, because a product like an engine cannot easily be marketed without user manuals.

Of course, it is true that the quality of many MT systems is low, and probably no existing system can produce really perfect translations.[2] However, this does not make MT useless.

First, not every translation has to be perfect. Imagine you have in front of you a Chinese newspaper which you suspect may contain some information of crucial importance to you or your company. Even a very rough translation would help you. Apart from anything else, you would be able to work out which, if any, parts of the paper would be worth getting translated properly. Second, a human translator normally does not immediately produce a perfect translation. It is normal to divide the job of translating a document into two stages. The first stage is to produce a draft translation, i.e. a piece of running text in the target language, which has the most obvious translation problems solved (e.g. choice of terminology, etc.), but which is not necessarily perfect. This is then revised – either by the same translator, or in some large organizations by another translator – with a view to producing something that is up to standard for the job in hand. This might involve no more than checking, or it

---

2 [Arnold *et al.*'s note] In fact, one can get perfect translations from one kind of system, but at the cost of radically restricting what an author can say, so one should perhaps think of such systems as (multilingual) text creation aids, rather than MT systems. The basic idea is similar to that of a phrase book, which provides the user with a collection of 'canned' phrases to use. This is fine, provided the canned text contains what the user wants to say. Fortunately, there are some situations where this is the case.

might involve quite radical revision aimed at producing something that reads as though written originally in the target language. For the most part, the aim of MT is only to automate the first, draft translation process.[3]

■ 'MT threatens the jobs of translators.'

The quality of translation that is currently possible with MT is one reason why it is wrong to think of MT systems as dehumanizing monsters which will eliminate human translators, or enslave them. It will not eliminate them, simply because the volume of translation to be performed is so huge, and constantly growing, and because of the limitations of current and forseeable MT systems. While not an immediate prospect, it could, of course, turn out that MT enslaves human translators, by controlling the translation process, and forcing them to work on the problems it throws up, at its speed. There are no doubt examples of this happening to other professions. However, there are not many such examples, and it is not likely to happen with MT. What is more likely is that the process of producing draft translations, along with the often tedious business of looking up unknown words in dictionaries, and ensuring terminological consistency, will become automated, leaving human translators free to spend time on increasing clarity and improving style, and to translate more important and interesting documents – editorials rather than weather reports, for example. This idea [is] borne out in practice: the job satisfaction of the human translators in the Canadian Meteorological Center improved when METEO was installed, and their job became one of checking and trying to find ways to improve the system output, rather than translating the weather bulletins by hand (the concrete effect of this was a greatly reduced turnover in translation staff at the Center).

[. . .]

Machine Translation started out with the hope and expectation that most of the work of translation could be handled by a system which contained all the information we find in a standard paper bilingual dictionary. Source language words would be replaced with their target language translational equivalents, as determined by the built-in dictionary, and where necessary the order of the words in the input sentences would be rearranged by special rules into something more characteristic of the target language. In effect, correct translations suitable for immediate use would be manufactured in two simple steps. This corresponds to the view that translation is nothing more than word substitution (determined by the dictionary) and reordering (determined by reordering rules).

Reason and experience show that 'good' MT cannot be produced by such delightfully simple means. As all translators know, word for word translation doesn't produce a satisfying target language text, not even when some local reordering rules (e.g. for the position of the adjective with regard to the noun which it modifies) have been included in the system. Translating a text requires not only a good knowledge of the vocabulary of both source and target language, but also of their grammar – the system of rules which specifies which sentences are well-formed in a particular language and which are not. Additionally it requires some element of **real world knowledge** – knowledge of the nature of things out in the world and how they work together – and technical knowledge of the text's subject area. Researchers certainly believe that much can be done to satisfy these requirements, but producing systems which actually do

Text B14.1
D. J. Arnold,
L. Balkan,
S. Meijer,
R. L. Humphreys
and L. Sadler

---

3 [Arnold *et al.*'s note] Of course, the sorts of errors one finds in draft translations produced by a human translator will be rather different from those that one finds in translations produced by machine.

Text B14.1
D. J. Arnold,
L. Balkan,
S. Meijer,
R. L. Humphreys
and L. Sadler

so is far from easy. Most effort in the past 10 years or so has gone into increasing the subtlety, breadth and depth of the linguistic or grammatical knowledge available to systems. We shall take a more detailed look at these developments in due course.

In growing into some sort of maturity, the MT world has also come to realize that the 'text in – translation out' assumption – the assumption that MT is solely a matter of switching on the machine and watching a faultless translation come flying out – was rather too naive. A translation process starts with providing the MT system with *usable* input. It is quite common that texts which are submitted for translation need to be adapted (for example, typographically, or in terms of format) before the system can deal with them. And when a text can actually be submitted to an MT system, and the system produces a translation, the output is almost invariably deemed to be grammatically and translationally imperfect. Despite the increased complexity of MT systems they will never – within the forseeable future – be able to handle all types of text reliably and accurately. This normally means that the translation will have to be corrected (post-edited) and usually the person best equipped to do this is a translator.

This means that MT will only be profitable in environments that can exploit the strong points to the full. As a consequence, we see that the main impact of MT in the immediate future will be in large corporate environments where substantial amounts of translation are performed. The implication of this is that MT is not (yet) for the individual self-employed translator working from home, or the untrained lay-person who has the occasional letter to write in French. This is not a matter of cost: MT systems sell at anywhere between a few hundred pounds and over £ 100 000. It is a matter of effective use. The aim of MT is to achieve faster, and thus cheaper, translation. The lay-person or self-employed translator would probably have to spend so much time on dictionary updating and/or postediting that MT would not be worthwhile. There is also the problem of getting input texts in machine readable form, otherwise the effort of typing will outweigh any gains of automation. The real gains come from integrating the MT system into the whole document processing environment, and they are greatest when several users can share, for example, the effort of updating dictionaries, efficiencies of avoiding unnecessary retranslation, and the benefits of terminological consistency.

 Task B14.1.2

➤ Text B14.1 talks of various important areas of **MT**: social/political, commercial, scientific and philosophical. Find current examples of MT that illustrate the significance of each of these. Are there any other areas that you would include?

➤ Arnold *et al.* mention the 'real-world knowledge' that computers lack. How far does this tie in with your own experience of **MT**? In many ways, real-world knowledge is related to ideas discussed in earlier units on pragmatics and the general concept of context. Look back at some of these earlier units. Do they help explain some of the acknowledged limitations of **MT**?

➤ Reread the limitations expressed by the authors in the last paragraph of the extract. Investigate what recent developments there have been since 1994 that might have altered the situation.

SECTION C
Exploration

Unit C1
What is translation?

Using the term of Roman Jakobson (see Text B 1.1), we can say that this book focuses on **interlingual** translation. However, the interdisciplinarity of Translation Studies and the crossover with techniques from other disciplines challenges the assertion of James Holmes (Text B1.2) of a separate identity for the discipline.

Task C1.1

Several definitions of translation were given in Sections A and B of Unit 1 but it is also true that translation is a shifting phenomenon.

➤ Look back at these definitions and establish the common denominators between them.

➤ Examine definitions in other dictionaries to find elements that have not been covered by the definitions so far.

➤ Look at examples of actual translations in your own culture to see the various kinds of translations that are described: what is the difference between 'translation', '**adaptation**', '**version**', etc.?

Task C1.2

Holmes's 'Name and Nature of Translation Studies' paper was originally delivered at an Applied Linguistics Conference. Since then, things have moved on and translation is of interest to a larger number of different research groupings.

➤ Refer to internet resources such as <http://www.monabaker.com/tsresources/> (Mona Baker's homepage) and <http://www.fut.es/%7Eapym/welcome.html> (Anthony Pym's homepage) and look at forthcoming conferences related to translation.

  ■ Note the disciplines under which they are categorized or from which they accept papers.
  ■ Try and explain any variation that you discover.

■ How far does it appear that Translation Studies has been accepted as a separate discipline or is it more an interdiscipline under the umbrella of another term?

■ Is a different term to Translation Studies used in other cultures or contexts?

 Task C1.3

Fig. A1.1, p. 8, Section A described the links between Translation Studies and other disciplines.

➤ Look at translation courses and degrees offered in your own country.

➤ What theoretical and practical aspects do they cover?

➤ How far do these links tally with what is set out in Fig. A1.1? Is there anything which could be added?

 Task C1.4

The interdisciplinary links discussed in Section A included an allusion to the visual image in film studies and multi-media. However, it is true that much work on written translation has followed the traditional path of focusing on the written text to the exclusion of the visual image that accompanies it. Yet there is no real reason for this exclusion especially now that the new media and advertising are the site of much translation. The task below is an example of translation research on new media:

➤ Find a website or a printed advert which is available in your language pair.

➤ Look at the way the image and text interact in the ST and compare this with the TT.

➤ Are there any noticeable changes or inconsistencies between this interaction in the two texts? What role does the image seem to play? Does the text seem to be affected by space constraints (e.g. to fit into a specific box size)?

➤ Look at further websites or advertisements to see how far these preliminary findings are supported.

Holmes's paper refers to many key aspects of translation. It talks of translation as:

■ a **process** – what happens in the act of translating the ST
■ a **product** – analysis of the TT
■ a **function** – how the TT operates in a particular context.

These are useful distinctions, even for a text, such as Example C1.1 below, which would sometimes be dismissed as simply deficient.

Task C1.5

The following text, Example C1.1, is to be found on a shoe-cleaning machine for use by passengers at a major international airport. In many ways, the English TT is typical of the often-quoted translation howlers from hotels or restaurants.

➤ What factors in the translation **process** might have contributed to its idiosyncrasies?

➤ What **function** do you think it was supposed to have in the TL in the context of the airport?

➤ Do you think it successfully fulfils that **function**? (Note that, in the airport, there were three illustrations above it corresponding to the different stages of the operation.)

➤ In what ways can it be called a 'translation'?

Example C1.1

For a good service of the máquina please read the instrucciones.

1° To clean your shoe, on the bottom side of the brush hold yourself in the bar of the maquine.
2° Put some shoe crème and put your shoe on the brush passing the top of your shoe, just a few drops of cream is enough.
3° Shine your shoe using the brush of the color of your shoe that you will find outside this maquine.

Please fallow these instrucciones and you will have an excelente polish of your shoe.

Task C1.6

As we saw in Section A, the postulated **universals** of translation might encompass reduced ambiguity (and greater **explicitation**) in translation, as well as Toury's **laws** of increased **standardization** in the TT and of **interference** from ST to TT.

➤ Example C1.2 below is an extract of a prepared speech made by Koïchiro Matsuura, the Director-General of UNESCO, in April 2002, concerning the situation in the Middle East. Examine the English TT, Example C1.2b, looking closely for the kind of **universals** mentioned above.

➤ Are there any different features of this text which confirm or counter the hypotheses of **universals**?

➤ The replicability of research, and the testing of hypotheses are central to the debate on **universals**. Look at some other texts in your own language pairs and see if your findings so far are supported. What does this short piece of research begin to suggest about **universals**?

Example C1.2a (Back-translation of ST French)

Appeals and declarations, letters, telephone communications to different political responsibles as well as to my colleagues of the United Nations system, including Secretary-General Kofi Annan, I have not spared any effort to denounce the bombing of schools or universities, the destruction of the cultural heritage or of communication infrastructure, the attacks carried out on places of worship, as well as all forms of obstacles to the freedom of expression.

Example C1.2b (Actual English TT)

Issuing appeals and declarations, writing letters and making telephone calls to various political officials and to my colleagues in the United Nations system, including Secretary-General Kofi Annan, I have spared no effort to denounce the bombing of schools and universities, the destruction of the cultural heritage and communication infrastructure, attacks on places of worship and all forms of obstacles to freedom of expression.

CONCLUSION

This unit has discussed the definition of translation and the different types of translation. Most written translation is understood as **interlingual** translation but we must acknowledge that the concept is more fuzzy in real life since other forms of translation (such as posters and street signs) often co-exist with the written text. In addition, the shoe-shine example shows that presentation of a TT, even a defective TT, as a translation immediately endows it with a certain status as long as it allows the user to work the machine successfully. In relation to the study of translation, the term **Translation Studies**, as coined by Holmes, has been discussed referring to the established discipline, or interdiscipline, which covers the varied phenomena around the **process**, **product** and **function**/context of translation. However, it remains debatable whether it is possible to determine any **universals** or, indeed, a general theory of translation that is valid for all texts and situations. Later units in this book examine closely the different contexts, **text-types** and participants which constrain translation.

PROJECT

1. Keep a notebook during a week and make a note of translation examples you come across in daily life of Jakobson's **interlingual**, **intralingual** and **inter-semiotic** translation. What links can you see between the different categories? Are there any examples which do not fit and which may show the need to modify the categories?

Unit C2
Translation strategies

As George Steiner notes, adherence to **literal** translation has been preferred for what is perceived to be the 'word of God'. For this reason, as well as provoking much heated debate not to say vicious persecution over the centuries, the many translations of sacred scriptures have also been the subject of numerous studies. A large selection of English language translations of the Bible are to be found on the internet at sites such as the Berean Christian stores (www.berean.com/). In 2003 the authors of the site illustrate their evaluation of the translation strategy adopted by the different versions by quoting the translation from each of a verse from Job (36: 33) and describing what they consider to be the translation strategy employed:

Example C2.1a Authorized King James Version (1611)

'The noise thereof sheweth concerning it; the cattle also concerning the vapour.'

The strategy, according to Berean, gives 'priority to word translation rather than meaning' and the purpose was 'to deliver God's book unto God's people in a tongue they can understand'.

Example C2.1b Revised King James Version (1982)

'His thunder announces His presence; the storm announces His indignant anger.'

The strategy is a modern language update of the King James Version.

Example C2.1c The New International Version (1978)

'His thunder announced the coming storm, even the cattle make known its approach.'

The idea was to find a balance between '**word-for-word**' and 'thought-for-thought'. The purpose was to 'produce an accurate translation, suitable for public and private reading, teaching, preaching, memorizing, and liturgical use'.

Example C2.1d The Living Bible (1971)

'We feel His presence in the thunder. May all sinners be warned.'
The goal was to provide a 'popular paraphrase' where 'meaning is all important'.

Task C2.1

➤ Look closely at the different TTs.

➤ How far can these TTs be categorized according to the 'literal-free' and 'form-content' clines discussed in Section A, Unit 2?

➤ How far do the strategies described relate to those clines?

➤ Have a look at the Berean or similar websites to see whether other strategic concepts are mentioned that may have influenced the translations.

The **form-content** and **literal-free** poles are still commonly used in the description of literary translations. Reviews of translations in the literary press, if they comment at all on the fact of translation, most likely make a criticism of the **form** or **style**. One example, from the review section of *The Guardian* on 23 February 2002, discussed the translation of Akimitsu Takagi's classic 1965 crime thriller *Mikkokusha*, translated as *The Informer* by Sadako Mizuguchi (Soho Press 1999). The reviewer damns it as follows: 'It sounds intriguingly noir, but sadly this translation is almost completely lacking in style, leaving us with a rather pedestrian and dated crime thriller.'

Task C2.2

Example C2.2 below is part of a review of the English translation of a Hungarian novel, Sándor Márai's *Embers*, published in *The Guardian* on 5 January 2002.

➤ Read the extract from the review and note the comments about the translation itself.

➤ How far do the comments on the translation fit with the discussion on **translatability** and 'literal-free' divisions in the first parts of this unit?

➤ How important do you feel it is to achieve consistency of **style** and terminology in the translation of a literary work?

Example C2.2

Much of Márai's style and patterning has been lost. While Hungarian doesn't have as rich a vocabulary as English, Márai's use of some pet words in an almost incantatory manner is no accident. On the first page of the original chapter three, for instance, he uses various forms of the verb *sértodni* four times. They are translated as 'suffers the wound', 'wound', 'offended pride' and 'offended': words that convey the sense well, but hide Márai's arrangement from the English reader.

Often, of course, the actual form of a word contributes to the content or meaning of a text. Example C2.3 sets challenging translation problems, since a change in the spelling of the names may alter the numeric value of its component letters. The narrator of this award-winning (mainly) children's detective story is an autistic teenager with a brilliant mathematical brain.

Example C2.3

I said that I wasn't clever. I was just noticing how things were, and that wasn't clever. [. . .] Being clever was when you looked at how things were and used the evidence to work out something new. [. . .] Like if you see someone's name and you give each letter a value from 1 to 26 (**a = 1**, **b = 2** etc.) and you add the numbers up in your head and you find that it makes a prime number, like **Jesus Christ** (151), or **Scooby Doo** (113), or **Sherlock Holmes** (163), or **Doctor Watson** (167).

(Mark Haddon (2003) *The Curious Incident of the Dog in the Night-Time*,
Oxford: David Fickling Books, p. 32 (emphasis is the original author's))

Task C2.3

➤ Try to translate this example into another language you know. How far does **literal** translation help you in creating a successful TT? At what point is a different strategy necessary?

Humour (or humor) is something that translates with notorious difficulty. This is even more so when the original involves a culture clash. The examples in Examples C2.4 and 2.5 are from the hit American sitcom *Frasier*, which has been **subtitled** or **dubbed** into many languages. The episode we shall discuss is *An Affair to Forget*.

Example C2.4   Frasier – the dialect of Bavaria

Frasier, a radio psychologist, receives a call from a German listener, Gretchen, who fears her husband Gunnar is having an affair. Frasier has already discovered that his brother Niles's wife is seeing a Bavarian fencing instructor called Gunnar. Frasier inadvertently reveals this knowledge, and tries to cover it up by saying that he recognizes Gretchen's German accent. But she then reveals she is from Austria not Bavaria!

Example C2.5   Frasier – A German family in Guatemala

Later on, Niles challenges Gunnar to a duel. Since Gunnar does not speak a word of English, their conversation is interpreted from German to Spanish by Marta, Niles's Guatemalan maid, and from Spanish to English by Frasier. Marta's unexpected knowledge of German is due to the fact that she had worked for a German family who, we are told, had arrived in Guatemala 'just after the war'.

Task C2.4

Imagine you were translating this episode for transmission in Germany.

➤ How would you deal with these two scenarios and the problems posed by the need for communication barriers to be constructed deliberately from the different nationalities of the characters?

➤ In what sense might these texts be 'untranslatable'?

THE ACTUAL GERMAN TRANSLATION

In fact, the broadcast German version alters the scenario and makes Gunnar and Gretchen Danish. This solves the problem of Gunnar's needing to speak a language which is unintelligible to the others and to the audience. Gunnar's Bavarian accent is displaced to Greenland and Gretchen is from Iceland rather than Austria. The translation of the second extract has Gunnar speaking in Danish, Marta in Spanish and Frasier **interpreting** from Spanish into German for Niles! Marta's explanation of her knowledge of Danish is that she had worked for some Danish people who had been . . . cultivating cannabis in Guatemala. The ST's reference to the Second World War and the implication of Nazism (potentially controversial in a German translation) is shifted to a different illegal activity which scandalizes Frasier. The major difficulty of this scenario is that **form** and **content** are inextricably linked for humorous effect and yet in translation the cultural context shifts, rendering **literal** translation impossible and perhaps necessitating **explicitation** to ensure the TT reader's comprehension, while retaining the humorous effect.

Making a text's meaning transparent and making it fit with the expectations of the TT **audience** is what the American theorist Lawrence Venuti (1995: 21) calls **domesticating translation** or **domestication**. This is the strategy Venuti says is preferred by Anglo-American publishers, and readers, and involves downplaying the foreign characteristics of the language and culture of the ST. This is opposed to the strategy of **foreignization** (1995: 20) that is proposed by Venuti. Closer to **literal** translation, a **foreignizing** strategy attempts to bring out the foreign in the TT itself, sometimes through **calquing** of ST **syntax** and lexis or through lexical **borrowings** that preserve SL items in the TT.

CONCLUSION

The dichotomies of **form–style, content**–sense and **literal–free** translation dominated translation theory for a very long time. But, as Steiner (1975/1998) says, this bi-polar perspective is ultimately sterile since it does not encourage further examination of the internal and external contextual constraints which affect the translation strategy and **function**. At the very least, the examples examined in this chapter have shown that **literal** and **free** cannot be considered as poles, but as a cline. The next units will examine some of these variables and show how translation theory has attempted to classify them.

PROJECTS

1. This unit has introduced some specific terminology related to translation and Translation Studies. Add these to the **glossary** that you commenced in Section A, Unit 1. Note particularly terms, such as **literal** translation, which may be used differently by different theorists.

2. Venuti's **domestication** and **foreignization** have exerted a central influence in translation over the past decade. Find examples of published translations in your own country which seem to have followed these two strategies. Try producing a **domesticating** and **foreignizing translation** of the same ST. Make a list of the methods you use to produce these translations.

3. This exploration section has discussed published reviews of translations. Have a look at other press reviews of a variety of works published in your own country. Note the comments they make about the translation itself. Summarize and try and categorize these statements. Is it possible to make generalizations about them? How far do they still adopt a dogmatic and **prescriptive** attitude to translation, favouring **domestication** over **foreignization**?

Unit C3
The unit of translation

In Example A3.2, we looked at the dictionary entry for the word *outbreak* and how some of the examples functioned as a single **translation unit** with a one-word translation. This lexicological unit of translation, to use Vinay and Darbelnet's term, can be further investigated using examples from electronic **corpora** (see Section A, Unit 14) or using a search for the term *outbreak* on any internet search engine (e.g. www.google.com).

Task C3.1

Examination of examples in monolingual **corpora** is now a firmly established lexicographical methodology.

➤ Look at the examples of *outbreak* in Text C3.1 below. These are from a range of sources accessed using the Google search engine (www.google.com).

➤ Think of what the **unit of translation** for each instance will be (e.g. is it just the word *outbreak* alone, or is it a longer word group?).

➤ Translate each instance into your language (or main foreign language).

➤ What do you learn about the way the **unit of translation** alters in these instances? In the light of your findings, would you modify the dictionary entry presented in Example A3.2?

Example C3.1 Examples of *outbreak*

1. Taiwan hit by sudden outbreak of rebranding madness.
2. It was the worst tornado outbreak in US history.
3. A Northumberland farmer is found guilty of animal cruelty and failing to tell officials of a foot-and-mouth outbreak among his pigs.
4. Bird flu outbreak started a year ago.
5. Historians believe there were several reasons for the outbreak of war during the summer of 1914.

6. Is there a way to stop the outbreak?

7. WHO post-outbreak biosafety guidelines for handling of SARS specimens.

Example C3.2a below is the beginning of an open letter from the British Prime Minister Tony Blair in March 2001. It was published at the height of the foot-and-mouth epidemic when large areas of the British countryside were closed to walkers and when the numbers of foreign tourists had plummeted. The Prime Minister is attempting to reassure potential visitors. The letter was published on British Embassy and Consulate websites around the world and, in translated form, appeared in the press in many countries.

Example C3.2a   Open letter from Tony Blair, Prime Minister of the UK

BRITAIN OPEN FOR BUSINESS

I want to use this article to put over two messages about Britain. First, that we are doing everything we can to contain and eliminate foot-and-mouth disease.

Secondly, that this outbreak, dreadful as it is for the farmers affected, has not closed Britain, that there is no danger to human health, that everyday life continues as normal for the overwhelming majority of people in our country – and that our great tourist attractions are open for visitors.

I know this may be at odds with what you have seen or read. TV pictures of slaughtered animals and funeral pyres have brought the tragedy of foot-and-mouth disease in Britain into homes in [Belgium/Czech Republic/Libya, etc.] and across the world . . .

 Task C3.2

➤ Imagine you have been asked to translate Tony Blair's address into your first language (or main foreign language if your first language is English).

- Decide what your **translation units** are, based on unit categories suggested by Vinay and Darbelnet (see Text B3.1).
- In your analysis, what seems to be the predominant unit and are there any units which are different from those we have covered?

Example C3.2b below is a **back-translation** of the French translation of Blair's letter which appeared in the Belgian daily *La Libre Belgique* on 13 April 2001:

Example C3.2b   Back-translation of French translation of Blair's letter

Great-Britain is greatly open

I would like in a few lines to convey two messages about the foot-and-mouth epidemic:

– firstly, we are doing everything to contain it and bring it to an end.

– secondly, as terrible as it may be for the farmers concerned, it has not closed the country; it is not a danger to human health and life continues as before for the overwhelming majority of my compatriots; our great tourist sites are open to visitors.

– I know that this is a little different from what you may have seen or heard. The pictures of bodies and pyres broadcast by television have brought this tragedy into all the homes in Belgium and elsewhere . . .

Task C3.3

Vinay and Darbelnet's analysis of translation **procedures**, which we shall explore in more depth in Unit 4, involves first determining the units of the ST and matching these with units observed in the TT. To understand how this may work:

➤ Look back at the 'unit of translation as a prelude to analysis' explanation in Section A, Unit 3, pp. 20–2.

➤ Look at the ST in Example C3.2a. Divide it into units and number them.

➤ Follow the same process with the TT, Example C3.2b, dividing the text into units and numbering them.

➤ Match the TT units to the ST units as best you can.

➤ Make a list of instances where it seems that the translator has used a different **unit of translation** from what you expected.

➤ Try the same method with your own TT from Task C3.2. What are the major differences between the units adopted in your translation and those adopted in the Belgian TT? Why do you think these differences may have occurred?

On the level of the word, note how *outbreak* in paragraph two of Example C3.2a is in fact not translated at all in the TT Example C3.2b. Rather, the object pronoun *it* ('contain *it* and bring *it* to an end') refers back to *the foot-and-mouth epidemic* of the previous sentence. This suggests that the **translation unit** is a shifting concept in the **process** of translation and can easily span sentence boundaries.

Task C3.4

Example C3.3 below is taken from the beginning of the short story *In Another Country* (1927) by Ernest Hemingway. Short sentences, or sentences linked by **paratactic** connectors such as *and* and *but*, are often considered to be typical of his bare style. Any alteration to that structure in translation could have an important bearing of the **style** of the TT.

➤ Look at the text and consider how far the sentence might function as a **unit of translation**.

➤ To test this, try translating the text into another language.

➤ Find published translations of this work in other languages. Look at the structure of the translation of this extract and of longer passages from the ST. How far do the translators seem to have used the sentence as their **unit of translation**, or has the **style** been altered, or, in your view, distorted in the TTs?

Example C3.3 *In Another Country*

In the fall the war was always there, but we did not go to it any more. It was cold in the fall in Milan and the dark came very early. Then the electric lights came on, and it was pleasant along the streets looking in the windows. There was much game hanging outside the shops, and the snow powdered in the fur of the foxes and the wind blew their tails. The deer hung stiff and heavy and empty, and small birds blew in the wind and the wind turned their feathers. It was a cold fall and the wind came down from the mountains.

In Section A, Unit 1, and later in Section A, Unit 11, we mention the unit at the **intertextual** level; all texts, and their readers, are affected and influenced by other texts. It is also true that no text stands in isolation from its communicative situation and that the choice of **translation unit** (in the sense of the structure and **content** of the TT) is motivated by extratextual considerations such as legal, ideological, cultural and even practical constraints.

 Task C3.5

Consider the following three scenarios and what has happened in translation.

➤ How would you analyse the **unit of translation** in this case?

➤ How far do your observations fit with or challenge the analysis of the **unit of translation** given earlier in this unit?

Example C3.4

Bio yoghurt is the name of a type of yoghurt made from active bifidus culture sold in many countries. However, in France, where the word *bio* means 'organic' (i.e. produced without the use of artificial pesticides and fertilizers, etc.), Danone's *Bio yoghurt* contains an explanation on the carton in French that the yoghurt 'is not from organic cultures'. This is omitted from packaging in the UK.

Example C3.5

A cycle helmet manufacturer provides a 10-point instruction leaflet in 12 languages. However, the Norwegian TT adds the following point:

'The helmet must not be used for play or climbing, since the helmet can get stuck and represents a hazard for the user with the danger of hanging.'

Example C3.6

There are some scenarios where documentation for a meeting will not be translated according to the **norms** of the TL. UNESCO's Guidelines for Translators (1997) make the following point regarding paragraph numbering: 'Documents need to be recognizably identical in all languages. [. . .] When paragraphs are numbered, the order of paragraphs must not be altered, even if, for instance, countries or organizations are dealt with in alphabetical order in the original and will not be in alphabetical order in [the TT].'

The methodology in this unit has been based on the reconstruction of the **unit of translation** from analysis of a ST–TT pair or on the presumption of what units would be used to produce a possible translation of a given ST. However, another approach is to observe the process of a translator working on a text. There are two ways of doing this: either by looking at draft translations where the revisions indicate some of the processes that have led to the final TT, or **Think-Aloud Protocols** (TAPs), where the researcher generally presents a translator (novice or professional) with a ST and records the translator as he or she 'thinks aloud' (see Krings 1986; Lörscher 1991; Tirkonnen-Condit and Jääskeläinen 2000). The last two tasks in this unit encourage experimentation with this method:

Task C3.6   Think-Aloud Protocol analysis

➤ Choose a suitable short ST and give it to a professional or trainee translator to translate.

➤ Ask him or her to talk through their thoughts as they carry out the translation.

➤ Observe and record the translator as s/he undertakes this task.

➤ Transcribe their comments (this can be very time-consuming, which is why a relatively short ST is best!).

➤ Analyse the comments and see how far it is possible to identify the **units of translation**.

➤ Try this task with a variety of informants with different levels of expertise to see if there is a difference in the unit they use. Try also with the informants translating into their second language to find what difference this makes (see Campbell 1998 for detailed treatment into the second language).

 Task C3.7   Draft translations

➤ Choose a suitable, longer ST and give it to a professional or trainee translator to take away and translate.

➤ Ask them to save the different drafts they make of the translation.

➤ Analyse the different drafts. Note the revisions at each stage.

➤ Try to identify the **units of translation** at each stage. How far does the translator operate at word, group, sentence or **text** level, and does this change at all as the translation **process** develops?

➤ Try this task with a variety of subjects with different levels of expertise to see if there is a difference in the unit they use.

CONCLUSION

More recent technical developments enable us to explore the notion of the **unit of translation** in exciting ways. In Section C we have used electronic **corpora** to help analyse the lexicological unit and **Think-Aloud Protocols** to research the thought processes of the translator. The results are inevitably fuzzy, because of the problems of analysing what is essentially a **cognitive** process. However, it does seem that translators operate on a variety of different levels and certainly very little translation can be carried out on a purely word level. As this section progresses, it will look at increasingly higher levels of translation where **text**, **discourse** and **ideology** play crucial roles. Unit C4, however, will first follow Vinay and Darbelnet in using the segmentation into units of translation as a necessary prelude to the analysis of **translation shifts**.

PROJECTS

1. The methodology described in Task C3.1, involving the examination of **concordance** lines of specific search terms and the determination of possible translation **equivalents** for the compilation of bilingual dictionary entries, can be used for any word-form. Try examining a range of different words, including different parts of speech, to see how the potential **unit of translation** varies from word to group and even to a higher level. How far is it possible to make generalizations about the **unit of translation**?

2. The translation of advertising is sometimes an example of translation at the level of full **text** or even culture, especially where the image is accompanied by a culturally specific slogan and little other textual material. Find examples of translated adverts in your country. Compare them to their originals and consider what the **unit of translation** has been in each case. Try to put together a **taxonomy** of the different **units of translation** employed in advertising translation (see Adab (2001) and Adab and Valdés (2004) for useful articles in this area).

Unit C4
Translation shifts

In Sections A and B of this unit, we discussed the important distinction made by Catford between **formal correspondence** and **textual equivalence**. The function of bilingual dictionaries lies somewhere between the two since they describe the relation between two different language systems but, in addition, they seek to provide **textual equivalents** for the likely contexts in which the headword occurs. The example below (adapted) shows part of the entry for *retirarse* in the *Collins Spanish Dictionary* (2000).

Example C4.1

retirarse *VPR*

1 a (= *moverse*) to move back *or* away (**de** from); **retírate de la entrada** move back *or* away from the door; **retirarse ante un peligro** to shrink back from a danger
2 (= *irse*) **puede usted retirarse** you may leave; **el testigo puede retirarse** the witness may stand down; **retirarse de las negociaciones** to withdraw from the negotiations; **se retiraron del torneo** (before start) they withdrew from *or* pulled out of the tournament; (after start) they retired from *or* pulled out of the tournament

 Task C4.1

➤ Look at this entry and the different English alternatives.

➤ What **formal correspondents** are presented in English for *retirarse*?

➤ If the example sentences given are to be taken as specific textual instances, what examples of **textual equivalents** are there in English for *retirarse*?

➤ Look at other dictionaries in other languages and evaluate how they present **correspondents** and **equivalents**.

The seven **procedures** listed by Vinay and Darbelnet in the reading presented in Section B of this Unit can be used in any translation situation. The following is part of a multilingual text to be found by the doors of trains on the Paris metro at the eye level of a young child. It is illustrated by a picture of a rabbit getting its paws caught as the doors close.

Example C4.2a   Paris metro French ST

Ne mets pas tes mains sur les portes. Tu risques de te faire pincer très fort.
[*Do not put your hands on the doors. You risk getting yourself nipped very hard.*]

Example 4.2b   English TT

Beware of trapping your fingers in the doors.

Task C4.2

Analyse this short text using the Vinay and Darbelnet model. Use the following methodology:

➤ Divide the French ST into units and number them.

➤ Divide the English TT into units and match them to the ST units.

➤ Decide which of Vinay and Darbelnet's translation **procedures** have been used and therefore what **shifts** have occurred.

➤ What conclusions can you draw about the translator's approach to this text?

➤ What difficulties do you find with this analysis?

Analysis of Task C4.2

The French–English translation shows a number of **shifts**. There is a grammar>lexis level **shift** with the French negative construction *ne . . . pas* translated lexically as *beware of . . .* and an interesting **textual equivalent** *fingers* for *mains*. In fact, only *your* for *tes* and *doors* for *portes* are clearly not **shifts**. Vinay and Darbelnet's model allows greater precision in the categorization of the **shifts**. Following them, we might match up the translation units as below:

1. Ne . . .   Beware of
2. mets   trapping
3. . . . pas

continued

4.	tes mains	your fingers
5.	sur	in
6.	les portes.	the doors.

Analysis might continue as follows:

1. and 3. *ne . . . pas* shifts to *beware of . . .*, which is **modulation** and negation of the opposite.
2. Explicative **modulation**, the effect (*trapping*) for the cause (*mets*).
4. Explicative **modulation**, the part (*fingers*) for the whole (*mains*).
5. **Modulation**, change of point of view.
6. **Literal** translation.

The second sentence from the French seems to be omitted entirely, though it could be claimed that *trapping* condenses the sense of *mets* with *pincer*. Similarly, *beware of* picks up some of the sense of *tu risques de* through **modulation** but with a change of point of view.

There are a number of difficulties with the analysis, not least in accurately assigning a **shift** to a specific category (the **shift** from *sur* to *in*, for instance) and in determining exactly which TT element has translated which ST element (*pincer* and *trapping*, or *beware* and *risques*). Another uncertainty concerns how to deal with the **register** of the text. The French ST is clearly directed at children with the informal *tu* form being used, an extended structure with no subordinate clauses, and a basic **lexicon**. The English cannot distinguish between formal and informal *you*, is more condensed and the **lexicon** is of a higher level (*beware*, *trapping*).

A key question in this type of analysis is whether we should really consider there to be a **shift** when the language systems have different **norms**? This enters the realm of what Vinay and Darbelnet call *option* and *servitude*.

Concept box *Option* and *servitude*

In **transfer** from ST to TT *servitude* refers to a **shift** that is unavoidable because of systemic differences between the languages; *option* refers to a non-obligatory variant that the translator has chosen for stylistic or other reasons. Clearly this is an important distinction. Of most interest to translation scholars are the **shifts** due to *option* since they indicate specific choices made by the translator in a specific translation situation.

Vinay and Darbelnet discuss some of the translation problems mentioned above. At the level of 'message', this includes ways of **compensating** (see Concept Box, p. 31) for the French informal form of address (Vinay and Darbelnet 1958/1995: 198–200). These include use of the forename or nickname in English, though it is true that the examples they give are from dialogue only.

Task C4.3

➤ Look again at the notice on the Paris metro train (Example C4.2a).

➤ Try and put together an English translation that **compensates** for the **loss** in Example C4.2b.

➤ If your first language is other than English or French, try producing a translation in that language too.

➤ What elements do you feel need consideration which have not appeared in the **shift** analysis so far?

Task C4.4

Compensation is a strategy often used in translation. You might want to add this to the list of possible **universals** of translation (Unit 1), or at least hypothesize as to its generality and begin to look for examples to test for it.

TRANSLATION EVALUATION SCHEME – A FIRST STEP

Translation shift analysis purports to be an objective analysis of the changes that have occurred between two texts. We will use it as a step in the construction of a toolkit for the evaluation of translation. It does, though, tend to focus above all on the word or small group level and neglects the wider **discourse** characteristics and the cultural contexts of translation. It makes little mention of the functions of language or of the acts of communication which take place between translator and reader. Analysis of Example C4.2 might indicate a preponderance of **literal** translation, **transposition** and **modulation**, but, some might say, 'so what?, what does it actually tell us about translation?' These are crucial issues that are discussed in later units of this book. Furthermore, the supposed objectivity of the analysis depends on the analyst's capacity to categorize with total precision, which is rather doubtful since there is inevitably some smoothing of fuzzy edges, and on being able to decide **equivalence** in meaning objectively. Unit 5 explores 'scientific' attempts to measure meaning in translation and Unit 6 begins the specific examination of forms of **equivalence**.

PROJECTS

1. In Text B4.2 in the Extension section, Vinay and Darbelnet give proverbs and idioms as examples of the '**equivalence' procedure** and book and film titles as examples of '**adaptation**'. Find examples of the translation of proverbs and titles between your own languages. How frequent in these translations are Vinay and Darbelnet's **equivalence** and **adaptation** compared with **literal** translation? What factors seem to be influencing the translations you look at?

2. In Section A, we mentioned the use of **translation shift** analysis in **Descriptive Translation Studies** as a means of producing hypotheses and making generalizations about translation. Find several ST–TT pairs in your own languages. Analyse them according to Vinay and Darbelnet's **procedures**. What general trends emerge in the analysis? What are the most frequent types of translation **procedures**? What hypotheses can you suggest concerning what is happening in these translations? How would it be possible to test these hypotheses?

Unit C5
The analysis of meaning

In Sections A and B of Unit 5 we described the forms of **semantic structure analysis**, including contrastive terms and **componential analysis**, that can be used to analyse meaning. Decisions have to be made about what are core elements of meaning and what are incidental. However, it is really only by carrying out such analysis that its efficacy and usefulness can be assessed.

Task C5.1

➤ Carry out a **semantic structure** or **componential analysis** to differentiate the following groups of words:

1 kidnap/abduct/hijack
2 table/desk/worktop/bench
3 detached house/semi-detached house/flat/maisonette/studio/bedsit/ apartment
4 swede/parsnip/turnip
5 fond/attached/devoted

and the following **polysemous** words:

6 bank
7 heart
8 file

➤ What works well with this analysis and what kinds of problems occur?

Task C5.2

➤ Try carrying out a similar analysis with sets of words from other languages that you know. For example, for the German *sollen/müssen/brauchen*.

Task C5.3

➤ Imagine you had to translate the following English terms, which are mostly of very new coinage:

1 booze cruise
2 congestion charging
3 school run
4 transfer window
5 benchmarking

➤ Analyse the meaning of the different expressions.

➤ If any of these are unfamiliar to you, decide how you will first of all discover their meaning.

➤ What translations in your languages would you suggest for these words?

 Task C5.4

➤ Analyse the following words according to their potential **connotative** meanings:

1 chance/possibility/opportunity
2 communist/anarchist/conservative/socialist
3 middle class
4 claim/say/assert
5 terrorist
6 white van man
7 middleman

➤ Try these words out on other respondents to make the results more objective. How much agreement is there on the **connotation** of these terms?

➤ Repeat the exercise with a set of words in another language you know.

The structural or **connotative** analysis of these examples is clearly useful in cases where the exact sense of the ST is in doubt or in lexicographical or terminological work where a precise definition or division of meaning is essential prior to a mapping on to TL terms.

Of course, even though the 'essential' core senses may be clear (or at least intuitively clear to native speakers) often there are fuzzy boundaries between members of groups which cloud the issue. This is the point of a famous article by Labov (1973) where respondents were asked to classify different containers (see Figure C5.1).

Task C5.5

Figure C5.1 A series of cup-like objects (from Labov 1973: 354)

➤ Look at the diagram and decide which you would term *cup*, which *glass*, which *mug*, which *bowl*, etc.

➤ Ask other respondents and see if there is any disagreement.

➤ Try and decide which are 'essential' or 'core' elements of the different terms, and where the fuzzy boundaries are.

➤ Carry out the same experiment using other languages that you know. Do the core and fuzzy characteristics alter?

There is a danger that the focus of analysis is on decontextualized lexis, the meaning of which may well alter according to context: so, a *cup* may normally have a handle, unless it is broken or comes out of a vending machine.

 Task C5.6

➤ Look back at your responses to Task C5.5.

➤ Try to identify the dimensions which cause the same object to be described differently (e.g. when is an object referred to as a *bowl* and when as a *cup*?).

The really interesting question for us is how useful such analysis can be for translation. It must be doubtful whether, in most cases, a translator will actually consciously adopt the types of analysis described above simply because of the time required and the fact that the translator is always working at the interface of two languages. Much of the **contrastive analysis** will also generally have been carried out in the compilation of good bilingual dictionaries, **glossaries** and **term banks** (see Unit A14). It may, though, be that the tendency is for translation to focus on the core meanings, to resort more frequently to generic nouns such as *the fact, issue, matter,* etc., or to use **explicitation**. Thus, in December 2002, oil from the wreck of the oil-tanker *Prestige* covered the coast of Galicia with what the Spanish called *chapapote*. **Parallel texts** in English simply referred to the generic *oil* or *oil slick,* or, in one instance, more precisely **explicated** it as *thick, tarry residue*. On other occasions, a foreign word is **borrowed** into the TL where no such item or concept existed: for instance, *tsunami* or *sushi* which have been imported from Japanese, and *triage* is an import from French that is used in many hospitals in the English-speaking world.

 Task C5.7

This task investigates what happens when an uncommon or new word suddenly appears in the news as a key element in a major international news story. For instance, the word *chad* was crucial in the US presidential elections in November 2000.

➤ How did the non-US media, and dictionaries, deal with the term?

➤ Was the term **borrowed** into the TL, was a new term coined or an existing term adapted?

➤ What does this show about how the TL deals with a new meaning from a powerful SL?

➤ Look at examples of other technical words that suddenly come to prominence in major international news stories.

When a **neologism** is created in a language, it is sometimes difficult to fix its **connotation**. The word *fashionista* is a recent creation of the English-language media and some examples suggest a positive slant, e.g. 'the must-have gifts on every fashionista's wish-list' (*Metro* – London edition – 3 December 2002). However, this is a word which would need to be investigated to see if there is any negative **connotation** in other contexts. Words can shift over time too. The Russian word *glasnost* appears in Dostoyevsky's *Crime and Punishment* and is translated as *beneficent publicity* by Constance Garnett (Dostoyevsky 1912/1966: 236). Yet in 1991, when the Russian term had become a political keyword, the new translation by David McDuff felt it appropriate to leave *glasnost* in the English (Dostoyevsky 1991: 339). Similarly, with cultural terms the analysis of the sense may be similar, but geographical, political or **genre** considerations may determine the translation.

Task C5.8

The festival of Halloween, the night of the witches, falls on 31 October and dates from the pre-Christian era. In translation from and into English, it is treated in many different ways:

■ An Italian translation of a guidebook to Ireland provides a description but emphasizes the Christian feast of All Souls that follows;
■ the Chinese translation of the first Harry Potter book explains the festival in an academic footnote;
■ the English **subtitles** of the film script of the French film *Les visiteurs* (Jean-Marie Poiré, 1993) give 'You're all dressed up for Halloween' whereas the original character speaks of dressing up for Mardi Gras.

➤ Reflect on the above translations and think of the possible motivations for the choice of the translation of *Halloween*.

➤ Find other examples of the translation of *Halloween* in your own languages. What trends can you identify?

➤ Explore the treatment of other culturally loaded terms. Is it possible to generalize about how these are translated and the elements of their meaning that are stressed?

KINSHIP TERMS

The mapping and comparison of **kinship terms** is an example of the successful analysis of decontextualized items. Of course, cultural knowledge is essential in order to draw up the list of relationships, but the format illustrated by Larson (see Text B5.1) is clear.

 Task C5.9

➤ Using Larson's example in Display 5.5 of Text B5.1, fill in the chart below with **kinship terms** in your own culture or in another culture that you know. Include lineal (e.g. *mother*), colineal (e.g. *aunt*) and ablineal (e.g. *cousin*) relationships of the different generations.

➤ How far does your chart map onto Larson's chart of English **kinship terms**?

➤ How useful do you think this would be for a translator?

	lineal		colineal		ablineal	
	masc.	fem.	masc.	fem.	masc.	fem.
second generation previous						
previous generation						
same generation		*ego*				
next generation						
second generation following						

While the mapping is useful for contrasting the two systems, it may still not solve specific translation problems. The following is typical: Yoruba, the major language of South-West Nigeria, has two words for the relationship of brother, namely *egbon* (elder brother) and *aburo* (younger brother). The translation into Yoruba of the sentence 'My brother phoned yesterday' would require **disambiguation**. The translator would need to look into the context to find out what exactly the meaning of *brother* was here. Only then could the correct Yoruba term be selected. The concepts exist in both languages, but they are not specifically lexicalized in English. This is a common problem, often associated with **kinship terms**. Thus, the German 'Hast du *Geschwister*?' would be translated as 'Do you have any *brothers and sisters*?' since, apart from the very formal *siblings*, English has no noun inclusive of both sexes.

Other considerations also need to be taken into account. Russian has two lexical terms for the English *daughter-in-law* (*snokha* for the daughter-in-law of a man and *nevestka* for the daughter-in-law of a woman), but these are now used less frequently than in the past partly because users would tend to confuse the terms but also because of the decline in the important cultural practice of the newly-married bride going to live with her husband at the home of his parents. The preferred term is now 'wife of son' (*zhena syna*). The current language in use would not therefore be predicted by a simple mapping of **kinship terms** in the two systems.

COLLOCATION

Since Nida's work on **referential** and **connotative meaning**, there have been significant developments in the analysis of lexical patterning. One of the most important has been in the area of **collocation**. **Collocation** refers to the way that words are typically used together. In English, to borrow the well-known example from Leech (1981: 17), *pretty woman* is a typical (or strong) **collocation**, and so is *handsome man*. This does not mean that *handsome woman* or *pretty man* is impossible, just that they are very unusual or **marked**. An interesting example using just this **collocation** occurs in the episode *Fathers and Sons* of the American sitcom *Frasier*. An old friend of the family turns up after many years and, looking for Niles, sees a female character, Ros. The friend at first thinks Niles must have undergone a sex change. When he is made aware of his error, he concludes by telling Ros 'You are a handsome woman' where the **marked collocation** is humorous because it shows that his initial perception continues.

Clearly, translation requires the strength of **collocation** to be identified in the ST and conveyed satisfactorily in the TT. **Collocation** is not a focus of Nida. However, it has been studied extensively in more recent years and Larson (1984/1998: 155–67) devotes a chapter to it. It has grown in importance with the growth of **corpus linguistics**, the computer-assisted study of electronic databases (**corpora**) of naturally occurring texts (see Section A, Unit 14 and Section C, Unit 3 for further discussion). It has become particularly relevant to the work of the bilingual lexicographer who is able to view a **concordance** of a given search term or statistics showing the significant frequencies of **collocates**. A **concordance** displays examples of the search term in the centre with a certain amount of context either side ordered alphabetically according to the first word right or left of the search term.

Task C5.10

Figures C5.2 and C5.3 are brief example **concordances** of the words *handsome* and *pretty* from the British National Corpus (BNC).

➤ Look at the lines in the two **concordances** with the surrounding **co-text**.

➤ Make a note of the **referential** senses of the two terms, their common collocates and **semantic** fields, and their **connotative meanings**.

➤ What conclusion do you come to from comparing the two terms in this way?

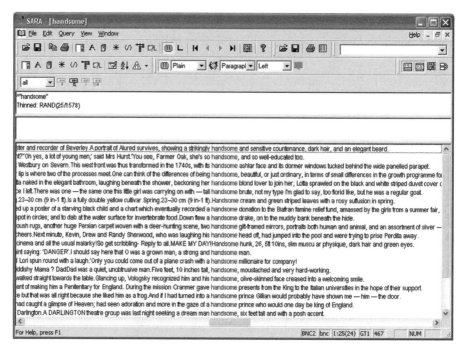

Figure C5.2 Example concordance of 'handsome'

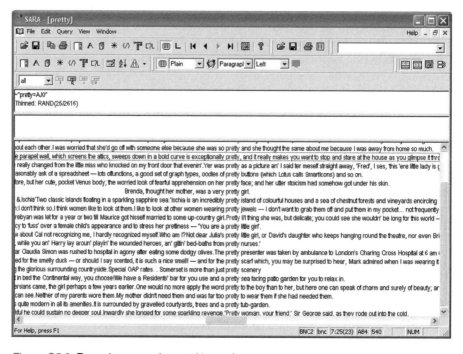

Figure C5.3 Example concordance of 'pretty'

➤ Carry out similar analyses using this or other **corpora** (note that 50 examples of search terms are freely accessible from the BNC website, http://thetis.bl.uk/lookup.html).

Larson (1984/1998: 159) makes the point that 'the **collocational** range of equivalent words between languages will not be identical. It will overlap but not match completely.' This is where **corpora** can help. By comparing with results from a **concordance** of related words in the TL, the lexicographer is able to map the two language systems onto each other and make more accurate decisions about **correspondences** between the two languages. This presupposes comparable **corpora** exist in the other language. The range of languages and **text-types** covered is increasing all the time.

Larson considers **collocation** primarily as a formal, structural device, looking at fixed combinations (*bread and butter, black and white*), including idioms, and the 'restrictions' on the **collocational** range of a word which 'only a native speaker of the language can judge' (1984/1998: 160). However, Leech (1981: 17) lists **collocative** meaning as one of his seven types of meaning, defining it as 'the associations a word acquires on account of the meanings of words which tend to occur in its environment'. This is very close to the concept of **semantic prosody** (see Louw 1993). **Semantic prosody** refers to the positive or negative **connotative meaning** which is transferred to the focus word by the **semantic fields** of its common **collocates**. Stubbs (1995, 1996: 173–4) examines collocates of causal verbs and finds in his **corpus** that the vast majority of collocates of *cause* are negative, e.g. *accident, cancer, commotion, crisis* and *delay*. On the other hand, the verb *provide* has a positive **semantic prosody** with collocates *care, food, help, jobs, relief* and *support*. This is an area which is beginning to be investigated between languages and in translation, the hypothesis being that in some cases the translator may not intuitively be aware of the **prosody** or may choose an **equivalent** which has a different **prosody** from the original.

Task C5.11

➤ Look at how the words *cause* and *provide* are presented in bilingual dictionaries featuring your languages. How, if at all, are **the prosodies** treated?

➤ Try and investigate the **prosodies** of similar verbs in your other languages using a **corpus** or examples accessed through an internet search engine. For example, in Portuguese the search terms *causar* and *provocar* could be used to find examples, and the grammatical subject or object collocates analysed (see Berber Sardinha 1999 for a more detailed description).

CONCLUSION

This unit has examined various attempts, adapted from English **semantics**, to examine meaning scientifically. The underlying assumption was that meaning is observable and measurable, and transferable in translation. The aim of these attempts was to assist the decision-making of the translator. However, there are many other factors that affect meaning and determine the choice of translation. These include the linguistic **co-text** and the context in which the TT is to function. Later units in this book pay greater attention to context and examine concepts in Translation Studies that are drawn from **pragmatics**.

PROJECTS

1. Most of the techniques and models explored in this unit derive from the analysis of English. Try out some of the techniques on other languages; how far does it seem that the analysis varies according to the TL studied? How valid do you think it is to use an English-language model of **semantics** for translation? What new forms of analysis may need to be developed?

2. The use of **corpora** is becoming increasingly common in Translation Studies. Follow up the readings given in the Further Reading section and investigate on the internet the availability of **corpora** in other languages. Try to repeat some of the studies in your own languages. An excellent starting point is Federico Zanettin's website (http://www.federicozanettin.net/sslmit/cl.htm) which has a wealth of useful links. For an overview of the use of **corpora** in Translation Studies, see Olohan (2004).

Unit C6
Dynamic equivalence and
the receptor of the message

LITERAL, FORMAL OR DYNAMIC?

Literal translation can work admirably in a range of contexts and for a variety of texts. In fact, the bulk of what we do as translators requires little more than **literal** translation. You can see this for yourself by going over a translation you have recently done and, using the Vinay and Darbelnet method of analysis (see Unit 4), tabulating how much of the ST was rendered using a predominantly **literal** approach.

But matters are not always so straightforward. SL and TL linguistic and rhetorical **norms** often clash, and the translator is normally left with a choice between two courses of action:

- Preserving ST **form**, no matter how odd it might sound. This is **formal equivalence**, a translation strategy strictly reserved for those situations in which ST **form** becomes inextricably linked to intended meaning and must therefore be preserved (e.g. preserving intended ambiguity of **form** or meaning, with a focus on the ST);
- Opting for various forms of **adjustment**, in an attempt to arrive at a wording that communicates ST meaning without in any way offending against TL linguistic and rhetorical **norms** (i.e. translating with naturalness and fluency). This is **dynamic equivalence** which focuses on the TT reader.

But whichever kind of **equivalence** we eventually settle on, the decision must always be 'contextually motivated' (i.e. taken on adequate linguistic, rhetorical or conceptual grounds). Unmotivated **formal equivalence** is a form of blind literalism, while unmotivated **dynamic equivalence** is a form of blatant **re-writing**.

Example C6.1

Preface

This book is about the rise of modern science and *how the world got to be the way it is*. The twentieth century has witnessed extraordinary collisions of societies, cultures, and civilizations . . .

Toby E. Huff (1993) *The Rise of Early Modern Science: Islam, China and The West*, Cambridge University Press. [italics added]

 Task C6.1

➤ Analyse the italicized informal and semi-dialectal (i.e. non-standard) feature in this example, from the preface to a scholarly monograph.

➤ Decide whether the use of this feature is significant (i.e. **contextually motivated**).

➤ Translate the text, preserving the significance of the dialectal use if motivated, or dealing with it appropriately if unmotivated.

➤ Describe and rationalize your decision. Apply similar evaluation procedures to a more extensive sample of texts in which the use of non-standard language is in all likelihood motivated (e.g. drama).

IS FORMAL EQUIVALENCE TANTAMOUNT TO LITERAL TRANSLATION?

What is meant by 'contextual motivatedness', and what does 'motivated' formal equivalence actually involve? In the case of Example C6.1, the 'dialectal' form *got to be the way it is* lacks motivatedness, and opting for **formal equivalence** would thus be inappropriate at best. On the other hand, any **explication** of *slyly protecting his own* in the Guinness example (Example A6.1) would have compromised intended meaning.

Motivated **formal equivalence** of the kind advocated here is an established procedure for dealing with such aspects of the ST as 'ambiguity'. But there are other contexts.

1. In his well-known model of **equivalence** relations, Werner Koller (1979: 186–91) deals with what Nida calls '**formal equivalence**' under '**expressive equivalence**' and relates it to the **form** and aesthetics of the text, including word plays and the individual stylistic features of the ST (see Section A, Unit 7).

2. From a **text-type** perspective, Katharina Reiss (1977/1989) also sees **formal equivalence** as ideal for engaging in the creative composition required for the translation of the '**expressive' text type** in which the aesthetic dimension of language is highlighted, and where the sender as well as the form of the message is foregrounded (see Section A, Unit 9).

But it is Peter Newmark's '**semantic translation**' that has perhaps come closest to what **formal equivalence** might actually entail. In **semantic translation**, 'the translator attempts, within the bare **syntactic** and **semantic** constraints of the TL, to reproduce *the precise contextual meaning* of the author' (1988: 22, italics added).

Example C6.2

The Syrian Ministry of Interior *announced* yesterday that *the topic of* travel between Syria and Iraq by identity card will be discussed at a meeting to be held *soon* by the Syrian–Iraqi *Joint* Commission, which was the *outcome* of the Agreement on [. . .]

    As is well known, the United Arab Republic, Iraq and Jordan recently signed agreements *between themselves* to allow [. . .]

    From another quarter, Mr Sami 'Attiyya, Minister of Communications, *announced* that Syria had started work on *the paving (i.e. with stones)* of the desert highway [. . .] *In like manner*, Iraq has commenced the paving [. . .]

    It is worthy of mention that the two countries lately agreed on the paving of. . . .

                                 (*Al-Jumhuriyya Daily*, Baghdad, 4 September 1967)

Task C6.2

➤ To clarify the difference between **literal, formal** and **dynamic equivalence**, examine the above translation of a news report. Pay special attention to the elements we have italicized.

➤ Now, evaluate the extent to which elements in italics are motivated **formal equivalents**.

➤ Edit and revise those elements that in your judgement carry no **motivatedness** and are therefore questionable literalisms.

WHEN FORMAL OR DYNAMIC EQUIVALENCE MISFIRE

In Example C6.2 above, target **norms** and conventions governing writing in this mode of news reporting are violated gratuitously, i.e. there is no **contextual motivatedness** for the **literal** approach adopted. But as a defining condition, is **contextual motivatedness** sufficiently stable for it always to be invoked with a reasonable degree of certainty? That is, can we always be sure when a ST feature is motivated, justifying a **formal** translation? This is a complex issue, and many factors are at work. Consider this example:

Example C6.3a   (Back-translation from Arabic)

At first we would *play for* walnuts. Then we began to *play for* poultry. And then came the day when I *played for* the three calves I had. And finally I *played for* the trees.

(A. Munif Al-Ashjar ('The Trees') (1973) [italics added])

In dealing with this example, two approaches may be adopted: one aiming for a **formal** rendering (preserving the repetition of *play for*), the other for **dynamic equivalence**. The latter approach may be illustrated by the published translation of the above text, which suppresses repetition and opts instead for fluent variation:

Example C6.3b

At first we used to *gamble* with walnuts; then we began to *play for* poultry; and then came the day when I *gambled* with the three calves I had. Finally I *threw the trees in*.

(A. Munif (The Trees) translation commissioned by
the Iraqi Cultural Centre, London [italics added])

The question is: has **formal equivalence** been given a fair chance in the English translation? Can there be sufficient grounds in this context for seeing the repetition as serving *no* **rhetorical purpose** worth preserving? Hatim and Mason suggest that, in this text, the repetition *is* **contextually motivated**:

> The **motivatedness** behind this exaggerated reiteration [of *play for*] may be explained in terms of the prominence which the concept of gambling assumes in the context of the passage and indeed the whole novel. The sin is magnified and the gradual lapse into frittering away all that one holds dear, including self-respect, is foregrounded.
>
> (1997: 32)

A translation sensitive to source culture, then, would preserve the repetition, thus forcing the reader to stop and ponder. This would be a case of **contextually motivated formal equivalence** on the grounds that what the ST involves is a particular stance or perspective that would be seriously compromised if the linguistic form of the message was not preserved.

★ Task C6.3

➤ Evaluate part of a translation of a modern literary work into or out of English and assess the kind of background knowledge (sociological, historical, and ideological) which the translator had (or needed to have) to do the ST justice.

➤ In dealing with Example C6.3a, for example, some basic knowledge is necessary regarding such socio-cultural values as attachment to the 'land', the significance of concepts such as honour and self-respect, etc. This is part of the *discours social* (Bruce 1994, Section B, Text B11.2), crucial to a fuller appreciation of the novel translated.

For an example which graphically shows how unmotivated **dynamic equivalence** may become simply aimless 're-writing', let us consider Example C6.4a:

Example C6.4a   (Back-translation from Arabic)

PERSONAL HOSPITALITY IS OUR TRADITION

Example C6.4b

RELIABILITY IS OUR TRADITION

Task C6.4

➤ Consider the above airline advertisement in C.6.4a.

➤ Compare this with how this text was rendered into English in C.6.4b.

➤ Examine a bilingual sample of locally produced advertisements. In cases where **literal** translation is used, assess whether there is any need for **adaptation**. How far are you prepared to go in adapting the ST? What are the criteria you would adopt?

RECEPTOR RESPONSE

In examining the licence often taken by translators in departing drastically from the source, one is immediately struck by the excesses of **dynamic equivalence**. The elusive nature of **equivalent effect** is the root cause of the problem. Consider Nida's original statement: 'What one must determine is the response of the receptor to the translated message. This response must then be compared with the way in which the original receptors presumably reacted to the message when it was given in its original setting' (Nida 1969: 1).

The last part of Nida's statement relating to **equivalence** of effect has been a serious bone of contention in Translation Studies. In a recent guide for practical translators, the following counter arguments are forcibly put:

To begin with, who is to know what the relationship between ST message and source-culture receptors is? For that matter, is it plausible to speak of *the* relationship, as if there were only one; are there not as many relationships as there are receptors? And who is to know what such relationships can have been in the past? In any case, few texts have a *single* effect, even in one reading by one person.

(Dickins et al. 2002: 30)

Nida would probably respond by suggesting that '**audience**' is such an unknown quantity in any case, and that, guided by a perspicuous reading of the ST and a keen eye on TT **comprehensibility**, translators have always fared well.

 Task C6.5

➤ Choose a translation aimed at overcoming serious problems of ST cultural references and preferences, drastically adapting these to comply with expectations in the target culture. Examine what has been justifiably or unjustifiably omitted from the ST or introduced to the TT.

➤ Focus on the changes justifiably made. Which aspects of the text have had to be **domesticated** through a **dynamic equivalence** of some kind? What justifies the decision? Write up your analysis, findings and conclusions.

WHEN COMPREHENSIBILITY IS COMPROMISED

From the perspective we adopt in this book, one thing is certain: excessive **dynamic equivalence** may compromise ST meaning so drastically in places that it is doubtful whether we can still legitimately call it translation. On the other hand, there are situations which strain TT **comprehensibility** to breaking point and thus leave the translator with no option but to resort to some form of **adjustment**, adding or taking away information as appropriate. Recall, for example, the Charity fund-raising text (Example A2.2), or the cash dispensing advert (Examples A2.4 and A2.5, p. 13).

Initially you may be offended or even enraged by the end result of **dynamically equivalent** translations. In fact, there is a tendency, often resorted to by translators whose command of the TL is superior to that of the source, to use **dynamic equivalence** as *carte blanche* in a kind of anything-goes attitude. Although the translations normally sound excellent, closer scrutiny immediately reveals that they relate to the ST only tangentially.

On reflection, however, you might have a great deal of sympathy with many translators who opt for such drastic departures in certain contexts.

Example C6.5

[This country], a unique federation and a unique experiment. An unparalleled experiment not known by the human society with compatible motives and constituents, where most political systems are proclaiming non-existence of such federation to that of [our country] through the history.

(Editorial, *Al-Jumruki*, in-house publication of the Customs Department, Sharjah, UAE (1999))

Task C6.6

In the particular case of the above English TT editorial, minimal modification of the translation would be simply unacceptable not only in terms of the kind of writing customary in English for this kind of text but also from the standpoint of general **cohesion** and **coherence**.

➤ Edit the example to highlight the argument more succinctly and in keeping with what is customary for this kind of text in English.

➤ Apply similar evaluation procedures to translations of editorials of the kind normally published by foreign English-medium newspapers and magazines, or on the internet.

THE TRANSLATION PROCESS

In the examples we have examined so far, the changes introduced are part of the so-called **restructuring** stage. In the **analysis** stage, which could occur before or after **transfer** and **restructuring** as the three stages are not necessarily sequential, grammar and lexis would obviously be under focus. As we saw in Section C, Unit 5, techniques such as **componential analysis** are available for the **analysis** of meaning in these areas. But this leaves us with the vexed question of what to do with **connotative** and stylistic meaning.

Task C6.7

➤ Translate a legal text into or out of English.

➤ Examine your own decision-making process as you progress through the translation.

➤ Make a list of the kind of stylistic parameters you need to work with (e.g. technicality of terminology, formality of tone, etc.).

➤ Illustrate each parameter by noting what a given grammatical or lexical choice was (as opposed to what it could have been).

➤ Are these decisions taken right from the start (i.e. in the **analysis** stage), during the **transfer** or in the revision (**restructuring**) stage?

In the **transfer** stage, what is involved seems to be more than a straightforward replacement of SL elements with their most **literal** TL **equivalents**. Take for example the important analytic distinction made between **contextual consistency** and **verbal consistency** in translation. According to Nida and Taber (1969: 199), contextual consistency is: 'the quality which results from translating a SL word by that expression in the receptor language which best fits each context rather than by the same expression in all contexts'.

⭐ Task C6.8

➤ Examine the translation of a sacred or sensitive text into English.

➤ Identify some key terms (e.g. *God, spirit*, even *war* or *home*).

➤ Chart the various renderings of a given term, noting the context of each rendering (using the criterion of contextual/verbal consistency).

➤ Even without access to the ST (e.g. for the Bible), you can still ascertain whether the criterion used has been verbal or contextual consistency: is the formal rendering *God* opted for systematically throughout, or are there any variations?

➤ What would happen if you were to impose verbal consistency on an entire portion of the text? Would the ST's sacred message be distorted in any way? If so, how?

Finally, stylistic appropriateness features prominently in **restructuring**. At this stage, the translator would be concerned with special effects and would thus focus on such features as choice of oral or written **mode**, the role of situational factors, the selection of appropriate **genre** and type of **text**, appropriate language varieties or styles, choice of formal features and lexical items.

⭐ Task C6.9

➤ Go through some of the TTs covered in this exploration unit and focus on the criteria invoked in **restructuring** the various texts. Make a checklist of the reasons why a change was made (i.e. what features of context have proved crucial in solving a particular problem). For example, the problems in Examples C6.2 and C6.5 are all related to the type of writing we conventionally associate with news reports.

Thus, we do not go through the translation **process** piecemeal (one stage at a time), nor do we deal with the various words and sentences as isolated entities. Rather, we seek all the time to relate these micro-level elements (words, phrases) to higher levels of text organization. Even when our immediate decision is to leave things as they are (because there is absolutely nothing to modify or change), or aim for a **formal** or a **dynamic** kind of **equivalence** (possibly despite an odd usage), we tend to ensure that words are assigned values that go beyond **referential** or even **associative** meanings. These values tend to cater for such aspects of text in context as subject matter and level of formality (which we shall deal with under **register** in Unit 9), as well as rhetorical conventions and a diverse range of textual **norms** (see **text**, **genre** and **discourse**, Unit 11). **Equivalence** is thus both relative and context-sensitive. It is the variable nature of **equivalence** that we shall now explore.

CONCLUSION

In this and related units (A6, B6), we have considered the issue of **equivalence** and found that, except in those cases where we deliberately choose to focus 'on the message itself, in both **form** and **content**' (Nida 1964: 159), any **form**-by-**form** translation is a kind of literalism that rarely works. This is simply because there can never be absolute **correspondence** between languages. The issue of **correspondence** is also an important consideration in judging extreme forms of **dynamic equivalence** and the kind of response it is supposed to elicit. Such a response can never be identical with that which the original has elicited from its readers, 'for no two people ever [. . .] understand words in exactly the same manner' (Nida 1969: 4).

How, then, is translation possible? Like all forms of intercultural communication, the **process** of translation works well at levels deeper than surface similarities and differences of structure or behaviour. Translators working within the framework of **dynamic equivalence** would thus be more concerned with the need to conjure up in the reader of a translation 'modes of behaviour relevant within the context of his own culture' (Nida 1964: 159). The same may be said of the motivated variety of **literal** translation (i.e. **formal equivalence**) which, in its own peculiar way, also focuses on context. In either kind of **equivalence**, there will be much less concern with matching TL message with SL message, a procedure typical of most **literal** translations. In Unit 7, we shall establish that **equivalence** is not only relative, but also hierarchical and context sensitive.

PROJECTS

1. Refine the Translation Evaluation Scheme commenced in Unit C4 by going through the various texts covered in the different sections of Unit 6. Recall the criteria you invoked in dealing with the various flawed translations. For instance, the criterion for Example C6.5 is **genre**.

    Categories such as 'genre' tend to *explain* why things go wrong. To *describe* a problem, however, we need initially to work with basic **syntactic**, **semantic** and textual categories. There will thus be two sets of categories, one subsumed under Description (**syntactic**, etc.), the other under Explanation (**genre, discourse, purpose** of translation, culture, etc.). Establish these two levels and the categories within each, and leave the entire analytic 'toolkit' open for other variables to be added as we progress through the book.

2. To appreciate the difference between **literal, formal** and **dynamic equivalence**, reflect on the translation of an entire article. Ideally, the translator will be (a) a professional, and (b) accessible. Conduct an informal interview asking the translator 'why like this, why here?'. Consider specifically how loss of TT authenticity (i.e. fluency) may be desirable in one place (through true **formal equivalence**) but not in others (when translation is blindly **literal**). Catalogue the constraints within which one type of **equivalence** works, and the other does not.

3. Poetry is an interesting translation domain to analyse.

   (a) You will be able to see **semantics** and **syntax** in a new way (i.e. not merely as a linguistic phenomenon, but both as a cultural and a conceptual phenomenon).
   (b) You will also see **dynamic equivalence** and **formal equivalence** at work.
   (c) You will be able to see how excessive 'fluency', 'authenticity', etc. can compromise the ST message.

   Find a collection of poems translated from your own language into English, and comment on (a), (b) and (c).

4. Editorials provide us with texts that often call for substantial **adjustment** towards **dynamic equivalence**. Collect a sample of this type of text probably from an internet source which caters for the translation of current affairs in your part of the world, or from an issue of your daily English-medium local newspaper.

   Focus in your assessment on the need for different types of **adjustment** to iron out structural, **semantic** or **stylistic** incongruities. You can do this by listing all the modifications that you have introduced and reflecting on whether they involve structure, **style**, etc.

5. *Newsweek* now appears in various bilingual editions. Examine the translation of the regular section, which features Quotable Quotes.

   (a) Reflect on the best way to deal with the 'point' of the quote, the most important element to preserve in translation.
   (b) Assess the translation of these quotable elements, and if translations are not available, reflect on the ST and attempt a translation of your own.

Bear in mind that the **formal** translations you will produce cannot simply be **literal** renderings: the focus is on the **form** and **content** of the 'message' (i.e. on the context of the utterance).

Unit C7
Textual pragmatics and equivalence

In Unit C6, we explored some of the contexts appropriate for **formal equivalence** through which the translator seeks to reflect in a motivated manner the linguistic or rhetorical prominence of an ST element. In the absence of such an aim, and when a **literal** translation would be unworkable due to incompatibility of **form** or **content**, the translator opts for **adjustment** of the ST in an endeavour to create on the TT reader a semblance of the effect which the ST could have had on its original receivers. This is **dynamic equivalence**, a valid **procedure** to circumvent problems of in**comprehensibility** and attain reasonable levels of **translatability** between languages.

COMPLEX DECISION-MAKING

But the **process** of translation is not as stable as the picture just presented might suggest. Translation involves a complex process of 'decision-making', where decisions are hierarchical and **iterative**, of the kind we saw with Koller's **equivalence** relations (Section A, Unit 7). It is safe to assume that, instinctively, translators start out with the most basic forms of what Koller calls '**formal equivalence**' (and what we shall continue to call '**literal**' translation since we reserve '**formal equivalence**' for those situations in which '**form**' is preserved in a **contextually motivated** manner). It is only when the **literal** proves insufficient that resort is made to other kinds of **equivalence** relations.

 Task C7.1

➤ Choose two kinds of text (a news report and an editorial, preferably on the same topic), and translate into your own language.

➤ Try out the idea of initially opting for a **literal** translation and of moving on to other forms of **equivalence** only when necessary.

➤ Go through the translation and reflect on the decisions you have made. Record these decisions and label them (L = literal, F = **formal** if **contextually motivated**, D = departure, Sy = **syntactic**, Se = **semantic**, P = **pragmatic**, etc.).

➤ Are departures from the **literal** fairly common and in which kind of text: the news report or the editorial?

➤ In addition to the type of text, what other factors can you identify as playing a role in departures from the **literal**? What aspects of language are affected most, and in which kind of text?

➤ You can now extend the sample to include other translations and, focusing on the editorial variety, examine the kind of complex decision-making necessitated specifically by (a) the need to capture **connotative meaning** and (b) the need to comply with textual and rhetorical **norms** relevant to editorials.

Pending further research, available evidence from process investigations (e.g. Lörscher 1991) points to the general validity of identifying this effortless **literal** option as the translator's first port of call in the bulk of what we do in translation. But decision-making is less straightforward than this 'sequential' model seems to indicate (i.e. if not **literal** or **formal**, then **pragmatic**, etc.). As we have shown in Section A, Unit 7, decisions tend to be hierarchical and **iterative**: the **literal** might work but for a variety of reasons you can and often do:

■ jump the loop and climb up the hierarchy to handle a particular element in, say, a '**norm**-oriented' way;
■ **iteratively** revisit decisions already made in one part of the text but valid only for that phase of the process;
■ revise your strategy in the light of subsequent decisions you take;
■ prioritize different kinds of **equivalence** relations such that what may be a priority to you in one situation may not be a priority in a different kind of situation or to another translator, in one kind of translation **commission** and not in another, and so on.

Example C7.1

The Definition of Jihad as a Term in Shari'a

The legal scholars have defined jihad in various closely connected ways. We will choose the definition of Ibn 'urfa, one of the Maliki legal scholars, when he says, '(Jihad is) a Muslim's fight against a disbeliever who does not have a covenant with the Muslims, in order to exalt the word of God or because the disbeliever has attacked him or entered his land.' [. . .]

From a translation commissioned by UNESCO for a scholarly monograph on Islam

Task C7.2

You are commissioned to produce a scholarly translation for a textbook, which may be illustrated by Example C7.1 which is a short extract from such a translation.

➤ You have been asked to re-work the text for publication in a mass-circulation magazine. Experiment with the above TT and modify with the new **purpose** (mass-circulation publication) in mind.

➤ Examine the decision-making involved in producing the two versions.

➤ What kind(s) of **equivalence** relations would dominate in one version and not in the other? This could probably be explained in terms of the nature of the 'commission'. Are there any other factors driving the decision-making: The kind of **audience** envisaged? The **text type** expected? The kind of language fulfilling the communicative requirements of one or other occasion?

In working through the above tasks, you will undoubtedly have noticed that several factors play a role in the decision-making characteristic of translation as a **process**. These include:

1. aesthetics (e.g. translator's 'aesthetic standards');
2. cognition (e.g. translator's '**cognitive** system');
3. knowledge base (i.e. epistemology);
4. task specification (e.g. agreed with clients).

 Task C7.3

➤ Examine the role of these criteria in motivating decisions in an area such as translating popular fiction (e.g. *Mills & Boon*) or a similar mass-produced text (*Goosebumps, Harry Potter*).

EQUIVALENCE OF TEXTS

Factors such as the kind of language appropriate to a given situation and the type of text or communicative act in question, which Koller discusses under **normative equivalence**, are crucial in **translational** decision-making.

Task C7.4

➤ Consider these flawed signs collected from around the world. What is wrong with them?

1. The lift is being fixed for the next day. During that time we regret that you will be unbearable. (Sign in a Bucharest hotel lobby)
2. Visitors are expected to complain at the office between the hours of 9 and 11 a.m. daily. (In a hotel in Athens)
3. Special today: no ice cream. (In a Swiss mountain inn)
4. Order your summer suit. Because is big rush we will execute customers in strict rotation. (At a Rhodes tailor shop)
5. If this is your first visit to the USSR, you are welcome to it. (On the door of a Moscow hotel room)

You will have noted that these texts are all poor, **literal**, unidiomatic translations.

➤ Are the problems simply lexical/ grammatical, or more deep-rooted, probably grounded in culture, the kind of text involved, etc.?

➤ What are the parameters within which these texts may be revised?

Below is an example of such a context/**text analysis** of the first sign:

Some basic language editing will see to it that the sign reads:

> *The lift is being fixed. We regret that you will be inconvenienced for the next 24 hours.*

Linguistic appropriateness is restored. But contextual appropriateness is still a problem. To see to that, we might first opt for:

> *The lift is being fixed. We regret any inconvenience.*

Then, perhaps:

> *Out of Order. We regret any inconvenience.*

Or even, simply

> *Out of Order.*

This leads us to a consideration of the kind of constraints under which translators operate in attempting to determine the types of **resemblance** that are most crucial for a given text/context in translation. Essentially, these constraints relate to the original text and the appropriateness of the TT. On both sides of the linguistic-cultural divide, these constraints have to do with

■ preference for a given **text type**
■ the nature of the **communicative event**
■ the kind of reader

Task C7.5

➤ Examine how far these factors have been taken into consideration by carefully studying this excerpt from a bilingual tourist brochure. Focus on elements in italics.

Example C7.2a   English version (italics added)

The reptile and insect house has exhibits of many of the Arabian snakes, lizards, amphibians, common insects and arachnids. *A huge aviary,* with a waterfall cascading down rocks into a small lake and river, *contains* several species of local songbirds as well as some small raptors.

(The Tourism Board, Government of Sharjah, UAE)

Example C7.2b   Arabic version (Back-translation. Italics added)

The visitor begins his tour by discovering the reptile department, which contains a variety of Arabian snakes and lizards. *Then he continues the journey* to find himself within a huge aviary, where waterfalls cascade on the rocks, a spacious place which contains different varieties of songbirds. *The visitor continues his journey* through a long corridor, which takes him to where there are baboons.

 Task C7.6

➤ Having worked through these examples, can you identify distinct patterns in how the two languages view the experience: Subjectively? Objectively? Test your hypothesis on a more extensive text example.

➤ Examine tourist brochures produced in your language.

➤ Translate (or assess existing translations).

➤ What kind of changes do you think are necessary to fulfil the requirements of the **text type**, the **communicative event**, the target reader, etc.?

DECISION-MAKING: THE TEXT FACTOR

In performing Task C7.6, you probably noted the 'objectivity' of the English version, compared with the 'subjectivity' of the Arabic version. For example,

English:

The reptile and insect house has exhibits of many of the Arabian snakes

Arabic:

The visitor begins his tour by discovering the reptile department

This disparity is to do with the issue of what we choose to make **salient** from the perspective of a particular language and culture. In some texts or parts of text, some elements inevitably exhibit more prominence than others. Textual **salience** is a crucial factor which, as we suggested in Section A, Unit 7, may best be explained in text-**pragmatic** ways. That is, the **equivalence** sought in this area of varying linguistic and/or conceptual prominence would be of a **text-normative** and **pragmatic** kind.

Marked word order is one way of displaying prominence. In well-written texts, prominence is often **functional**, that is, purposeful within the text. Consider, for example, the following text by Oliver Sacks, a writer renowned for his human perspective on those aspects of near-psychology, which his 'medical novellas' so graphically portray. This is how Sacks describes his patient's suffering:

Example C7.3

But it was not merely the cognition, the gnosis, at fault; there was something radically wrong with the whole way he proceeded. For he approached these faces – even of those near and dear – as if they were abstract puzzles or tests. *He did not relate to them, he did not behold. No face was familiar to him, seen as a 'thou', being just identified as a set of features, an 'it'.*

(Oliver Sacks (1985) *The Man Who Mistook His Wife for a Hat*,
London: Picador [italics added])

Note in particular the recurrent use of **mental clauses** (added in italics). Compare this with how a core neuropsychologist would have described a similar phenomenon:

Example C7.4

Neurological examination was essentially negative, apart from her recent memory deficit and visual performance. Her visual acuity was difficult to determine because of her agnosia, but using the open E method, and the occasional letter identification, it was found to be 20/20 bilaterally.

(Andrew Kertesz (1979) *Aphasia and Associated
Disorders*, New York: Grune and Stratton)

Task C7.7

➤ Translate the above Example C7.3 by Sacks and focus on how **markedness** may be best preserved. Compare your translation with an existing translation, if one is available.

This leads us to a consideration of the kind of constraints under which we operate in attempting to determine the types of **resemblance** that are most crucial for a given text/context in translation. This will be the subject of subsequent units. Before we can do this, it is perhaps instructive to shift the focus from **text type** to **cognitive** models of the translation **process**. **Relevance** and **inferencing** are issues to be tackled in the next unit.

CONCLUSION

What this discussion of **pragmatics** and translator decision-making has made clear is that, as we suggested in Unit 3, ultimately the word cannot be a legitimate **unit of translation**. What we translate may indeed be words, etc., but all the time these have to be seen as the building blocks of larger texts. In other words, we deal with grammar and vocabulary not in isolation but as part of text in communication. This is why words (and, by extension, texts) do not yield one definite meaning only but rather an increasing range of possible meanings. Within this framework, it is no longer possible to entertain the curious translation dichotomy of **formal** vs **pragmatic resemblance**. Instead, what is needed is a set of criteria by which we can determine which types of **resemblance** are most crucial for a given text or part of a text.

Clearly emphasized here is the fact that it is the ST and its linguistic–stylistic structure and meaning potential which is regarded as the fundamental factor in translation. However, the link which exists between the translation and the conditions on the receiver's side does not disappear. Factors other than the source which contribute to the production and **reception** of a translation remain crucial. From a focus on texts and text fragments, we shift the focus and concentrate in the next unit on such aspects of dealing with texts as **relevance**, inference and similar **cognitive** factors.

PROJECTS

1. What motivates decision-making?

    a) The translator's own 'aesthetic standards'?
    b) The translator's '**cognitive** system'?
    c) Task specification as agreed with clients?

Children's literature in translation is ideal for the study of some or all of these factors. Examine a popular children's book and study the kind of decisions taken in response to aesthetic criteria (the translator's own, or the preferences of the culture), problems of cognition (the translator's or the reader's) and other task-specific criteria (the publisher, the nature of the medium, etc.).

2. Surely there would be no point translating Oliver Sacks if the human perspective was not preserved in the translation. Find a translation of Oliver Sacks into a language with which you are familiar. Assess the translation to ascertain if Sacks's 'human perspective' has been adequately conveyed and, if not, why not? If no translations are available, experiment with a translation you would make.

Unit C8
Translation and relevance

Within the **relevance** theory of translation (presented in Units A8 and B8), interest in textual **pragmatics** ebbed, and attention to a different set of **cognitive** pragmatic abilities such as **inferencing** heightened. Translation came to be seen as a case of **interpretive** use of language (with the translator functioning as an observer/ spokesperson-like), and anything which smacked of **descriptive** use (with translations attaining the status of full participation in the communicative act) was discouraged.

THE BEST OF BOTH WORLDS

The thorny issue which confronted **relevance** theoreticians was precisely this: what if we wanted to render the 'letter and the spirit'? It was at this point that the notion of the **communicative clue** was proposed in an attempt to reconcile the fact that enormous **semantic, syntactic** and cultural differences exist between languages with the need on the part of the translator sometimes to preserve not only what is said but also how it is said (in the translation of sacred and sensitive texts, for example). Before exploring the implications of the decision to preserve **form** and **content**, let us re-visit the basic translation dichotomy **descriptive** vs **interpretive**.

Example C8.1a   English ST

Access all areas
Wherever you want to be

Land Rover's entry into the fiercely competitive SUV market raised more than a few eyebrows.
    Make no mistake; it's a real Land Rover. The car you can drive down the highway can negotiate adrenaline-pumping steep, muddy hills and rough ground with similar quiet authority.

Example C8.1b   Back-translation of Arabic TT

You take it anywhere you want
You drive it any way you want
Many put question marks and were wondering when Land Rover *(known for its large and luxurious cars) decided to enter the multi-purpose small-sized sports car market (SUV).*

Nevertheless, the response from Land Rover came loud and clear to dispel all doubts and answer all questions. Freelander was born to prove that it is a real Landrover (in form and content), regardless of size. Sceptics tried it on smoothly paved roads, and it coursed down smoothly and quietly. Sceptics also tried it on rough roads with their mud, sand and rocks, and it conquered these with strength and confidence. Now there is no room for doubt: Freelander IS a Landrover in all senses of the word.

(From the publicity material for Freelander (Arabic version))

Task C8.1

Consider Example C8.1a from a sample of publicity material for Freelander in English, alongside a back-translation of the parallel Arabic version.

Note how almost the entire Arabic version is an 'addition', drastically rewording the original. This is an extreme case of '**descriptive**' translation.

➤   What kind of effect might this TT have on the target reader in a language with which you are familiar? Is the effect compatible with the **function** of the text?

➤   Translate the above English ST '**interpretively**' (adhering as far as possible to the ST structure, etc.) into a language of your choice. What difference in effect can you discern when comparing your version with the Arabic TT above? Would you still regard your '**interpretive**' version as a piece of effective advertising?

DIRECT COMMUNICATION

Relevance theoreticians had no problem responding to the question: what if we needed to translate the Bible or Dickens for children? This, according to Gutt (1991) would be a case of **descriptive** translation, and is therefore not acceptable as 'translation' but may well be called by another name (e.g. **adaptation**).

Task C8.2

➤ Consider the following extract from the Koran, a popularized translation (Example C8.2a), and compare it with two other more scholarly English versions of the 'original' (C8.2b and C8.2c). Assess the choices made in the light of the need to move away from the **formal** end, and towards the **dynamic** end.

Example C8.2a

Say: 'God is One, the Eternal God. He begot none, nor was He begotten. None is equal to Him.'

(N. J. Dawood)

Example C8.2b

Say, O Mohammad: He is Allah the one. Allah As-Samad (the self-sufficient master, whom all creatures need, he neither eats nor drinks). He begets not, nor was He begotten. And there is none co-equal or comparable unto Him.

(Al-Hilali and Khan)

Example C8.2c

SAY: He is God alone: God the eternal! He begetteth not, and He is not begotten. And there is none like unto Him.

(Rodwell)

But, what if within the **interpretive** mode, we needed to preserve both **form** and **function**, as we explained above? **Relevance** theory caters for such aims within what came to be known as **direct translation**, a type of **interpretive** translation veering more towards the **formal** end.

Direct translations are those in which the translator has somehow to stick to 'the explicit contents of the original' (Gutt 1991: 122). Although this kind of translation is still a case of **interpretive** use, the translator would make choices in such a way that the TT *resembles* the ST 'closely enough in relevant respects' (Sperber and Wilson 1988: 137). This **resemblance** or closeness is a requirement which is not strictly complied with in normal **interpretive translation**, and which, when responding in **direct translation**, entails that we identify and preserve **communicative clues**.

Task C8.3

In line with the **Minimax** Principle, which we looked at in Section A of this unit, the various 'focal' elements (i.e. **semantic**ally or **syntactic**ally **marked** elements – see Section A, Unit 9) are treated as **communicative clue**s to specific meanings.

➤ Example C8.3 is actually a text that has been translated into English. Treat it now as a possible ST to translate into your own language. Aim for a translation which recognizes:

- ■ the need in this kind of text to preserve both 'what is said' and 'how something is said', **form** and **content**;
- ■ the difficulties encountered in straightforward **form**-by-**form** translation.

➤ Apply insights you have gained in this kind of exercise to the assessment of actual translations. Identify a sample of argumentative texts and their translations, and examine these, focusing on preserving **functional markedness**.

Example C8.3

[. . .]

Always on the side of the teaching profession and the people, and *never on the side of* institutions, he wrote in 1908: 'The schools, teachers and students will be freed by *those who* are ready to dedicate *their work, their sacrifices and their enthusiasm* to the development of education; *those who* rise and fall with it; *those who* are the soul of every school; they will be freed *by the teachers who teach school and by the folk who send their children* to school.' *Out of this passionate personal adherence to liberty developed* gradually a philosophical concept of freedom as man's highest ideal and aim . . .

(UNESCO *Prospects*, (1986) [italics added])

SEMANTIC REPRESENTATIONS

A **semantic** representation is a mental/linguistic formula, not yet developed into a properly **functional** instance of language use. But even at this rudimentary stage of development, a **semantic** representation of a word, for example, is not the same as the 'meaning' of that word. It is meaning plus contextual implications (effect, etc.).

To become proper language use, **semantic** representations need to be **inferentially** enriched. Only then can meaning become derivable, not from the stimulus alone but from the interaction of this with the **cognitive environment**. By **cognitive environment** what is meant is all the assumptions and **implicature**s which utterances convey in a given context of use. Ideally, there will be a reasonable degree of fit between what we infer to be the interpretation (e.g. when we know what is being implied) and the **communicative clue**s provided.

Example C8.4

An example of parallel-text publicity material is a booklet issued by the government of Sharjah, United Arab Emirates, entitled:

Al-Ihtisham wa al-*Suluuk al-'aam: Decency and Public Conduct* (English), *La Pudeur et le comportement* (French), *Der Anstand und das allgemeine Verhalten* (German) . . .

 ### Task C8.4

In Arabic, *ihtisham* is certainly 'decency', but the **semantic** representation of the concept would in addition have such elements of 'meaning' as 'humility', 'modesty', even 'submissiveness'.

➤ Do the other renderings preserve these added contextual implications?

Task C8.5

➤ Find similar multilingual publicity material, and identify salient concepts.

➤ Focus on ST **semantic** representations and use 'contextual implications' as **communicative clue**s.

➤ Check how these concepts have been dealt with, and whether the various TTs do justice to this aspect of ST meaning and at the same time uphold **relevance** for the target reader.

GRAMMAR IS MEANINGFUL

Like **semantics, syntax** can generate its own **communicative clue**s. Syntactic structures can be vehicles for the expression of a diverse range of **pragmatic** meanings. But how can we be even marginally sure that changing or preserving a given **syntactic** arrangement would ensure **equivalence of effect**? To break this question down to two main sub-issues: Do we know enough about how the different languages and cultures do their **pragmatics**? And, assuming that certain pragmatic acts do enjoy a reasonable degree of universality, how can we be sure that the TT reader will or will not appreciate, say, the irony conveyed through similar or different **syntax**?

Task C8.6

As a research technique, in addition to accessing the translator's thoughts (see Section C, Unit 3, pp. 235–6), **Think-Aloud Protocols** may be useful in gathering **empirical** evidence from reader response.

➤ Experiment with texts that are **marked** in different ways. Give a group of readers two translated versions, one preserving ST **syntactic** arrangement, the other abstracting or somehow modifying the **syntax**. See if the **reception** of certain effects (e.g. irony) is affected at all.

As we pointed out above, languages differ not only in the patterns of structure employed but also in the values they assign to these patterns. Is repetition in Arabic as sensitive and curiosity-arousing as it is, say, in English? The answer is probably no, certainly not as often.

A TYPOLOGY OF COMMUNICATIVE CLUES

Writers employ **communicative clue**s as sign-posts to guide the reader through the maze of communicative values conveyed by the text. Readers/translators must therefore learn to:

■ identify what constitutes a 'clue';
■ define the **function**, which the clue might conceivably serve.

At this stage, the translator must go a step further and

■ identify a suitable **communicative clue** capable of conveying ST **function**.

This is an ideal scenario. Often, translators have to settle for less than this theoretical ideal when they

■ opt for some form of re-wording that often does not have the making of a **communicative clue**.

In this last-resort option, we would be translating the 'what' and not necessarily the 'how'.

Task C8.7

➤ To appreciate the **form** and **function** of **communicative clue**s, obtain a play by Shakespeare (or a similarly 'sensitive' text) translated into a language with which you are familiar. Identify whatever strikes you as **communicative clue**s, retrieve the functions they are meant to convey, assess the translation **equivalent**s and see if the **function** is preserved and if the translator has achieved this with or without the clue.

 Task C8.8

In the area of formulaic expressions (greetings, good wishes, etc.), we tend to look for expressions that have similar 'encyclopaedic' information in the other language (the target rendering *nice hair cut*, to cater for a communicative occasion where the hearer, having just had a hair cut, is being 'congratulated' with an expression in Arabic which literally translates 'bless you'). This is a serious problem in literary translation.

➤ Examine the Shakespearean translation you have selected, and identify the various strategies used in coping with this level of **style**.

In the area of phonology and **style**, the working principle in this area is: If **semantic** meaning behind sound is felt to be particularly relevant, the need to select from a range of possible clues becomes important.

For example, ST sounds may be replicated in TT if they belong to the class of so-called onomatopoeia. Onomatopoeia must not be confused with alliteration and assonance. Onomatopoeia is a word whose phonic form imitates a sound – *splish, splosh, bang, cuckoo*, etc.

Two kinds of onomatopoeia have been distinguished by Levý (1967): *ad hoc* and **functional**. The latter type is likely to be thematically significant, and must therefore be preserved in translation.

 Task C8.9

➤ Focus on the **functional** variety of onomatopoeia, and identify examples in the Shakespearean translation you are looking at.

➤ Examine the problem and the solutions opted for by the translator.

Finally, sound-based **poetics** (rhyme, rhythm, etc.) is another category of utterances involving expression without **semantic** properties.

 Task C8.10

➤ Is sound-based poetics translatable? Show by finding real examples from the Shakespearean translation you are assessing.

PITFALLS IN DEALING WITH COMMUNICATIVE CLUES

Languages differ not only in the patterns of structure employed but also in the values assigned to what could be a similar pattern (e.g. repetition). Cumulative effects conveyed by sequences of elements also tend to vary across languages and cultures (does parallelism, together with other relevant devices within a given configuration in English, perform a similar role as it does in other languages?). In addition to this factor of complexity, there is 'frequency of use' in the TL to consider. Take the case of repetition or parallelism, for example. From the perspective of **relevance** theory, the effect of these structures is seen in terms of 'the cost–benefit correlation between the effort needed to process a stimulus and the contextual effects to be expected as a reward' (Gutt 1991: 140). With repetition or parallelism being 'fashions of speaking' used frequently almost by default in a range of Eastern languages, will such a structure be as 'noteworthy' in these languages compared, say, to English?

Gutt puts forward the following **relevance** principle which accounts for both complexity and frequency of use:

> if a communicator uses a stimulus that manifestly requires *more* processing effort than some other stimulus equally available to him, the hearer can expect that the benefits of this stimulus will *outweigh* the increase in processing cost – otherwise the communicator would have failed to achieve optimal relevance.
>
> (Gutt 1991)

Thus, if focalization in English, for example, has stress as a fairly common realization (thus requiring minimal processing effort), the alternative of **clefting** in a TL such as Arabic would only be adequate if clefting also happens to be as commonly used in this language. Imbalance would otherwise set in, and the disparity between cost and benefit across languages would become unmanageable.

CONCLUSION

Can this **cognitive** feat of **inferencing** (as the **relevance** model insists) be achieved without recourse to such templates as **text typologies** and communicative acts (Gutt 1991)? Despite the insistence by **relevance** theoreticians that this is possible, distinctions such as **descriptive** vs **interpretive** use, **direct** vs **indirect** translation and so on all seem to involve concepts that are not binary but rather points on a sliding scale: the relationships involved are 'more or less' and 'probabilistic'. And to be meaningful for the translator, these dichotomies have to be seen in terms of a complex set of factors, with some correlation, albeit fairly weak, inevitably existing between orientation (say, **interpretive** use), translation strategy (**indirect**) and **text-type** and **purpose** constraints. This is an area to be explored next.

PROJECTS

1. Extreme **interpretive** translations (like those exhibiting extreme **formal equiv-alence**) and extreme **descriptive** translations (like those produced through drastic forms of **dynamic equivalence**) are certainly rare, but they do occur, sometimes with justification, and often in one and the same translated text. Examine a sample of translated texts drawn from a particular domain such as promotional literature and see if you can identify examples of some of these extreme cases: from cases of **transliteration** to cases of **re-writing**, etc. What is it that motivates this fluctuation in decision-making?

2. Examine a sample of translations of the Koran or the Bible, or another religious text, that have been made for children, and compare these versions with translations done for scholarly purposes. Assess the choices made in order to ensure that '**interpretive**' translation moves away from the **formal** end, in the case of children's translation, and towards the **formal** end in the case of more scholarly translations.

3. Particularly in working from languages with a great deal of orality, the iden-tification of genuine **communicative clue**s becomes a serious problem. Texts will abound with repetition, parallelism, etc. But most of these clues will not be **functional**; that is, they may be ascribed to general linguistic incompetence, or to being part of speaking fashions in vogue within those languages and cultures. **Relevance** is an ideal framework for adjudicating over the issue of **functionality**, and the **Minimax** will be an ideal translation **procedure**. To study this phenomenon:

   1 Make a list of possible '**marked**' structures.
   2 Collect a sample of texts (preferably from a neutral body of materials in a language such as English) and their translations into a language known for its preference for overly emotive expression.
   3 See how **markedness** creeps into the TT, often in an unmotivated manner.

Unit C9
Text type in translation

The **text typology** presented in Section A, Unit 9 draws upon text research conducted within both applied linguistics (e.g. Werlich 1976) and translation theory (e.g. Beaugrande 1978). With English/Arabic/French in mind, this body of work has been the basis on which Basil Hatim and Ian Mason have developed their own **text-type** model of the translation **process** (1990, 1997). Prior to this, however, another influential **text typology** had been in circulation within Translation Studies for some time. This had been proposed and developed by German translation theorist Katherina Reiss (Section B, Unit 9). The model goes back to the early 1970s, and takes as its foundations the much earlier work of linguists such as Karl Bühler.

TEXT PURPOSE AND TEXT FUNCTION

Reiss's **text typology** was originally intended as a set of guidelines for the practising translator. Three basic types of text are recognized (**informative, expressive** and **operative**) and are distinguished one from the other in terms of such factors as the **intention** or the **rhetorical purpose** of the text producer, and the 'function' which a text performs in actual use. These factors (roughly **intentionality** and **acceptability** in Beaugrande's terminology) have a direct consequence on the kind of lexical/**semantic**, grammatical/**syntactic** and rhetorical/**stylistic** features in use. Text intention and **function** also influence the way texts are structured in accordance with, or in rhetorically motivated violation of, set compositional plans and patterns.

Task C9.1

➤ Examine these three text examples below and answer the following questions for each text, producing linguistic evidence (actual words, grammar, etc.) to support your views:

■ What in your estimation is the writer's ultimate aim (i.e. **rhetorical purpose**)?
■ How does the text, or the language used, affect you as a reader (in response to 'text **function**')?

Example C9.1

Summary

The present report . . . has been prepared in response to General Assembly Resolution 51/186. In accordance with resolution 54/93, the report comprises a review of the implementation and results of the World Declaration and Plan of Action . . . It draws upon a wide range of sources . . . It also draws upon earlier reports . . .

From the *Report to the General Assembly by the UN Secretary-General* 4 May 2001, concerning follow-up to the World Summit for Children (available online at <http://www.unicef.org/specialsession/documentation/documents/a-s-27-3e.pdf>)

Example C9.2

She talked all the time and at first it was about people and places.

She was working on a piece of needlepoint when we first met them and she worked on this and saw *to* the food and drink and talked to my wife.

(E. Hemingway *A Moveable Feast* (1964/1994) Arrow: London)

Example C9.3

The Cohesion of OPEC

Tomorrow's meeting of OPEC is a different affair. Certainly, it is formally about prices and about Saudi Arabia's determination to keep them down. Certainly, it will also have immediate implications for the price of petrol, especially for Britain which recently lowered its price of North Sea oil and may now have to raise it again. But this meeting, called at short notice, and confirmed only after the most intensive round of preliminary discussions between the parties concerned, is not primarily about selling arrangements between the producer and consumer. It is primarily about the future cohesion of the organization itself.

(*The Times* 31 March 1998)

Let us now examine each of the examples in more detail. Example C9.1 is a summary, a **rhetorical purpose** which is realized by a particular kind of language use that essentially reflects the **informative function** in question (e.g. *The report comprises . . .*). However, in the UN published translation into Arabic, this **informative purpose** and **function** were drastically misconstrued, with the translator opting for a form of words so inappropriate that the end result is a style more suited for an editorial than a summary report. This text is discussed further in Task C11.1.

Task C9.2

➤ Re-write Example C9.1 to make it suitable for an editorial.

Example C9.2 is a creative description, a **rhetorical purpose** which finds expression in the kind of language used. **Salient** characteristics of Hemingway's style include short sentences, action verbs in acts involving men, and patientive verbs in acts involving women (see Fowler 1986).

This **expressive** text has seen two translations into Arabic: one properly renders ST **style**, the other radically misappreciates it. In the latter version, the expressive **purpose** and **function** have not been fully appreciated by the translator who seems oblivious to the significance of features as subtle as the short pithy sentence structure, action verbs in relation to the main protagonist's activities, and patientive verbs to indicate female (in)activity. This aspect of Hemingway's language will also be discussed further in Tasks C11.5 and C11.6.

Task C9.3

➤ Choose extracts from a Hemingway story, and examine the language, specifically the **agents** used, together with the actions performed by them.

Example C9.3 is a counter-**argument**, a **rhetorical purpose** adequately served by the text structure employed (e.g. *Certainly*). This '**operative**' text, however, is erroneously rendered into Arabic. The **operative purpose** and **function** have been almost totally misunderstood, when the signal *certainly* is perceived not as intended (a 'concessive' connector), but as an emphatic device (equivalent to 'there is absolutely no doubt that . . .'). This is probably why the adversative *but*, in the fourth sentence, is seen as unimportant and is therefore omitted. These are 'structure' signals, which serve an important cohesive **function**, an aspect of **texture** that is seriously compromised.

Task C9.4

➤ Is this counter-argumentative format (e.g. *Certainly . . . However . . .*) known or common in other languages? If not, what other counter-argumentative forms are in use?

➤ Do you foresee any problems translating the English (or these other) counter-argumentative structures into or out of English?

These three examples illustrate Reiss's **typology**. Texts of type A ('**informative**') are primarily intended to convey information, type B '**expressive**' texts tend to communicate inner thoughts through narrating a series of events in a creative way, and Type C '**operative**' texts seek to persuade.

Task C9.5

One important difference between the **typology** proposed by Reiss and that of Hatim and Mason is in the area of the 'operative' kind of text. Reiss conflates under 'operative' what Hatim and Mason keep distinct as 'argumentative' and 'instructional'. Conflating the two types feels intuitively right in the area of advertising.

➤ Examine this 'operative' text (Example C9.4) and show how the **instructional purpose/function** is fused with persuasion.

Example C9.4

Shop with your Visa card and win US$ 40,000.

TEXT TYPE AND TRANSLATION STRATEGY

The **typology** proposed by Reiss has made its mark on the strength of a correlation rather boldly established between **text type** and translation method. To start with, it is argued that the type of text correlates with the nature of the demands made on the translator. For example, **operative** texts are particularly challenging to translate. Furthermore, it is suggested that the predominant **function** of the ST must invariably be preserved in the translation. Thus, translators of **informative** texts should aim primarily for 'semantic equivalence', and only then for **connotative meanings** and aesthetic values. In the case of **expressive** texts, the main concern of the translator should be to preserve aesthetic effect alongside relevant aspects of **semantic content**. Finally, **operative** texts should be dealt with in terms of **extra-linguistic** effect (e.g. persuasiveness), a level of **equivalence** normally achieved at the expense of both **form** and **content**.

 Task C9.6

➤ Can you think of situations in which the above trends (e.g. **informative** texts translated for information) may simply be unworkable?

➤ Identify texts or translation **commissions** which challenge the above tendencies (e.g. when an **informative** text has to be translated as creative fiction, a piece of propaganda, an advertisement, etc.).

➤ Experiment with any of the examples in this unit, attending to **purposes** for which a text would not be normally intended.

In fact, it was Reiss herself who, some twenty years later, modified **equivalence** of the kind identified above along **text-type** lines. Specifically under the *skopos* (translation **purpose**) régime, **equivalence** of **function** is not abandoned altogether, but is now related to adequacy, a term used in a non-technical sense simply to mean 'adequate to the job'. This is related to the translation **brief**, and the nature of the **commission**.

THE COMMISSION OR TRANSLATION PURPOSE

Within the framework of *skopos* theory (or translation **purpose**), Reiss tones down the correlation between type of text, nature of demand on the translator and method of translation. It is suggested that the correlation applies only in the translation of texts that call for **functional** invariance, that is, when, due to all sorts of factors, there is nothing to justify **functional** change. The UN text, Example C9.1 above, is a good example of this kind of text.

In cases which call for **functional** change, however, ST **function** may be adjusted. Although this is rare, the predominance of **content** in **informative** texts, of **form** in **expressive** texts and of effect in **operative** texts are in theory not sacrosanct and the translation *skopos* begins to play a crucial role in what happens across linguistic and cultural boundaries.

Task C9.7

➤ To acquire facility in dealing with the two basic notions of **functional** 'variance' and 'invariance', find a text that has been authoritatively translated in full by such translation institutions as the BBC Monitoring Service or the UN translation department.

➤ Using such a document as a basis, try to work to a specific set of instructions, perhaps to translate the text for a tabloid newspaper.

➤ What kind of changes would you introduce, and what would the implications of such decisions be for ST original **function**?

CONCLUSION

What has long been the subject of debate in Translation Studies (e.g. Emery 1991) is whether classifying texts is at all feasible or indeed useful for the 'practical' translator. Two problems are identified with the kind of **text typologies** currently available. First, the notion of **text type** is of such a wide scope that it can subsume a huge array of text-form variants. In one study, for example, the **text-type** 'instruction' is shown to include '**genres**' as varied as Acts of Parliament, technical instructions, political speeches, sermons and advertisements (Zydatiss 1983). The second problem with current **typologies** has to do with the issue of **hybridization** discussed earlier: a particular text can and often does consist of different 'types' (e.g. an instruction manual may include conceptual **exposition** and description, as well as **instruction**).

Yet **text typologies**, and the identification of text **purpose** and text **function**, continue to be seen as valuable tools for translators in their attempts to specify the appropriate hierarchy of **equivalence** levels needed for a particular translation assignment. Indeed, as German theorist Christiane Nord (1997: 38) observes, even in the case of a much-needed **functional** change with a given *skopos* in mind, one would still be talking about **text type** and **function** in the TL: 'Text-type classifications sharpen the translator's awareness of linguistic markers of communicative function.'

PROJECTS

1. Consider the following kind of criticism usually levelled at **text typologies**:

    The idea of **rhetorical purpose** is of dubious validity, as it is difficult to link particular text samples with particular **text types** in a plausible and systematic way.

    Assess the validity of such criticisms by carrying out a **text analysis** of a whole feature article in a magazine such as *The Economist* or *Newsweek*. If well selected, such a lengthy piece of writing can include a variety of **text types**. Set a translator or a group of translators the task of translating this article (or use published translations if such exist). Going by the kind of problems which the analysis has anticipated in theory and which the translators will have encountered in practice, can you reach some conclusions regarding the value of **text-type** classifications and the status of **text type** in the translation **process**?

2. Perhaps rightly, models of text classification which view **field of discourse** almost exclusively in terms of 'subject matter' are called into question. Examine a sample of texts all dealing with one particular topic (e.g. the war on terrorism), and attempt a classification of these texts in terms of such categories as **rhetorical purpose** (**informative exposition**, **operative argumentation** and expressive creativity). If any of these texts has been translated, assess the quality of the translation in terms of the extent to which a **text type** specification is heeded. In other words, can the problems encountered in the translation of these texts be accounted for in **text type** terms?

3. Focus on features of Hemingway's style such as short sentences and the use of action verbs for men and inactivity for women. Evaluate translations of one of Hemingway's novels or short stories published in a TL you are familiar with: are these features heeded and preserved? If not, why do you think the translator has opted for a different strategy? Is it anything to do with TL conventions?

Unit C10
Text register in translation

In Sections A and B of Unit 10 we were concerned with how awareness of textual **registers** features prominently in any attempt to ensure that a translation adequately reflects subtle aspects of **cohesion** and **coherence**. Preserving the integrity of text in this way upholds appropriateness in terms of such standard factors of the communication process as who is speaking to whom, where, when, and so on.

RHETORICAL PURPOSE VS TEXT FUNCTION

To focus on **register** in practice, and to examine the wider implications of research in this area, let us now look in some detail at translation quality assessment, and specifically at a model proposed for this purpose by German linguist and translation theorist Juliane House (1977, 1997). In this approach, which is largely based on **register** theory, **equivalence** is defined in terms of:

- the linguistic and situational features of the ST and TT
- a comparison of the two texts
- an assessment of ST–TT relative match.

Example C10.1

The Hamas Charter

Preamble

'Israel will rise and will remain erect until Islam eliminates it as it had eliminated its predecessors.'

(The Imam and Martyr Hasan al-Bana)

'This is the Charter of the Islamic Resistance (Hamas) which will reveal its face, unveil its identity, state its position, clarify its purpose, discuss its hopes, call for support to its cause and reinforcement, and for joining its ranks. [. . .]'

(From *The Hamas Charter (1990)* (trans Prof. R. Israeli), in *The 1988–1989 Annual on Terrorism*, Dordrecht, Netherlands: Kluwer Academic Publishers)

Task C10.1

➤ Consider this extract from a translation of a charter, and reflect on some of the problems the text might have for its English target readers:

➤ The translation of the full text is available on the Internet as well as from the printed source. Examine the document and work out a strategy which does justice to the ST and at the same time serves as a 'proper' charter in terms of format.

Example C10.1 is almost a **word-for-word** translation from Arabic. To invoke **register** theory for purposes of a ST–TT comparison, we would presumably start with **field**, **tenor** and **mode**, only to conclude that, by and large, there are no significant problems. But if we were to probe more deeply and inquire into whether this TT can ever function as a charter in English, the answer would be a resounding 'no!'.

The notion of **equivalence** adopted in House's approach to quality assessment is underpinned by the idea of text **function**. This is certainly related to **register** and to such linguistic-situational factors as subject matter and level of formality. **Function**, however, cannot be seen solely in terms of the minutiae of a text's grammar and vocabulary. It is a higher level category and is more closely linked to **text type**. Recall how in Section A, Unit 9, the accepted sender-oriented specification of **function** as **rhetorical purpose** was proposed as the defining feature of **text type**. This may now be extended to cater for the receiver end, with **function** seen as 'the application or use which the text has in the particular context of a situation' (Lyons 1968: 434). The receiver orientation ensures that subtle variations at this end of the communication process are not overlooked as a very important part of source and target 'textual profiles'.

 Task C10.2

Rhetorical purpose and text **function** on the one hand, and translation **function** on the other, can be (and often are) similar, if not identical. There are, however, situations where ST **purpose/function** and translation **function** part company in significant ways.

➤ What would you say is the **rhetorical purpose/text function** of the Hamas text in Arabic?

➤ What **function** does the Hamas text perform in the English translation?

➤ What criteria would you invoke to assess this ST–TT **purpose–function** disparity?

As a comparative reference point, consider the following excerpt from the UN Charter.

Example C10.2

The UN Charter

Preamble

WE THE PEOPLES OF THE UNITED NATIONS
DETERMINED
To save succeeding generations from the scourge of war, which twice in our lifetime has brought untold sorrow to mankind,
[. . .]

AND FOR THESE ENDS
To practise tolerance and live together in peace with one another as good neighbours,
[. . .]

(UN Charter)

To draw up a textual profile, then, texts are placed in their situational context. That is, some form of correlation is established between language and situation. For this situationalization to be useful, however, it must go beyond the use and user of language to include such factors as the conventionalized ways of speaking or writing typical of certain **communicative events** or social activities (or what we can collectively refer to as **genre**). In deciding that, as it stands, the Hamas text cannot conceivably be used as a charter in English, several factors are involved: the **instructional** tone (a **text** issue) is far too emotive (a **discourse** issue). The single most important factor, however, would be **genre**, a category that will receive full attention in the next unit.

Task C10.3

The Hamas text all but fails as a charter in English.

➤ Can you, nevertheless, find situations in which a translation of the Hamas text as it stands might be valid and acceptable?

COVERT AND OVERT TRANSLATION

Different translations (each with its own unique **function**) may be produced for one and the same text. A legal document may be translated as intended (i.e. as a set of instructions) or may indeed be turned into a news report, a description, an explanation or even an argument in an editorial. This underlines the importance of translation **purpose**.

Translators use a number of parameters for this 'matching' between how the ST might be intended, and how it should be received, with ST **function** preserved, modified or altogether jettisoned. Crucially, there is the issue of ST status: does the text rely for its relevance on such aspects of the SL and culture as traditions, social or institutional structures, etc.? If it does (as in the case of most sacred and sensitive texts), there is no way we can hope that the TT will be as **functional** in the TL as the ST has been for its readers (i.e. there is no way that ST **function** can be preserved intact in the TT). In such cases, the best we can hope for is to produce what House (1977) calls **overt translation**. Variously labelled as **literal, semantic, foreignizing, documentary**, this translation method entails that signs are simply substituted for signs, and that quite a portion of the cultural **content** is left for the target reader to sort out.

Like the Hamas text, a letter by Saddam Hussein to the people of Iraq (Example C10.3) is an example of the kind of text that lends itself to (and has received) an **overt translation** treatment. With footnotes explaining that Hulaku, the grandson of Genghis Khan, sacked Baghdad in 1258 AD, and that Alqami was a non-Arab Shia who betrayed Baghdad to the Mongols, this is how *The Guardian* translation began:

Example C10.3

From Saddam Hussein to the great Iraqi people, the sons of the Arab and Islamic nation, and honourable people everywhere.

Peace be upon you, and the mercy and blessings of God.

Just as Hulaku entered Baghdad, the criminal Bush entered it, with Alqami, or rather, more than one Alqami.
[. . .]

(*The Guardian* 30 April 2003 (trans. Brian Whitaker))

The full translation of this letter is available on the Internet at (http://www.guardian.co.uk/Iraq/Story/0,2763,946805,00.html).

 Task C10.4

➤ Examine the text and suggest ways of turning it into one that is perhaps more 'reader-friendly'.

Your edited version would certainly have earned the indictment 'not really a translation' by translation scholars such as Gutt. However, the strategy can be optimally viable in a different kind of context. **Covert translation**, as this strategy is called by House, is chosen for when the ST does not depend for its relevance so much on the SL and culture (a letter from the President of an international company to the shareholders, for example). Here, translators produce a TT that is as immediately relevant for the target reader as the ST has been for the SL reader. This is achieved through heavy **adjustment**, which conceals whatever betrays the origin of the translated text.

In this kind of **covert** translation, preserving ST **function** is conceivable but only through varying degrees of 'cultural filtering' (varying degrees of mediation on the part of the translator). The translator engages in heavy mediation in an attempt to recreate in the TL a cultural model, which, to all intents and purposes, is equivalent to that of the ST. This process is informed by an awareness of the differences (as well as the similarities) which exist between the source and target cultures in areas such as socio-cultural predisposition and communicative preferences.

Task C10.5

➤ Choose a text of the kind that is least dependent on its SL and culture (this might be a global advertisement, a journalistic text, technical material, etc.) and examine aspects of the text which give it this sense of autonomy. Translate into your own language to reflect this 'independent status'.

➤ Examine your translation and reflect on how, to preserve ST **function**, a number of **covert** strategies would have to be used, involving various degrees of cultural filtering. You might want to consider situations in which 'touring the city' and 'sampling the culture' are inseparable in a tourist guide, for example.

If an intervention on behalf of the ST producer, usually for the benefit of the TT user, turns out to be unjustified (e.g. a misreading of the original's intention or a miscalculation of likely target reactions), we no longer have translation proper, but at best a **covert version**. Covert versions are said to be inadequate as translations almost by definition.

CASE STUDY

House analyses the text of a letter in English from the president of an investment company encouraging shareholders to adopt changes in the set-up of the company which, if truth were told, would not exactly be to their advantage. The use of language is cleverly manipulated to relay a carefully evasive and distantly polite tone (e.g. *Your assistance is required; it is anticipated that . . .*).

Task C10.6

Example C10.4 below is an extract from the company president's letter.

➤ Examine it carefully and identify features through which the polite, yet evasive, tone is conveyed. Use these categories:

- On the **ideational** front, the **function** of the text is to inform the addressee of a set of facts as succinctly as possible and to request action.
- In the **interpersonal** domain, on the other hand, the **function** is to mollify the reader through generating positive rapport and impressing on the reader the soundness of the company's policy in instituting the changes. It is also to give the reader a feeling of importance, even power, and to achieve all these communicative aims in a non-committal, almost detached fashion.

Example C10.4   (from House 1997: 170)

As you will note, we have asked that you designate a bank (or broker) to which your dividend certificates will be sent. Your bank (or broker) should indicate its confirmation of your signature by executing the bottom half of the 'Dividend Instruction Form' including its official signature and stamp.

Obviously, this is suitable material for **covert translation**. The translator has to accommodate likely cultural differences by placing a 'cultural filter' between the ST and the translation, re-negotiating the ST **function** in terms acceptable to the TL user of the translation. But such a strategy can be risky, and proved to be so in this particular translation. House (1997: 49–57) shows that translation into German of this commercial correspondence seemed to have catered neither for the **interpersonal** nor for the **ideational** functional components in the same manner as the ST did (e.g. *your bank (or broker) should indicate* . . . is translated as *Sie müssen die Bank (oder einen Makler) bitten* . . . – literally, 'you must ask the bank (or a broker) . . .').

The German rendering was thus erroneous in that it presented the writer as someone much more forceful, active and direct than indicated by the ST where the action requested of the addressee was cast in a highly abstract and indirect way (e.g. nominally). In short, while the translation seemed more like a direct request presented in a much more forward, blunt, and undiplomatic tone, the overall **illocutionary force** of the English ST is one of subtle suggestion, with the original text producer trying to intimate that it is not the company but some 'benign' external **agency** which is proposing a particular course of action.

This is the conclusion which House reached at the time. The assumptions entertained concerning the different expectations of the German shareholders with regard to such a letter were thought to be unwarranted since they were stereotypical and not substantiated by facts. But such evidence has now come to light. A number of cross-cultural (German–English) studies have since been carried out suggesting that communicative preferences exist and that these differ along five basic dimensions: directness, self-reference, **content**-focus, explicitness and reliance on communicative routines.

Task C10.7

➤ Having appreciated the commercial text for what it is, try now either to retrieve the letter from House (1997: 169–73) or collect examples of similar letters originating in English.

➤ Attempt an analysis and translation into languages which you know to be more 'direct' and 'forceful'.

Researching TL preferences is obviously crucial, but, as translators working to deadlines under pressure, rarely if ever can we afford such luxuries. We must therefore opt for a **heuristics** of some kind, a practical way of assessing likely target reader response. **Text type** and textual practices related to such macro-structures as **genre** are important parameters for making this **heuristics** less subjective.

CONCLUSION

In this unit, we have explored variables such as the use and user of language from the perspective of both **register** analysis and **translation quality assessment**. The latter is an important application of **register** theory and one which has provided translation analysts and practitioners with useful tools for judging the adequacy of a given translation strategy for a particular kind of text. But the choice of a translation strategy is not just a ST issue, nor is it exclusively a **context of situation** matter. Rather, it is bound up with the entire **context of culture** within which texts and their translation are produced. It is these issues that will occupy us in the next unit.

PROJECTS

1. Find a translation with a dialect problem (e.g. George Bernard Shaw's *Pygmalion*, 1916) and examine two or three versions translating the same text. Analyse and assess the strategy adopted.

2. Investigate a language which varies little in time or space (e.g. Arabic), and examine how the language can cope with subtle dialect and **register** variations in STs belonging to variation-sensitive languages (e.g. English).

3.   Investigate a language with abundant terminology in a certain area (e.g. falconry in Arabic, information technology in English) or with formality markers (such as honorifics in Japanese) and study how languages with deficits in their repertoires cope.

4.   **Rhetorical purpose** and text **function** can be (and often are) similar, if not identical. However, there are situations where **purpose** and **function** may be at variance: what we want the translation to 'function' as (as detailed in the 'commission' for example) may not be the same as the **purpose** intended for the ST by the text producer.

     Examine the work of a translation agency or a satellite TV station and investigate in detail the changes undergone by texts imported from other (perhaps more neutral) translation agencies.

5.   Several cross-cultural studies (e.g. German–English) have been carried out, suggesting that communicative preferences exist and that these differ along five basic dimensions: directness, self-reference, **content**-focus, explicitness and reliance on communicative routines. Apply this model to the analysis of how your language and culture prefer to handle a sample of texts of a similar kind to the commercial letter analysed by House.

Unit C11
Text, genre and discourse shifts in translation

EXPLORING TEXT SHIFTS IN TRANSLATION

Task C11.1

➤ Examine the following two texts (one of which you have already seen in Example C9.1) and try to determine:

1. the **field** or subject matter
2. **tenor** of level of formality
3. the writer's intention to **monitor** or **manage** a situation
4. the **text-type** orientation as reflected by the contextual focus on **exposition** or **argumentation**.

Example C11.1a   English ST

Summary

The present report . . . has been prepared in response to General Assembly Resolution 51/186. In accordance with resolution 54/93, the report comprises a review of the implementation and results of the World Declaration and Plan of Action . . . It draws upon a wide range of sources . . . It also draws upon earlier reports . . .

(From the *Report to the General Assembly by the UN Secretary-General* 4 May 2001)

Example C11.1b   Back-translation of Arabic translation, italics added

Summary

It is the present report . . . *which* has been prepared by the Preparatory Committee in response to the General Assembly Resolution 51/186. In accordance with resolution 54/93, *what* the report comprises *is* a review of the implementation and results of the World Declaration and Plan of Action . . . It draws upon a wide range of sources *as well as* earlier reports . . .

International affairs as **field** and a formal style as **tenor**, are aspects of **register** optimally preserved by Example C11.1b. These contextual specifications certainly tell us a great deal about the level of technicality (or terminology) and formality (or authority) shared as important features by the ST and TT in question, but can hardly identify precisely where the TT has gone wrong. To establish real differences or similarities, we must therefore invoke another set of criteria to do with **intentionality**. The pragmatic orientation of Example C11.1a is to **monitor** a situation impartially by producing a fairly detached summary, while that of Example C11.1b is to **manage** a situation by arguing for the merits or demerits of a particular scheme. **Monitoring** and **managing** lead us to another basic distinction: Examples 'a' and 'b' above are likely to be found in the summary section and the evaluation section of a UN document respectively. The fact that a text is a summary or a commentary has to do with **intertextuality**, which establishes how texts (and utterances within texts) can conjure up images of other texts, much in the same way as signs point us in the direction of what they refer to. This level of context is ultimately responsible for creating texts and for the evolution of **text types**.

 Task C11.2

Due to a shortage of translators in particular language pairs, a practice not uncommon in organizations such as the UN is to translate from already translated texts and not from originals.

➤ If you were to use the above TT (Example C11.1b) as a ST to translate into your own language, what would your translation strategy be: to preserve this level of emotiveness, to neutralize it partially or to jettison it completely? What is your rationale?

GENRE SHIFTS

For the various interrelationships (**register**-related and **pragmatic**) to make sense in the wider context of communication, then, we need to see a given sequence of sentences in terms of a dominant contextual focus which points to the overall **rhetorical purpose** of the writer or the **function** of the text. But there are other vantage points from which to approach a text.

Task C11.3

➤ Consider this piece of narration (Example C11.2a). By focusing on the elements in added italics, what strikes you as somewhat unusual in this kind of narration?

Example C11.2a

There was another soft rustling, then silence. *Gabrielle's ears strained* against it as she tried to hear Doyle's breathing, just to reassure herself that he was still there, but the harder she listened, the more strange sounds she could hear – sounds that she couldn't identify but which her mind went spinning off to make sense.

Was that soft, slithering sound a snake moving across the ground towards her? And *that light insistent tapping – could it be . . .?*

(Jennifer Taylor, Jungle Fever, Richmond, Surrey:
Harlequin Mills & Boon, 1995: 45–6)

A salient feature of this narrative (and of the entire novel from which it is drawn) is the predominantly **inanimate agency** (*Gabrielle's ears strained*) which threads its way throughout. For the rationale behind the choice of **inanimate** themes in subject position in this text, we need to see the narrative at another level of text organization. This would focus not so much on narration (a **rhetorical purpose** taken care of on the text level) as on the narrative as a **communicative event**. We would here focus on the participants in the event, their goals, and the style and conventions governing writing in this particular mode. The above text is drawn from a Mills & Boon novel, a **genre** which, to enhance the entertainment value, does a number of things with language, including the hijacking of other **genres** (e.g. the **Gothic** and straight Horror in the above example). Like these other **genres**, although probably for different reasons, Mills & Boon tends to be heavy on the **suppression** of human **agency**, deliberately letting **actors** other than the human take over. There is also a clear tendency to use what Carter and Nash (1990) call 'core' verbs, strikingly colourful adjectives, and so on.

It is perhaps helpful at this juncture to comment on the translation of this and similar chunks of narrative in one particular Mills & Boon novel examined in Arabic translation. Quite a number of the inanimate subjects were turned into animate ones, and many of the 'core' verbs lost their 'coreness', probably because inanimate **agency** and a proliferation of 'core' verbs are stylistic features favoured by the fictional **register** in the TL. Inanimate **agency** or core verbs are not unknown in this language, but in the absence of a clear rationale for why this **defamiliarizing** style is used, the decision is likely to be for the default option of resorting to animate **agency** and core verbs. Example C11.2b is a **back-translation** from Arabic of part of the above passage:

Example C11.2b

She started to hear another kind of rustling, then silence. So she strained her ears as she tried to hear Doyle's breathing, just to reassure herself that he was still there . . .

Task C11.4

➤ Examine this kind of popular fiction writing translated into a language with which you are familiar. Are features we associate with the popular fiction **genre** as developed in English preserved, or are they explained away in an attempt to remove any traces that make the story-telling 'vulgar' and 'popular'?

DISCOURSE SHIFTS IN TRANSLATION

What could the Mills & Boon text producer intend by deliberately suppressing human **agency** and resorting to the impersonal mode of narration noted in Example C11.2a above (an effect which was lost in the translation C11.2b)? To answer this question, we will find it helpful to invoke the communicative requirements of the **genre** in question: 'In the domain of popular fiction, there is an implicit supposition that men like their stories to be "action-packed", whereas women prefer a "heart-warming" tale' (Carter and Nash 1990: 100).

But behind the 'heart-warming' lurks a paradox: women make up the majority of those who avidly 'consume' this essentially sexist **discourse**. Carter and Nash (1990) explain this very well: '[Sentences with inanimate or impersonal agents as subjects] occur again and again in contexts presenting the character as a victim-object of uncontrollable forces . . . When soldier Sam is in a spot, his stomach tightens; when nurse Nancy is alone in the fog-bound clinic, fear grips her with an icy claw . . .'

(p. 106)

> ### Example C11.3a (Italics added)
>
> She *talked* all the time and at first it was about people and places.
>
> She *was working* on a piece of needlepoint when we first met them and she *worked* on this and *saw to* the food and drink and *talked* to my wife.
>
> I cannot remember whether she was *walking her dog* or not.
>
> And she always *gave* me the natural eau-de-vie.
>
> She *talked*, mostly, and she *told* me about modern pictures and about painters – more about them as people than as painters – and she *talked* about what she had written and what her companion typed each day.
>
> (E. Hemingway *A Moveable Feast* (1964/1994) Arrow: London)

 Task C11.5

Staying with the interface between **genre** and **discourse**, and with the concept of **shifts** which, if unjustified, constitute an important source of translation problems, consider the excerpt above, culled from what has legitimately become a **genre** in its own right – the Hemingway novella.

➤ What kind of narrative do we have here? Does anything strike you as 'unusual' or marked about it? Why do you think this kind of narrative has been used and what effect does it have?

Hemingway's intention in this or similar texts is certainly to tell a story. However, a pattern emerges in the work of this particular writer, which reveals a tendency to treat men and women differently (Fowler 1986). While men are seen always as 'active' (doing things, picking up bags, etc.), women are relegated to a 'passive' existence (i.e. always at the receiving end, sitting, smiling, etc.).

Cumulatively, this shift in attitude turns a narrative into a forum for ideological statement, and an act of **monitoring** into an act of **managing**. This kind of language use, together with such general stylistic features as short, pithy sentences, have become the trademark of Hemingway, the hallmark of a **genre**. Ultimately, however, what we have is the expression of an attitude towards the sexes, specifically a sexist **ideology** which is a **discourse** matter: how the American Dream is essentially the work of the white American male.

To see this from a translation perspective, a relevant question is whether Hemingway's translators are aware of the implications of such innocent-sounding manifestations such as fairly passive verbs for women and dynamic, active verbs for men. Do translators notice these peculiarities and attitude shifts, or seek to preserve them in their translations?

Task C11.6

➤ Examine a Hemingway story, analyse the **style**, and evaluate a translation made into a language with which you are familiar.

We have performed this kind of analysis on Hemingway's *A Moveable Feast*. This novel has seen two major translations into Arabic. One translation shows a remarkable sensitivity to the stylistic features identified above. In the other translation, the translator does not only gloss over these features by indifferently doing nothing, but seems to go out of the way to convey the opposite effect to what is intended. Consider (Example C11.3b) these **back-translations** (in **bold**) of how the translator of the second version approached the issues involved, and our own **glosses** [in brackets] of the level of 'activity' assigned to the various actions.

Example C11.3b

She talked all the time [actively, as in holding the floor] and **begins by talking** about people and places . . .

She *was* [actively] **preoccupied with** [immersed in] **embroidering a piece of cloth** when we first met them, she was **embroidering** this and [actively] **taking care** of the food and drink and [actively] talked to my wife.

It was she who always talked [actively], **and thus talked to me** about modern pictures and about painters – more about them as people than as painters – and she talked and **showed me** [actively] **the many volumes of a manuscript she was working on and which her companion was typing.**

It is safe to assume that this strategy was influenced by TL linguistic and stylistic **norms** and conventions which prefer (indeed encourage) such features as longer and more complex sentences closely linked to each other within the text, as well as predominantly 'active' verbs across the board.

ANARCHIST DISCOURSE

Phenomena such as **text** and **genre shifts** in Hemingway or Mills & Boon texts, then, inevitably involve **discourse** as 'statement of attitude'. To illustrate discursive practices, in Section B, Unit 11 we included an extract by Donald Bruce (Text B11.2), who looked into the reasons for the state of critical neglect suffered by the French writer Jules Vallès's trilogy *L'Enfant, Le Bachelier* and *L'Insurgé*.

To understand the nature of this specific problem, we need to inquire into the anarchist counter-**discourse** which the work of Vallès represents. Let us explore an important set of discursive features which revolve around what Bruce labels 'radical decentralization'. This manifests itself in a general fragmentation of the narrative, for example. Milan Kundera (discussed in Section A, Unit 11) provides us with an excellent example of this device at work.

 ### Task C11.7

To research fragmented narration and similar **defamiliarizing** uses of language:

➤ Find a translation of Kundera done into your own language or a language with which you are familiar (and assess the translation).

➤ Does the language seem to have been 'normalized' in the TT and the sense of fragmentation lost?

➤ Modify the TT and attempt to increase the **defamiliarization**.

➤ Extend your sample to include works you know have suffered the same kind of imposition of western narrative order at the hands of their translators.

Vallès's novels exhibit another set of discursive features representative of the **discourse** of the Commune. This involves tense shifts which cumulatively prop up the fragmentation motif, this time through the 'sense of spontaneity and immediacy which the shifts relay'. As Bruce (1994: 66) explains, the French text is often written in the present historic and verb tense shifts can be quite abrupt to cater for the different narrative 'voices'.

Third, we have the 'binary dialectic' in the area of the **lexicon**. As Bruce observes, oppositional terms in any text generally 'function to sustain narrative and ideological tension without attaining any level of resolution' (1992: 66). This binary dialectic is compatible with anarchistic vision. What is involved, however, could cover structures beyond the lexical item: oppositional key **semantic** fields, juxtaposed **discourses** or competing enunciative positions.

Next, Bruce discusses word play as another important characteristic 'which metaphorizes the inherent notions of **dynamism** in the **discourse** of the Commune' (1992: 67). It is here also that what Bruce terms 'ideologems' emerge in abundance. Although these are often phrase-length expressions usually embedded in larger **syntactic** structures, the way they discursively function is pervasive: **discourse** can be made to confront **discourse** in a syntagmatically restricted space governed by ambiguity.

Finally, 'interdiscursive mixing' provides us with another area of textual activity where anarchist **discourse** optimizes its effect. Mixing is an ideological weapon which draws heavily on the way signs signify. Subsumed under this category are most of the features discussed so far: the ambiguity of competing **discourses** in the ideologem, discursive juxtaposition and conflict, the hijacking of other **discourses** and the subversion of the currently unfolding **discourse**.

Task C11.8

➤ Consider examples of tense **shifts**, word play, interdiscursive mixing, etc. in works by Vallès, Kundera or writers in your own language and culture who serve similar ideologies.

➤ Assess translations of such works.

➤ How far do you find that the strategy seems to be one of tidying these anomalies?

Task C11.9

To show that the **discourse** model outlined above is not exclusively applicable to literature, you may want to focus on one of the variables commonly taken to be characteristic of a range of styles – interdiscursive mixing.

To illustrate this from a currently topical issue, let us consider translated extracts from speeches by Bin Laden and Saddam Hussein. Both speakers systematically employ religious **discourse** to harness the political **discourse**. These speeches are available on the internet.

➤ Examine the examples below and assess the effectiveness of the translations provided in dealing with the way the two **discourses** compete and ultimately merge.

➤ Examine this phenomenon in these examples, then in extensive samples of interdiscursive mixing in speeches by political leaders such as Bush and Blair.

Full texts of such speeches are also available on the Internet.

Example C11.4

Allah willing, the day of liberation and victory will come, for us, for the nation, and for Islam above all else. This time, as always when right triumphs, the days to come will be better.

(From a Letter by Saddam Hussein, trans. MEMRI
(The Middle East Media Research Institute), 1 May 2003)

Example C11.5

A small group of young Islamic [fighters] managed . . . to provide people with [concrete] proof of the fact that it is possible to wage war upon and fight against a so-called great power. They managed to protect their religion and effectively to serve the objectives of their nation better than the governments and peoples of the fifty-odd countries of the Muslim world, because they used Jihad as a means to defend their faith.

(From a speech by Bin Laden, trans. MEMRI, 14 March 2003)

CONCLUSION

This unit has supplemented the previous units in showing that the status enjoyed by **text type** in the translation **process** may best be appreciated when text is seen in terms of **register** and as part of the socio-textual practices which make up the **context of culture**. This is the **semiotic** dimension of **context** which caters for the diverse range of **rhetorical purposes**, modes of speaking and writing, and statements of attitudes towards aspects of socio-cultural life. **Texts**, **genres** and **discourses** are **macro-signs** within which we do things with words. Words thus become instruments of **power** and **ideology**. These issues are explored fully in the next unit.

PROJECTS

1. Examine texts of news reports originally produced by international news agencies such as Reuters, but translated by foreign news organizations and slanted to serve a diverse range of political agenda. News of conflict in places such as Palestine or Iraq is a rich source. The news is handled in a particular way by western news agencies, but undergoes an interesting process of transformation when translated.

2. A sample such as Mills & Boon novels is ideal for the study of **genre**, and how this interacts with **discourse** on the one hand (e.g. sexism) and **text** on the other (the fragmentary narrative). This type of popular fiction is being translated into a variety of foreign languages, and may thus be researched for **translation shifts** of a textual, generic and discoursal kind.

3. Further research into the translation of publicity materials is needed. A hypothesis worth testing (particularly in working between English and languages with a great deal of orality) relates to how English tourist brochures tend to 'objectify' experience, while those of other languages 'subjectify' experience.

4. **Vertical intertextuality** is a powerful mechanism for the establishment and maintenance of **genres**, **discourses** and **text types**. Comment on and illustrate how this **norm** evolution has been happening in your own language. For example, Spanish is said to have only fairly recently acquired the **genre** Job Advert (Beeby 1996). Similarly, feminist **discourse** is bound to be a newcomer in many languages and cultures. Finally, Arabic is said to have re-discovered the counter-argument text form only recently.

5. The case of excluding the French anarchist writer Vallès is repeated in so many cultures in different parts of the world. The Arab writer Abdul Rahman Munif (whose writings span half a century) has only recently been re-discovered by western translators. In all cases, the reasons seem to be **discourse**-based. Identify such a case of exclusion and examine the linguistic reasons for this state of neglect. Bruce's study of Vallès is an ideal framework to adopt.

6. Units 7 to 11 have introduced many new factors into the translation equation. Look back at the evaluation scheme/toolkit constructed on pp. 241 and 261, and amend in the light of the new variables that have been encountered.

Unit C12
Agents of power in translation

THE TRANSLATOR AND POWER

In the introductory section of this unit, we spoke about how translators find themselves part of a commercial network or 'cash nexus' where they are often the least powerful members. This is not just the case for the translators of literary fiction, of course, but also for the freelance translator of everyday documentary texts and manuals, as described in the **translational action model** of Holz-Mänttäri (1984). Other scenarios add extra layers of power. Thus, translators for the stage will undoubtedly see their texts modified by the director and the actors in the very process of rehearsal and performance. The translator is often not consulted and sometimes not even mentioned in the theatre programme.

 Task C12.1

➤ Investigate how many translated plays are currently being performed in your own locality or capital city.

➤ What types of plays are they and what languages are they translated from?

➤ Collect examples of reviews or other discussions of some of these plays.

➤ What appreciation is there of the translator's work compared to that of the ST playwright?

THE ETHICS AND RESPONSIBILITIES OF THE TRANSLATOR

Translators' organizations have pushed for due recognition of their work and status, but they are also aware of their responsibilities. The European Council of Literary Translators' Associations CEATL (Le Conseil Européen des Associations de Traducteurs Littéraires) adopted a code of ethics at its annual general meeting of 5–6 October 2001 in Helsinki 'in consideration of the vital role played by literary translators in the circulation of ideas and information between cultures . . .' (Schwartz 2002: 43).

Task C12.2

Below (Example C12.1) are some of the main clauses from the code of ethics.

➤ Read through the clauses of the code.

➤ How valuable do you feel the code to be? How far do you think it is possible for a translator to adhere to these clauses?

➤ Investigate if there is a code of ethics in your own country for literary (or non-literary) translators and how it may differ from this one.

➤ If possible, discuss with practising translators the benefits or problems associated with such codes.

Example C12.1

European Code of Ethics for Literary Translators from CEATL

1. Anyone practising the profession of Translator confirms that they have a very sound knowledge of the language from which s/he translates (the SL), and of the language into which s/he is working (the TL). The TL should be their mother tongue, or a language in which they have mother-tongue competence, as any writer must master the language in which s/he writes.
2. The translator must be aware of his/her limitations and refrain from translating material which is outside his/her scope or the sphere of knowledge required.
3. The translator shall refrain from introducing any tendentious modifications to the thoughts or words of the author, and from cutting or adding to the text without the express permission of the author or rights holder.
4. When it is not possible to translate from the original language and the translator is obliged to translate from a translation, the translator must obtain the permission of the author and cite the name of the translator whose work is being used . . .
[. . .]
7. The translator undertakes not to do anything that may be damaging to the profession by agreeing to conditions that jeopardise the quality of the work or deliberately harm a colleague.

EXCLUDED READER, AUTHOR OR TRANSLATOR?

Task C12.3

A phenomenon all too common in newspapers, magazines, etc. is the publication of advertisements, announcements, invitations to tender, etc., in languages other than the 'official' language of publication or of the country (see Pym 1992).

➤ Examine a sample of such 'alien' material.

■ What prompts the decision to do this in the first place?
■ What are the implications for readers who can lingually work out the content of these adverts, and for others who can do so only through a '**gloss**' of what the advert is about?
■ Can the latter kind of reader participate equally effectively in, say, invitations possibly issued by these adverts?

The choice of what to translate (e.g. announcement placed in a French newspaper, but translated from Arabic into English and not French) and how to translate (**gloss** or full) are all decisions taken strategically and carry serious **pragmatic** implications – essentially to be inclusive or exclusive of a certain kind of reader, etc.

 Task C12.4

➤ Collect a sizeable sample of material translated into your own language and, just by examining the TTs, reflect on areas in which the average target reader would be somehow 'excluded' (e.g. through a term **transliterated**, **calqu**ed, left un**gloss**ed despite being incomprehensible, covering an area of social reality alien to the target reader, etc.). In the light of the catalogue of features which your search would yield, reflect on the implications of this exclusion. Why have the particular choices been made in the first place? Are the reasons linguistic, political, editorial?

➤ To give you an example from a translation of a *Newsweek* article (Example C12.2), the Arabic renderings of those elements in bold were phrased in such a way that the average Arabic-speaking target reader would most probably feel a sense of **loss** (i.e. feel excluded). Read through the text and try to answer these questions:

■ Is this intentional or unintentional, what for and on whose part?
■ Assuming that it is the translator who is likely to be the culprit, what motivates him or her to be exclusive like this?
■ Is the decision politically motivated or is it a simple case of lack of sensitivity to the needs of a particular **audience**?

Example C12.2

Blame it on yourselves

Who cost the United States its seat on the UN Human Rights Commission in the recent secret vote? Theories abound. **Was there a European Judas – or three, or five?** Is the world tired of **being bullied by U.S. strong-arm human-rights tactics?** Or did China help **bring the Bush administration down to earth?**

In the above example, a particular kind of reading experience is excluded and a different one included. This is a serious matter. But in such an exercise of power over the reader, in all likelihood by the translator, authors can also be the targets of exclusion. Invoked here by the exclusive translator would be real or imagined textual-rhetorical as well as social/cultural **norms** operative in the TL.

THE TRANSLATOR'S VOICE REMODELLED

In Section A of this unit we looked at the notion of **voice** and the translator's discursive presence which insinuates itself into the TT even if the aim of the translator has been to produce a 'transparent' translation. In this way, it is suggested, the translator's voice gains strength, even if that voice is not immediately recognized by the reader. Yet, an indication of the relative strength of the translator's voice and that of the original author is the retranslation of **canonical** authors after a period of time, a phenomenon studied, amongst others, by polysystems theorists such as Even-Zohar and Toury (see Section A, Unit 13). Rarely, a translation is so widely accepted it achieves the status of an original, as with the King James Version of the Bible in English, a seventeenth-century translation against which new translations are still measured and often criticized for failing to meet its literary standards (see Task C2.1). Or a self-translation which is carried out by the ST author may also be considered to be 'definitive': Samuel Beckett, for example, wrote in both his native English and in French and translated each work into the other language. However, most frequently new translations of classic works are commissioned as the tastes or **norms** of the target culture change and when the author goes out of copyright. Marcel Proust's *A la Recherche du Temps Perdu* was retranslated in 2002 by a team of seven translators. This new translation will now vie with the 'established' Scott-Moncrieff 1920s translation and the revised Kilmartin–Enright translation of the 1980s. One of the major differences noted by reviewers (e.g. Davis 2002) was the breaking of the reverence customarily afforded to Proust with the inclusion of down-to-earth terms and, especially, the informality of the new translation compared to the 'cascades of Edwardian purple prose' of Scott-Moncrieff.

Similarly, new translations of the Russian classics were produced in the 1990s. The first translations of the Russian greats (Chekhov, Dostoyevsky, Gogol, Tolstoy, Turgenev) were nearly all the work of one woman, Constance Garnett, in the early twentieth century. Her achievements were remarkable (see Simon 1996: 68–71) but she has also been criticized for linguistic inaccuracy and for adopting a uniform prose that flattens the stylistic differences of the authors. The modern translators have the advantage of being able to consult her work but it is illuminating to see the kinds of changes they have made as an illustration of the underlying form of literary expression to which they aspire.

Task C12.5

➤ Look at the following extracts from translations of the first chapter of Dostoyevsky's *Brothers Karamazov* (published in Russian in 1880).

➤ What elements of the translator's **voice** come through in these excerpts?

➤ What does this tell us about the way the translators have read and interpreted the text?

➤ Choose another work which has several translations in your own language. What differences do you find between the translations? Is it possible to identify the 'voice' of the translators?

Example C12.3a Back-translation of ST Russian

They used to relate that the young bride demonstrated in that context incomparably more nobility and loftiness than Feduor Pavlovish, who, as is known now, filched from her at that very moment all her little monies, up to twenty five thousand, as soon as she received them, so that these little thousands decisively as if vanished for her into the water. The little VILLAGE [emphatic] and quite a good town house, which had also gone to her in a dowry, he for a long time and out of all his strength tried to transfer into his own name through the completion of some kind of suitable act [. . .]

Example C12.3b Translation by Constance Garnett (Heinemann 1912, Random House Modern Library 1995)

It was said that the young wife showed incomparably more generosity and dignity than Fyodor Pavlovich, who, as is now known, got hold of her money up to twenty-five thousand roubles as soon as she received it, so that those thousands were lost to her for ever. The little village and the rather fine town house which formed part of her dowry he did his utmost for a long time to transfer to his name, by means of some deed of conveyance [. . .]

Example C12.3c Translation by Richard Pevear and Larissa Volokhonsky (San Francisco: North Point Press 1990)

It was said that in the circumstances the young wife showed far more dignity and high-mindedness than did Fyodor Pavlovich, who, as is now known, filched all her cash from her, as much as twenty-five thousand roubles, the moment she got it, so that from then on as far as she was concerned all those thousands positively vanished, as it were, into thin air. As for the little village and the rather fine town house that came with her dowry, for a long time he tried very hard to have them transferred to his name by means of some appropriate deed [. . .]

Example 12.3d Translation by Ignat Avsey (Oxford University Press 1998)

It was said that during this time the young wife displayed immeasurably more honour and rectitude than Fyodor Pavlovich, who, as we now know, pocketed her twenty-five thousand roubles at one stroke as soon as she received it, so that, as far as she was concerned, her few thousand vanished into thin air. He made numerous and strenuous attempts to have transferred to his own name the title to the hamlet and the rather fine town house that had come with the dowry [. . .]

TRANSLATED OR MANIPULATED?

One way of seeing this whole exercise of power in context is to see translation as a form of 're-writing', even **manipulation**. Power structures such as **ideology** and **poetics** are consistently invoked to account for this phenomenon which, although condoned and even encouraged in certain sectors of Translation Studies (see Unit 13), are nonetheless rarely if ever innocent.

Task C12.6

➤ What kind of status do such forms of writing as children's literature, popular fiction, translations, enjoy in your own language and culture? Why should this be so? If the status is low, has this anything to do with the 'dominant **poetics**', the '**canon**', etc.?

➤ A novel and useful approach to researching these issues might be to study book reviews which denigrate the use of such 'vulgarisms' as journalistic devices, **translationese** and popular fiction gimmicks, etc. Examine how the kind of critical remarks made tend invariably to betray an élitist attitude which looks down upon 'derivative' forms of writing such as translations.

Consideration as to why translations or children's literature, for example, enjoy low status is likely to point to the struggle for domination which is a constant in all systems, not only in translation.

Task C12.7

➤ Identify specific **genres** (some enjoying high status, others being marginalized) and examine the system struggle at work.

➤ What form does this struggle take?

➤ To focus your research on the relevant issues, you might want to consider languages and cultures in which translation happens to be a favoured **genre** (e.g. Hebrew). Also consider the phenomenon of **pseudo-translation** in contexts such as post-Soviet Russia. What light does this kind of translation shed on the power play which is all too clear in translation?

In this respect, consider also how the Anglo-American translation tradition has fared, presenting itself as the custodian of all that is valued in the English language and culture. You might entertain the notion that, here, the English reader is included, not excluded. But at whose expense? Could it be at the expense of a ST author, his or her reader, his or her translator? Does this have any implications for the issue of one person's 'identity' usually promoted at the expense of someone else's?

 Task C12.8

➤ Choose an author whose work you are familiar with and who has been translated widely into English.

➤ What appealed to publishers/translators in this particular author?

➤ Is the author already '**domesticated**' in the way he or she naturally favours target social and literary mores, or consciously **domesticated** and brought into line with these target preferences? If the latter is the case, who or what will be 'excluded' in the process, and what forms of exclusion does this **domestication** take?

 Task C12.9

Domesticating foreign authors invariably involves **re-writing** and image construction. Image is the desire through translation to promote an author who is perhaps less known in his or her own language. Of course this is not a bad thing in itself. But whose interest does this image-building ultimately serve? Is it the image of an entire way of thinking or set of cultural mores which belong to the TL and culture that is the ultimate winner? Does this intimately relate to political and literary power structures operative in a given society or culture?

➤ Do you agree with the claim that texts are consciously or unconsciously made compatible with dominant world views and/or dominant literary structures? If this is the case, what are the advantages and disadvantages?

CONCLUSION

The use of language to exclude some parties and include others is not something new, and translation is no exception. **Literal** translation is one way of achieving this kind of power on the part of the translator. Is this manifested through **transcription**, **word-for-word** translation, or deliberate avoidance of **paratextual** features?

But 'free' translation is not necessarily more innocent. It is likely that the author would probably be the real victim of such translations. And the ideological weapon of exclusion here is the unthinking use of TL **norms** or in-house conventions.

Finally, it is perhaps worth noting that translators themselves are by no means more immune to power displays than are the reader, the original text and the author. But as Fawcett (1995) points out, many published translations would be more incomprehensible were they to come to us totally unrevised.

PROJECTS

1. We have looked in this unit at how literary translators in the English-speaking world have tended to be overlooked. They are invisible to the general public, they are few in number (because relatively few translations are commissioned) and their work is generally undervalued. Investigate literary translation practices in your own country to see how active and visible literary translation is. Find out what societies operate for literary translators. How many translators do they represent? Look at literary journals to see how much is written about literary translators. Contact a literary translator in your country and interview him or her about their work.

2. Aspects of a ST's **poetics** or **ideology** can and often do condemn works to oblivion or lead to their rejection. Find a class of texts condemned in this way, and another 'welcomed' by a powerful translation tradition (e.g. the Anglo-American). Analyse the power dynamics at work.

3. **Literal** translations avoid **paratexts** of any kind, and often fail to point the reader to sources of information likely to be useful for a fuller understanding of a translation. Choose a sample translated in a reader-inclusive way. Identify types of paratextual features serving as guides in the form of footnotes, etc. Then choose a sample of an academically oriented translation that illustrates **paratext-***less* renderings. Edit, making suggestions as to where paratexts may be inserted.

4. The map of Translation Studies presented by Holmes (1988/2000, see Section A, Unit 1) divided translation theory into 'general' and 'partial' (restricted by **genre**, time, etc.). This unit has focused on one **genre** – literary translation. How applicable do you think the concepts studied in this unit are to non-literary

translation? In other words, could concepts such as 'voice' and 'agents of power' also be applied to non-literary translation? Are they part of a 'general' theory of translation?

Investigate this by examining some non-literary texts which are seeking to persuade the reader (e.g. annual business reports of companies, marketing material, travel brochures). These will contain evaluation that may be mediated by the translator. Study a ST–TT pair and see if the translator's voice can be discerned in alterations to the evaluation of the text (additions, **omissions**, pronoun referents, evaluative adjectives, etc.).

Unit C13
Ideology and translation

THE CULTURAL TURN IN TRANSLATION STUDIES

'The translator who takes a text and transposes it into another culture needs to consider carefully the ideological implications of that transposition', warns Bassnett (1980/1991: xv). Even though the **cultural turn** has been a given in Translation Studies for many years, there is, perhaps inevitably, disagreement as to what 'cultural' and 'ideological' really mean (see Fawcett 1998: 106). Though '**cultural turn**' may be used as a catch-all expression for non-linguistic study of translation, Sherry Simon describes how she sees culture and language interacting at the point of translation:

> Translators must constantly make decisions about the cultural meanings which language carries, and evaluate the degree to which the two different worlds they inhabit are 'the same' . . . In fact the process of meaning transfer has less to do with *finding* the cultural inscription of a term than in *reconstructing* its value.
>
> (Simon 1996: 139, italics in original)

Simon illustrates these cultural inequalities with an example from religion: in sixteenth-century South America, the Catholic Church suppressed indigenous people's pictorial representations of the Catholic God and their native language terms for religious concepts. With this analysis, Simon moves beyond the kind of socio-linguistic examination of differences that preoccupy Nida (see Unit 6) to include a consideration of the relative power relations at play.

Task C13.1

➤ What do you understand by the phrase 'reconstructing its value'?

➤ Can you find examples of other translations in which this process seems to have occurred?

➤ How does this differ from the goal of **equivalent effect** employed by Nida when translating the Bible into indigenous languages (see Unit 6)?

LES BELLES INFIDÈLES

As we saw in Section A of this unit, feminist writers react against such a male-oriented view by directing fidelity towards the **translation project** and by adopting a translation strategy that makes the feminine visible. To a lesser extent, most large organizations are now aware of the need to avoid sexist and gender-marked terms when a neutral **equivalent** is possible.

 Task C13.2

➤ Investigate the translation policy of some large organizations (for example, the United Nations) and translation agencies.

➤ How many of these organizations include a policy concerning gender marking on their websites or in their publications?

➤ Look at translations produced by such organizations. What linguistic or writing strategies are followed to avoid gender marking?

➤ Examine a variety of languages to see if the trend is general or if there is greater marking in certain languages or cultures.

Gender-neutral, or 'inclusive', translation has extended to some **canonical** works, such as the New Revised Standard version of the Bible (1989) which has attempted to avoid just such a use of the masculine gender, as in Example C13.1:

Example C13.1

'Let anyone with ears listen!' (Matthew 11.15) instead of
'He that hath ears to hear, let him hear!' (King James Version)
and
'Follow me and I will make you fish for people' (Mark 1.17) instead of
'Follow me and I will make you become fishers of men' (King James Version)

It is perhaps not surprising that such a translation strategy has proved controversial. The quotations and extract in C13.1 and C13.2 are taken from a letter critical of the new translation and published in the journal of the London-based Society of Authors (*The Author* (Spring 2002) vol. CXIII, no. 1: 38–9).

Example C13.2

The English language that we know and love is being inflicted with damage to its most basic resources for the expression of general ideas about the human condition, as well as being rendered much less capable than previously of being used as a medium for close translation from ancient Greek, and equally from Hebrew . . .

Task C13.3

➤ Look at Example C13.1 and the quotation in Example C13.2 above.

➤ Do you think it is valid to criticize the gender-neutral **translation project** in this way?

➤ Compare with translations of sacred texts in your own culture. Is gender or other ideological marking avoided or not? Why do you think this occurs?

Task C13.4

Below is an extract from the English version of the Universal Declaration of Human Rights approved by the United Nations on 10 December 1948. A landmark in human politics, it is said to be the most translated document in the world and is freely available in all its languages at http://www.unhchr.ch/udhr/index.htm. However, some of its gender marking in English is still masculine, with references to *mankind, man,* and 'a spirit of *brotherhood*'.

➤ Look carefully at the gender marking of the English text below.

➤ Compare it to translations in other languages you know. Are these also strongly gender marked?

➤ How important and/or acceptable in your culture do you think it would be to update the language?

Example C13.3

Universal Declaration of Human Rights

From the preamble [. . .]

Whereas disregard and contempt for human rights have resulted in barbarous acts which have outraged the conscience of mankind, and the advent of a world in which human beings shall enjoy freedom of speech and belief and freedom from fear and want has been proclaimed as the highest aspiration of the common people, [. . .]

Whereas it is essential, if man is not to be compelled to have recourse, as a last resort, to rebellion against tyranny and oppression, that human rights should be protected by the rule of law, [. . .]

Article 1

All human beings are born free and equal in dignity and rights. They are endowed with reason and conscience and should act towards one another in a spirit of brotherhood.

★ **Task C13.5**

➤ The Canadian feminists place loyalty to the **translation project** above loyalty to the ST. Investigate the case of such projects in your own culture.

➤ Look at the translation of a potentially problematic and sensitive texts in your own languages (these might be religious or political texts, biographies of controversial figures, literary works that are potentially divisive or offensive – e.g. the Bible, Hitler's *Mein Kampf* or the work of Marx and Engels).

➤ Who are the translators (male/female, well-known writers?) and does the presentation of the book (blurb, preface, etc.) suggest any 'project' or 'agenda'?

➤ Compare the ST and the TT to see what the strategy of the translator has been. Are there important additions or alterations?

➤ Is it possible to discern a trend in these translations? If so, what do you think is motivating this trend?

★ **Task C13.6**

In Section A of this unit, we looked at Harvey's (1998/2000) discussion of camp talk and how the gay had become obscured in translation.

➤ Look at translations of other gay writers or subjects into your own languages. Possible starting points are Thomas Mann's *Tod in Venedig* (*Death in Venice*), Patricia Highsmith's *The Talented Mr Ripley*, André Gide's *L'Immoraliste* (*The Immoralist*) or work by authors such as Oscar Wilde or Sappho.

➤ How far does the gayness of the subject seem to be erased in translation? If possible, look at the film versions of some of the above to see how the process works on-screen and through **subtitles** or **dubbing**.

POSTCOLONIALISM AND TRANSLATION STUDIES

As we saw in Section A, the translation practices associated with intercultural transfer have been the subject of some debate. Spivak has attacked '**translatese**' that erases the differences and identity of third world voices; Venuti calls for a foreignizing translation practice, similar in many respects to Niranjana's radical **re-translation** that brings Kannada lexical and cultural items into the English translation. Nevertheless, Niranjana's attack on the translator and poet A. K. Ramanujan for his westernized translations has in turn been persuasively criticized by Dharwadker (1999).

Example C13.4

Apart from demonstrating that Ramanujan actually used a slightly different ST to the one analysed by Niranjana, Dharwadker sheds important light on the way Ramanujan viewed his two languages, quoting the translator himself:

> English and my disciplines (linguistics, anthropology) give me my 'outer' forms – linguistic, metrical, logical and other such ways of shaping experience; and my first thirty years in India, my frequent visits and fieldtrips, my personal and professional preoccupations with Kannada, Tamil, the classics and folklore gave me my substance, my 'inner' forms, images and symbols. They are continuous with each other, and I no longer can tell what comes from where.
>
> (quoted in Dharwadker 1999: 118)

Task C13.7

➤ Look at A. K. Ramanujan's statement about his background in the text above.

➤ What effects do you think such a background has at the moment of writing and of translating?

➤ Look at the work of other authors who have lived and worked in different languages and cultures (e.g. Chinua Achebe, Samuel Beckett, Carlos Fuentes, Milan Kundera, Ngugi wa Thiong'o, Arundhati Roy, Salman Rushdie, Max Sebald).

➤ How do the authors' varied backgrounds manifest themselves in their work?

➤ How far is this background visible in translations of the authors into languages you know?

TRANSLATION AND CULTURAL IN-BETWEENNESS

Of course, the standpoint projected by cultural theorists is itself conditioned by their own ideological biases, whether feminist, gay, Marxist, **poststructuralist**, anti-colonial, **postcolonial** or any other. Spivak's assertion to western feminists that 'if you are interested in talking about the other, and in making a claim to be the other, it is crucial to learn other languages' (Spivak 1993/2000: 190) may be understandable from her perspective but would be potentially inflammatory if applied in reverse in border cultures where a minority language is struggling for its identity and were the argument to be used as a means of prohibiting translation or minority language use, as has happened with the English-only legislation in over twenty states in the USA.

 Task C13.8

➤ Investigate how language policy, specifically the prohibition of the use of a language, is used for political reasons by the dominant group in a culture.

➤ Carry out a web-based search on English-only legislation in the USA. What are the official statements about the use of languages other than English?

➤ Consider what public opinion says. How visible is the voice of the minority groups?

➤ Compare your findings with the situation in your own city, region or country.

Extensive migration and the growing recognition of border cultures means that more translation, and **interpreting**, is occurring worldwide, and this includes the home countries of the former colonizers. In the United Kingdom, for instance, this can involve **interpreting** for asylum seekers at the point of entry but also a wide range of information leaflets, especially on health, in the minority languages of the local communities.

Task C13.9

In the United Kingdom and Australia, among others, one of the main areas of translation for minority groups is health care. Information leaflets are provided by local authorities on a large range of topics from infant nutrition and illnesses to caring for the elderly. Two sample websites which contain many translations of this type of material are those of Tower Hamlets Primary Care Trust in London (http://www.hiel.nhs.uk/resourceproduction/Factsheets/index. html) and New South Wales Health in Australia (http://www.health.nsw.gov.au/health-public-affairs/mhcs/).

➤ Look at the information available on these two websites.

➤ How many languages are provided? How do these languages vary between the two sites? Are you surprised by the inclusion or omission of any languages?

➤ How do the topics covered differ between the sites?

➤ Examine some of the TTs in languages that you know. What alterations, addition or **omission** of information do you find? How much cultural adaptation to the environment of the minority groups does there seem to be (e.g. regarding care for the elderly or babies or regarding diet)?

➤ Compare with the situation of minority groups in your own geographical location (country, city, neighbourhood). Investigate what translation and **interpreting** services are provided for them or needed by them.

CONCLUSION

The unit on the **cultural turn** in Translation Studies has examined a range of approaches that have dealt with the central theme of power relations between languages and cultures as highlighted by translation. This has pushed the debate on the context of translation beyond the immediate linguistic or textual context and importantly has fostered very fruitful interdisciplinary links within Cultural Studies. It will be pursued in the final unit which moves on to consider these issues in relation to new technologies.

PROJECTS

1. This unit has looked briefly at some of the metaphors of translation such as 'les belles infidèles' and Steiner's four-part **hermeneutic** motion which includes an act of aggression/penetration. Chamberlain (1989/2000: 322) sees the 'metaphorics of translation [as] a symptom of larger issues of western culture: of the power relations as they divide in terms of gender; of a persistent (though not always hegemonic) desire to equate language or language use with morality'. It is interesting to investigate the range of metaphors that have been used and how these have developed.

    Read Chamberlain (1998), Evans (1998) and Robinson (1997, Chapter 3) for a discussion of metaphors of translation. List the main types of metaphor and their uses. How far do you agree with the analysis that accompanies the descriptions?

    Investigate other metaphors, proposed by other theorists and other translators, in your own culture. A good starting-point would be the summaries of different translation traditions in Delisle and Woodsworth (1995) and in Baker (1998), as well as prefaces written by translators and articles written in journals of literary translators societies: in the UK, this could be the publication *In Other Words*, produced by the British Centre for Literary Translation and the Translators Association; in the USA, *Translation Review* publishes many articles by translators.

What different types of metaphor do you find? Is there a difference according to whether the writer is a translator or theorist? How far do you think these metaphors are indicative of larger issues?

2. For Suzanne Jill Levine (1991: 4) 'The good translator performs a balancing act, attempting to push language beyond its limits while at the same time maintaining a common ground of dialogue between writer and reader, speaker and listener.' On the other hand, for Niranjana and Venuti, amongst others, the preferred translation strategy to counter the hegemonic language is a **foreignizing** 'resistant' one, with foreign **borrowings** or stylistic **calques** employed to make the foreign visible.

    Investigate some literary translations to see how common this translation strategy is in your own culture. You could start by looking at the translations of Emily Brontë's *Wuthering Heights*, Arundhati Roy's *The God of Small Things*, Nick Hornby's *Fever Pitch* or J. K. Rowling's Harry Potter books. Each of these has many cultural and linguistic characteristics that are specific to the source culture.

    Examine the frequency of lexical and **syntactic borrowings** and cultural **adaptation**s in these TTs.

    Look also at translations of books from other languages and countries, particularly from lesser-used languages or **postcolonial** environments. Are similar translation strategies exhibited?

3. Consider how applicable the writing on **postcolonial** theory and translation is to your own country.

    List the languages that are spoken or otherwise used in your country. How many of these are official languages?

    Investigate the power relations that exist between these languages. Which languages are dominant (in the legal, administrative and education systems, for example) and which have greatest prestige?

    What is the role of 'international' languages such as English? How widely are these spoken and used?

    How do all these factors affect translation? Into and out of which languages does translation most frequently take place? What is the position of minority or lesser-used languages as far as translation goes?

Unit C14
Translation in the information technology era

GLOBALIZATION AND LOCALIZATION

Task C14.1

> The acronym GILT (Globalization, Internationalization, **Localization**, Translation) is frequently used in commercial circles in English-speaking countries.

➤ Look at how the term is used on English-language commercial websites (you might start by searching for 'GILT' using a search engine).

➤ What mention is there of the practical **process** of translation on these sites?

➤ How important does the role of 'translation' seem to be in these companies? How far does it seem to be replaced by '**localization**'?

➤ Investigate the terms (or similar terms) on company and agency websites in your own country.

The **localization** process models used by commercial companies may contain anything up to fourteen steps (Esselink 2000: 17–8) and translation is just one of those. Example C14.1 shows the four-phase process model used by the milengo **localization** alliance (http://www.milengo.com/cto/) mentioned in Section A, Unit 14.

Example C14.1 Milengo localization alliance project

A project is usually divided in four phases:

1. Preparation tasks:
Creation of a project schedule; Setup of the project team; Analysis of the product and terminology research; Pre-production planning; **Glossary** development

2. **Linguistic and translation tasks:**
Translation of software strings; Translation of online help; Online documentation; Tutorials; Demos; Printed documentation; Incorporating TL screen captures; Disk labels; Packaging; Add-ons

3. **Engineering tasks:**
Extraction of text strings from the software; DTP layouting of the translated documentation because of text swell; Dialog box resizing because of text swell; Adaptation of accelerator keys, tooltips, tab order, menu options, buttons; Adaptation of sorting orders in list boxes; Compiling of the help files using help authoring tools; **Localization** of multimedia files and embedded graphics containing text; Re-creation of sound effects containing text

4. **Testing tasks:**
Consistency checks against localized software; User interface testing; Functional testing; Cosmetic testing

Task C14.2

➤ Read through Example C14.1 and note the references to translation.

➤ Consider the phases and tasks where translation is not present. Have any of these been touched upon in this book when discussing different aspects of translation?

➤ Look at the remaining phases that are not directly translation-related. Is it possible to assign them to other disciplines (e.g. some of the phase 3 tasks are specifically related to information technology).

COMPUTER-ASSISTED TRANSLATION

In the introduction we briefly discussed some of the IT tools, such as **translation memory** and **term banks**, that are available to translators.

Task C14.3   Investigating translation memory tools

This task can be used to investigate TRADOS's *Translator's workbench* (www. trados.com), ATRIL's *Déjà Vu* (www.atril.com) or any other memory tool.

➤ Look at the description of the products on the product websites.

➤ Make a note of the different software available and the likely uses and the advantages claimed.

➤ Contact professional translators who use this or similar products. Ask them to state the advantages and disadvantages of the program as applied to the languages in which they work.

➤ How far does it facilitate the work of the individual translator or the translator working as part of a team?

➤ What additional features might be usefully incorporated?

One of the most widely known terminology databases in Europe is EURODICAUTOM, run by the European Commission (http://europa.eu.int/eurodicautom/Controller), though this is due to be replaced in the near future by the new Inter-Agency Terminology Exchange database (IATE). As is crucial in terminology work, search terms carry a definition in each language and the different established **correspondent**s are presented. See the example below for *cold calling by telephone*, taken from the EURODICAUTOM database:

Example C14.2

Cold calling by telephone

definition: practice of approaching potential clients by telephone without their prior written consent to offer them financial services

English cold calling

Danish telefonsalg

French démarchage par téléphone

German telefonische Kundenwerbung

Greek τηλεφωνική προσέγγιση πελατών

Italian marketing telefonico

Portuguese venda por telefone

Spanish venta a domicilio por teléfono

Task C14.4

This definition of *cold calling* and its translations date from 1995.

➤ Investigate how far the sense given here is still used in current day English. You might consult dictionaries, on-line **glossaries**, **corpora**, search engines, or contact marketing companies.

➤ Check some of the other languages to see if the **correspondent**s are still used or if they have been supplanted.

➤ Find out what terms are used in any other languages you know.

In Unit 5, Task C5.3, we briefly mentioned the use of *congestion charging* in London, a scheme that was introduced in 2003 imposing a charge on drivers travelling into the centre of the city. The term appears in EURODICAUTOM but with the definition of 'scheme for road pricing according to the amount of time drivers spend behind the wheel'. The French term is as follows:

Example C14.3

French taxation des comportements sources de congestion [*taxation for behaviours that are sources of congestion*]

 ### Task C14.5

➤ Consult EURODICAUTOM or other **glossaries** to see the corresponding terms in other EU languages. Is there any discrepancy?

➤ Check, using other databases, newspaper archives or internet search engines, whether both the new and old sense of *congestion charging* are still in use in English.

➤ Use other databases, glossaries or news articles to see how the new sense is translated into other languages.

➤ Is it possible to say that there is a standard term for the new sense of *congestion charging* in the languages you are examining?

MACHINE TRANSLATION

The introduction to this unit discussed some of the obstacles to fully automatic **Machine Translation (MT)**. As we then saw, Bar-Hillel even claimed **MT** was impossible because translation requires 'real-world knowledge'. Below is a short extract from UNESCO's world heritage presskit (http://whc.unesco.org/nwhc/pages/doc/main.htm) in French together with an English MT version and the published English version.

Example C14.4a UNESCO heritage presskit

Le patrimoine est l'héritage du passé, dont nous profitons aujourd'hui et que nous transmettrons aux générations à venir. Nos patrimoines culturel et naturel sont deux sources irremplaçables de vie et d'inspiration. Ce sont nos pierres de touche, nos points de référence, les éléments de notre identité. Ce qui rend exceptionnel le concept de patrimoine mondial est son application universelle. Les sites du patrimoine mondial appartiennent à tous les peuples du monde, sans tenir compte du territoire sur lequel ils sont situés.

Example C14.4b English MT version using online SYTRAN (http://www.systranbox.com/systran/box)

The inheritance is the legacy of the past, from which we profit today and who we will transmit to the generations to come. Our inheritances cultural and natural are two irreplaceable sources of life and inspiration. They are our stones of key, our points of reference, the elements of our identity. What makes exceptional the concept of world inheritance is its universal application. The sites of the world inheritance belong to all the people of the world, without holding account of the territory on which they are located.

Example C14.4c Published English version

Heritage is our legacy from the past, what we live with today, and what we pass on to future generations. Our cultural and natural heritage are both irreplaceable sources of life and inspiration. They are our touchstones, our points of reference, our identity. What makes the concept of World Heritage exceptional is its universal application. World Heritage sites belong to all the peoples of the world, irrespective of the territory on which they are located.

Task C14.6

➤ Compare the three texts above.

➤ Identify the particular features of the MT text.

➤ In what ways does the MT text differ from the actual English version?

➤ Investigate other texts from this and other **genre**s, using SYSTRAN and other automatic online translation software, using your own languages and others of which you have no knowledge.

➤ Evaluate the strengths and weaknesses of such software. How much post-editing is needed?

➤ Arnold *et al.* (Text B14.1) say that 'the aim of MT is only to automate the first draft translation **process**' but that the kinds of errors made by human translators at that stage are 'rather different' from those produced by machines. In what ways do your findings here support or undermine these claims?

THE CORPUS-BASED APPROACH

In Unit 5 we explored some of the uses of **corpora** in dictionary design, specifically in identifying senses of terms and typical **syntactic** patterns. The two tasks in this sub-section look at how **concordances** may be used to investigate translation.

 Task C14.7

➤ Have a look at some of the **corpora** mentioned in Section A of this unit (e.g. the BNC or the BoE). Many are either freely available or offer short trial access.

➤ Investigate a range of search terms and parts of speech and see the patterns in which they are used (it may be useful to start by examining **near-synonym**s such as *entail* and *involve*, *refute* and *reject*, *devoted* and *attached*, *need* and *necessity*).

➤ Search in a representative **corpus** of English (such as the BNC, BoE) and draw up a profile of the competing terms (relative frequencies, common **collocates** and **syntactic** patterns, **connotations**, etc.).

➤ Look at **concordances** of potential **equivalent**s of the English search terms in a **corpus** of your other languages. Make a profile of these **equivalents**. How useful is this process in matching the profiles in the two languages? How easy is it to find the **equivalent**s?

 Task C14.8

Although many professional translators may not be directly aware of **corpus linguistics**, most do use a form of **corpus** in their translation memory software or in web-based searches for **parallel text**s and translation **equivalents**.

➤ Contact and 'shadow' a professional translator for a day as he or she works on a text.

➤ Keep a note of the specific searches the translator makes on internet search engines.

➤ Ask the translator to indicate the purpose of each search.

➤ Which searches are most (and least) successful (e.g. leading to the identification of a suitable **parallel text** or translation **equivalent**)?

➤ Compare your results with results obtained by other students or by studying other translators. What seems to be the best method of extracting useful translation information from the web?

CONCLUSION

Information technology has transformed not only the working practice of the professional translator but also the way in which translation is studied. Although the goal of fully automatic translation may still lie in the future (and some would say will always remain a pipe-dream), technology is already allowing research into areas that previously relied on anecdotal evidence. This is particularly the case with the rapid rise in **corpus linguistics** which means that large amounts of naturally occurring language can be examined rapidly and accurately. The possibilities are enormous for **contrastive analysis** of languages, **Descriptive Translation Studies** (ST–TT comparisons) and the study of **universal** features of translation (see Project 1 below) as well as the generation of new texts (Bateman, Matthiessen and Zeng 1999).

PROJECTS

1. Develop Task C14.7 by examining features of translated language. Look up the same or similar terms using a **parallel corpus** (the Canadian Hansard, for instance, <www.tsrali.com/index.cgi?UTLanguage=en>) or a **corpus** of translated language (such as the TEC **corpus**, <www.monabaker.com/tsresources/).

   Investigate other **corpora** of translated language. These are being developed all the time, so it is always worth searching for *corpora/corpus + translation* in an internet search engine and following the many web links.

   Baker (1995) suggests that **corpora** are valuable in identifying '**universals** of translation' (see Section A, Unit 1). To what extent is this suggested by the findings of your own research here?

2. Use EURODICAUTOM, IATE or other databases to search for other terms in the transport field and their corresponding terms in other languages (e.g. *dual carriageway, toll charge, articulated vehicle, breathalyser*).

   Investigate how the presentation in the different databases treats various terms and identify what kind of terms (e.g. concepts, parts of speech) seem to pose most problems for the format of the database.

What kind of terms are not found in the databases? Why do you think this is?
Try investigating other fields and databases that are local to you. Do you find
similar results? How are the local databases put together and are they more
useful than more general ones?

Developing words and cultures
– some concluding remarks

In Unit 1 we started off by asking the questions 'what is translation?' and 'what is Translation Studies?'. In the course of the book we have explored a large number of concepts and theories of translation that have illustrated the breadth and interdisciplinarity of the subject. The earlier units investigated more linguistic theories such as the unit of translation, translation shift and the measurement of meaning. One of the most interesting points there were the rejection of a simplistic 'literal vs free' polarity and the acceptance of clines and 'fuzziness' of meaning. Furthermore, the actual form of investigation illustrated the huge variety of often innovative theoretical approaches that can be employed: concepts from semantics and Chomskyan and Hallidayan linguistics, but allied to the use of electronic corpora and think-aloud protocols, amongst others.

Units 6 to 11 interrogated the idea of text and context in many different guises coinciding with the evolution of Translation Studies through the second half of the twentieth century and into the new millennium. The important development in the 1960s was the acknowledgement that a text is not static but plays a communicative role and functions within a specific socio-cultural context. Nida's proposal of securing 'equivalent effect' in translation was vital in switching the focus towards the dynamic communication relationship between text producer and receptor. Later theorists such as Koller, Reiss and Vermeer, House and Gutt continued to incorporate concepts from socio-linguistics, but also pragmatics, cognitive linguistics and the growing interest in text types and function. The shifts that were analysed in Unit 4 on the word or phrase level were then seen to occur on the higher levels of text, genre and discourse (Unit 11).

The levels dealt with in Units C12 and C13 are in one sense of a different order, since they are based on a Cultural Studies approach, exploring translation as power, manipulation, re-writing, and then from a gender, postcolonial or poststructuralist perspective. Translation is recognized as possessing an ideological power, not only reflecting the dominant forces at work in the society but also performing an active role in the formation and interpretation of ideology. In Niranjana's case, translation is considered to be an active tool in the colonial process and in the translation of the image and identity of the colonized people. Yet it is the 'in-betweenness' of the 'third space', as described by Bhabha, which perhaps best points to the extraordinary cross-cultural phenomenon of translation in today's world. Translation occurs between languages, between texts, between writers and readers and between cultures. The complexity of these varied relationships accounts for the fuzziness of much of translation and the difficulty of reliably pinning down any of the elusive 'universals' of translation. Thus, just as meaning is often a cline, so texts are hybrids, composed of many different elements, and cross-cultural communication can end up being as much about the hybrid 'third space' in-between as about the discrete cultures that commission translation.

Despite the apparent dominance of English globally, the need for translation continues to grow and the actual and virtual movement of peoples means that even previously monolingual societies are increasingly adapting to the presence of other languages and cultures in their travels through the internet or within their local community. Translation in the information technology age was explored in the final unit. There are many exciting possibilities that will surely develop further in future years. On the one hand, the ready availability of online translation software has made translation more visible for the general net-surfer and represents an astounding evolution in the use of machine translation. On the other hand, increased computer power and the popularity of electronic texts is enabling corpus-based analysis that will doubtless shed much new light on what goes on linguistically in the translation process. The challenge for Translation Studies now is to encompass this range of approaches and to encourage collaboration between researchers in complementary areas. In this respect, the authors firmly hope that this volume will give translators and new researchers not only the tools to evaluate translation but also the enthusiasm to research new ideas and data related to a complex linguistic, socio-cultural and ideological practice.

Further reading

UNIT A1

Williams and Chesterman (2002, chapter 1); Munday (2001, chapter 1).

UNIT A2

Bassnett (2002, Chapter 1); Berman (1985/2000); Fawcett (1997, Chapter 2); Kelly (1979, Chapters 7, 8 and 9).

UNIT A3

Barkhudarov (1993), Hervey and Higgins (1992, Chapter 4), Kelly (1979, Chapter 4), Newmark (1988, chapter 6), Snell-Hornby (1990)

UNIT A4

Ivir (1981) and Snell-Hornby (1990) for more on correspondence and equivalence, van Leuven Zwart (1989, 1990), Toury (1995: 84–9) and Koster (2000) for translation shifts.

UNIT A5

The analysis of meaning in key works on **semantics** in English (e.g. Lyons 1977, Leech 1981) differs from Nida. Leech, for example, considers seven types of meaning whereas Nida only looks at two. See also Carter (1998) for a valuable analysis of vocabulary, especially Chapter 3 (words and patterns) and Chapter 9 (**style**, lexis and the dictionary). Stubbs (2001) is an insightful corpus-based study of lexical semantics.

UNIT A6

Fawcett (1997). See Chapter 5 in particular.

Hu (1994). This is one of a series of articles in which the author discusses the implausibility of **dynamic** response.

UNIT A7

Chesterman (1989). The chapter by Koller is particularly relevant.

Delisle (1982, translated 1988) is an influential work that advocates a discourse analytic approach for the teaching of translation.

Pym (1995). A balanced critique of approaches supporting or rejecting **equivalence**.

UNIT A8

Fawcett (1997). Chapter 12 on **relevance** provides a useful summary of the complex issues surrounding this notion.

Malmkjær (1992). A critical assessment of the translation model which has evolved out of Gutt's original work on **relevance**.

UNIT A9

Fawcett (1997). Chapters 7, 8 and 9 place **text type** within a **register**, text structure and text **function** framework.

Emery (1991). This article provides a critique of current text classifications and proposes a pragmatically oriented alternative.

UNIT A10

Gregory and Carroll (1978). An important introductory book which covers the various aspects of **register**: **field**, **tenor** and **mode**.

Eggins (1994). A practical guide to doing **register** analysis.

Crystal and Davy (1969). The introductory chapters provide one of the earliest critique of situational **registers**.

UNIT A11

Bassnett and Lefevere (1990). In particular, see Introduction and Kuhiwczak's chapter on Milan Kundera.

Fairclough (1989). Chapters 1–4.

Hatim and Mason (1997). Particularly the chapter on ideology.

UNIT A12

Bassnett and Lefevere (1990). See in particular the Introduction and Chapters 3 and 4. Classe (2000) and France (2000) are excellent sources of information on literary translation into English. Warren (1989) contains interesting essays by well-known translators, while papers in Boase-Beier and Holman (1999) cover a wide range of topics (see especially articles by Coates and Sturge). Information on literary translation in the UK is also available on the British Arts Council website at http://www.literarytranslation.com

UNIT A13

For feminist writing, see Simon (1996) and van Flotow (1997, Chapter 2). For **postcolonialism**, Robinson (1997) gives an overview of writing in this field. See also Talib (2002) for an interesting discussion of language and **postcolonialism**.

UNIT A14

Austermühl (2001) for electronic tools; Esselink (2000) for **localization**; Hutchins (1986) for a detailed online discussion of the history of MT, now with updated references; Somers (2003) for a wide range of papers covering computers and translation; Olohan (2004) for **corpus-based** Translation Studies; Stubbs (2001) and McEnery, Tono and Xiao (forthcoming) for **corpus-based** language studies.

Glossary

Items in non-bold upper case cross-reference to definitions located at the alphabetically ordered entry for the item elsewhere in this Glossary.

ACCEPTABILITY
See INTENTIONALITY.

ADAPTATION
A TT where many textual modifications have been made, including modifications for a different audience (cf. VERSION). In Vinay and Darbelnet's list of TRANSLATION PROCEDURES, adaptation involves modifying a cultural reference for the TT readership.

ADJUSTMENT
Techniques for producing correct EQUIVALENTs and achieving DYNAMIC EQUIVALENCE in translation.

AGENT DELETION
The omission in a passive sentence of the noun or noun phrase which follows *by*, e.g. *The reasons outlined* (by the writer). Such uses of the grammar can be ideologically motivated.

ALIGNMENT
The juxtaposition of a ST sentence with its TT EQUIVALENT. A tool of CORPUS LINGUISTICS that allows rapid comparison of ST–TT elements.

ANALYSIS
The first of three stages constituting the translation PROCESS according to Eugene Nida. In this process, we analyse the source message into its simplest and structurally clearest forms, TRANSFER it at this level, and then restructure it to a level stylistically acceptable to the target reader.

ARGUMENTATION, ARGUMENTATIVE
A TEXT TYPE in which concepts and/or beliefs are evaluated. The two basic forms are counter-argumentation, where a thesis is presented and then challenged, and through-argumentation, where a thesis is presented and defended.

ASSOCIATIVE MEANING
See CONNOTATION.

AUDIENCE
The readership of the text.

AUDIOVISUAL TRANSLATION
Translation of any audiovisual medium, such as film, DVD, etc. This typically involves DUBBING or SUB-TITLING.

BACK-TRANSFORMATION	A kind of paraphrase in which surface structures are replaced by other, more basic structures (e.g. event nouns into verbal expressions: *wrath > X is angry*).
BACK-TRANSLATION	A WORD-FOR-WORD translation of a TT back into the SL, often retaining the structure of the TT. This can be used to explain the translation PROCESS for an audience that does not understand the TL.
BORROWING	The use of a SL item in the TL. Typically, these are cultural items such as French *baguette* or Russian *rouble* which do not exist in the SL or which are used to give a foreign character to the TT.
BRIEF	Specifications relating to the purpose for which a translation is needed provided by those who commission translations.
CALQUE	The process whereby the individual elements of an SL item are translated literally to produce a TL EQUIVALENT (e.g. *Ministère des Finances – Ministry of Finance*).
CANON, CANONICAL, CANONIZED TEXT	Texts or text considered part of the heritage of a particular community and thus mandatory reading in school and university curricula.
CATAPHORA	The use of a linguistic item to refer forward to subsequent elements in the text (e.g. In *his* speech, the King said . . .).
CATEGORY SHIFT	A translation at a different RANK in the TT (e.g. ST word by TT group).
CHOMSKYAN LINGUISTICS	See TRANSFORMATIONAL-GENERATIVE GRAMMAR.
CLEFT SENTENCE	A sentence structured in two parts. The first part, comprised of *it + be*, is intended to emphasize a particular piece of information, e.g. *It was Mrs Smith who gave Mary the book.*
COGNITIVE ENVIRONMENT	In RELEVANCE theory, this is the interaction between the contextual assumptions regarding the meaning of an utterance and the interpretation yielded, or, to put it differently, between 'purpose' and 'use'.
COGNITIVE LINGUISTICS	A branch of linguistics which studies the role of such mental processes as inference (see INFERENCING) in the reasoning necessary for processing texts.
COHERENCE	A standard which all well-formed texts must meet and which stipulates that the grammatical and/or lexical relationships 'hang together' and make overall sense as TEXT.

COHESION	The requirement that a sequence of sentences display grammatical and/or lexical relationships which ensure the surface continuity of TEXT structure.
COLLOCATION, COLLOCATE, COLLOCATIVE MEANING	The co-occurrence of two lexical items, known as collocates (e.g. *greenhouse gas* is a strong collocation).
COMMISSION	See BRIEF.
COMMUNICATIVE CLUE	In RELEVANCE theory, a stimulus to interpretation supplied by the formal properties of the ST.
COMMUNICATIVE EVENT	See GENRE.
COMPENSATE, COMPENSATION	An ADJUSTMENT technique resorted to with the aim of making up for the LOSS of important ST features in translation with a gain at the same or other points in the TT. The fourth part of Steiner's (1975/1998) HERMENEUTIC MOVEMENT which restores life to the TT.
COMPONENTIAL ANALYSIS	Breaking down lexical items into their basic meaning components.
COMPREHENSIBILITY	The accessibility and transparency of a TT in conveying ST meaning efficiently, effectively and appropriately.
COMPUTER-ASSISTED TRANSLATION (CAT)	Translation in which computerized tools such as TERM BANKs and TRANSLATION MEMORY TOOLs are used to assist the human translator.
CONCORDANCE	In CORPUS LINGUISTICS, this is an on-screen or printed-out list of occurrences of the search term with surrounding CO-TEXT.
CONNOTATION, CONNOTATIVE MEANING	Additional meanings which a lexical item acquires beyond its primary, REFERENTIAL MEANING, e.g. *notorious* means 'famous' but with negative connotations.
CONTENT	The level of lexical and SEMANTIC meaning of an expression.
CONTEXT	The multi-layered extra-textual environment which exerts a determining influence on the language used. The subject matter of a given text, for example, is part of a context of situation. The ideology of the speaker, on the other hand, would form part of the context of culture. Finally, context of utilization caters for such factors as whether the translation is in written form, orally done (INTERPRETING) or as SUBTITLING/DUBBING, etc.
CONTEXT OF CULTURE	See CONTEXT.
CONTEXT OF SITUATION	See CONTEXT.

CONTEXT OF UTILIZATION	See CONTEXT.
CONTEXTUAL MOTIVATEDNESS, CONTEXTUALLY MOTIVATED	The intention to produce certain rhetorical effects, using language in a conscious, deliberate manner for that purpose.
CONTRASTIVE ANALYSIS	Analysis of two (or more) different languages with the aim of identifying places where meaning and use coincide or differ.
CORPUS (plural CORPORA)	An electronically readable database of naturally produced texts (i.e. texts which have been written for genuine communicative purposes and not invented for analysis) which can be analysed for word frequency, COLLOCATION, etc. by computer.
CORPUS-BASED TRANSLATION STUDIES	An increasingly important branch of Translation Studies which analyses translation using corpora (see CORPUS) and tools derived from CORPUS LINGUISTICS.
CORPUS LINGUISTICS	A branch of linguistics that bases analysis on corpora (see CORPUS) using tools such as CONCORDANCEs and statistical analyses of phenomena such as COLLOCATION.
CORRESPONDENCE, CORRESPONDENT	See FORMAL CORRESPONDENCE.
CO-TEXT	The other lexical items that occur before and after a word.
COVERT TRANSLATION	Term coined by Juliane House (1977). A translation which conceals anything that betrays the foreignness of a ST. Unlike OVERT TRANSLATION, a covert translation approximates as far as possible to original writing.
CRITICAL DISCOURSE ANALYSIS, CRITICAL LINGUISTICS	The analysis of language use with the aim of discovering concealed ideological bias, and underlying power structures.
CROSS-CULTURAL PRAGMATICS	The study of culturally different ways of using language, and of different expectations among different members of linguistic communities regarding how meaning is negotiated.
CULTURAL TURN	A metaphor that has been adopted by Cultural Studies oriented translation theorists to refer to the analysis of translation in its cultural, political and ideological context.
DECONSTRUCTION	A philosophical theory, centred in the work of Jacques Derrida and allied to POSTSTRUCTURALISM and POSTMODERNISM, which interrogates language,

discovers the multiple interpretations of texts and challenges the stability of concepts and terms.

DEEP STRUCTURE | See TRANSFORMATIONAL-GENERATIVE GRAMMAR.

DEFAMILIARIZATION, DEHABITUALIZATION | The effect produced by opting for MARKED (i.e. expectation-defying) structures (e.g. repetition, parallelism).

DENOTATION | Covers the decontextualized, dictionary meaning of a given lexical item.

DESCRIPTIVE TRANSLATION | In RELEVANCE theory, this is the use of language normally as true or false of a given state of affairs. In translation, this mode amounts to a 'free' translation. Compare COVERT TRANSLATION.

DESCRIPTIVE TRANSLATION STUDIES (DTS) | A branch of Translation Studies, developed in most detail by Toury (1995), that involves the EMPIRICAL, non-PRESCRIPTIVE analysis of STs and TTs with the aim of identifying general characteristics and LAWS OF TRANSLATION.

DIFFERENTIATED | See PATRONAGE.

DIRECT TRANSLATION | In Vinay and Darbelnet's TAXONOMY, it is a translation method that encompasses CALQUE, BORROWING and LITERAL TRANSLATION. In RELEVANCE theory, direct translation is a kind of translation performed in situations where we need to translate not only what is said, but also how it is said. In MACHINE TRANSLATION, it is the replacement of a ST item by a TL item as a WORD-FOR-WORD translation.

DISAMBIGUATION | Differentiation of different senses of a word.

DISCOURSE | Modes of speaking and writing which involve participants in adopting a particular attitude towards areas of socio-cultural activity (e.g. racist discourse, bureaucratese, etc.). See also SHIFT.

DOCUMENTARY TRANSLATION | A term used by Nord (e.g. 1997) to describe a translation method which does not conceal the fact that it is a translation.

DOMESTICATING TRANSLATION, DOMESTICATION | A translation strategy, discussed by Venuti (1995), in which a transparent, fluent style is adopted in order to minimize the foreignness of an ST. See FOREIGNIZING TRANSLATION.

DUBBING | A technique used in the translation of foreign films. It involves substitution of the ST actors' voices in translation with a new TT voice, often attempting to synchronize the original lip movements with the TT sounds.

DYNAMIC EQUIVALENCE	A translation which preserves the effect the ST had on its readers and which tries to elicit a similar response from the target reader.
DYNAMISM	See MARKED, MARKEDNESS.
EMOTIVE MEANING	See CONNOTATION.
EMPIRICAL	Based on experiment and observation rather than theory.
EQUIVALENCE	A central term in linguistics-based Translation Studies, relating to the relationship of similarity between ST and TT segments. Also one of Vinay and Darbelnet's TRANSLATION PROCEDURES, referring to the translation of fixed expressions such as idioms with an EQUIVALENT that is very different in FORM.
EQUIVALENT	A TT segment or even full text which functions as an equivalent of the ST segment.
EQUIVALENT EFFECT	A translation aim in Nida's writing, where the TT should create 'substantially the same' effect on the TT audience as the ST had on its readership.
EVALUATIVENESS	The comparison or assessment of concepts, belief systems, etc. See MARKED, MARKEDNESS.
EXPLICATE, EXPLICITATION	Explanation in the TT that renders the sense or intention clearer than in the ST.
EXPOSITION, EXPOSITORY	A TEXT TYPE in which concepts, objects or events are presented in a non-evaluative manner (e.g. explanations).
EXPRESSIVE TEXTS	Texts which include an aesthetic component in which the writer exploits the expressive and ASSOCIATIVE MEANING possibilities of language in order to communicate thoughts and feelings in a creative way.
EXTRA-LINGUISTIC	Not part of or deducible from the ST.
FAITHFUL(NESS), FIDELITY	A general term, now less used in translation theory, which describes the close mirroring of ST sense by the TT.
FIELD (OF DISCOURSE)	Subject matter, including aspects of perceiving the world influenced by social institutions and social processes at work.
FOREIGNIZING TRANSLATION, FOREIGNIZATION	A translation which seeks to preserve 'alien' features of a ST in order to convey the 'foreignness' of the original. Discussed in Venuti (1995). See also DOMESTICATING TRANSLATION, DOMESTICATION.
FORM	The shape or appearance of a linguistic unit, in contrast to its content.

FORMAL CORRESPONDENCE | The general, systemic relationship between an SL and TL element, out of context (e.g. there may be formal correspondence between *este* in Spanish and *this* in English; however, in real examples in the practice of translation, *este* may be translated in another way). See TEXTUAL EQUIVALENCE.

FORMAL CORRESPONDENT | A TL item which generally fulfils the same function in the TL as the SL item does in the SL, or vice versa (e.g. *this* may be a formal correspondent of *este*).

FORMAL EQUIVALENCE | A translation that adheres closely to the linguistic FORM of a ST.

FRAME | See SCRIPT.

FREE TRANSLATION | A translation that modifies surface expression and keeps intact only deeper levels of meaning.

FUNCTION | The use of language for a particular purpose.

FUNCTIONAL | Having a role to perform in the development of a TEXT. Functional signals are in contrast with other purely formal devices whose role is, as the term suggests, merely 'organizational' rather than rhetorically motivated.

FUNCTIONALITY | The communicative or contextual motivation of a ST element.

FUNCTIONAL SENTENCE PERSPECTIVE | A form of sentence analysis devised by the Prague School of linguists. The major element contributing to sentence structure is 'communicative dynamism', which is more important even than word order. See INFORMATION STRUCTURE.

FUNCTIONAL TENOR | An aspect of tenor (see TENOR OF DISCOURSE) or level of formality used to describe what language is used for (e.g. persuading), and is thus very much akin to the notion of TEXT.

FUZZY MATCH | A close but non-perfect translation match located in an electronic translation memory.

GAIN | See COMPENSATE, COMPENSATION.

GENRE | Conventional forms of TEXT associated with particular types of social occasion or communicative events (e.g. the news report, the editorial, the cooking recipe). See SHIFT.

GIST TRANSLATION, GISTING | A translation which reproduces the main points of a ST, and thus serves as a synopsis.

GIVEN INFORMATION | See INFORMATION STRUCTURE.

GLOSS TRANSLATION | The kind of translation which aims to re-produce as literally and meaningfully as possible the FORM and

CONTENT of the original (as a study aid, for example). Alternatively, at the level of the individual word or phrase, a gloss is an addition of information, necessary for the understanding of the ST term, but which does not interrupt the flow of the TT (e.g. in translation, the term *10 Downing Street* might be rendered with a gloss as *10 Downing Street, the Office of the British Prime Minister*).

GLOSSARY

In professional translation, this refers to online or tailor-made lists of SL technical terms with definitions and their TL CORRESPONDENTs (see CORRESPONDENCE).

GOTHIC

A fictional genre which makes salient the characters' morbid feelings and general passivity.

HALLIDAYAN LINGUISTICS

A systemic-functional theory of language advanced by M. A. K. Halliday in the latter part of the twentieth century. Halliday focuses on language in use, as a communicative act, and describes three strands of functional meaning co-occurring in a text IDEATIONAL MEANING, INTERPERSONAL MEANING and TEXTUAL (see TEXT).

HERMENEUTIC MOVEMENT

The four-phase description of the interpretation and transfer of meaning from ST to TT (Steiner 1975/1998).

HEURISTICS

A set of analytic principles that rely on variable and not categorical rules in dealing with texts.

HOMONYM

A word that has the same sound and spelling as another word, but a different meaning (e.g. *bank* meaning a side of a river and *bank* meaning a financial institution). See POLYSEMY.

HORIZONTAL

See INTERTEXTUALITY.

HYBRIDITY

The dynamic cultural and linguistic environment of migrant or border communities, where interaction and overlap highlights cultural difference and interrogates identity. Also known as 'in-betweenness'.

HYBRIDIZATION

TEXT TYPEs are rarely if ever pure. More than one text-type focus is normally discernible in a given TEXT. This is known as hybridization.

HYPONYM, HYPONYMY

The inclusion of one meaning within another. For example, the sense of *walk* is included within the sense of *move*; hence, *walk* is a hyponym of the superordinate *move*.

IDEATIONAL MEANING

Language used to convey information, ideas or experience. It is a means of giving structure to our experience of inner feelings and emotions as well as of the external world around us.

IDEOLOGY	A body of ideas that reflects the beliefs and interests of an individual, a group of individuals, a societal institution, etc., and that ultimately finds expression in language. See DISCOURSE.
ILLOCUTIONARY FORCE	See SPEECH ACT.
IMPLICATURE	The implied meaning conveyed by deliberate non-compliance with rhetorical or linguistic conventions.
INANIMATE AGENCY	Use of a non-human agent or 'doer' of a process or action, e.g. '*Tears* coursed down her cheeks'. See TRANSITIVITY and AGENT DELETION.
IN-BETWEENNESS	See HYBRIDITY.
INDIRECT TRANSLATION	A translation which responds to the urge to communicate as clearly as possible. See DIRECT TRANSLATION.
INFERENCING, INFERENTIAL	A cognitive-linguistic mechanism which utilizes contextual assumptions in the process of reasoning surrounding language use. See COGNITIVE LINGUISTICS
INFORMATION STRUCTURE	The way that information is structured in a sentence. This has been addressed in slightly different ways in FUNCTIONAL SENTENCE PERSPECTIVE and HALLIDAYAN LINGUISTICS. The sentence, or clause, is divided into a theme (which, in English, commonly starts a clause and deals with 'given' or known information) and a rheme (which normally ends a clause and supplies 'new' information).
INFORMATIVE TEXT	See EXPOSITION.
INFORMATIVITY	The degree of unexpectedness which an item or an utterance displays in some CONTEXT.
INSTRUCTIONAL	A TEXT TYPE in which the focus is on the formation of future behaviour, either 'with option' as in advertising or 'without option' as in Legal Instruction (e.g. Treaties, Resolutions, Contracts, etc.).
INTENTIONALITY	A feature of human language which determines the appropriateness of a linguistic form to the achievement of a pragmatic purpose (see PRAGMATICS).
INTERFERENCE	Excessive influence of ST lexis or syntax on the TT (see SYNTACTIC STRUCTURES, SYNTAX). One of Toury's two LAWS OF TRANSLATION.
INTERLINEAR TRANSLATION	A type of extremely LITERAL, WORD-FOR-WORD TRANSLATION in which TL words are arranged item by item below the ST words to which they correspond.

INTERLINGUAL TRANSLATION	Translation between two different languages.
INTERPELLATION	Used in POSTCOLONIALISM to refer to the process of stereotyping and subjection of the DISCOURSE and image of the colonized.
INTERPERSONAL MEANING	Language used to establish a relationship between text producer and text receiver.
INTERPRETING	Spoken translation, sometimes also called 'interpretation'.
INTERPRETIVE	In RELEVANCE theory, this is the use of language in an observer-like manner. In translation, this mode seeks to resemble the original in all relevant aspects.
INTERTEXTUALITY	A precondition for the intelligibility of texts, involving the dependence of one text upon another. Horizontal intertexuality involves direct reference to another text. Vertical intertexuality is more an allusion and can refer to a mode of writing, a STYLE, etc.
INTERSEMIOTIC TRANSLATION	Translation between the written word and another medium (e.g. music, art, photography).
INTRALINGUAL TRANSLATION	Translation within the same language (e.g. paraphrase or rewording).
INVISIBILITY	A term used by Venuti (1995) to describe translations which tend to be heavily domesticated (i.e. which conform to the expected linguistic and cultural patterns of the target culture). See DOMESTICATING TRANSLATION, DOMESTICATION.
ITERATIVE	A repeated process.
KERNEL	In Nida's ANALYSIS, kernels are the most basic syntactic elements to which a sentence may be reduced.
KINSHIP TERMS	Terms that are used to describe blood or family relations within a group.
LANGUE	Saussure's term for the abstract linguistic system that underlies a language in use. See also *PAROLE*.
LAWS OF TRANSLATION	Probabilistic statements as to patterns of translation behaviour. See INTERFERENCE, STANDARDIZATION.
LEVEL SHIFT	A SHIFT between ST grammar and TT lexis, or vice versa.
LEXICOGRAMMAR	A Hallidayan term for the lexis (vocabulary) and grammar of a language. See HALLIDAYAN LINGUISTICS.
LEXICON	The vocabulary at the disposal of a user.

LITERAL TRANSLATION	A rendering which preserves surface aspects of the message both semantically and syntactically, adhering closely to ST mode of expression. See SEMANTICS and SYNTACTIC STRUCTURES.
LOCALIZATION	A term in commercial translation referring to making a product linguistically and culturally appropriate to the target country and language.
LOSS	See COMPENSATE, COMPENSATION.
MACHINE TRANSLATION (MT)	Automatic translation by a computer.
MACRO-SIGN	See SIGN.
MANAGING	See MONITORING.
MANIPULATION	See RE-WRITING.
MARKED, MARKEDNESS	An aspect of language use where some linguistic features may be considered less 'basic' or less 'preferred' than others. These marked features are used in a CONTEXTUALLY MOTIVATED manner, i.e. to yield a range of effects. (e.g. *It was Mary who stole the purse* as a 'marked' variant of the 'unmarked' *Mary stole the purse*).
MENTAL PROCESS	See TRANSITIVITY.
MICRO-SIGN	See SIGN.
MINIMAX	In the PROCESS of translation, decisions that yield maximal effect for minimal effort.
MODALITY	Expressing distinctions such as that between 'possibility' and 'actuality', and, in the process, indicating an attitude towards the state or event involved. See INTERPERSONAL MEANING.
MODE OF DISCOURSE	An aspect of REGISTER which builds on the basic distinction spoken vs written.
MODULATION	A translation PROCEDURE, where the TT presents the information from a different point of view (e.g. negation of opposites as in *it is difficult* instead of *it isn't easy*).
MONITORING	Expounding in a non-evaluative manner. This is in contrast with managing, which involves steering the discourse towards speaker's goals.
MT	See MACHINE TRANSLATION.
NEAR-SYNONYMS	Two words that have a very similar sense. SL near-synonyms will require DISAMBIGUATION, while TL near-synonyms are potential EQUIVALENTS for a ST term.

NOMINALIZATION | The condensed reformulation of a verbal process and the various participants involved as a Noun Phrase. This is an important grammatical resource for the expression of IDEOLOGY. For example, by saying '*The net inflow is . . .*', a government spokesperson could avoid having to state that '*there are large imports flowing into the country*'.

NORMALIZATION | See STANDARDIZATION.

NORMATIVE | A type of EQUIVALENCE relation which focuses on the conventions governing language use (e.g. the rhetorical preference in writing within a particular GENRE).

NORMS | 1. The conventions (in the sense of implicitly agreed-upon standards) of 'acceptable' content and rhetorical organization. 2. Observed and repeated patterns of translation (or other) behaviour in a linguistic and cultural context.

OBLIQUE TRANSLATION | One of two translation methods described by Vinay and Darbelnet (the other is DIRECT TRANSLATION). It is used to cope with stylistic problems and covers MODULATION, TRANSPOSITION, EQUIVALENCE, ADAPTATION.

OMISSION | Deliberate, or accidental, absence of a ST element or aspect of sense in the TT.

OPERATIVE TEXT | A type of text which aims at the formation of future behaviour and is thus part of persuasion. See also INSTRUCTION.

OPTION | Used by Vinay and Darbelnet to denote TT segments that are the result of real translator stylistic choice, as opposed to *servitude*, which are wordings governed by the TL system where the translator has no choice.

OVERT TRANSLATION | See COVERT TRANSLATION.

PARALLEL CORPUS | A normally electronically readable collection of PARALLEL TEXTS. See CORPUS.

PARALLEL TEXTS | Texts in two languages. They may be ST–TT pairs (i.e. STs with their translation), or non-translated texts in the two languages on the same topic.

PARATEXT | Those elements in addition to the main body of text, such as titles, headings and footnotes.

PAROLE | Language in use, as it is spoken, or written. See also LANGUE.

PATRONAGE | The powers that can further or hinder the reading, writing or RE-WRITING of literature, which has implications for what may or may not get translated.

	The typical powers concern finance and IDEOLOGY. Where the same patron controls both of these, patronage is said to be undifferentiated; if finance and ideology are separate, patronage is differentiated.
POETICS	Favoured genres, popular motifs and canonized texts making up the literary repertoire of a given language and culture.
POLYSEMY, POLYSEMOUS	Where one word has two or more senses (e.g. *mouth* as part of the body and as part of a river).
POSTCOLONIALISM	A broad cultural approach to the study of power relations between different groups, cultures or peoples where language, literature and translation may play a role.
POSTMODERNISM	A complex critical and artistic movement of the second half of the twentieth century highlighting fragmentation of perspective, subject and voice, in opposition to the 'rational' thought of older western philosophical and literary traditions. See DECON-STRUCTION, POSTSTRUCTURALISM.
POSTSTRUCTURALISM	A reaction to the ordered 'scientific' views of structuralism, poststructuralism emerged in the 1960s as a critical philosophical movement based on theorization and destabilization of language, subject and literary text.
POWER	In the analysis of INTERPERSONAL MEANING, two basic types of relationship may be distinguished: power and solidarity. Power emanates from the text producer's ability to impose his or her plans at the expense of the text receiver's plans. Solidarity, on the other hand, is the willingness of the text producer genuinely to relinquish power and work with his or her interlocutors as members of a team.
PRAGMATICS, PRAGMATIC MEANING	The domain of INTENTIONALITY or the purposes for which utterances are used in real CONTEXTs.
PRESCRIPTIVE	An approach to translation which seeks to dictate rules for 'correct' translation. Compare DESCRIPTIVE TRANSLATION STUDIES.
PROCEDURE	See TRANSLATION PROCEDURES.
PROCESS (OF TRANSLATION)	What happens linguistically and cognitively as the translator works on a translation.
PRODUCT (OF TRANSLATION)	The finished TT resulting from the translation PROCESS.
PROPOSITIONAL CONTENT	What is involved in saying something that is meaningful and can be understood. Not included

here is the function which the particular sentence performs in some specified CONTEXT.

PSEUDO-TRANSLATIONS	TTs regarded as translations, though no genuine STs exist for them.
PURPOSE OF TRANSLATION	See *SKOPOS*.
RANK	Term used by Halliday (see HALLIDAYAN LINGUISTICS) to refer to different linguistic units, namely morpheme, word, group, clause and sentence.
RANK-BOUND TRANSLATION	A translation that translates on the same RANK as the ST (e.g. WORD-FOR-WORD).
RECEPTION	The reaction a TT receives from its readers. Published reviews are one instance of reception in the TT culture.
REDUNDANCY	The amount of information communicated over and above the required minimum. See EXPLICATE, EXPLICITATION.
REFERENTIAL MEANING	See DENOTATION.
REGISTER	The set of features which distinguishes one stretch of language from another in terms of variation in CONTEXT, relating to the language user (geographical dialect, idiolect, etc.) and/or language use (FIELD or subject matter, TENOR or level of formality and MODE or speaking vs writing). Examination of a TEXT using these parameters is known as Register Analysis.
RELEVANCE	Sperber and Wilson (1986) define this as an expectation on the part of the hearer that an attempt at interpretation will yield adequate contextual effects at minimal processing cost. This has been applied to translation, yielding such important distinctions as INTERPRETIVE, DESCRIPTIVE, DIRECT and INDIRECT TRANSLATION.
RESEMBLANCE	The relationship between ST and TT segment achieved through adherence to RELEVANCE.
RESTRUCTURING	See ANALYSIS.
RE-TRANSLATION	In POSTCOLONIALISM, a practice of 'resistance' by translating anew key texts to subvert colonialist DISCOURSE. The less technical meaning of 're-translation' refers to the new translation of (normally) CANONICAL works.
RE-WRITING	Metalinguistic processes, including translation, which can be said to reinterpret, alter or generally

	manipulate text to serve a variety of ideological motives.
RHEME	See INFORMATION STRUCTURE.
RHETORICAL PURPOSE	The intention behind the production of a TEXT.
SALIENCE, TEXTUAL SALIENCE	See MARKED, MARKEDNESS.
SCHEMA (plural SCHEMATA)	A global pattern representing the underlying structure which accounts for the organization of a text. A story schema, for example, may consist of a setting and a number of episodes, each of which would include events and reactions.
SCRIPT	Another term for 'frame'. These are global patterns realized by units of meaning that consist of events and actions related to particular situations. For example, a text may be structured around the 'restaurant script' which represents our knowledge of how restaurants work: waiters, waitresses, cooks, tables where customers sit, peruse menus, order their meals and pay the bill at the end.
SEMANTICS	The study of meaning.
SEMANTIC FIELD	A category of words related by topic or sense. Thus, the semantic field of politics would include words such as *government, parliament, Prime Minister, political party*.
SEMANTIC PROSODY	The positive or negative CONNOTATION which is transferred to a word by the SEMANTIC FIELDs of its common collocates (see COLLOCATION).
SEMANTIC STRUCTURE ANALYSIS	See COMPONENTIAL ANALYSIS, CONTRASTIVE ANALYSIS, DISAMBIGUATION.
SEMANTIC TRANSLATION	One of two types of translation described by Newmark, the other being communicative translation. Semantic translation attempts to reproduce ST FORM and sense as precisely as possible while complying with the formal requirements of the TL.
SEMIOTICS	A dimension of CONTEXT which regulates the relationship of texts to each other as SIGNs. Semiotics thus relies on the interaction not only between speaker and hearer but also between speaker/hearer and their texts, and between text and text. This INTERTEXTUALITY is governed by a variety of socio-cultural factors and rhetorical conventions (e.g. the way news reporting is handled in a given language).
SEMOTACTIC	See CO-TEXT.
SERVITUDE	See *OPTION*.

SHIFT	A shift is said to occur if a ST element is rendered by a TL element that is different from the expected TL CORRESPONDENT (e.g. if English *development* is translated by French *mise en place* rather than *développement*). Shifts can occur at all levels, including TEXT, GENRE and DISCOURSE. See also *TERTIUM COMPARATIONIS*.
SIGN	A unit of signifier and signified, in which the linguistic form (signifier) stands for a concrete object or concept (signified). When the notion of sign is extended to include anything which means something to somebody in some respect or capacity, signs could then be used to refer to cultural objects such as *honour* (micro-sign), as well as to more global structures such as TEXT, GENRE and DISCOURSE (macro-sign), and to even more global structures such as that of the myth.
SIGNIFIED	See SIGN.
SIGNIFIER	See SIGN.
SITUATION	See CONTEXT.
SITUATIONALITY	See CONTEXT.
SKOPOS	A term, used by Reiss and Vermeer, referring to the purpose of the translation as stated in a BRIEF or COMMISSION.
SL	See SOURCE LANGUAGE.
SOCIO-COGNITIVE SYSTEM	Culture, ideology and system of values and beliefs.
SOCIO-SEMIOTIC	A system of SIGNs used for social communication. Language and translation can both be seen as socio-semiotics.
SOURCE LANGUAGE (SL)	The language of the original text.
SOURCE TEXT (ST)	The original text for translation.
SPEECH ACT	An action performed by the use of an utterance to communicate in speech or writing, involving reference, force and effect. This level of meaning is also referred to as the illocutionary force of the utterance.
ST	See SOURCE TEXT.
STANDARDIZATION	The practice by which TT linguistic choices tend to be less varied than in the ST. One of Toury's LAWS OF TRANSLATION.
STANDARDS OF TEXTUALITY	See COHESION, COHERENCE, INTERTEXTUALITY, INTENTIONALITY, etc.

STRUCTURAL CORRESPONDENCE	See FORMAL EQUIVALENCE.
STRUCTURE	The linguistic form, grammatical or lexical.
STYLE, STYLISTIC	The patterns of deliberate or subconscious choices made by speakers or writers from among the lexico-grammatical resources of language (see LEXICO-GRAMMAR). In Translation Studies, style is often linked to FORM as opposed to CONTENT.
STYLISTICS	A branch of literary criticism that analyses STYLE using interpretive tools from linguistics.
SUBTITLES, SUBTITLING	A method of language transfer used in translating types of mass audio-visual communication such as film and television.
SUPERORDINATE	See HYPONYM.
SUPPRESSION OF AGENCY	See NOMINALIZATION.
SURFACE STRUCTURE	See TRANSFORMATIONAL-GENERATIVE GRAMMAR.
SYNTACTIC STRUCTURES, SYNTAX	The grammatical structures and arrangements of elements in a language or text.
TARGET LANGUAGE (TL)	The language of the translation.
TARGET TEXT (TT)	The translated text.
TAXONOMY	A classification of TRANSLATION PROCEDURES, etc.
TENOR OF DISCOURSE	Formality or informality as an aspect of the REGISTER to which a TEXT belongs.
TERM BANK	Machine-readable technical glossary of TERMINOLOGY.
TERMINOLOGY	Specialized vocabulary relating to a specific field of translation.
TERTIUM COMPARATIONIS	A non-linguistic, intermediate form of the meaning of a ST and TT used for evaluation of sense TRANSFER.
TEXT	A sequence of cohesive and coherent sentences realizing a set of mutually relevant intentions (see COHESION, COHERENCE, INTENTIONALITY). A text exhibits features which serve a particular CONTEXTUAL FOCUS and identify the text as a token of a given TEXT TYPE.
TEXT ANALYSIS	The analysis of lexicogrammatical features and communicative FUNCTIONs of real TEXTs.
TEXT LINGUISTICS	Analytical research within linguistics which focuses on the TEXT rather than lower-level units such as word or phrase.

TEXT-NORMATIVE EQUIVALENCE	One of Koller's EQUIVALENCE types, referring to features specific to the TEXT TYPE and the appropriate stylistic usage.
TEXT TYPE	Classification of TEXTs according to broad type. Proposed by Reiss, who sees type determining translation strategy. See EXPRESSIVE, INFORMATIVE and OPERATIVE TEXTs.
TEXTUAL COMPETENCE	The ability not only to apply the LEXICOGRAMMATICAL rules of a language in order to produce well-formed sentences, and not only to know when, where and to whom to use these sentences, but to know how to make the sentence play a role within a sequence that is eventually part of a well-formed TEXT, DISCOURSE and GENRE.
TEXTUAL EQUIVALENCE	For Catford, this kind of equivalence is encountered in situations where FORMAL EQUIVALENCE is unworkable and where there is a need for a TRANSLATION SHIFT of some kind. Other authors (e.g. Beaugrande, Koller) define it in terms of pragmatic equivalence (see PRAGMATICS, EQUIVALENCE) obtaining at the level of TEXT.
TEXTUAL EQUIVALENT	See EQUIVALENT.
TEXTUAL FUNCTION	The use of language in the creation of well-formed texts.
TEXTUALITY	See STANDARDS OF TEXTUALITY.
TEXTUAL PRAGMATICS	See TEXTUAL EQUIVALENCE.
TEXTURE	The successful organization of a TEXT in its CONTEXT achieved by COHESION, COHERENCE, TEXTUAL FUNCTION, etc.
THEME	See INFORMATION STRUCTURE.
THINK-ALOUD PROTOCOL (TAP)	A technique for recording reactions elicited from translators or users of translations regarding the PROCESS of translation.
TL	See TARGET LANGUAGE.
TRANSCRIPTION	Translation that retains the form of the ST item in the TT, frequently used for names.
TRANSFER	See ANALYSIS.
TRANSFORMATIONAL-GENERATIVE GRAMMAR	A theory of grammar proposed by the American linguist Noam Chomsky in 1957. Chomsky attempted to show how, with a system of internalized rules, native speakers of a language put their knowledge to use in forming grammatical sentences. He proposed a two-level structure for the sentence: the

SURFACE STRUCTURE, which is the linguistic structure we see or hear, and the abstract DEEP STRUCTURE of basic elements that is used for SEMANTIC analysis.

TRANSITIVITY

A linguistic system in which a small set of presumably universal categories characterize different kinds of events and processes, different kinds of participants in these events, and the varying circumstances of place and times within which events occur. These variations are closely bound up with different world views and ideological slants. Three main processes may be distinguished:

1. Material process, including action process ('Ana *lifted* the suitcase');
2. Mental process ('John *recognized* it');
3. Relational process ('Such a perspective *is lacking*').

TRANSLATABILITY

The extent to which it is possible to translate from one language to another. Those who argue for the possibility suggest that anything which can be said in one language can be said in another.

TRANSLATESE

See TRANSLATIONESE.

TRANSLATIONAL

A term denoting 'specific or pertaining to translation' as opposed to 'original or creative writing'.

TRANSLATIONAL ACTION MODEL

Model proposed by Holz-Mänttäri which describes translation as purpose-driven co-operation between several participants.

TRANSLATION CRITICISM

See TRANSLATION QUALITY ASSESSMENT.

TRANSLATIONESE

Peculiarities of language use in translation.

TRANSLATION MEMORY TOOL

Computerized software which stores previous translations and assists in recycling them to achieve consistency and speed.

TRANSLATION PROCEDURES

Vinay and Darbelnet identify seven main techniques of translation which they term 'procedures'.

TRANSLATION PROJECT

A systematic approach to literary translation, initiated in Canada, in which feminist translators openly foreground the feminist in the TT.

TRANSLATION QUALITY ASSESSMENT

The systematic evaluation of a TT by comparison with a ST.

TRANSLATION SHIFT

See SHIFT.

TRANSLATOR AIDS

All kinds of computerized and non-computerized aids for translation (e.g. TRANSLATION MEMORY TOOLs, dictionaries, GLOSSARIES).

TRANSLATORY	See TRANSLATIONAL.
TRANSLITERATION	The letter-by-letter rendering of a SL name or word in the TL when the two languages have distinct scripts (e.g. Russian and English).
TRANSPOSITION	One of Vinay and Darbelnet's TRANSLATION PROCEDURES which involves a grammatical but not a meaning change (e.g. *dès mon retour* [on my return] = *as soon as I get back*).
TT	See TARGET TEXT.
TYPOLOGY	See TEXT TYPE.
UNBOUNDED TRANSLATION	See FREE TRANSLATION; cf. RANK-BOUND TRANSLATION.
UNDIFFERENTIATED	See PATRONAGE.
UNIT OF TRANSLATION	The linguistic element (word, clause, sentence, TEXT) used by the translator in the PROCESS of translation.
UNIVERSALIST	A philosophy of how intercultural communication works, endorsing TRANSLATABILITY, for example.
UNIVERSALS OF TRANSLATION	Specific characteristics that, it is hypothesized, are typical of translated language as distinct from non-translated language (cf. LAWS OF TRANSLATION).
UNIVERSE OF DISCOURSE	The entire domain, field, institutional framework and cultural context surrounding a text.
VERSION	Its technical use denotes a TT in which so many modifications, additions or cuts have been made that it cannot properly be called a translation.
VERTICAL	See INTERTEXTUALITY.
VOICE	An abstract concept often used by literary translators to refer to the narrative STYLE and rhythm of the ST author which must be grasped in order to produce a successful TT. Used also (e.g. Hermans 1996) in the sense of the translator's voice to refer to the underlying and potentially distorting presence of the translator's choices in the TL.
WORD-FOR-WORD TRANSLATION	A TT in which each word of the ST is replaced by its close correspondent in the TL (see CORRESPONDENCE, CORRESPONDENT).
ZERO TRANSLATION	A case where the TT contains no EQUIVALENT of a ST item. Often represented by the symbol Ø.

Bibliography

Adab, B. (2001) 'The Translation of Advertising: A Framework for Evaluation', *Babel* 47(2): 133–57.

Adab, B. and C. Valdés (2004) *Key Debates in the Translation of Advertising Material: The Translator* (special issue) 10.2.

ALPAC (Automatic Language Processing Advisory Committee) (1966) *Language and Machines: Computers in Translation and Linguistics*, Washington DC: National Academy of Sciences. Online available <http://www.nap.edu/books/ARC000005/html/R1. html> (accessed 15 October 2003).

Amos, F. (1920/1973) *Early Theories of Translation*, New York: Octagon Books.

Angenot, M. (1983) 'Intertextualité, interdiscursivité, discours social', *Texte* 2: 101–12.

—— (1989) *Un Etat du discours social*, Longueuil, Quebec: Préamble.

Arnold, D. J., L. Balkan, S. Meijer, R. L. Humphreys and L. Sadler (1994) *Machine Translation: an Introductory Guide*, London: Blackwells–NCC. Online available <http:// www.essex.ac.uk/linguistics/clmt/MTbook/PostScript/> (accessed 4 August 2003).

Austermühl, F. (2001) *Electronic Tools for Translators*, Manchester: St Jerome.

Baker, M. (1992) *In Other Words: A Coursebook on Translation*, London and New York: Routledge.

—— (1993) 'Corpus Linguistics and Translation Studies: Implications and Applications', in: M. Baker, G. Francis and E. Tognini-Bonelli (eds) *Text and Technology: In Honour of John Sinclair*, Amsterdam and Philadelphia: John Benjamins, pp. 233–50.

—— (1995) 'Corpora in Translation Studies: An Overview and Suggestions for Future Research', *Target* 7.2: 223–43.

Baker, M. (ed.) (1998) *Routledge Encyclopedia of Translation Studies*, London and New York: Routledge.

Bakhtin M. M. (1981) *The Dialogic Imagination: Four Essays*, University of Texas Press Slavic Series, vol. 1 (trans. Caryl Emerson and Michael Holoquist), Austin: University of Texas Press.

Bar-Hillel, Y. (1959) *Report on the State of Machine Translation in the United States and Great Britain: Technical Report 15 February 1959*, Jerusalem: Hebrew University.

Barkhudarov, L. (1993) 'The Problem of the Unit of Translation', in P. Zlateva (ed.) *Translation as Social Action: Russian and Bulgarian Perspectives*, London and New York: Routledge, pp. 39–46.

Barlow, M. (forthcoming) *ParaConc*, software available online from <http://www.athel. com>

Bassnett, S. (1980/1991) *Translation Studies*, London and New York: Routledge, 2nd edn.

—— (2002) *Translation Studies*, London and New York: Routledge, 3rd edn.

Bassnett, S. and A. Lefevere (eds) (1990) *Translation, History and Culture*, London and New York: Pinter.

—— (1990a) 'Introduction: Proust's Grandmother and the Thousand and One Nights: The "cultural turn" in Translation Studies', in Bassnett and Lefevere (eds) (1990), pp. 1–13.

Bateman, J. A., C. M. Matthiessen and Zeng, L. (1999) 'Multilingual Natural Language Generation for Multilingual Software: A Functional Linguistic Approach', *Applied Artificial Intelligence*, 13.6: 607–39.

Beaugrande, R. de (1978) *Factors in a Theory of Poetic Translation*, Assen: Van Gorcum.

—— (1980) *Text, Discourse and Process*, ed. R. O. Freedle, in *Advances in Discourse Processes*, Series IV, Norwood NJ: Ablex.

Beaugrande, R. de and W. Dressler (1981) *Introduction to Text Linguistics*, London: Longman.

—— (2004) *A New Introduction to the Study of Text and Discourse*. Online available: <http://beaugrande.bizland.com/new_intro_to_study.htm>

Beeby, A. (1996) 'Course Profile: Licenciatura en traducción e interpretación, Universitat Autónoma de Barcelona, Spain', *The Translator* 1: 113–26.

Beekman, J. and J. Callow (1974) *Translating the Word of God*, Michigan: Zondervan.

Bell, A. (1984) 'Language Style as Audience Design', *Language in Society* 13: 145–204.

Belloc, H. (1931) *On Translation*, Oxford: Oxford University Press.

—— (1931a) 'On Translation', *Bookman* 74: 179–85; reprinted in *The Bible Translator* 10 (1959): 83–100.

Belsey, C. (2002) *Poststructuralism: A Very Short Introduction*, Oxford: Oxford University Press.

Benjamin, W. (1923/1969) 'The Task of the Translator', in *Illuminations*, Frankfurt: Suhrkamp Verlag, trans. by H. Zohn (1969), in M. Bullock and M. Jennings (eds) *Walter Benjamin: Selected Writings Volume I: 1913–1926*, Cambridge, MA: The Belknap Press of Harvard University Press, reprinted in L. Venuti (ed. 2000), pp.15–25.

Berber Sardinha, T. (1999) 'Semantic Prosodies in English and Portuguese: A Contrastive Study', *Cuadernos de Filología Inglesa* (Murcia, Spain), 9.1: 93–110. Online available: <lael.pucsp.br/~tony/2000murcia_prosodies.pdf> (accessed 19 July 2003).

Berman, A. (1985/2000) 'La traduction comme épreuve de l'étranger', *Texte* 4: 67–81, trans. L. Venuti as 'Translation and the Trials of the Foreign', in L. Venuti (ed.) (2000) *The Translation Studies Reader*, London and New York: Routledge, pp. 284–97.

Bhabha, H. (1994) *The Location of Culture*, London and New York: Routledge.

Bloomfield, L. (1933) *Language*, New York: Henry Holt & Co.

Blum-Kulka, S. and E. Levenson (1983) 'Universals of Lexical Simplification', in. C. Faerch and G. Kasper (eds) *Strategies in Interlanguage Communication*, London and New York: Longman, pp. 119–39.

Boase-Beier, J. and M. Holman (1999) *The Practices of Literary Translation*, Manchester: St Jerome.

Boutsis, S., S. Piperidis and I. Demiros (1999) 'Generating Bilingual Lexical Equivalences from Parallel Texts', *Applied Artificial Intelligence* 13.6: 583–606.

Bruce, D. (1994) 'Translating the Commune: Cultural Politics and the Historical Specificity of the Anarchist text', *Traduction, Terminologie, Rédaction* 1: 47–76.

Bühler, K. (1934/1965) *Sprachtheorie: Die Darstellungsfunktion der Sprache*, Stuttgart: Gustav Fischer.

Bush, P. (1997) 'The Translator as Reader and Writer', *Donaire* 8: 13–18.

Campbell, J. (1993) 'Culture and Ideology in the Translation of Poetry', in Y. Gambier and J. Tommola (eds) *Translation and Knowledge: Proceedings of the 1992 Scandinavian Symposium on Translation Theory*, Turku: Tampere University Centre for Translation and Interpreting, pp. 139–53.

Campbell, S. (1998) *Translation into the Second Language*, London: Longman.

Carter, R. (1998) *Vocabulary: Applied Linguistic Perspectives*, London and New York: Routledge, 2nd edn.

Carter, R. and W. Nash (1990) *Seeing Through Language: A Guide to Styles of English Writing*, Oxford: Basil Blackwell.

Cary, E. (1959) 'La traduction dans les congrès internationaux', *International Associations* vol. II: 27–32.

Catford, J. C. (1965) *A Linguistic Theory of Translation*, Oxford: Oxford University Press.

Chamberlain, L. (1988/2000) 'Gender and the Metaphorics of Translation', *Signs* 13: 454–72, reprinted in L. Venuti (ed.) (2000), pp. 314–29.

—— (1998) 'Gender Metaphorics in Translation', in M. Baker (ed.) (1998), pp. 93–6.

Chau, S. (1984) *Aspects of Translation Pedagogy: The Grammatical, Cultural and Interpretive Teaching Models*, Ph.D. thesis, University of Edinburgh.

Chesterman, A. (ed.) (1989) *Readings in Translation Theory*, Helsinki: Finn Lectura.

—— (1997) *Memes of Translation: The Spread of Ideas in Translation Theory*, Amsterdam and Philadelphia: John Benjamins.

Chesterman, A. and J. Williams (2002) *The Map: A Beginner's Guide to Doing Research in Translation*, Manchester: St Jerome.

Cicero (46 BC/1960 CE) 'De optimo genere oratorum', in Cicero *De inventione, De optimo genere oratorum, topica*, trans. H. M. Hubbell, Cambridge MA: Harvard University Press, London: Heinemann, pp. 347–73.

Classe, O. (ed.) (2000) *The Encyclopedia of Literary Translation into English*, London: Fitzroy Dearbon.

Coates, J. (1999) 'Changing Horses: Nabokov and Translation', in J. Boase-Beier and M. Holman (eds) (1999), pp. 91–108.

Connor, U. and R. Kaplan (1987) *Writing Across Languages and Cultures*, Reading, Mass.: Addison Wesley.

Copeland, R. (1991) *Rhetoric, Hermeneutics and Translation in the Middle Ages: Academic Traditions and Vernacular Texts*, Cambridge: Cambridge University Press.

Coseriu, E. (1970) *Einführung in die transformationelle Grammatik*, Autorisierte Nachschrift, Tübingen: Gunter Narr.

Cronin, M. (1996) *Translating Ireland: Translation, Languages, Cultures*, Cork: Cork University Press.

—— (2003) *Translation and Globalization*, London and New York: Routledge.

Crystal, D. and D. Davy (1969) *Investigating English Style*, Harlow: Longman.

Davis, P. (2002) 'Reviving the Dread Deity', Review of the new Marcel Proust *In Search of Lost Time, The Guardian* 2.11 2002; also available <http://books.guardian.co.uk/review/story/0,12084,824010,00.html>

Delabastita, D. (1989) 'Translation and Mass-Communication: Film and TV Translation as Evidence of Cross-cultural Dynamics', *Babel* 35:4, 193–218.

Delisle, J. (1982) *L'analyse du discours comme méthode de traduction*, Ottawa: Presses de l'Université d'Ottawa, 2nd edn.

—— (1988) *Translation: An Interpretive Approach* (trans. P. Logan and M. Creery), Ottawa: University of Ottawa Press.

Delisle, J. and J. Woodsworth (eds) (1995) *Translators through History*, Amsterdam and Philadelphia: John Benjamins.

Derrida, J. (1985) 'Des Tours de Babel', in J. Graham (ed.) (1985) *Difference in Translation*, Ithaca: Cornell University Press, pp. 209–48, trans. by J. F. Graham, pp. 165–207.

Dharwadker, V. (1999) 'A. K. Ramanujan's Theory and Practice of Translation', in S. Bassnett and H. Trivedi (eds), 114–40.

Dickins, J., S. Hervey and I. Higgins (2002) *Thinking Arabic Translation: A Course in Translation Method: Arabic to English*, London and New York: Routledge.

Dostoyevsky, F. (1912/1966) *Crime and Punishment*, trans. Constance Garnett, New York: Bantam Classics.

—— (1991) *Crime and Punishment*, trans. D. McDuff, London: Penguin.

Dryden, J. (1697/1992) 'Dedication of the *Aeneis*', in R. Schulte and J. Biguenet (eds) (1992) *Theories of Translation*, Chicago and London: University of Chicago Press, pp. 17–31.

—— (1697/1997) 'Dedication of the Aeneis', in D. Robinson (ed.) (1997) *Western Translation Theory from Herodotus to Nietzsche*, Manchester: St Jerome.

Duff, A. (1981) *The Third Language: Recurrent Problems of Translating into English*, Oxford: Pergamon.

Eggins, S. (1994) *An Introduction to Systemic Functional Linguistics*, London and New York: Pinter.

Emery, P. (1991) 'Text Classification and Text Analysis in Advanced Translation Teaching', *Meta*, 35.4: 567–77.

Esselink, B. (2000) *A Practical Guide to Localization*, Amsterdam and Philadelphia: John Benjamins, 2nd edn.

European Communities Court of Auditors (2002) *Report on the Financial Statements of the Translation Centre for the Bodies of the European Union for the Financial Year 2001*. Online available: <http://www.eca.eu.int/audit_reports/specific_reports/2001/ctou_en.pdf> (accessed 20 September 2003).

Evans, R. (1998) 'Metaphor of Translation', in M. Baker (ed.) (1998), pp. 149–53.

Even-Zohar, I. (1978/2000) 'The Position of Translated Literature within the Literary Polysystem', *Poetics Today* 11: 45–51, reprinted in L. Venuti (ed.) (2000), pp. 192–7.

Ezard, J. (2000) 'Error Led to Bombing of Monte Cassino', *The Guardian* 4.4.2000: 5.

Fairclough, N. (1989) *Language and Power*, London: Longman.

—— (1992) *Discourse and Social Change*, Cambridge: Polity Press.

Fawcett, P. (1995) 'Translation and Power Play', *The Translator* 1.2: 177–92.

—— (1997) *Translation and Linguistics: Linguistic Theories Explained*, Manchester: St Jerome.

—— (1998) 'Ideology and Translation' in M. Baker (ed.) (1998), pp. 106–11.

Felstiner, J. (1980) *Translating Neruda: The Way to Macchu Picchu*, Stanford: Stanford University Press.

Firbas, J. (1992) *Functional Sentence Perspective in Written and Spoken Communication*, Cambridge: Cambridge University Press.

Flotow, L. van (1997) *Translation and Gender: Translation in the 'Era of Feminism'*, Manchester: St Jerome.

Fowler, R. (1986) *Linguistic Criticism*, Oxford: Oxford University Press.

France, P. (2000) *The Oxford Guide to Literature in English Translation*, Oxford: Oxford University Press.

Gentzler, E. (2001) *Contemporary Translation Theories*, Clevedon: Multilingual Matters, 2nd edn.

Gniffke-Hubrig, C. (1972) 'Textsorten. Erarbeiten einer Typologie von Gebrauchstexten in der 11. Klasse des Gymnasiums', *Der Deutschunterricht* 24.1: 39–52.

Gregory, M. (1980) 'Perspectives on Translation from the Firthian Tradition', *Meta* 25.4: 455–66.

Gregory, M. and S. Carroll (1978) *Language and Situation: Language Varieties and their Social Contexts*, London: Routledge & Kegan Paul.

Grice, P. (1975) 'Logic and Conversation', in P. Cole and J. Morgan (eds) *Syntax and Semantics 3: Speech Acts*, New York: Academic Press, pp. 41–58.

Gulich, E. and W. Raible (1975) 'Textsorten-Probleme', in H. Moser (ed.) *Linguistische Probleme der Textanalyse*, Jahrbuch des Instituts fur Deutsche Sprache, Düsseldorf: Pädagogischer Verlag Schwann, pp. 144–97.

Gutt, Ernst-August (1991) *Translation and Relevance: Cognition and Context*, Oxford: Blackwell.

—— (1998) 'Pragmatic Aspects of Translation: Some Relevance-Theory Observations', in L. Hickey *The Pragmatics of Translation*, Clevedon: Multilingual Matters, pp. 41–53.

Halliday, M. A. K. (1978) *Language as Social Semiotic*, London: Edward Arnold.

—— (1985/1994) *An Introduction to Functional Grammar*, London, Melbourne and Auckland: Edward Arnold, 2nd edn.

Halliday, M. A. K., A. McIntosh and P. Strevens (1964) *The Linguistic Sciences and Language Teaching*, London: Longman.

Hartmann, R. R. K. (1980) *Contrastive Textology*, Heidelberg: Julius Groos Verlag.

Harvey, K. (1998/2000) 'Translating Camp Talk: Gay Identities and Cultural Transfer', *The Translator* 4.2: 295–320, reprinted in L. Venuti (ed.) (2000), pp. 446–67.

Hatim, B. (1984) 'A Text Typological Approach to Syllabus Design in Translator Training', *The Incorporated Linguist*: 146–9.

Hatim, B. and I. Mason (1990) *Discourse and the Translator*, London: Longman.

—— (1997) *The Translator as Communicator*, London and New York: Routledge.

Hawkins, R. (1962) 'Waiwai Translation', *The Bible Translator* 13.3: 164–6.

Hermans, T. (1985) *The Manipulation of Literature*, Beckenham, UK: Croom Helm.

—— (1996) 'The Translator's Voice in Translated Narrative', *Target* 8.2: 23–48.

Hervey, S. and I. Higgins (1992) *Thinking French Translation: A Course in Translation Method*, London and New York: Routledge.

Hines, B. (1969) *Kes*, Harmondsworth: Penguin, trans. L. Tranec-Dubled (1982) Paris: Gallimard.

Hinsley, F. H. and A. Strip (eds) (1993) *Codebreakers: The Inside Story of Bletchley Park*, Oxford: Oxford University Press.

Holmes, J. S. (1988/2000) 'The Name and Nature of Translation Studies', in *Translated! Papers on Literary Translation and Translation Studies*, 2nd edn, pp. 67–80; reprinted in L. Venuti (ed.) (2000), pp. 172–85.

Holz-Mänttäri, J. (1984) *Translatorisches Handeln: Theorie und Methode*, Helsinki: Suomalainen Tiedeakatemia.

House, J. (1977) *A Model for Translation Quality Assessment*, Tübinger Beiträge zur Linguistik 88.

—— (1997) *Translation Quality Assessment: A Model Revised*, Tübingen: Gunter Narr.

Hu, Q. (1994) 'On the Implausibility of Equivalent Response (Part V)', *Meta* 39.3: 418–32.

Hutchins, W. J. (1986) *Machine Translation: Past, Present and Future*, Chichester, UK: Ellis Horwood. Online available: <http://ourworld.compuserve.com/homepages/WJHutchins/PPF-8.pdf> (accessed 4 August 2003).

Ivir, V. (1981) 'Formal Correspondence vs Translation Equivalence Revisited', *Poetics Today* 2.4: 51–9.

Jakobson, R. (1959/2000) 'On Linguistic Aspects of Translation', in R. Brower (ed.) (1959) *On Translation*, Cambridge MA: Harvard University Press, 232–9, reprinted in L. Venuti (ed.) (2000), pp. 113–18.

James, C. (1989) 'Genre Analysis and the Translator', *Target* 1.1: 21–41.

Jerome, E. H. (St Jerome) (395/1997) 'De optime genere interpretandi' (Letter 101, to Pammachius), in *Epistolae D. Hieronymi Stridoniensis* (1565), Rome: Aldi F., pp. 285–91, trans. by P. Carroll as 'On the Best Kind of Translator', in D. Robinson (ed.) (1997a), pp. 22–30.

Katz, J. and J. Fodor (1963) 'The Structure of Semantic Theory', *Language* 39: 170–210.

Kay, M. (1980/2003) 'The Proper Place of Men and Machines in Language Translation', Research Report CSL-80–11, Palo Alto, California: Xerox Palo Alto Research Center; reprinted in S. Nirenburg, H. Somers and Y. Wilks (eds) (2003) *Readings in Machine Translation*, Cambridge, MA: MIT Press.

—— (2003) 'Machine Translation'. Online available at: <www.lsadc.org/fields/index. php?aaa=/__ translation.html> (accessed 20 September 2003).

Kelly, L. (1979) *The True Interpreter: A History of Translation Theory and Practice in the West*, New York: St Martin's Press.

Kenny, D. (2001) *Lexical Creativity in Translation*, Manchester: St Jerome.

Klein, W. (1991) 'Was kann sich die Übersetzungswissenschaft von der Linguistik erwarten?' *Zeitschrift für Literaturwissenschaft und Linguistik*, 21: 104–23.

Koller, W. (1972) *Grundprobleme der Übersetzungstheorie: Unter besonderer Berücksichtigung schwedischdeutscher Übersetzungsfälle*, Bern and Munich: Francke.

—— (1979) *Einführung in die Übersetzungwissenschaft*, Heidelberg: Quelle & Meyer, [the English translation of the chapter appears in A. Chesterman (ed.), (1989), pp. 99–104].

—— (1981) 'Textgattungen und Übersetzungsäquivalenz', in W. Kühlwein, G. Thome and W. Wilss (eds), *Kontrastive Linguistik und Übersetzungswissenschaft*, Munich, 272–9.

—— (1989) 'Equivalence in translation theory', in A. Chesterman (ed.) *Readings in Translation Theory*, Helsinki: Finn Lectura, pp. 99–104.

—— (1995) 'The Concept of Equivalence and the Object of Translation Studies', *Target* 7.2.: 191–222.

Koster, C. (2000) *From World to World. An Armamentarium: For the Study of Poetic Discourse in Translation*, Amsterdam: Rodopi.

—— (1992) *Einführung in die Übersetzungswissenschaft*, Heidelberg and Wiesbaden, Quelle Meyer.

Kress, G. (1985) *Linguistic Processes in Sociocultural Practice*, Victoria: Deakin University Press.

Kress, G. and G. Jones (1981) 'Classification at Work: The case of Middle Management', *Text* 1.1.

Kuhiwczak, P. (1990) 'Translation as Appropriation: The Case of Milan Kundera's *The Joke*', in S. Bassnett and A. Lefevere (eds) (1990), pp. 118–30.

Labov, W. (1973) 'The Boundaries of Words and Their Meaning', in C. J. Bailey and R. Shuy (eds) *New Ways of Analyzing Variation of English*, Washington DC: Georgetown Press, pp. 340–73.

Ladmiral, J-R. (1979) *Traduire: théorèmes pour la traduction*, Paris: Payot.

Larson, M. (1984/1998) *Meaning-Based Translation: A Guide to Cross-Language Equivalence*, Lanham, New York & London: University Press of America, 2nd edn.

Leech, G. (1981) *Semantics: The Study of Meaning*, Harmondsworth: Penguin.

Lefevere, A. (1992) *Translation, Rewriting and the Manipulation of the Literary Fame*, London and New York: Routledge.

Leuven-Zwart, K. van (1989) 'Translation and Original: Similarities and Dissimilarities, I', *Target* 1.2: 151–81.

—— (1990) 'Translation and Original: Similarities and Dissimilarities, II', *Target* 2.1: 69–95.

Levine, S. J. (1991) *The Subversive Scribe: Translating Latin American Fiction*, St Paul, Minnesota: Graywolf Press.

Levý, J. (1967/2000) 'Translation as a Decision Process', *To Honour Roman Jakobson: Essays on the Occasion of his 70th Birthday*, vol. 2. The Hague: Mouton, 1171–82, reprinted in L. Venuti (ed.) (2000), pp. 148–59.

Localisation Standards Industry Association (2003) *Frequently Asked Questions.* Online available at: <http://www.lisa.org/info/faqs.html#trans> (accessed 20 September 2003).

Lörscher, W. (1991) *Translation Performance, Translation Process, and Translation Strategies. A Psycholinguistic Investigation,* Tübingen: Gunter Narr.

Lotmann, J. (1972) *Die Struktur literarischer Texte,* Munich.

Lounsbury, F. (1956) 'A Semantic Analysis of Pawnee Kinship Usage', *Language* 32: 158–94.

Louw, W. (1993) 'Irony in the Text or Insincerity in the Writer?: The Diagnostic Potential of Semantic Prosodies', in M. Baker, G. Francis and E. Tognini-Bonelli (eds) *Text and Technology: In honour of John Sinclair,* Amsterdam and Philadelphia: John Benjamins, pp. 157–76.

Lyons, J. (1977), *Semantics,* Vols. 1 and 2, Cambridge: Cambridge University Press.

McEnery, A., Y. Tono and Z. Xiao (forthcoming) *Corpus-Based Language Studies* [Routledge Applied Linguistics Series]. London and New York: Routledge.

McEnery, A. and A. Wilson (2001) *Corpus Linguistics,* Edinburgh: Edinburgh University Press, 2nd edn.

Malmkjær, K. (1992) 'Review of *Translation and Relevance* by E. A. Gutt', *Mind and Language* 7.3: 298–309.

Mauranen, A. and P. Kujamäki (eds) (2004) *Translation Universals: Do They Exist?,* Amsterdam and Philadelphia: John Benjamins.

Mira, A. (1999) 'Pushing the Limits of Faithfulness: A Case for Gay Translation', in J. Boase-Beier and M. Holman (eds) (1999), pp. 109–24.

Munday, J. (2001) *Introducing Translation Studies,* London and New York: Routledge.

Nabokov, V. (1955/2000) 'Problems of Translation: *Onegin* in English', *Partisan Review* 22: 496–512, reprinted in L. Venuti (ed.) (2000), pp. 71–83.

Newmark, P. (1981) *Approaches to Translation.* Oxford: Pergamon.

—— (1988) *A Textbook of Translation,* New York and London: Prentice Hall.

—— (2003) 'Translation now – 24', *The Linguist* 42.3: 95–6.

Nida, E. A. (1964) *Towards a Science of Translating.* Leiden: E. J. Brill.

—— (1969) 'Science of Translation', *Language* 43.3: 483–98.

—— (1975) 'A Framework for the Analysis and Evaluation of Theories of Translation', in R. Brislin (ed.) *Translation Application and Research,* Gardner Press, New York, 47–91.

Nida, E. A. and C. Taber (1969) *The Theory and Practice of Translation,* Leiden: Brill.

Niranjana, T. (1992) *Siting Translation: History, Post-structuralism, and the Colonial Context,* Berkeley, Los Angeles and Oxford: University of California Press.

Nirenburg, S., H. Somers and Y. Wilks (eds) (2003) *Readings in Machine Translation,* Cambridge MA: MIT Press.

Nord, C. (1997) *Translating as a Purposeful Activity: Functionalist Approaches Explained,* Manchester: St Jerome.

Oakes, M. (1998) *Statistics for Corpus Linguistics,* Edinburgh: Edinburgh University Press.

Ogden, C. P. and I. A. Richards (1923) *The Meaning of Meaning: A Study of the Influence of Language upon Thought and of the Science of Symbolism,* New York: Harcourt Brace.

Olohan, M. (2004) *Corpus-Based Translation Studies,* London and New York: Routledge.

Ong, W. (1971) *Rhetoric, Romance and Technology,* Ithaca, NY: Cornell University Press.

Ortega y Gasset, J. (1937/1965) 'Miseria y esplendor en la traducción', Langewiesche-Brand edition (1965), Munich: Ebenhausen. In English as 'The Misery and the Splendor of Translation', trans. E. G. Miller, in L. Venuti (ed.) (2000), pp. 49–62.

Osgood, C., G. Suci and R. Tannenbaum (1957) *The Measurement of Meaning,* Urbana, IL: University of Illinois Press.

Peden, M. S. (1987) 'Telling Others' Tales', *Translation Review* 24–5: 9–12.

Pennycook, A. (1994) *The Cultural Politics of English as an International Language*, Harlow: Longman.

Pergnier, M. (1990) 'Comment dénaturer une traduction', *Meta* 35.1: 219–25.

Phillips, H. P. (1959) 'Problems of Translation and Meaning in Field Work', *Human Organization* 18: 184–92.

Pratt, M-L. (1992) *Imperial Eyes: Travel Writing and Transculturation*, London and New York: Routledge.

Pym, A. (1992) 'The Relations Between Translation and Material Text Transfer', *Target* 4.2: 171–89.

—— (1995) 'European Translation Studies, une science qui dérange, and Why Equivalence Needn't be a Dirty Word', *Traduction, Terminologie, Rédaction* 8.1: 153–76.

Rabassa, G. (1984) 'The Silk Purse Business: A Translator's Conflicting Responsibilities', in W. Frawley (ed.) (1984) *Translation: Literary, Linguistic and Philosophical Perspectives*, Newark, London and Toronto: Associated University Presses, pp. 35–40.

Rafael, V. (1993) *Contracting Colonialism: Translation and Christian Conversion in Tagalog Society Under Early Spanish Rule*, Durham, NC: Duke University Press.

Ramanujan, A. K. (1989) 'On Translating a Tamil Poem', in R.Warren (ed.) (1989), pp. 47–63.

Reiss, K. (1971) *Möglichkeiten und Grenzen der Übersetzungskritik*, Munich: M. Hueber, trans. (2000) by E. F. Rhodes as *Translation Criticism: Potential and Limitations*, Manchester: St Jerome and American Bible Society.

—— (1974) 'Das Problem der Textklassification in angewandt-linguistischer Sicht', *Linguistica Antverpiensia* 8: 43–60.

—— (1975) 'Einige Elemente des Textverstehens', *IRAL-Sonderbrand* 1: *Übersetzungswissenschaft*.

—— (1977/1989) 'Text-types, Translation Types and Translation Assessment', (in A. Chesterman (ed.) 1989), pp. 105–15.

Reiss, K. and H. J. Vermeer (1984) *Grundlegung einer allgemeinen Translationstheorie*, Tübingen: Niemeyer.

Rener, F. (1989) *Interpretatio: Language and Translation from Cicero to Tytler*, Amsterdam: Rodopi.

Riccardi, A. (2002) *Translation Studies: Perspectives on an Emerging Discipline*, Cambridge: Cambridge University Press.

Rieu, E. V. and J. B. Phillips (1954) 'Translating the Gospels', *Concordia Theological Monthly* 25: 754–65.

Robinson, D. (1997) *Translation and Empire: Postcolonial Theories Explained*, Manchester: St Jerome.

—— (ed.) (1997a) *Western Translation Theory from Herodotus to Nietzsche*, Manchester: St Jerome.

Sacks, O. (1986) *The Man who Mistook his Wife for a Hat*, London: Picador.

Said, E. (1978/1995) *Orientalism*, London: Penguin, revised edn.

Saussure, F. de (1916/1983) *Course in General Linguistics*, ed. C. Bally, A. Sechehaye and A. Riedlinger, trans. and annotated by R. Harris, London: Duckworth. [The 1960 translation by W. Burkin, published in London by Peter Owen.]

Savory, T. (1957/1968) *The Art of Translation*, London: Cape.

Schwartz, R. (2002) 'CEATL: A code of ethics for literary translators', *In Other Words*, No. 19 (Autumn): 43–4.

Scott, M. (2003) *WordSmith Tools*, software. Online available: <www.lexically.net/wordsmith>.

Shuttleworth, M. and M. Cowie (1997) *Dictionary of Translation Studies*, Manchester: St Jerome.

Simon, S. (1996) *Gender in Translation: Cultural Identity and the Politics of Transmission*, London and New York: Routledge.

Sinclair, J. (1991) *Corpus, Concordance, Collocation*, Oxford: Oxford University Press.

Snell-Hornby, M. (ed.) (1986) *Übersetzungswissenschaft – Eine Neuorientierung*, Tübingen: Francke.

—— (1990) 'Linguistic Transcoding or Cultural Transfer: A Critique of Translation Theory in Germany', in S. Bassnett and A. Lefevere (eds) (1990), pp. 79–86.

Somers, H. (1998) 'Machine Translation: History', in M. Baker (ed.) (1998), 140–3.

—— (ed.) (2003) *Computers and Translation*, Amsterdam and Philadelphia: John Benjamins.

Sperber, D. and D. Wilson (1986/1995) *Relevance: Communication and Cognition*, Oxford: Blackwell, 2nd edn.

Spivak, G. (1993/2000) 'The Politics of Translation', in G. Spivak *Outside in the Teaching Machine*, London and New York: Routledge, reprinted in L. Venuti (ed.) (2000), pp. 397–416.

Steiner, G. (1975/1998) *After Babel: Aspects of Language and Translation*, London, Oxford and New York: Oxford University Press, 3rd edn.

Stiehler, U. (1970) *Einführung in die allgemeine Semantik*, Bern.

Stubbs, M. (1995) 'Collocations and Semantic Profiles: On the Cause of the Trouble with Quantitative Studies', *Functions of Language*, 2.1: 23–36.

—— (1996) *Text and Corpus Analysis: Computer-assisted Studies of Language and Culture*, Oxford: Blackwell.

—— (2001) *Words and Phrases: Corpus Studies of Lexical Semantics*, Oxford: Blackwell.

Strange, D. and E. Deibler (1974) *Papua New Guinea Translators' Course*, Ukarumpa, Papua New Guinea: Summer Institute of Linguistics.

Sturge, K. (1999) '"A Danger and a Veiled Attack": Translating into Nazi Germany', in J. Boase-Beier and M. Holman (eds) (1999), pp. 135–46.

Sucic, Daria Sito (1996) 'The Fragmentation of Serbo–Croat into three new languages', *Transition* 2.24.

Talib, I. (2002) *The Language of Postcolonial Literature: An Introduction*, London and New York: Routledge.

Tannen, D. (ed.) (1984) *Coherence in Written and Spoken Discourse*, Norwood, NJ: Ablex.

Thomas, J. (1995) *Meaning in Interaction: An Introduction to Pragmatics*, London: Longman.

Tirkkonen-Condit, S. and R. Jääskeläinen (eds) (2000) *Tapping and Mapping the Processes of Translation and Interpreting*, Amsterdam and Philadelphia: John Benjamins.

Todd, O. (1996) *Albert Camus: Une vie*, Paris: Gallimard.

Toury, G. (1980) *In Search of a Theory of Translation*, Tel Aviv: The Porter Institute for Poetics and Semiotics, Tel Aviv University.

—— (1982) 'A Rationale for Descriptive Translation Studies', in A. Lefevere and K. Jackson (eds) *The Art and Science of Translation, Dispositio* 7, special issue, pp. 22–39.

—— (1982a) 'Transfer as a Universal of Verbal Performance of L2 Learners in Situations of Communication in Translated Utterances,' *FINLANCE* II: 63–78.

—— (1995) *Descriptive Translation Studies – and Beyond*, Amsterdam and Philadelphia: John Benjamins.

Unbegaun, B. O. (1951) *Grammaire russe*, Lyon: AIC.

Upton, C-A (ed.) (2000) *Moving Target: Theatre Translation and Cultural Relocation*, Manchester: St Jerome.

Venuti, L. (1995) *The Translator's Invisibility: A History of Translation*, London and New York: Routledge.

—— (1998) *The Scandals of Translation*, London and New York: Routledge.

—— (ed.) (1992) *Rethinking Translation: Discourse, Subjectivity, Ideology*, London and New York: Routledge.

—— (ed.) (2000) *The Translation Studies Reader*, London and New York: Routledge.

Vermeer H. J. (1976) Review of *La traduzione. Saggi e studi* (1973), *Göttingische Gelehrte Anzeigen* 228, 1–2: 147–62.

—— (1989) 'Skopos and Commission in Translational Action' (trans. A. Chesterman), in A. Chesterman (ed.) (1989), 173–87.

Véronis, J. (ed.) (2000) *Parallel Text Processing: Alignment and Use of Translation Corpora*, Dordrecht: Kluwer.

Vinay, J. P. and J. Darbelnet (1958/1995) *Stylistique comparée du français et de l'anglais. Méthode de traduction*, Paris: Didier, trans. and ed. J. C. Sager and M.-J. Hamel (1995) as *Comparative Stylistics of French and English: A Methodology for Translation*, Amsterdam and Philadelphia: John Benjamins.

von Keller, A. (ed.) (1861) *Translation von Niclas von Wyle*, Stuttgart: Bibliothek des Literarischen Vereins 57.

von Stackelberg, J. (1971) '*Das Ende der* belles infidèles', in K-R. Bausch and H-M. Geiger (eds) *Interlinguistica Sprachvergleich und Übersetzung, Festschrift zum 60. Geburtstag von Mario Wandruszka*, Tübingen: Max Niemeyer.

Walter, H. (1988) *Le Français dans tous les sens*, Paris: Robert Laffont.

Warren, R. (1989) *The Art of Translation: Voices from the Field*, Boston: Northeastern University Press.

Wechsler, R. (1998) *Performing Without a Stage: The Art of Literary Translation*, North Haven, CT: Catbird Press.

Werlich, E. (1976) *A Text Grammar of English*, Heidelberg: Quelle & Meyer.

Wilson, D. and D. Sperber (1988) 'Representation and Relevance', in: R. M. Kempson (ed.) *Mental Representations: The Interface between Language and Reality*, Cambridge: Cambridge University Press, pp. 133–53.

Wilss, W. (1982) *The Science of Translation: Problems and Methods*, Tübingen: Gunter Narr.

Yule, G. (1996) *Pragmatics*, Oxford: Oxford University Press.

Zydatiss, W. (1983) 'Text Typologies and Translation', *The Incorporated Linguist* 22.4: 212–21.

Index

field (of discourse) 80, 81, 83, 85, 189, 191, 286, 288, 295–6
film studies 8
Firbas, J. 22
Firth, JR. 188
Flaubert, G. 197
Flemish 30
Flotow, L. van 105
Fodor, J. 38
foreignizing translation, foreignization 12, 103, 107, 210, 230, 290, 317, 320
form and content 10–11, 164, 168, 169, 227, 229, 230, 263, 264, 272; direct translation 64; disambiguation 36; formal equivalence 42, 48, 70–2, 253–4, 261, 275, 284; and function 61, 65, 67; resemblance 56
formal correspondence 27–29, 33, 238
formal equivalence 40–2, 47, 50, 59, 65, 66, 70, 161, 167, 170, 251, 253–7, 261–2, 264, 274, 280
Fowler, R. 283, 299
frame *see* script
France, P.
free translation 11–14, 16, 17, 95, 104, 132, 148, 161, 200, 226, 230, 329
French 11, 13, 15, 17, 18–20, 20–21, 23, 26, 27, 28, 30, 116, 118, 133, 137–41, 144, 145, 146–7, 148–51, 167, 201, 209, 216, 223, 235, 239, 281, 285, 307, 325
Fuentes, C. 317
function: and context 68, 72; dynamic equivalence 40, 288; vs form 65, 67; preservation of 290–2; politeness 20; and relevance 64; and text type 24, 281, 286
functional markedness 275
functionality 60–1, 280
functional sentence perspective (FSP) 22–3
fuzzy match 115

Gaelic 145
Gain 31 *see also* compensation
Galician 110
García Márquez, G. 95–6
Garnett, C. 247, 307–8
Gay studies 8, 106, 316
gender: marking 314–6; -neutral translation 314–5; studies 8, 103–6, 111, 206, 329
genre 9, 88, 92, 192, 297–8; analysis of 161, 194–6; context of culture 86; and corpora 120; criterion for 261; intertextuality 87; in polysystems 309; and register 76, 78, 83;

in Reiss 285'; relevance 67; secondary 98; selection of 260; as sign 193; translation as genre 98–9; type of 98, 289; as unit of translation 56 *see also* shifts
Gentile, G. 134
Gentzler, E. 126
German 26, 28–29, 36, 209, 243, 248, 292–3, 294
Gide, A. 318
GILT (Globalization, Internationalization, Localization, Translation) 113, 321
gist translation, gisting 43, 95
given information *see* information structure
globalization 112–3, 213, 321
GLOBALINK 216
gloss translation 95, 305
glossary 9, 246, 323
Gniffke-Hubrig, C. 185
Godard, B. 105
Gogol 307
Gothic 188
Greek 11, 38, 133, 154, 209, 314
Gregory, M. 81, 188–91
Grice, P. 176, 180
Guaica 39
Gutt, Ernst-August 57–66, 67, 176–80, 273, 279, 290, 329
Halliday, M.A.K. 22, 23, 76, 81, 91, 145, 191
Hallidayan linguistics 22, 23, 329
Hamas 74
Hamel, M.-J. 137
Harry Potter 4–5, 11, 266, 320
Harvey, K. 106, 316
Hatim, B. 78, 82, 102–3, 181, 198, 281, 284
Hawkins, R. 158
Hebrew 16, 99, 194, 310, 314
Hegel, C. 211
Heine, H. 133
Hemingway, E. 24, 234, 282–3, 286, 298–300
Hempel, C. 127
Hermans, T. 96, 102
Hermeneutics 8, 31
Hervey, S. 65
hierarchical structuring 37–8
Higgins, I. 65
Highsmith, P. 316
Hines, B. 204
Hinsley, F.H. 115
Hitler, A. 316
Holman, M.
Holmes, J.S. 7, 8, 9, 126–31, 221, 224, 311
Holz-Mänttäri, J. 304

Related titles from Routledge

Introducing Translation Studies
Theories and Applications
Jeremy Munday

'Jeremy Munday's book presents a snapshot of a rapidly developing discipline in a clear, concise and graphic way. This is a book which raises strong awareness of current issues in the field and will be of interest to translation trainers and trainees alike'

Basil Hatim, *Heriot-Watt University, UK*

Introducing Translation Studies is a practical, introductory textbook providing an accessible overview of the key contributions to translation studies.

Munday explores each theory chapter by chapter and test the different approaches by applying them to texts. The texts discussed are taken from a broad range of languages – English, French, German, Spanish, Italian, Punjabi and Portuguese – and English translations are provided.

Each chapter includes the following features:

- A table presenting the key concepts
- An introduction outlining the translation theory or theories
- Illustrative texts, including a tourist brochure, a children's cookery book, a Harry Potter novel, the Bible, literary reviews, film translations and a European Parliament speech, with translations
- A chapter summary
- Discussion points and exercises

Hb: 0–415–22926–X
Pb: 0–415–22927–8

Available at all good bookshops
For ordering and further information please visit:
http://www.routledge.com/textbooks/its.html

Related titles from Routledge

The Translation Studies Reader
Second Edition
Edited by Lawrence Venuti

'This is bound to be the most authoritative anthology of theoretical reflection on translation currently available in English. The selection of primary documents is varied and imaginative, the editorial introductions lucid and informed.'

Theo Hermans, *University College London*, UK

This new and fully revised edition of *The Translation Studies Reader* provides a definitive survey of the most important and influential approaches to translation theory and research, with an emphasis on the developments of the last thirty years. With introductory essays prefacing each section, the book places a wide range of seminal and innovative readings within their thematic, cultural and historical contexts.

The new edition features nine new readings, by authors such as Jerome and Derrida. These provide an historical dimension as well as exploring the interdisciplinary nature of translation studies through readings in fields such as philosophy and film studies.

Contributors: Kwame Anthony Appiah, Walter Benjamin, Antoine Berman, Shoshana Blum-Kulka, Jorge Luis Borges, Annie Brisset, Lori Chamberlain, Jean Darbelnet, Jacques Derrida, John Dryden, Itamar Even-Zohar, Johann Wolfgang von Goethe, Keith Harvey, James S. Holmes, Roman Jakobson, Jerome, André Lefevere, Philip E. Lewis, Ian Mason, Vladimir Nabokov, Eugene Nida, Friedrich Nietzsche, Abé Mark Nornes, Nicolas Perrot D'Ablancourt, Ezra Pound, Katharina Reiss, Steven Rendall, Friedrich Schleiermacher, Gayatri Spivak, George Steiner, Gideon Toury, Hans J. Vermeer, Jean-Paul Vinay

Hb: 0–415–31919–6
Pb: 0–415–31920–X

Available at all good bookshops
For ordering and further information please visit:
www.routledge.com